SUPREME COURT
AND
APPELLATE ADVOCACY

MASTERING ORAL ARGUMENT

*

SUPREME COURT AND APPELLATE ADVOCACY

MASTERING ORAL ARGUMENT

By

David C. Frederick
Kellogg, Huber Hansen, Todd & Evans
Washington, D.C.

FOREWORD

By

Ruth Bader Ginsburg
Associate Justice
Supreme Court of the United States

Mat #40105907

West Group has created this publication to provide you with accurate and authoritative information concerning the subject matter covered. However, this publication was not necessarily prepared by persons licensed to practice law in a particular jurisdiction. West Group is not engaged in rendering legal or other professional advice, and this publication is not a substitute for the advice of an attorney. If you require legal or other expert advice, you should seek the services of a competent attorney or other professional.

Practitioner Treatise Series and West Group are
registered trademarks used herein under license.

COPYRIGHT © 2003 By WEST GROUP
610 Opperman Drive
P.O. Box 64526
St. Paul, MN 55164–0526
1–800–328–9352

ISBN 0–314–14414–5

TEXT IS PRINTED ON 10% POST
CONSUMER RECYCLED PAPER

To Aaron and James

*

Foreword

Oral advocacy is an art, but it is one that can be learned by determined effort. Still vibrant in my mind is the first of my six 1970s arguments before the Supreme Court. In those years, the Court regularly heard four arguments in a sitting day. I was scheduled to appear in the afternoon. Anxiety mounted as I observed the morning's arguments. I skipped lunch to guard against the butterflies fluttering inside. Then, after delivering a well-rehearsed opening sentence, I looked up at the bench and experienced a feeling of extraordinary power. There sat the nine top judges in the land. They had no place to go. They were my captive audience for the next several minutes. Then a teacher by trade, I relished the opportunity to persuade them that my cause was just, my legal argument sound.

Having observed oral argument for some 22 years from the other side of the bench (13 years at the D.C. Circuit, 9 at the Supreme Court), I applaud the publication of *Supreme Court and Appellate Advocacy*. It is a well-designed guide, offering sound advice on preparing and delivering oral arguments capable of capturing the Court's sympathetic attention.

The author, David Frederick, is an accomplished advocate, veteran of twelve arguments in the Supreme Court and numerous appearances in courts of appeals. He has drawn on his own experiences, encounters of his colleagues in the Office of the Solicitor General, and interviews with skilled practitioners in the private bar. His book is comprehensive in scope, novel in approach, and engagingly instructive. Frederick first traces the history of advocacy before the Court from two centuries ago, when Daniel Webster and other Bar luminaries would argue a case for days on end, to today's precious half hour per side. He describes in detail how the careful advocate prepares for oral argument and then, what counsel must do to use that preparation effectively.

To reach the nine minds, Frederick conveys, the advocate must be agile. He or she must appreciate that oral argument nowadays seldom accommodates set speeches. At best, oral argument is a conversation, a discussion between knowledgeable attorneys and jurists who have done their homework, a "hot bench," as appellate advocates say. The justices' homework generally starts with the decision the Court is reviewing, then proceeds to the relevant portions of the record, the statutes and other judicial decisions in point, the briefs filed by the parties, and, depending upon their quality, the briefs of supporting amici. Frederick counsels lawyers not to resent questions from the bench as annoying interruptions of an argument's flow. Instead, he cautions advocates to address the Court's concerns directly, while remaining alert to opportunities to use a question to advance a key point. Not many cases, it is true, are won on the oral argument alone, but a case can be lost if a lawyer is unable or unwilling to answer a justice's question honestly and persuasively.

Although a conversational exchange with nine justices can be a daunting endeavor, in essence, oral argument at the Supreme Court is what it generally is in most U.S. appellate tribunals, both federal and state. Our appellate courts, unlike many appellate forums abroad, do not assign reporting judges. The presiding judge does not decide who may speak or when inquiries may be made. Any justice or judge asks a question whenever he or she pleases within the allotted argument time. Frederick's step-by-step analysis, his account of the components of oral argument, can arm an attorney to perform to best effect before any of our nation's multi-judge courts. He knows that examples work more forcibly on the mind than precepts. His text is rich in illustrations showing how an advocate can rise or fall with the occasion. Constantly informative, the book is also laced with humor that eases the reader's way.

In sum, in chapters and verse, Frederick teaches advocates how to achieve what Justice Joseph Story counseled nearly two centuries ago (in words I borrow, with some editing):

Be brief, be pointed
Lucid in style and order
Spend no words on trifles
Condense
Strike but a few blows, strike them to the heart
Scattered fires smother in smoke and noise
Keep this your main guide
Short be your speech, your matter strong and clear
And leave off, leave off when done.[*]

RUTH BADER GINSBURG

*

---

[*] I have several times recounted this concise advice. See, e.g., "Remarks on Appellate Advocacy," 50 S.C. L. REV. 567, 670–71 (1999).

Preface

This book came about at the suggestion of several friends. Between October 2000 and April 2001, I argued three cases in the Supreme Court of the United States and *United States v. Microsoft Corporation* in the U.S. Court of Appeals for the District of Columbia Circuit. In the midst of those argument preparations, I also worked on a number of briefs. It was one of the most work-intensive periods of my life. As I emerged from the self-imposed monasticism caused by the need to do that work as well as I could, I had an opportunity to reconnect with friends who were naturally curious about the toll it had taken on me and what it was like. One friend, in particular, was curious about how I had gone about preparing for those arguments.

Those conversations spurred me to thinking about how to describe the process of preparing for and presenting oral argument in the Supreme Court and the courts of appeals. I quickly discovered that no one had written a book dedicated exclusively to the art of oral advocacy, with a focus on presenting arguments to the Supreme Court and appellate courts. I started to have more in-depth conversations with experienced advocates, both to learn their secrets and to test theories of my own. As I heard stories about arguments and compared them to my own, it occurred to me that using examples from actual arguments would be a potentially useful way to illustrate the various points of advocacy I thought were most important.

The timing of these conversations coincided with my decision to leave the Office of the Solicitor General, where I had served for more than five years as an Assistant to the Solicitor General and argued twelve cases in the Supreme Court. I wrote the vast bulk of the manuscript during a break between leaving the government and joining the Washington, D.C., law firm of Kellogg, Huber, Hansen, Todd & Evans, P.L.L.C., which generously allowed me to defer my start and provided a wonderful place from which to complete the book. My colleagues both at the Office of the Solicitor General and at the firm aided me immeasurably in discussing the finer points of advocacy and offering suggestions of key points to make and examples to use.

In putting together this book, my aims have been to instruct on the best principles of oral advocacy, to provide some additional insights about the Supreme Court and the courts of appeals, and to make the book readable and accessible. I have tried to mix practical advice with illustrations, on the theory that this is not a paint-by-the-numbers exercise, but rather an art form that should vary in its execution. For me, the illustrations from real cases serve as a reminder of the humbling nature of the experience and the inspiring ways in which advocates can perform when at their best.

I have also tried to be sensitive to gender usages. To avoid references to gender is impossible in a book like this, where I am attempting to describe what a hypothetical person—the advocate—should do. I have adopted the compromise of referring to the "advocate" in odd-numbered chapters in the male form and in even-numbered chapters in the female form. I hope whatever awkwardness the reader may experience will be compensated for by a sense of balance.

A number of people contributed in large and small ways to the development of this project. The following advocates generously agreed to speak to me about their process for preparation and their approaches to the presentation of oral argument: Lisa Blatt, Michael Dreeben, Irving Gornstein, Michael Kellogg, Jeffrey Lamken, Edwin Kneedler, Maureen Mahoney, Jeffrey Minear, Theodore Olson, John Roberts, Malcolm Stewart, and Seth Waxman. I learned a great deal from each of them. Linda Greenhouse and Tony Mauro shared their perspectives as seasoned journalists who have observed hundreds of oral arguments in the Supreme Court. And William Suter not only permitted me to interview him, but he also provided historical materials and carefully read the manuscript in draft. The following persons read all or part of the manuscript and offered much helpful advice: David Bederman, Harold Bruff, E. Christi Cunningham, Mark Evans, Dennis Hutchinson, Michael Kellogg, Richard Lazarus, Daniel Marcus, Maeva Marcus, David Meyer, Michael Ross, Michael Sturley, William Suter, Richard Taranto, and Seth Waxman. Meagan Jeronimo provided invaluable assistance through many changes to the manuscript and offered a number of stylistic suggestions. David Burke also carefully reviewed the book for consistency and accuracy in citations; he contributed a vast number of useful ideas. Tracey Erwin also provided assistance for which I'm grateful. Pamela Siege Chandler has been a wonderful editor in every facet of the process and Jon Olson of West Group offered special assistance and many important insights. Tim Payne nursed the manuscript through the production process with care and skill.

Finally, I would like to thank Justice Ruth Bader Ginsburg for contributing the Foreword. From my very first Supreme Court argument, she and I have had a number of memorable colloquies in arguments, and I have long admired her. Given her own considerable experience as an oral advocate and writer on the subject, it is a special thrill for me that she agreed to write the Foreword.

My two sons, Aaron and James, provide daily inspiration. To them, I gratefully dedicate this book, with the hope that the promise they now show as advocates will develop in the years ahead in whatever endeavors they choose to pursue.

D.C.F.

Washington, D.C.
October 2002

*

WESTLAW® Overview

Supreme Court and Appellate Advocacy: Mastering Oral Argument offers a detailed and comprehensive treatment of the basic rules, principles, and issues relating to oral argument at the appellate level. To supplement the information contained in this book, you can access Westlaw, West's computer-assisted legal research service. Westlaw contains a broad array of legal resources, including case law, statutes, expert commentary, current developments, and various other types of information.

Learning how to use these materials effectively will enhance your legal research abilities. To help you coordinate the information in the book with your Westlaw research, this volume contains an appendix listing Westlaw databases, search techniques, and sample problems.

The instructions and features described in this Westlaw overview are based on accessing Westlaw via westlaw.com® at **www.westlaw.com**.

THE PUBLISHER

*

Summary of Contents

xvii

Table of Contents

PART IV. APPENDICES

*

SUPREME COURT
AND
APPELLATE ADVOCACY

MASTERING ORAL ARGUMENT

*

Part I
INTRODUCTION AND HISTORICAL OVERVIEW

Chapter One

INTRODUCTION

Analysis

From the inception of the American judicial system, oral advocacy has played a critical role in how judges decide cases and make law. For the first 50 years of its history, the Supreme Court of the United States allowed attorneys to argue for as long as they wanted. Many cases consumed days of oral argument as attorneys read portions of cited cases and delivered elaborate orations. Over time, the court has placed increasingly stricter time limits on oral arguments. For the past 30 years, the Supreme Court has formally limited the time for oral argument in most cases to one-half hour per side—one hour total—and the courts of appeals have followed that lead. From arguments in the late nineteenth century that could occupy hours, or even days on occasion, the courts of appeals now routinely limit oral argument to 30 minutes—15 minutes per side.

That transformation has had a profound effect on the nature and quality of oral argument. If that trend continues, by later in the twenty-first century the Supreme Court may eliminate oral argument altogether except in the most important cases, thereby following the trend of courts of appeals that are deciding an ever-larger percentage of cases solely on the basis of written submissions.[1]

---

1. According to statistics compiled by the Administrative Office for United States Courts (AOUSC), in the twelve-month period ending September 30,

If the Supreme Court were to take that drastic step, and the courts of appeals to limit still further the availability of oral argument, a principal reason would be long-expressed disappointment by judges and justices with the quality of oral advocacy. Justices have long complained about the inadequacy of a high percentage of the attorneys who argue in the Supreme Court. In the early nineteenth century, Chief Justice John Marshall spoke of arguments so stultifying that the "acme of judicial distinction" consisted of "the ability to look a lawyer straight in the eyes for two hours and not hear a damned word he says."[2] In 1948, Frederick B. Wiener wrote in the *Harvard Law Review* that "[w]ithin the [past] year I have been told by a justice of the Supreme Court of the United States that four out of every five arguments to which he must listen are 'not good.'"[3] In 1973, Chief Justice Warren E. Burger expressed the opinion that "from one-third to one-half of the lawyers who appear in the serious cases are not really qualified to render fully adequate representation."[4] And Justice William O. Douglas complained in his memoirs that 40 percent of the lawyers who argued in the Supreme Court were "incompetent."[5]

Circuit judges have echoed those sentiments. Judge Laurence J. Silberman of U.S. Court of Appeals for the District of Columbia Circuit, for example, has written that although "the D.C. Circuit reputedly hears the best appellate advocates in the nation, * * * it is astonishing how many cases are presented by lawyers who are simply not up to the task."[6]

When done well, however, oral argument performs critical functions. The better the advocate, the more fully those functions are served. Wholly apart from its effect on the court's deliberative process and the interests of the parties in shaping that process, oral argument advances important public purposes. It demonstrates that the court is operating openly and without furtive influences.

2001, 19,525 cases were decided by the courts of appeals on the briefs, and 9,315 after oral argument. *See* AOUSC, *Judicial Business of United States Courts 2001,* at Table B–5.

2. 4 Alfred Beveridge, *The Life of John Marshall* 83 (1919).

3. Frederick Bernays Wiener, "Oral Advocacy," 62 HARV. L. REV. 56, 56 (1948).

4. Warren E. Burger, "The Special Skills of Advocacy," 42 FORDHAM L. REV. 227, 234 (1973).

5. William O. Douglas, *The Court Years, 1939–1945* 183 (1980).

6. Laurence H. Silberman, "From the Bench: Plain Talk on Appellate Advocacy," 20 LITIGATION 3 (Spring 1994).

For the parties and the public alike, the opportunity to view the proceedings is one component of the credibility earned by the judiciary. It allows them to gauge for themselves the attentiveness and receptivity of the court to the arguments, as well as whether the issues addressed in the court's opinions adequately dealt with the arguments of the parties. Oral argument also enforces a level of accountability: lawyers and the press alike can usually discern the prepared judge or justice from the unprepared (except when the jurist is totally silent throughout the argument). A prepared bench operating in a transparent manner instills confidence in the process and increases the public's respect for the rule of law.

§ 1.1   The Importance of Oral Argument

Writing in the 1920s, Chief Justice Charles Evans Hughes commented that oral argument helps the justices "separate the wheat from the chaff" and that, in most cases, "the impression that a judge has at the close of a full oral argument accords with the conviction which controls his final vote."[1] In a discrete number of cases, oral argument makes the difference between winning and losing a case. Justice Ruth Bader Ginsburg notes that, in her years as a circuit judge and Supreme Court justice, "I have seen few victories snatched at oral argument from a total defeat the judges had anticipated on the basis of the briefs. But I have seen several potential winners become losers in whole or in part because of clarification elicited at oral argument."[2] Chief Justice William H. Rehnquist has written that, "[i]n a significant minority of the cases in which I have heard oral argument, I have left the bench feeling different about a case than I did when I came on the bench."[3] He cautions, however, that "[t]he change is seldom a full one-hundred-and-eighty-degree swing, and I find that it is most likely to occur in cases involving areas of law with which I am least familiar."[4]

Circuit judges have also written of the importance of oral argument to the court's deliberative process. Judge Myron H. Bright of the U.S. Court of Appeals for the Eighth Circuit has written emphatically that "oral argument is *helpful* in a *substantial*

---

§ 1.1

1. Charles Evans Hughes, *The Supreme Court of the United States* 61, 63 (1928).

2. Ruth Bader Ginsburg, "Remarks on Appellate Advocacy," 50 S.C. L. Rev. 567, 570 (1999).

3. William H. Rehnquist, *The Supreme Court: How It Was, How It Is* 243–244 (2d ed. 2001).

4. *Id.*

number of appeals" because "[t]he argument can isolate and clarify the core issues."[5] Judge Irving R. Kaufman of the Second Circuit notes that "[t]he oral argument is counsel's opportunity to persuade, to turn the heads of the judge a little, to leave them with the working hypothesis that his client deserves to win."[6]

Oral argument also matters to a court's internal functioning for an entirely different reason. When the court sits in multi-judge panels or, like the Supreme Court, with all nine justices present, the oral argument presents the first opportunity for the members of the court to focus their collective attention on the merits of the case. At oral argument, the members of the court can communicate with each other and probe their respective views on the issues raised in the case prior to conference. That dynamic can be important because, once they have voted at conference, the justices have made up their minds and are unlikely to change them (even after written opinions in the case circulate). And although a three-judge court of appeals panel can operate in a more informal manner, the argument gives the court a collective opportunity to hear how counsel responds to questions that may raise common concerns.

§ 1.2 How Courts Use Oral Argument

The contemporary use of oral argument in the Supreme Court as a "pre-conference" may reflect how Chief Justice Rehnquist is said to conduct the conferences at which the justices decide cases. Although only the justices themselves attend and it is therefore impossible to say for certain what happens in the conference room, word has filtered out that the conferences do not produce real dialogue in the sense of the justices exchanging views. Rather, conference in the Rehnquist era provides each justice with an opportunity to state views about a case, without a substantial amount of give and take. Thus, the oral argument can become the forum for the justices to "talk" to each other in ways that the conference does not. They can express their thoughts or float various theories to gauge the reactions of other justices without necessarily being committed to a particular viewpoint. As Justice Ginsburg has written, "[o]ral argument, at its best, is an exchange

---

5. Myron H. Bright, "The Power of the Spoken Word: In Defense of Oral Argument," 72 Iowa L. Rev. 35, 36 (1986).

6. Irving R. Kaufman, *Appellate Advocacy in the Federal Courts*, 79 F.R.D. 165, 171 (1977).

of ideas about the case, a dialogue or discussion between court and counsel."[1]

The process of dialogue—however helpful it might be for the court—can only be helpful for the advocate who is attentive and flexible in presenting argument. The severest types of pre-conference discussions among the judges or justices are more likely to occur when an argument is going badly because the court is, in effect, using that time to analyze the case without the benefit of the advocate's considered synthesis. The advocate becomes a mere conduit for the members of the bench to speak to one another. When that dialogue occurs in its most extreme form, the attorney no longer has any control over the direction of the argument and gets forced into the position of either agreeing or disagreeing with propositions put forth from the bench. A good advocate will apprehend the dangers of too readily assenting to a proposition advanced by a judge and of becoming the ball in a ping-pong match between members of the court who disagree with one another and use counsel's answers to advance their own positions. When the latter happens, the advocate has lost the opportunity to present a case and the arguments that support it.

Courts also use oral argument to get a better sense of the outer limits of an advocate's position. Especially at the Supreme Court level, but also at times in a court of appeals or state supreme court argument, judges and justices often ask hypothetical questions to understand more fully the implications of a rule they are being asked to adopt. Frequently, those hypothetical questions take the legal principle being advanced by the advocate and extend it to other logical factual scenarios. If handled well, the advocate may use the hypothetical examples to convince the court that the extension of a legal rule being sought in the case presents an orderly progression to a desired set of future rules that will be posed in subsequent cases. Or, if the rule itself is desirable but further extensions may be problematic, a skilled advocate may find persuasive ways for the court to draw lines that retain the useful rule but foreclose an extension of that rule.

Members of the court themselves can be quite explicit about using oral argument to flesh out issues that shape the opinion. Judges often muse openly at oral argument about the consequences

1. Ginsburg, "Remarks on Appellate Advocacy," 50 S.C. L. Rev. at 569.

of the court's decision. Keenly aware that only a handful of court of appeals cases will be reviewed by the Supreme Court, circuit judges ask such questions because they know their decisions will functionally be the final word in the vast majority of the cases they decide. Even Supreme Court justices, who know that each case before them will have far-reaching significance, will nonetheless emphasize at oral argument that the advocate must help the court understand more completely the consequences of its decision. And when counsel does not provide a satisfactory response, the court at times will self-consciously limit the scope of its opinion.[2]

Oral argument also provides an opportunity for clarification so that matters in the record, the facts, the claims being asserted, and the expected scope of the decision can be fully vetted. An advocate may face questions about where certain matters may be found in the record, what parts of a lower court opinion are the most problematic, what the party's position is with respect to a related policy, how a similarly situated entity addresses an analogous situation, and whether the party is now prepared to take a position on an issue about which it had been silent in the briefs. Members of the court also routinely pose questions about how far a particular line of doctrine should extend, whether the court in a prior case has properly construed a statute, and whether language in a prior decision of the court is dicta or part of the holding. All of those types of questions seek clarification of the advocate's case and help the court to frame the parameters of its opinion.

---

2. For example, in *Wilson v. Arkansas*, which concerned whether the Fourth Amendment requires officers to knock and announce their presence before entering a dwelling to execute a warrant, the Arkansas Attorney General put forth two theories, one of which was that the manner of entry never should have a bearing on the reasonableness inquiry under the Fourth Amendment. That position sparked heated questions from the bench, with one justice interrupting with this statement: "[W]e have to write the opinion. I want to know what the consequences of my opinion are, and I'm asking you whether or not the manner of entry is ever relevant as to reasonableness, the same question Justice Souter's question asked." *Wilson v. Arkansas*, No. 94–5707, 1995 WL 243487 at *34 (Mar. 28, 1995). In a follow-on case under the knock-and-announce rule, Justice Anthony Kennedy said at oral argument that, if the court were to hold that officers do not need any higher level of proof than reasonable suspicion (such as probable cause) if they damage property on making an unannounced entry, "it seems to me that * * * we would still say, if we agreed with you, that the ultimate standard is reasonableness, that * * * you cannot destroy more property than is reasonably necessary, given all of the circumstances and given the necessity to protect your officers." *United States v. Ramirez*, No. 96–1469, 1998 WL 15476 at *18 (Jan. 13, 1998). Chief Justice Rehnquist's unanimous opinion for the court picked up on that theme. *See United States v. Ramirez*, 523 U.S. 65, 71, 118 S.Ct. 992, 996 (1998).

§ 1.3 Oral Argument From the Parties' Perspective

To the parties, oral argument can be critically important. Ordinarily, it is their only chance to stand face to face with the court and plead their case directly, without the filter of a written brief. That opportunity will be the culmination of a long process of litigation, which begins with the filing of a complaint and proceeds through discovery, argument over motions, and trial. As a case makes its way up the ladder of appellate courts, the issues narrow and become more focused. By the time a case gets to the Supreme Court, it typically involves only one or two issues that are analyzed in great depth. How the court disposes of those issues can completely resolve the case or spark the continuation of protracted litigation under a different set of legal principles.

After what may be thousands of hours spent developing a case, investigating the facts, litigating over motions, and conducting a trial, a court of appeals argument in most cases forces the parties to articulate their positions and to respond to the judges' concerns in 15 minutes or less. Even in the Supreme Court, where the nine justices often seem almost to compete with one another to ask their questions of counsel, 30 minutes of oral argument seem to elapse very quickly. The attorneys' presentation of oral argument, therefore, becomes the culminating event in a highly charged hour just prior to the justices' votes on how to resolve the case.

The compression of time in Supreme Court and court of appeals arguments puts a high premium on preparation. The adage that it takes only five minutes to prepare an hour-long presentation, but hours to prepare a five-minute speech, applies with even greater force to a Supreme Court or court of appeals argument. The oral advocate has to make the right points in the shortest amount of time possible. Each question must be met with a precise answer, and the advocate has to know how to move from a hostile question to a point that will help advance the client's cause. Because of the time pressure, there is scarcely room for error. An erroneous answer can get the court off course, damage the advocate's credibility, or simply be a missed opportunity to persuade the court that the advocate's side should prevail.

Because of the limited number of minutes per side, that time is made even more valuable by the unstructured nature of the argument itself. In neither the Supreme Court nor the courts of appeal are the times an advocate may speak further sub-divided to address particular issues, except in the rarest circumstances. Those courts do not, for example, allot 5 minutes for an opening presentation, 20 minutes for questions and answers, and 5 minutes for a rebuttal. Rather, the time elapses in whatever manner the advocate and judges decide in the spur of the moment.

An attorney stands up to address the court and typically opens with, "May it please the Court." Once those words are spoken, every oral argument differs in form, purpose, and effect. Like a blank canvas, the argument becomes what the participants—the lawyers and members of the court—make of it. If done badly, the argument will not facilitate the court's understanding of the issues, and may even confuse the court. Indeed, cases are lost every year in the Supreme Court and the courts of appeals due to poor oral arguments. If done well, the argument may transform a losing case into a winner. In between lay a range of possibilities that can only be imperfectly envisioned prior to the argument itself.

Just as the judges and justices come to court with certain objectives, so too do skilled advocates. They seek to strengthen the position presented in their briefs through reason and personal credibility, to answer the court's questions in as straightforward a manner as possible, and to reassure the court that a ruling in their client's favor is the most reasonable outcome. Courts rarely respond well to histrionics in either briefing or oral argument. The best advocates thus recognize that it is in their client's interest to conduct a reasoned, and reasonable, dialogue in an appellate argument. In this respect, the advocate is a personification of the client represented. A well-prepared presentation is a further signal to the court that it should take that party's interests especially seriously.

An advocate seeks in oral argument to boil a case down to its essence. Under the Federal Rules of Appellate Procedure, an appellant's or appellee's opening brief on the merits can be as long as 14,000 words, which can translate to 60 or more double-spaced pages, with appellant having an opportunity to file a reply brief of up to 7,000 words.[1] The merits briefs in a Supreme Court case are up to 50 printed pages apiece, with an additional 20–page reply brief also permitted.[2] Whether in court of appeals cases, which typically involve multiple issues, or in Supreme Court cases raising just a single issue, those dense briefs do not readily lend themselves to easy distillation. Yet the best advocates are able to summarize in one or two sentences what the case is about and why they should

§ 1.3   2. Sup. Ct. R. 33(g).
1. Fed. R. App. P. 32(a)(7).

prevail. Numerous examples given in this book show how the best advocates succeed in that synthesis, and how the worst advocates fail—even after 30 minutes of argument—to explain why the court should rule in their favor.

Finally, an advocate seeks to allay any concerns the court might have about ruling for his client. Members of the court routinely ask questions that reveal the problems they perceive with the advocate's case. An advocate who can address those concerns will improve the odds of winning the case or aid in shaping a rule that does not harm its interests.

When public spectators observe oral arguments in the Supreme Court or the court of appeals, they can tell the difference between a good advocate and a mediocre one, but rarely can appreciate the distinction between a good oral argument and a great one. In the past three decades, that distinction has become increasingly important—and ever more elusive—as oral advocacy in the Supreme Court and courts of appeals has become more challenging. The complexity of the questions addressed by the federal courts paradoxically places a premium on the advocate's ability to synthesize and to simplify without distorting the nuances inherent in the law. That ability is what elevates oral advocacy to an art form. Like any art form, natural talent is a help, but the performance of a great argument—like the creation of a master painting—is far more the product of hard work than innate inspiration. Preparation, properly focused, is the surest way to thrive in the courtroom. The very best advocates appreciate the extra effort that goes into a great argument, as well as the element of nuance that transforms an adequate answer to a question from the bench into a case-winning colloquy.

§ 1.4   The Approach of This Book to Oral Argument

This book is about oral advocacy in the Supreme Court and the courts of appeals: how to prepare for an oral argument, how to conduct practice sessions to refine the argument, and what approaches to take when presenting a case. Many books have addressed the subject of appellate advocacy and may contain a chapter on oral argument. They generally take a "how to" approach without illustrating in practical terms the consequences that flow from decisions an advocate must make.[1] Over the years, a few excellent

---

§ 1.4

1. *See, e.g.*, Marshall Houts & Walter Rogesheske, *Art of Advocacy: Appeals*

40–1 to 42–8 (2001); Carole C. Berry, *Effective Appellate Advocacy: Brief Writing and Oral Argument* 122–88 (2d ed.

articles have been written about Supreme Court and appellate advocacy,[2] but those efforts have tended to suffer from two principal shortcomings. One is that they reflect advice that was timely for the era in which it was written—advice that with the evolution of practices in the Supreme Court and courts of appeals is now out of date. A second has tended to be an absence of real-world examples from cases that can sharpen the analysis and make it more immediate in explaining not only how to improve in this form of advocacy, but also how to understand better why the members of the court perform as they do at oral argument.

The approach taken here is to explain the various principles of effective Supreme Court and appellate advocacy, drawn from the collective experiences of members of the Solicitor General's Office as well as the finest private practitioners before the Supreme Court and the courts of appeals. To illustrate those principles, the book uses examples selected from Supreme Court and court of appeals cases, and tries to show how the oral argument may have affected the court's decision. Even those who never set foot behind the podium in the Supreme Court or a court of appeals may gain a better understanding of how those courts work as institutions and how an attorney may improve as an advocate in any forum. As a laboratory for such lessons, the Supreme Court is ideal. Just as baseball players of all abilities refine their skills from watching and imitating major leaguers, so too may attorneys who argue a legal motion in any tribunal learn about oral advocacy from experienced

1999); Edward D. Re & Joseph R. Re, *Brief Writing & Oral Argument* 137–69 (8th ed. 1999); Michael E. Tigar & Jane B. Tigar, *Federal Appeals: Jurisdiction and Practice* 475–541 (3d ed. 1999); Nancy L. Schultz & Louis J. Sirico, Jr., *Legal Writing and Other Lawyering Skills* 321–43 (3d ed. 1998); Ruggero J. Aldisert, *Winning on Appeal: Better Briefs and Oral Argument* 293–341 (rev. 1st ed. 1996); *Handbook of Appellate Advocacy* 84–102 (Frank R. Acuña et al., eds., 2d ed. 1986).

2. *See, e.g.*, Robert Stern, Eugene Gressman, Stephen M. Shapiro & Kenneth S. Geller, *Supreme Court Practice* 569–609 (7th ed. 1993); Stephen M. Shapiro, "Oral Argument in the Supreme Court of the United States," 33 CATHOLIC

U. L. REV. 529 (1984); E. Barrett Prettyman, Jr., "The Supreme Court's Use of Hypothetical Questions at Oral Argument," 33 CATHOLIC U. L. REV. 555 (1984); William H. Rehnquist, "Oral Advocacy: A Disappearing Art," 35 MERCER L. REV. 1015 (1984); Russell A. Kolsrud, "Preparing for a Supreme Court Argument: Do What Your Mother Told You," 66 A.B.A. J. 855 (July 1980); E. Barrett Prettyman, Jr., "Supreme Court Advocacy: Random Thoughts in a Day of Time Restrictions," 4 LITIGATION 16 (1978); Robert H. Jackson, "Advocacy Before the Supreme Court: Suggestions for Effective Case Presentations," 37 A.B.A. J. 801 (Nov. 1951); Wiener, "Oral Advocacy," *supra*; John W. Davis, "The Argument of an Appeal," 26 A.B.A. J. 895 (Dec. 1940).

Supreme Court practitioners. Virtually all of the approaches to oral advocacy suggested in this book have universal application to any court that puts exacting questions to the advocates in resolving legal issues.

The process of preparation can be tedious, but arguing in the Supreme Court or court of appeals is likely to be an attorney's most intense professional experience. In no other area of law must the attorney be as comprehensively prepared, quick to react, and focused. Oral appellate advocacy is, unquestionably, the toughest test any attorney can face in a courtroom and the most exacting art form in the law. A trial attorney can refer to notes in making arguments or questioning witnesses and, in most trial settings, control the agenda of what he says and asks in the courtroom. In an oral argument, the advocate has only partial control. There is scarcely time to refer to notes, so the argument must be fully internalized. The judges can knock the advocate off-stride with a single question. If the attorney does not recover quickly or adequately, the court may continue to badger the advocate with hostile questions until the case is decisively lost.

In the Supreme Court and appellate courts, oral argument is almost always difficult and potentially humiliating or exhilarating. Difficult because every case in the Supreme Court involves a genuinely complex legal issue. Except in the rarest cases, the Supreme Court does not review issues unless there is a division of authority among the courts that have ruled on that issue in prior cases. The comparatively easier ability to cope with precedent in a court of appeals is more than offset by the challenge of mastering a voluminous trial record. Oral argument can be potentially humiliating because no attorney wants to suffer public embarrassment in front of a large gallery of spectators, friends, colleagues, the press, and the country's highest-ranking judges in a matter of national importance. And it can be potentially exhilarating because there is the opportunity to excel and succeed. Given those stakes, the pressure to perform at the highest possible level is enormous.

* * *

The great lawyer, Solicitor General, and Supreme Court Justice Robert H. Jackson once said that he gave three arguments in each Supreme Court case: "First came the one that I planned—as I thought, logical, coherent, complete. Second was the one actually presented—interrupted, incoherent, disjointed, disappointing. The third was the utterly devastating argument that I thought of after going to bed that night."[3] The advocate will prepare for the experience, live it, and then relive it in the days afterward. As the argument fades through the occupation of the mind with other matters, it becomes possible to put the experience in its proper perspective. But that takes time. Anyone serious about becoming a great oral advocate, therefore, must accept the responsibility of preparation, the risk of putting everything on the line, and the agony of post-argument angst. The reward for engaging in that kind of work and undergoing that amount of stress is the thrill of being alone in the well of a court composed of some of the smartest humans on Earth, the satisfaction of passing an exacting and demanding test of personal skill and fortitude, and the honor of playing at least a small part in the development of the law.

3. Jackson, "Advocacy Before the Supreme Court," 37 A.B.A. J. at 803.

Chapter Two

A BRIEF HISTORY OF ORAL ARGUMENT IN THE SUPREME COURT

Analysis

The nature and purpose of oral argument in the Supreme Court and the courts of appeals have evolved dramatically since the Supreme Court issued its first rules of practice in February 1790. From its inception, the Supreme Court and the subordinate district and circuit courts followed the English oral tradition of argument, by which the arguing attorneys supplied the court, through their oral presentations, with virtually all of the information needed to resolve the case. The attorneys did not write briefs either before or after oral argument. As time went on, the inefficiencies of that practice persuaded the Supreme Court to institute a number of changes that resulted in a compression in the time allotted to oral argument and a reliance on written briefs to expound the positions of the parties.

From days-long, set-piece orations, oral arguments in the Supreme Court today demand of the attorney an ability to articulate in 30 minutes the most important principles of the case and to respond to dozens of questions from the justices. In the United States Courts of Appeals, which were formed in 1891 amidst this process of transformation, the need for succinctness and clarity is also present, as advocates in those courts generally have fifteen minutes or less in which to present their case. Throughout that

14

period of refinement over the course of nearly two centuries, important developments in style, practice, and institutional reform influenced the role of oral advocacy in the Supreme Court's decision-making. This chapter focuses on the evolution of oral argument practices in the Supreme Court over the past two centuries. As oral argument has changed in that court, so, too, have those transformations filtered down to federal and state courts.

§ 2.1 Early Practice of Oral Argument in the Supreme Court

In the first year and a half of the Supreme Court's existence, the rules of practice led to much uncertainty among practitioners.[1] On August 8, 1791, the court issued an order in response to a motion from the Attorney General attempting to obtain clarification. The order advised that "this court consider[s] the practice of the courts of king's bench, and of chancery, in England, as affording outlines for the practice of this court; and that they will, from time to time, make such alterations therein as circumstances may render necessary."[2]

By long-standing tradition, advocates at the King's Bench presented their material orally to the court. For arguments to the House of Lords, the highest tribunal in Britain, advocates would even go so far as to state orally the decision of the court from which the appeal was being taken, and then proceed with a long presentation of the facts and precedents on which they relied in making their appellate argument.[3] For the modern American lawyer, schooled in the traditions of voluminous written briefs, such practice would seem highly inefficient and impracticable. But the rationale for that practice in England has been that the entire judicial process is completely open to public scrutiny: everything the judge

---

§ 2.1

1. In the 1790s, the Rules of the Supreme Court were issued by orders of the court on an ad hoc basis. In 1803, William Cranch compiled the first set of rules of the Supreme Court and published them in what is now 5 U.S. (1 Cranch) xv–xvii. Henceforth, when a new Reporter of Decisions was appointed, that Reporter published a compilation of the Rules of the Supreme Court as they then existed in the first volume of that Reporter's series. *See* 14 U.S. (1 Wheat.) xiii–xix (1816); 26 U.S. (1 Pet.)

v–xi (1828); 42 U.S. (1 How.) xxiii–xxxvii (1843). From the earliest set of Cranch's rules, before being admitted to practice, attorneys had to swear an oath in terms that are remarkably similar to the oath required of attorneys in the present day.

2. 5 U.S. (1 Cranch) xvi (1803) (Rule VII, issued Aug. 8, 1791).

3. *See* Robert J. Martineau, *Appellate Justice in England and the United States: A Comparative Analysis* 101–03 (1990).

learns about the case is presented in open court, which thus diminishes the possibility of out-of-court influence.

In its first decade, the Supreme Court hewed to the English oral tradition of appellate litigation. As a practical matter, however, even that tradition was rather informal and somewhat irregular throughout the 1790s. In *Hayburn's Case*,[4] for example, Attorney General Edmund Randolph appeared on his own motion to argue in favor of relief for a disabled veteran of the Revolutionary War. Because no counsel showed up to argue against him, the members of the court apparently took it upon themselves to construct a case against his authority to make such a request.[5] In so doing, they must have posed a reasonable number of questions to Randolph, although the records of the argument are insufficient to know precisely how the argument unfolded.

From another early case, *Georgia v. Brailsford*,[6] it is possible to glean something about the oral argument and, through that, to make inferences about argument practice more generally. Justice James Iredell took extensive notes of the argument that capture its substance rather than its procedure. From all the references to legal sources contained in those notes, however, it is fair to infer that counsel spent a good part of the seven-hour argument (spanning two days) citing cases and treatises to the court.[7] Less clear is how active the court was in questioning counsel. That practice of having counsel read swatches of prepared treatise and case material, however, was not consistently followed. Some advocates resorted to such sources as scripture, history, and Roman law in arguing their cases, rather than the particular matters presented in the case. Hence, in 1795, a change in the rules advised that "[t]he Court gave notice to the gentlemen of the bar, that hereafter they will expect to be furnished with a statement of the material points of the case."[8] That rule might be read by modern eyes to be an invitation to file a written brief, but it was instead treated during this era as a requirement by counsel to fill their oral presentations with citations and long excerpts of learned treatises in support of the argument.

---

4. *Hayburn's Case*, 2 U.S. (2 Dallas) 408 (1792).

5. *See* 6 *The Documentary History of the Supreme Court of the United States, 1789–1790* at 38 (Maeva Marcus, ed., 1998).

6. *Georgia v. Brailsford*, 2 U.S. (2 Dallas) 402 (1792).

7. 6 Marcus, *The Documentary History of the Supreme Court* at 119–126.

8. *See* 5 U.S. (1 Cranch) xvi (Rule VIII, issued February 4, 1795).

As befitting other changes in the Supreme Court under the leadership of Chief Justice John Marshall, oral advocacy practice also evolved in the decades between 1803 and 1835. In 1812, the court issued a rule limiting oral argument to only two counsel per side.[9] That rule contributed to a growing trend of Supreme Court specialists who came to dominate advocacy before the court. In the 1814 Term, for example, one of the most celebrated early Supreme Court advocates, William Pinkney, argued more than half of the cases decided by the court that term.[10] A contemporary of Pinkney's, Luther Martin, was known for his "iron memory" and the "fullness of his legal knowledge" notwithstanding the fact that he "often appeared in [the Supreme] Court evidently intoxicated."[11] Despite that weakness, Chief Justice Roger Brooke Taney remembered him as a "profound lawyer" who "never missed the strong points of his case."[12] Martin was one of the losing advocates in the celebrated case of *McCulloch v. Maryland*,[13] a case whose importance was acknowledged at the time by the court itself, in waiving its rule limiting argument to two counsel per side.

In *McCulloch*, six advocates presented arguments, including the greatest of the day, Daniel Webster, as well as Pinkney, Martin, William Wirt, Walter Jones, and Joseph Hopkinson. All six were regarded as among the most prominent attorneys of the era. Jones, in fact, is said to hold the record for most arguments in the Supreme Court, with more than 300.[14] Though advocating a losing cause, Martin's argument was thought to have been one of his finest, particularly given his age (he was 71 years old at the time). Interestingly, his argument invoked the Constitutional Convention, of which he had been a participant in 1787, thus creating a rare merger between the role of an attorney as both shaper of the historical record and expositer of it in court.[15]

The court made no effort at this time, however, to limit the length of attorney presentations. Oral argument could and did consume numerous days in important cases. In *McCulloch*, for

---

9. *See* 14 U.S. (1 Wheat.) xviii (1816) (Rule XXIII, issued February Term, 1812).

10. G. Edward White, III–IV The Oliver Wendell Holmes Devise, *History of the Supreme Court of the United States, The Marshall Court and Cultural Change, 1815–1835*, at 208 (1988).

11. *Id.* at 230.

12. Samuel Tyler, *Memoir of Roger Brooke Taney* 66 (1872).

13. *McCulloch v. Maryland*, 17 U.S. (4 Wheat.) 316 (1819).

14. William O. Douglas, *The Court Years, 1939–1975*, at 178 (1980).

15. White, *The Marshall Court*, at 238–240.

example, the argument began on February 22 and did not end until February 27, a Saturday afternoon. And in *Gibbons v. Ogden*,[16] the famous case that announced the rule that States may not interfere with interstate commerce under the Commerce Clause of the Constitution, the attorneys argued for six days. That case was touted to have been the "high point of advocacy on the Marshall Court."[17] The attorney who represented the State of New York in *Gibbons*, Thomas Addis Emmet, earned recognition as a preeminent Supreme Court advocate. Renowned for an eloquence that sometimes contributed to his own undoing, Emmet approached his preparation with a zeal matched by few advocates. He was known for his passionate commitment to his legal causes and for "putting his whole soul" into his cases. He collapsed from a stroke in the middle of an argument in 1827, leading one newspaper to record that there was "something glorious and consolatory" in the manner of his death.[18]

Emmet's maiden argument as a Supreme Court advocate in *The Mary*[19] was auspicious only for the fact that his opposing counsel, William Pinkney, leveled a rather vicious and ungentlemanly slur at Emmet for having been an immigrant to the United States.[20] It is well to recall that, even in today's supposedly less civil times, it is completely unthinkable that one advocate would criticize another in such openly derogatory terms. One of the cardinal rules of Supreme Court advocacy is not to attack opposing counsel. Such a calumny was all the more remarkable coming from an attorney of the stature of Pinkney, who at the time was at the height of his career as a Supreme Court advocate and who was described by former Deputy Solicitor General Stephen M. Shapiro as "The Supreme Court's Greatest Advocate."[21] Pinkney would be retained

---

16. *Gibbons v. Ogden,* 19 U.S. (6 Wheat.) 448 (1821).

17. White, *The Marshall Court,* at 211.

18. *Id.* at 213–14. Emmet was not the only attorney to expire from an oral argument experience. According to Justice William O. Douglas, one advocate passed out in 1973 while arguing a Fourth Amendment case, which was reargued the following week by a different lawyer. And another lawyer, Prew Savoy, insisted on arguing *Soriano* v. *United States,* 352 U.S. 270, 77 S.Ct. 269 (1957), even though he was in the last

stages of lung cancer. He died within 36 hours of arguing, leading Justice Douglas to write: "[H]e had lived with his case a long time and felt so keenly about it that he wanted to argue it even on his last day on this earth." Douglas, *The Court Years,* at 181.

19. *The Mary,* 13 U.S. (9 Cranch) 126 (1815).

20. White, *The Marshall Court,* at 208 (describing argument in *The Mary*).

21. Stephen M. Shapiro, "William Pinkney: The Supreme Court's Greatest Advocate," Y.B. Sup. Ct. Hist. Soc. 40 (1988).

to argue some of the most celebrated cases in the history of the Supreme Court, such as *Trustees of Dartmouth College v. Woodward*,[22] *McCulloch v. Maryland, Cohens v. Virginia*,[23] and *Gibbons v. Ogden*. Pinkney's fame extended not just to his advocacy in important cases, but also to his manner of dress. He was known as such a fancy dresser that Chief Justice Taney once wrote that Pinkney's *haute couture* "approached dandyism, if it did not reach it."[24] Notwithstanding his appearance, Pinkney was a successful advocate because his presentations were rich in substance. The distinguished Supreme Court historian G. Edward White notes that a comparison between Pinkney's arguments (as recorded by the Reporter of Decisions) and Chief Justice Marshall's famous opinions in *McCulloch* and *Cohens* reveals a striking parallel between the language and content of Pinkney's arguments and the court's opinions.[25]

One of Pinkney's frequent opponents in the Supreme Court was William Wirt, who, as the longest serving Attorney General in the history of the United States (1817–1829) and as a member of the private bar, argued in even more of the Marshall Court's important constitutional cases than Pinkney: *Dartmouth College, Sturges v. Crowninshield*,[26] *McCulloch, Cohens, Gibbons, Ogden v. Saunders*,[27] *Cherokee Nation v. Georgia*,[28] and *Proprietors of the Charles River Bridge v. Proprietors of the Warren Bridge*.[29] He is believed to have argued some 50 cases in the Supreme Court, 25 while serving as Attorney General.[30] White use adjectives to describe Wirt's ability in court that would make any advocate proud: "calm," "deliberate," "smooth," "pleasant," "agreeable," and "gentlemanly."[31]

22. *Trustees of Dartmouth College v. Woodward*, 17 U.S. (4 Wheat.) 518 (1819).

23. *Cohens v. Virginia*, 19 U.S. (6 Wheat.) 264 (1821).

24. Tyler, *Memoir of Taney*, at 64.

25. White, *The Marshall Court*, at 247–50.

26. *Sturges v. Crowninshield*, 17 U.S. (4 Wheat.) 122 (1819).

27. *Ogden v. Saunders*, 25 U.S. (12 Wheat.) 213 (1827).

28. *Cherokee Nation v. Georgia*, 30 U.S. (5 Pet.) 1 (1831).

29. *Proprietors of the Charles River Bridge v. Proprietors of the Warren Bridge*, 36 U.S. (11 Pet.) 420 (1837).

30. This information is drawn from Debra M. Lessin, *Cases Argued by United States Attorneys General Before the Supreme Court of the United States, 1789–1998*, at 10–13 (Aug. 1999) (available from the Clerk, Supreme Court of the United States). William K. Suter, Clerk of the Supreme Court, generously made this document available.

31. White, *The Marshall Court*, at 265.

Wirt's advice on advocacy in 1815 bears some resemblance to the process the modern advocate must endure before feeling fully ready to appear in the Supreme Court, even while his plea to emotionalism speaks from an entirely different age:

> You must read and meditate, like a Conastoga horse,—no disparagement to the horse by the simile. You must read like Jefferson, and speak like Henry. If you ask me how you are to do this, *I* cannot tell you, but you are nevertheless to do it. * * * [M]aster the cause in all its points, of fact and law; digest a profound, comprehensive, simple, and glowing speech for the occasion—not strained beyond the occasion, nor beyond the capacity of your audience;— and make upon the world the impression of strength, of vigor, of great energy, combined with a fluent, animated, nervous elocution; no puerile, out-of-the-way, far-fetched, or pedantic ornaments or illustrations, but *simple, strong,* and *manly—level yourself* to *the capacity of your hearers,* and insinuate yourself among the heart-strings, the bones and marrow * * * .[32]

Wirt was not the only Attorney General to be a frequent advocate before the Supreme Court. President George Washington's last Attorney General, Charles Lee, is believed to have argued 8 cases as Attorney General, and another 49 after he left office.[33] Caesar Rodney, who served as Attorney General under Presidents Thomas Jefferson and James Madison, and Roger Brooke Taney, who later would become Chief Justice of the United States, both argued numerous cases while serving as Attorney General. Indeed, the role of the Attorney General as an advocate before the Supreme Court was so important that, between John Breckenridge, who left office in 1806, and Joseph McKenna, who served for barely a year as Attorney General from 1897 to 1898 prior to being appointed Associate Justice, every single Attorney General argued at least one case on behalf of the United States.

Some of those lawyers who served as Attorney General, like Rodney and Taney, are still remembered as among the finest lawyers in American history. But the advocate often described as the greatest in Supreme Court history was Daniel Webster.[34] He

---

32. John P. Kennedy, I *Memoirs of the Life of William Wirt* 385–86 (1849).

33. *See* Lessin, *Cases Argued by United States Attorneys General,* at iii, 16–18.

34. *See, e.g.,* Seth P. Waxman, "In the Shadow of Daniel Webster: Arguing

was the winning attorney in such cases as *Trustees of Dartmouth College, McCulloch, Cohens, Gibbons, Osborn v. Bank of the United States*,[35] and *Mason v. Haile*.[36] Webster's only loss in a major constitutional case during the period in which those cases were decided was *Ogden v. Saunders*. Even in an era when Emmet, Wirt, and Pinkney were lions at the bar, Webster was arguably the most important advocate during the Marshall Court years, not only for the many significant cases he argued but also for his frequent public orations that served to promote the nationalist constitutional principles announced by the Supreme Court under Chief Justice Marshall's leadership.[37]

It is hard to speculate on how Webster would have fared in today's climate of half-hour arguments, characterized by the quick thrust and parry of questions. From the summaries of his arguments, however, it is fair to infer that he would have been as formidable today as he was in the nineteenth century. His arguments displayed an understanding of the basic tenets of great Supreme Court advocacy, albeit in a rhetorical style that fit the times.

For example, in *Bank of Augusta v. Earle*,[38] a case from 1839 that raised the question of the Supreme Court's power to protect commercial interests against the intrusive authority of states that had enacted statutes forbidding certain acts by foreign corporations, Webster had a very simple mantra: whatever individuals can do under a state's law, a corporation can do as well. In advancing that basic theme, Webster also was careful to articulate a limiting principle—simply because of its legal status, a corporation does not have carte blanche to exercise privileges not enjoyed by individuals: "We say, undoubtedly, that [corporations] cannot acquire power under the Pennsylvania charter to do acts in Alabama which they cannot do as individuals; but we say that the corporation may do in their corporate character in Alabama, all such acts authorized by their charter, as the members thereof would have a right to perform as individuals."[39] And even though in this case Webster's

---

Appeals in the Twenty–First Century," 3 J. APP. PRAC. & PROCESS 521 (Fall 2001).

35. *Osborn v. Bank of the United States*, 22 U.S. (9 Wheat.) 738 (1824).

36. *Mason v. Haile*, 25 U.S. (12 Wheat.) 370 (1827).

37. *See generally* Kennedy, *Memoirs of William Wirt*, at 267–89.

38. *Bank of Augusta v. Earle*, 38 U.S. (13 Pet.) 519 (1839).

39. *Id.* at 550 (reporter's summary of Webster's argument).

client was the Sergeant for the Bank of the United States, he conveyed the humility before the court that is an unchanging attribute of the finest Supreme Court advocates:

> It is not, however, for the learned gentleman, nor for myself, to say here that we speak for the country. We advance our sentiments and our arguments, but they are without authority. But it is for you, Mr. Chief Justice and Judges, on this, as on other occasions of high importance, to speak and to decide for the country. The guardianship of her commercial interests; the preservation of the harmonious intercourse of all her citizens; the fulfilling, in this respect, of the great object of the Constitution, are in your hands; and I am not to doubt that the trust will be so performed as to sustain at once high national objects and the character of this tribunal.[40]

In other words, an advocate must stand before the Supreme Court in full knowledge that the justices control the forum. Even in Webster's day and age, when the oral tradition of argument meant that the justices had to wait patiently for counsel to propound the argument—even for days on end—the advocate was still a supplicant to the court, which necessarily imposed certain rhetorical limits.

§ 2.2 Transitional Efforts to Regulate Oral Argument

In 1830, toward the end of the Marshall Court years, the court issued a rule to promote further regularity in oral argument practice. Until that time, the docket was less formalized. The court not infrequently called cases in which only one side was ready to make an appearance. The difficulties of travel and communication clearly contributed to the need to hold over cases for a certain period of time, or indeed even to the next term of court. In 1830, however, the Supreme Court issued a rule requiring that cases be called for argument in the order in which they were placed on the docket. Counsel was to be ready for the following case so that the court's handling of cases could proceed in an orderly pace.[1] That require-

---

40. *Id.* at 567.

§ **2.2**

1. *See* 42 U.S. (1 How.) xxxiii (1843) (Rule XXXVI, issued Jan. Term, 1830).

ment must have caused no small controversy between Supreme Court lawyers and their clients, because arguments in major cases were still occupying days. Clients and attorneys alike must have chafed at the requirement of sitting in the courtroom waiting for the next case to be called.

In 1833, the Supreme Court indicated that attorneys had suggested that "it would in many cases accommodate Counsel, and save expense to parties, to submit causes upon printed arguments."[2] For that reason, the court ordered that, "in all cases brought here on appeal, writ of error, or otherwise, the court will receive printed arguments, if the Counsel on either or both sides shall choose so to submit the same."[3] Thus began the practice of submitting written briefs to the court, but the hortatory nature of the "order" meant that change was to proceed at the pace promoted by the bar. In time, that order led to a profound change in the manner of oral argument in the Supreme Court, because the availability of written briefs rendered unnecessary the long, pedantic orations that had marked Supreme Court practice up to that time.

Even so, some celebrated cases continued to be marked by extended oral arguments. The new rule was in effect in 1841, for example, when the famous case of the *Amistad*[4] was argued. This was the first slavery case argued to the Supreme Court and, as such, drew as much national attention at the time as it has in historical curiosity. The case concerned the fate of slaves aboard a slave trade ship, the Amistad. The African natives had killed the captain and taken over the ship out of port from Havana, Cuba. The slave traders managed to trick the slaves into steering the vessel to the United States, rather than back to Africa, where it was seized by a United States war vessel and brought into district court. A protracted litigation ensued, leading to the Supreme Court. Abolitionists convinced John Quincy Adams, at that time a member of the House of Representatives after his presidency, to represent the Africans who sought their freedom from slavery. For eight days, Adams argued the case with his colleague, Roger D. Baldwin, while Attorney General Henry D. Gilpin represented the United States on the other side. Though much celebrated in a film by Steven Spielberg, Adams' argument did not do much to help the cause.

---

2. *Id.* at xxxv (Rule XL, issued Jan. Term, 1833).

3. *Id.*

4. *United States v. Libellants of Schooner Amistad*, 40 U.S. (15 Pet.) 518 (1841).

According to one historian, the court reporter "observed that the court did not consider much of [Adams' argument] essential to the decision"[5]—not exactly the type of historical epigraph desired by a Supreme Court advocate. The distinguished Supreme Court historian Carl B. Swisher went even further, commenting that "[t]he case enabled [Adams] to demonstrate in the court room the techniques which he used in the House of Representatives, denouncing to his heart's content the policy followed by the Van Buren administration."[6] That kind of approach, however, rarely helps the Supreme Court decide cases. However much the abolitionists gained politically by Adams' involvement, as a matter of Supreme Court advocacy his participation likely was tolerated by the justices, even if it did not help them resolve the issues in the case. As Justice Joseph Story described in a letter to his wife, Adams' argument was "[e]xtraordinary, I say, for its power, for its bitter sarcasm, and its dealing with topics far beyond the record and points of discussion."[7]

After the *Amistad* case, a number of competing pressures combined to culminate in the issuance of a rule limiting the time for argument of a case to two hours.[8] One such pressure was occasioned by the Supreme Court's workload, which increased from 98 cases in 1810 to 253 cases in 1850. That growing caseload forced the court to increase the time set aside on its calendar for oral argument, from 43 days in 1825 to 99 days in 1845.[9] Not only was the court's docket increasing, but the justices were not receiving any relief from their circuit-riding duties, which forced them to spend long periods outside of Washington hearing cases.

A second dynamic was the susceptibility of the justices to illness, which could cause interruptions in a justice's ability to hear the entire argument and which meant that evenly divided cases had to be reargued, at great expense to the litigants and the court. For example, Justice John McKinley was in ill health throughout his career on the court and Justice Story missed the entire 1843 Term. Shortly after Justice Story returned from that bout of illness, Chief

5. Charles Grove Haines & Foster H. Sherwood, *The Role of the Supreme Court in American Government and Politics, 1835–1864*, at 101 (1957).

6. Carl B. Swisher, *Roger B. Taney* 417 (1935).

7. 2 Charles A. Warren, *The Supreme Court in United States History* 76 (Rev. ed. 1928).

8. *See* 48 U.S. (7 How.) I (1849) (Rule 53, issued Jan. Term, 1849).

9. *See* Gerhard Casper & Richard Posner, *The Workload of the Supreme Court* 12–13 (1976).

Justice Taney fell ill and missed most of the 1844 Term. Those absences caused a severe backlog of cases to develop.

Finally, oral argument was perceived by some of the justices as overly long and not particularly helpful to the court's decision-making process. Justice Story complained to members of the bar about the length and quality of Supreme Court arguments. Justice John Catron attempted to persuade Chief Justice Taney to "take responsibility for suppression of irrelevant oratory," but, according to Swisher, "Catron was asking him for an authoritarian type of performance that was out of character with Taney's gentle and courteous if sometimes highly persistent personality."[10]

Faced with a growing backlog of cases and opposition among some justices to protracted arguments, the court adopted a change in the rules in 1849, providing that "no counsel will be permitted to speak, in the argument of any case in this court, more than two hours, without the special leave of the court, granted before the argument begins."[11] The rule also stated that no counsel would be permitted to speak in a case unless having first filed a printed abstract of points and authorities. Importantly, the new rule prohibited an attorney from referring to any other book or case not referenced in the points and authorities, and informed the bar that the court would proceed *ex parte* with the hearing if counsel for a party did not conform to this rule.[12]

Such special leave of court, however, was granted in numerous cases in succeeding years. The *Dred Scott* case,[13] infamous in the history of the Supreme Court, was one such example. Like other great constitutional cases, *Dred Scott* drew as advocates some of the leaders of the Supreme Court bar, including Reverdy Johnson, Montgomery Blair, Henry S. Geyer, and, eventually, George T. Curtis. Blair took Scott's case pro bono, having arranged for the court costs to be picked up by others. Johnson and Geyer, two Marylanders, represented John Sanford, who claimed to be Scott's

---

10. Carl B. Swisher, V The Oliver Wendell Holmes Devise, *History of the Supreme Court of the United States, The Taney Period, 1836–64,* at 278 (1974).

11. *See* 48 U.S. (7 How.) i (1849) (Rule 53, issued Jan. Term, 1849).

12. *See id. See also* 51 U.S. (10 How.) v (1851) (Rule 58, issued Dec. Term, 1850; establishing that the print-

ed argument had to be filed before the oral argument, if the court was to receive it).

13. *Dred Scott v. Sandford,* 60 U.S. (19 How.) 393 (1857). According to Professor Wright, the Supreme Court simply misspelled Sanford's name in its official reports. See 20 Charles Alan Wright and Mary Kay Kane, *Federal Practice and Procedure* § 57 n. 5 (2000).

owner and master. At the time, Geyer was a United States Senator well-known for his pro-slavery stance. Johnson would subsequently become a Senator from Maryland and still later would be involved in the representation of Mary Surratt, who was convicted and hanged as a co-conspirator in the assassination of President Abraham Lincoln.

The first argument in the case occurred in February 1856, during which Johnson secured three hours' time for each counsel. (At that point, Curtis was not involved in the case.) The parties also filed written briefs. Blair's brief for Scott was incredibly short for a case of this magnitude, running to a mere 11 printed pages.[14] The court deadlocked at conference and set the case for reargument on the questions of whether it had jurisdiction to decide the case and, if it did, on the merits of whether Scott was a citizen of Missouri in light of the facts appearing on the record. By the time of reargument, the case was drawing significant national attention. Shortly before the reargument, Blair filed 2 more briefs (for reasons that remain obscure), one of 8 pages, the other of 40. Three days before the second argument, Blair persuaded Curtis to participate, a decision that appears to have caused no procedural difficulties. (Today, except in cases of the most extraordinary nature—such as *Bush v. Gore*,[15] which was granted review on a Saturday and argued two days later on a Monday—it would be highly unusual to add an arguing counsel at such a late date.) The decision to add Curtis, who argued for the last hour of the case, was also interesting for the fact that he was the brother of Justice Benjamin Curtis, whose dissent would be characterized by Swisher as "a performance in juristic art."[16] (Justice Curtis is reported to have later said charitably that "his brother had conducted himself in a manner exceedingly creditable to himself and to the bar of New England, and quoted Justice Catron as saying that his was the best argument on a question of constitutional law he had heard in the court."[17])

§ 2.3   Creation of the Office of the Solicitor General

The subsequent onset of the Civil War ushered in a new era in Supreme Court advocacy. Although various Attorneys General had pushed for decades for the creation of an officer whose responsibili-

---

14. Swisher, *The Taney Period*, at 605–606.

15. *Bush v. Gore*, 531 U.S. 98, 121 S.Ct. 525 (200).

16. Swisher, *The Taney Period*, at 630.

17. *Id.* at 614.

ty would be the efficient handling of the government's Supreme Court litigation, those efforts had come to naught. In the decades immediately preceding the Civil War, the government was represented in the Supreme Court in a somewhat ad hoc manner. Sometimes cases were argued by the Attorney General, sometimes by a district attorney, sometimes by a government lawyer from one of the executive departments, and sometimes by private outside counsel retained to represent the government. As Civil War-related litigation rose, the United States became involved in increasingly significant cases before the Supreme Court. The Attorney General simply could not conduct it all. The short-gap solution was to hire private lawyers. From 1861 to 1867, the Attorney General paid nearly $50,000 to hire outside counsel just to argue the federal government's cases in the Supreme Court.[1] Not only was that approach prohibitively expensive, it also diminished the effectiveness of the government's advocacy, because outside counsel could not be expected necessarily to consider the full range of institutional interests an executive officer could.

In that period arose *Ex parte Milligan*,[2] one of the most important cases of constitutional law concerning the authority of the military over civilians. Lamdin Milligan was a resident of Indiana who was arrested by the military commandant of his district in Indiana and imprisoned. Charged with conspiracy against the United States, disloyalty, and insurrection, Milligan was found guilty by a military commission and sentenced to death by hanging. The case came to the Supreme Court in 1866 on appeal of a circuit court's denial of a petition for a writ of habeas corpus. David Dudley Field, brother of Justice Stephen Field and one of the most prominent attorneys of the last half of the nineteenth century, represented Milligan. He contended that the military commission lacked jurisdiction over Milligan, who was a civilian and had never been in the military, and that the writ of habeas corpus therefore should issue. The argument was transcribed, and it is noteworthy for the extent to which the practice of extended oral arguments still carried the day. It also contains rather unusual interruptions of Field's argument not by one of the justices, but by his opponent, Assistant Attorney General Henry Stanbery, who the following year (1867) would become Attorney General of the United States:

---

1. H.R. Exec. Doc. No. 40–198, at 3–4 (1868).

2. *Ex parte Milligan*, 71 U.S. (4 Wall.) 2 (1866).

MR. FIELD: * * * It was decided by this Court, in *Holmes v. Jennison*[3] that a proceeding on habeas corpus is a suit, and suit is a more comprehensive word than cause.

MR. STANBERY: Will the gentleman allow me a word?

MR. FIELD: Certainly.

MR. STANBERY: I never said that a habeas corpus, after the return, when the parties appear and begin to try the case, is not a suit; and that was Holmes and Jennison.

MR. FIELD: Then the argument is that it is not a cause until the adverse party comes in. Is not a suit commenced before the defendant is brought into Court?[4]

That exchange may well have been somewhat atypical for oral argument in that (or any) era, although at a later point in the *Milligan* argument Stanbery again interrupted Field, this time to ask his opponent a question![5] (Some evidence exists from a celebrated case in the Ninth Circuit argued in 1895 that the practice of arguing counsel interrupting each other may not have been out of the norm.[6])

In 1867, a year after the *Milligan* case was argued and decided, the court considered another important case for the administration of justice with implications for oral argument practice. At first blush, the case of *The Gray Jacket*[7] was a simple prize case concerning who was to receive the proceeds of a ship arrested for trying to run the blockade during the Civil War. But the claimant's attorney schemed to get the government to remit the seized assets to the claimant rather than to give the proceeds to the seizing crew or naval pension fund, as was required by statute. The claimant's attorney, Benjamin Butler, failed to persuade the Attorney General of his concocted theory, but he did manage to convince the Secretary of the Treasury that his position had some merit. As a result, the oral argument contained the rather unusual lineup of both the

---

3. *Holmes v. Jennison*, 39 U.S. (14 Pet.) 540 (1840).

4. I *Speeches, Arguments, and Miscellaneous Papers of David Dudley Field* 10 (A.P. Sprague, ed., 1884) (footnote omitted) (reprint of oral argument transcript in *Ex parte Milligan*).

5. *Id.* at 16–17.

6. *See* David C. Frederick, *Rugged Justice: The Ninth Circuit Court of Appeals and the American West, 1891–1941*, at 44 (1994) (describing oral argument in *United States v. Stanford*, the case in the mid–1890s that saved Stanford University).

7. *The Gray Jacket*, 72 U.S. (5 Wall.) 342 (1867).

claimant and the Secretary of the Treasury aligned against the Attorney General. The argument may have convinced the court of the havoc such multiple representations by the government could wreak. In an opinion issued in April 1867, the Supreme Court held that, "in causes where the United States is a party, and is represented by the Attorney General [or an attorney under the Attorney General's supervision], no counsel can be heard in opposition on behalf of any other of the departments of the government."[8]

The importance of that precedent, coupled with others in subsequent years of a similar vein,[9] became clear after 1870, when Congress enacted a law to create the Department of Justice, with a special provision for the establishment of "an officer learned in the law, to assist the Attorney-General in the performance of his duties, to be called the solicitor-general."[10] Henceforth, through the Attorney General or designee, the Solicitor General, the authority to litigate on behalf of the United States would rest with the Department of Justice.

The first Solicitor General was Benjamin Bristow, who quickly established himself as a Supreme Court advocate of the first rank. Whereas in the December 1869 Term the government was represented in 15 cases by private outside counsel, by the December 1872 Term government lawyers under Bristow's supervision argued all of the cases in which the United States participated. Bristow himself argued 13 cases in the December 1870 Term: 3 alone, 5 with Attorney General Amos T. Ackerman, and 5 with various Assistant Attorneys General. The following term, Bristow argued 27 Supreme Court cases: 7 alone, and 20 with either the Attorney General or an Assistant Attorney General.[11] As a Supreme Court advocate, Bristow earned a reputation for his level of preparation

---

8. *Id.* at 370–71.

9. *See, e.g., Confiscation Cases,* 74 U.S. (7 Wall.) 454 (1869) (holding that Attorney General has the power to dismiss any action brought in the name of the United States); *United States v. Throckmorton,* 98 U.S. 61 (1878) (holding that suit by the United States or any of its agencies to set aside a land patent could be brought only at the direction of the Attorney General); *United States v. San Jacinto Tin Co.,* 125 U.S. 273, 8 S.Ct. 850 (1888) (holding that Attorney General, or his designate, has authority to bring action on behalf of the United

States to set aside a patent or other instrument).

10. Act of June 22, 1870, ch. 150, § 2, 16 Stat. 162. The history of the origins of the Solicitor General's Office is recounted by Solicitor General Seth P. Waxman, " 'Presenting the Case of the United States As It Should Be': The Solicitor General in Historical Context," 2 J. Sup. Ct. Hist. 3–25 (1998).

11. *See* Waxman, "Presenting the Case of the United States As It Should Be," at 11–12.

and judgment. One of his successors, Seth P. Waxman, published this description of Bristow, from papers in the Library of Congress:

> One marked characteristic of Mr. Bristow's arguments was an absence of all attempt at display. He always thoroughly prepared himself, going over every case in which he did not make the brief, with as much care as if nothing had been done in its preparation, and making voluminous notes and memoranda. But when he came to speak he would never make any further use of these than the posture of the case demanded; and if he thought the case had been sufficiently argued by his associate, would add but a few remarks on one or two of the most vital points. The great judgment he thus showed in arguing the important questions and leaving the others alone, and never unnecessarily taking up the time of the overworked judges, was one reason why he was so great a favorite with them, and was always listened to with respectful attention.[12]

Samuel Field Phillips, who immediately followed Bristow as Solicitor General, earned a similar reputation. Phillips' "habit was to discard the minor points of a case, and address himself to the great questions upon which [the court's] decision ought to rest; and then he was so candid in stating the position of his opponents and the facts appearing in the record, and so lucid and strong in his argument, that he commanded the entire confidence, as well as the respect, of the court."[13]

Those attributes mark many attorneys who have served as Solicitor General, including some lawyers already regarded as among the greatest in American history, such as William Howard Taft, John W. Davis, Charles Fahy, Robert Jackson, Archibald Cox, Thurgood Marshall, and Erwin Griswold. Still others, such as Robert Bork, Rex Lee, Kenneth Starr, Drew Days, Seth Waxman, and Theodore Olson have achieved great prominence in their day. The Office of the Solicitor General has also produced some of the country's finest attorneys, many of whom subsequently served as judges: Oscar Davis, Myron Bright, Paul Freund, Daniel Friedman, Richard Posner, Frank Easterbrook, Charles Wyzanski, Robert Stern, Warner Gardner, and William Bryson. Others, such as John

---

12. *Id.* at 13.

13. R.H. Battle, "Obituary of Samuel Field Phillips, LL.D.," 1 N.C.J.L. 22,

26–27 (1904) (quoted in Waxman, "Presenting the Case of the United States As It Should Be," at 12–13).

Roberts, Miguel Estrada, Maureen Mahoney, and Barbara Under-wood all served with great distinction in the Office of the Solicitor General and were either nominated or considered for judgeships. As Justice Douglas would later recall, many of the finest advocates before the Supreme Court have been staff lawyers in the Office of the Solicitor General: "lesser lights and lawyers not well known brought greater distinction to advocacy at the appellate level."[14] Such attorneys "made more enduring contributions to the art of advocacy before [the Supreme Court] than most of the 'big-name' lawyers."[15]

In singling out lesser-known advocates for special praise, Justice Douglas wrote in his memoirs about the unique contributions of female lawyers who served in the government. And although female government lawyers brought greater equality and diversity among the ranks of advocates in the twentieth century, they all owed a debt to the pioneering efforts of Belva A. Lockwood in the nineteenth century. In the 1870s, Lockwood spent considerable time and energy seeking admission to the Supreme Court bar. After the Court of Claims turned down her application for admission to the bar, Lockwood even went so far as to lobby Congress for legislation that a woman otherwise admitted to the bar of a state could not be "debarred from practice before any United States Court on account of sex or coverture."[16] She then scoured the rules of the Supreme Court bar, discovering that an attorney could be admitted after practicing in a state for three years. Lockwood believed that if she could get admitted to the Supreme Court bar, she could use that credential to win admission to the bar of the Court of Claims, where she was attracting business for her representation of soldiers and their families after the Civil War. After her third year of practice in the District of Columbia elapsed, Lockwood persuaded a supporter of women's suffrage, Albert G. Riddle, to move her admission. But the Supreme Court denied the motion, on the ground that, "[b]y the uniform practice of the court from its organization to the present time, and by the fair construction of its rules, none but men are permitted to practice before it as attorneys and counselors," further stating that "the court does not feel called upon to make a change until such a change is required

---

14. Douglas, *The Court Years*, at 186.

15. *Id.*

16. Jill Norgren, "Before It Was Merely Difficult: Belva Lockwood's Life

in Law and Politics," 3 J. Sup. Ct. Hist. 16, 28–29 (1999) (quoting Lockwood's proposed legislation).

by statute or a more extended practice in the highest courts of the State."[17]

Lockwood stubbornly returned to Congress where, within two years, she secured passage of a bill providing that any woman in good standing of a bar of the highest court of any state or the District of Columbia shall be admitted to practice in the Supreme Court of the United States. On March 3, 1879, the Supreme Court admitted her to practice. Twenty months later, on December 1, 1880, Belva Lockwood became the first woman to argue a case on the merits in the Supreme Court, *Kaiser v. Stickney*.[18] She later would represent an Indian tribe's members in oral argument before the court in *United States v. Cherokee Nation*.[19]

By the mid-twentieth century, it was not quite such a rarity for female advocates to be arguing in the court, but virtually all were in public service. Beatrice Rosenberg, for example, may have been the greatest woman advocate of the twentieth century, arguing in some 30 criminal cases in the Supreme Court. She was not a member of the Solicitor General's Office, however, but represented the government as an attorney on the Criminal Division Appellate Staff. The extent of government litigation in the twentieth century was so great that the Solicitor General often delegated responsibility for arguing cases to skilled lawyers in other agencies or departments. Hence, Helen R. Carloss, whom Justice Douglas described as "an advocate *par excellence*—brief, lucid, relevant and powerful," represented the Tax Division of the Department of Justice in cases from the 1920s to the 1940s.[20] And Bessie Margolin of the Department of Labor argued a number of Fair Labor Standards Act cases. She was said to have been "crisp in her speech and penetrating in her analyses, reducing complex factual situations to simple, orderly problems."[21] In 1972, Harriet Shapiro became the first woman appointed to the Office of the Solicitor General. She argued 17 cases for the government and worked on the merits briefs in some 72 others before going into a part-time status for the last decade of her nearly 40–year career as a government lawyer.[22]

---

17. *Id.* at 29–30 (quoting Minutes of the Supreme Court).

18. *See* 131 U.S. App. clxxxvii (1880) (Appendix of "Omitted Cases in the Reports of the Decisions of the Supreme Court") (1889)).

19. *United States v. Cherokee Nation*, 202 U.S. 101, 41 Ct.Cl. 507, 26 S.Ct. 588 (1906).

20. Douglas, *The Court Years*, at 184.

21. *Id.*

22. *See* "In re Harriet S. Shapiro, Esq.: Petition for a Writ of Apprecia-

Although not as frequent an advocate before the Supreme Court in the 1970s as Shapiro, Ruth Bader Ginsburg also contributed significantly to the development of the law as an advocate. She would later serve with distinction as a circuit judge on the U.S. Court of Appeals for the District of Columbia Circuit and as an associate justice on the Supreme Court, but for a stretch in the 1970s, Ginsburg was one of the most important advocates for equal rights in the country. Just as Thurgood Marshall's victories in the 1950s had advanced the cause of racial equality, Ginsburg's victories in a string of cases furthered gender equality. Those cases—*Frontiero v. Richardson*,[23] *Weinberger v. Wiesenfeld*,[24] *Craig v. Boren*,[25] and *Califano v. Goldfarb*[26]—are staples of the constitutional law curriculum decades later.[27]

§ 2.4   Twentieth Century Developments

The increasing diversity among advocates in the Supreme Court was not the only important development affecting oral argument in the twentieth century. By 1911, the rules of the court provided that each side would have one-and-a-half hours for oral argument, with the petitioner being given an opportunity to open and close the argument. In certain cases, such as those certified from the circuit courts of appeals that had been created under the Evarts Act of 1891, the Supreme Court limited argument to 45 minutes per side. The theory behind that limitation was the expectation that the recently created circuit courts of appeals would help to filter the issues that the Supreme Court needed to resolve. In both instances, the court had the discretion to provide leave for an expansion of time. The court retained the rule limiting arguing

---

tion," prepared by the Office of the Solicitor General, March 21, 2001.

23. *Frontiero v. Richardson*, 411 U.S. 677, 93 S.Ct. 1764 (1973) (holding unconstitutional federal statutes that provided that spouses of male members of the armed forces were "dependents" for purposes of obtaining military benefits, but that spouses of female members were not "dependents" unless they in fact depended on their wives for more than one-half of their support).

24. *Weinberger v. Wiesenfeld*, 420 U.S. 636, 95 S.Ct. 1225 (1975) (striking down provision of Social Security Act that awarded survivor's benefits only to widows, and not widowers).

25. *Craig v. Boren*, 429 U.S. 190, 97 S.Ct. 451 (1976) (invalidating prohibition on sale of 3.2% beer to men under age of 21 and women under age of 18 as discrimination on the basis of gender).

26. *Califano v. Goldfarb*, 430 U.S. 199, 97 S.Ct. 1021 (1977) (striking down as gender discrimination provision of Social Security Act that paid survivor's benefits to widowers only if they could show substantial reliance on the deceased's income while not imposing same requirement to widows).

27. *See generally* Lawrence H. Tribe, *American Constitutional Law* §§ 16–25 to 16–27 (2d ed. 1988).

counsel to two advocates per side.[1] In the 1920s, the court divided its docket between the "regular" docket and the "summary" docket. Cases on the "regular" docket were allotted one hour per side, and no more than two counsel per side were permitted to argue. In cases on the "summary" docket, only one-half hour per side was apportioned, and the court permitted no more than one counsel per side, except by special leave of court. For cases certified to the Supreme Court for decision, the justices heard 45 minutes of oral argument per side.[2] Interestingly, the rules still provided—as they had in the 1830s—that if a party chose to rest its submission on the briefs without appearing at oral argument, the opposing side was permitted to make an appearance.[3]

Just as the rules were changing, with a steady contraction in the amount of time allotted to oral argument, so, too, the manner of argument also evolved. In 1926, the Supreme Court decided *Village of Euclid v. Ambler Realty Co.*,[4] which concerned the constitutionality of zoning.[5] Apart from its enduring importance to constitutional law, the case also illuminates certain aspects of practice in the 1920s. The case was set for argument on January 27, 1926, only a few days, it turned out, after the respondent had filed its merits brief responding to Euclid's 142–page opening brief. Euclid's counsel, James Metzenbaum, was so disturbed by the supposed inaccuracies in the argument of the respondent's counsel, Newton D. Baker (one of the founders of the firm now known as Baker & Hostetler), that he scribbled a telegram to Chief Justice William Howard Taft on the train ride back to Cleveland in which he requested leave to file a reply brief, wrapped the money to pay for it around the message, and trustingly threw it off the moving train to a man who was shoveling snow by the side of the tracks. When, on February 2, 1926, Metzenbaum received a telegram back from the Supreme Court giving him one week in which to file his reply brief, he knew that his trust in the snow shoveler had been

§ 2.2

1. See 222 U.S. App. 28 (1912) (Rule 22, promulgated Dec. 22, 1911).

2. See 266 U.S. 673 (1925) (Rule 26).

3. See 275 U.S. 616 (1928) (Rule 28); 42 U.S. (1 How.) xxxvi (1843) (Rule XLIV, issued in 1837).

4. *Village of Euclid v. Ambler Realty Co.*, 272 U.S. 365, 47 S.Ct. 114 (1926).

5. See Michael Allan Wolf, "'Compelled by Conscientious Duty': *Village of Euclid v. Ambler Realty Co.* as Romance," 2 J. Sup. Ct. Hist. 88–100 (1997); Michael Allan Wolf, "*Euclid* at Threescore Years and Ten: Is This the Twilight of Environmental and Land—Use Regulation?" 30 U. Rich. L. Rev. 961 (1996).

rewarded. The court also allowed the respondent to file a sur-reply brief and, eventually, set the case down for reargument.[6]

Justice Harlan Fiske Stone's law clerk that Term, Milton Handler, later described Metzenbaum's argument as a "disaster," because he spent "a substantial part of his limited time in denouncing the trial judge who had decided the case."[7] As Handler related, "[i]t was a total waste of time to attack the trial judge in an important case before the Supreme Court," because the "Court was not going to reverse on that ground alone and the importance of the appeal was to get a determination on the legality of zoning. * * * I know that this was poor advocacy and a waste of the limited time allotted to counsel for the presentation of his case."[8] Such was hardly surprising, given Metzenbaum's background and experience. A local lawyer from Euclid, Ohio, Metzenbaum assumed the duty of defending the village's ordinance by virtue of his being the only attorney on the town council, hardly the kind of credential one would expect in the advocate defending the constitutional authority of municipalities to impose zoning restrictions on landowners' use of property. Notwithstanding his shortcomings as an advocate, the Supreme Court upheld Metzenbaum's argument that the Village of Euclid could constitutionally promulgate its zoning ordinance.

The change in the rules limiting the time for oral argument affected advocacy in the Supreme Court, particularly during the New Deal era. Although the court occasionally heard extended arguments in important cases, increasingly the court used the limited time for argument to put questions to counsel. By the 1930s, the transformation of oral argument from oration to question-and-answer was not quite complete, but the signs of that trend were well in evidence in some of the most prominent constitutional cases of the era.

In *Helvering v. Davis*,[9] for example, Robert H. Jackson defended the constitutionality of the Social Security Act's imposition of a tax on employers and employees so that funds would be available for the payment of old-age benefits by the government. At that time, Jackson was Assistant Attorney General in charge of the Justice Department's Antitrust Division. The case did not arise out of his division, but Jackson was perceived to be so skilled that,

---

6. *See* Wolf, "'Compelled by Conscientious Duty,'" at 93–95.

7. Letter to the Editor by Milton C. Handler, 2 J. Sup. Ct. Hist. (1998).

8. *Id.*

9. *Helvering v. Davis*, 301 U.S. 619, 57 S.Ct. 904 (1937).

during the period in which he headed the Antitrust Division, he argued ten cases for the government in the Supreme Court, only one of which had to do with antitrust law. The others concerned taxation, administrative law, and constitutional law.[10]

The transcript of *Helvering* is one of only two of Jackson's Supreme Court arguments that apparently still exists.[11] Both date from his service as Assistant Attorney General. Neither recordings nor transcripts of his appearances as Solicitor General or Attorney General apparently exist. The transcript in *Helvering* conveys the impression of a confident advocate with extremely precise locution who is quick on his feet:

JUSTICE STONE: Are you going to deal with the equity jurisdiction, Mr. Jackson?

MR. JACKSON: I had not intended to; but, of course, if there is a question about it, I shall be glad to. I may say that we waived any question as to equity jurisdiction; that we waived because of the vital importance to the Government of an early decision in this case. * * *

JUSTICE STONE: So that the Government is in the position of saying here that a suit to enjoin a tax is properly here, although provision is made for payment of the tax and for a suit to recover it, which would give adequate relief, would it not, to the taxpayer?

MR. JACKSON: We think that question, if raised by the Government or by the defendant in the case, would have to be decided against the stockholder. We believe that the *Norman* case,[12] decided in the second circuit (Apr. 12, 1937), is good law, but we also believe that it is a question not of jurisdiction, but of fact, as to whether the stockholder is irreparably injured under the circumstances, and that it can be waived by the Government, as was done in

10. *See* Warner Gardner, "Government Attorney," 55 Colum. L. Rev. 438, 440 nn. 3–7 (1955).

11. *See* "Oral Arguments in *Helvering et al.* v. *Davis,* involving the Old Age Benefit Provisions of the Social Security Act before the Supreme Court of the United States," S. Doc. No. 71, 75th Cong., 1st Sess. (May 5, 1937). The other is *Charles C. Steward Machine Co. v.*

Davis, 301 U.S. 548, 57 S.Ct. 883 (1937). *See* "Arguments in the cases arising under the Social Security Act and the Alabama Unemployment Compensation Law before the Supreme Court of the United States," S. Doc. No. 53, 75th Cong., 1st Sess. 99–122 (Apr. 15, 1937).

12. *Norman v. Consolidated Edison Co.,* 89 F.2d 619 (2d Cir.1937).

Pollock v. Farmers' Loan & Trust Co. (157 U.S. 429), and I think in *Brushaber v. Union Pacific R.R.* (240 U.S. 1).

JUSTICE STONE: Conceding that is so, he would be equally protected by a direction to pay the tax and sue to get it back?

MR. JACKSON: Perhaps that is true.

JUSTICE STONE: That is the procedure which the Government has insisted should be followed in most of these tax cases.

MR. JACKSON: We have insisted on that in many cases.

JUSTICE STONE: And having been disposed to be with them on that, I wonder whether I should recede from that position now.

MR. JACKSON: I should very much dislike to say anything that would discourage you in that position, Your Honor. Our position is that it can be waived, that it is not jurisdictional, and we waived it in this case.

JUSTICE STONE: Equity jurisdiction cannot be conferred by consent, on the other hand.

MR. JACKSON: I think, however, that the jurisdiction which depends upon the question of fact as to irreparable injury can be waived, so as to permit the cause to proceed. It is not a situation where the court has no jurisdiction to proceed to inquire into the facts. It is a case where, if the facts are found to establish irreparable injury, as in *Ashwander v. Tennessee Valley Authority* (297 U.S. 288) and other cases, then it is held that the court may enter judgment.

JUSTICE STONE: Is it not a little more than that? It has always seemed to me that it was a question of large public policy, and a very important one, that when a taxpayer is called upon to pay taxes and there is an adequate remedy at law whereby he can pay the tax and sue to get it back, the courts should keep away from granting injunctions.

MR. JACKSON: I certainly agree that that should be the law, but we have been subjected to many such injunctions. The law is unsettled upon this subject of injunctions to restrain collection of taxes.

JUSTICE STONE: This may unsettle it further, if you succeed.

MR. JACKSON: I would not think so, if we succeed upon the ground of waiver.[13]

Given the quickness of mind and insistence on his position demonstrated by Jackson in that passage, it is easy to imagine Justice Douglas's description of Jackson's "piercing look over his spectacles" as he argued with "greater intensity, precision and force" than any other advocate in his time.[14]

As that colloquy also showed, the Supreme Court was much more willing than at any previous time in its history to use the time at oral argument to put questions to counsel. Part of that dynamic resulted from the increasing pressures on time placed on the advocates; part of it was the disposition of the justices themselves. Justice Pierce Butler, for instance, was incessant in his questioning, particularly of government counsel during Franklin Roosevelt's Administration.[15] And when he served on the court, Justice Felix Frankfurter could dominate oral arguments with his questions, leading Justice Douglas to recall that "[s]ome of us would often squirm at Frankfurter's seemingly endless questions that took the advocate round and round and round."[16]

Unfortunately, the bar did not rise to the challenge of the new conditions for oral argument in the Supreme Court, as justices continued to complain about the performance of advocates.[17] Part of the problem must have stemmed from the increasing tendency of the justices to question counsel and the concomitant difficulties of being interrupted in mid-thought with a question, formulating a precise and persuasive answer, and transitioning back to an affirmative point. Of the 60 minutes per side allotted to counsel, Frederick Wiener recommended that counsel prepare to speak for 40 minutes, because the justices ask "many, many questions."[18] Although to Wiener the questioning might have seemed intense,

---

13. S. Doc. No. 71, at 2–3.

14. Douglas, *The Court Years*, at 182.

15. *See* E. Barrett Prettyman, Jr., "Robert H. Jackson: 'Solicitor General for Life,' " J. Sup. Ct. Hist. 1992, at 80 (noting that Justice Butler interrupted Jackson 79 times in *Helvering* and *Steward Machine*, a total that was 15 more than the rest of the justices combined).

16. Douglas, *The Court Years*, at 181.

17. Frederick Bernays Wiener, "Oral Advocacy," 62 Harv. L. Rev. 56, 56 (1948); Douglas, *The Court Years*, at 183.

18. Douglas, *The Court Years*, at 74.

except in the rare case it was still quite mild by the standards of a typical argument at the turn of the twenty-first century. But the time constraints in this mid-century period were nonetheless causing an increasing focus at oral argument on addressing the concerns of justices.

The *Steel Seizure Case*[19] provides a nice illustration of this transitional period in oral advocacy before the court. The case concerned the constitutionality of President Harry Truman's controversial seizure of the steel mills on April 8, 1952, in response to labor unrest in the midst of the Korean War. The case proceeded on a very fast track. After the district court issued an injunction against the government on April 29, 1952, the case quickly went through the court of appeals and into the Supreme Court, which granted certiorari on Saturday, May 3. The court set down the case for argument, three hours per side, on May 12. Unhappy with how divided argument in the district court had proceeded, the steel industry apparently could agree on only one advocate to present its case: John W. Davis. This 79-year-old former Solicitor General and presidential candidate had been one of the greatest Supreme Court advocates of the twentieth century. The *Steel Seizure Case* was Davis's 138th argument in the Supreme Court, a number exceeded in the twentieth century only by Deputy Solicitor General Lawrence G. Wallace.

The argument in the *Steel Seizure Case* was noteworthy in several respects, and bears brief elaboration for the themes to be developed elsewhere in this book. First, even though he was allotted 3 hours for argument, Davis' opening presentation consumed less than half that, 87 minutes. During his argument, Davis received only one question, from Justice Frankfurter. Rather confidently, Davis asked the justice whether he could defer answering it until a more convenient point in his argument. (Interestingly, Davis never did adequately address the question, which concerned an inconsistency between Davis's argument in the *Steel Seizure Case* and a position he had advocated as Solicitor General in a prior case.[20])

When Solicitor General Philip Perlman rose to defend President Truman's seizure of the steel mills, on the other hand, "there

---

19. *Youngstown Sheet & Tube Co. v. Sawyer*, 343 U.S. 579, 72 S.Ct. 863 (1952).

20. Maeva Marcus, *Truman and the Steel Seizure Case: The Limits of Presidential Power* 166–170 (1994).

was a perceptible change in attitude among the Justices," according to the Supreme Court historian Maeva Marcus.[21] The justices peppered Perlman with questions for more than two-and-a-half hours, with the argument extending until the 4:30 p.m. hour of adjournment when, "in the middle of a comment by Justice Frankfurter, the other Justices left the courtroom."[22] The next day, when argument resumed, Perlman had only 20 minutes remaining, but Chief Justice Fred M. Vinson extended his time so that he could field yet more questions from the court. Perlman's argument ended on a very weak note, with Justices Jackson and Frankfurter sharply questioning the Solicitor General's apparent inconsistency in dramatically defending the President's exercise of power because this was "wartime," while on the other hand conceding that Congress had not declared war.[23]

Even though he had more than an hour for rebuttal, Davis used only ten minutes, a demonstration of supreme confidence that no more needed to be said in support of his position. Notwithstanding press accounts, which noted how emotional Davis had gotten during the argument, Justice Frankfurter very much admired his skill as an advocate. In terms that echo what many modern-day justices and judges have said about oral advocacy, Frankfurter subsequently wrote in a letter to a friend:

> What miserable reporting even the best of our papers do when there aren't any handouts. Précis writing seems to be an unknown art with us. On the whole what you get from an account of the argument like that in the *Steel* case are what to the reporters seem quips or brushes between court and counsel. You rightly surmise, however, that the S.G. was better the second day, though to me it is absurd that his argument should have taken more than three hours. To me it is a constant surprise that lawyers resent questioning from the Bench. Of course an English barrister should be allowed to develop his argument and quote from the cases and all the rest of the business, since the judges must take it all in by ear. But I see no excuse whatever for allowing them here to tell us by word of mouth what they have submitted in print. With us the

21. *Id.* at 170.

22. *Id.* at 173.

23. *Id. See also* Alan F. Westin, *The Anatomy of a Constitutional Law Case:*

Youngstown Sheet and Tube Co. v. Sawyer 116–22 (1958) (excerpting transcripts of Perlman's argument).

function of oral argument is that of supplementing the printed briefs, by cross-examination as it were, of counsel on what is in the briefs. Of course an artist at the business, like Davis, knows how to exercise his art and holds the court's attention by it. Incidentally, although he had two-and-a-half hours I don't think he used more than half of it. One of the differences between good advocates and others is what R.L. Stevenson said was the difference between Homer and other poets: "Homer knew what to omit."[24]

The arguments produced a fractured court, which ruled 6–3 that the President lacked the constitutional authority to seize the steel mills. Chief Justice Vinson led the dissenters.

Though of advanced age, Davis was not done arguing in the Supreme Court. Barely six months later, on December 9, 1952, Davis represented the State of South Carolina in one of the lead cases that would become famous as *Brown v. Board of Education.*[25] In that era, the court heard argument promptly at noon, recessed at 2:00 for lunch for 30 minutes, and then reconvened at 2:30 for 2 more hours of oral argument. In defending segregation, Davis argued with no small confidence that his position was correct as a matter of constitutional law and social policy. The questioning from the bench was quite active in the *Brown* series of cases. The fissures on the Vinson Court evident in the *Steel Seizure Case* were, if anything, even more pronounced in the school desegregation cases. The 1952 Term ended without a decision, with the court issuing an order setting down the cases for reargument in the fall of 1953.

The reargument order sent the parties in a mad scramble to research the history of the Fourteenth Amendment. By the time the cases were reargued, beginning on December 7, 1953, Chief Justice Vinson had died and was replaced by Earl Warren. The court was at least as active, if not more so, than it had been for the first argument the prior year. And, as in the *Steel Seizure Case,* the now–80–year–old Davis spoke in the courtroom with great emotion, tears said to have been running down his cheeks during the

---

24. Letter from Felix Frankfurter to Charles C. Burlingham (May 19, 1952) (Box 36, Felix Frankfurter Papers, Library of Congress), *quoted in* Marcus, *Truman and the Steel Seizure Case,* at 330.

25. *Brown v. Board of Education,* 347 U.S. 483, 74 S.Ct. 686 (1954).

argument.[26] (Davis's show of emotion apparently caused one disgusted member of the Solicitor General's Office to whisper in the courtroom to a colleague, "That sonofabitch cries in every case he argues."[27]) Thurgood Marshall delivered one of his least effective performances, focusing on matters of little interest to the justices, such as the court's old precedents, and not addressing adequately the questions of the propriety of the court exercising judicial power put to him by Justice Jackson, whose vote was perceived to be critical to the NAACP's cause.[28]

Notwithstanding his lackluster performance in the reargument of the *Brown* cases, Thurgood Marshall has to be considered one of the greatest Supreme Court advocates. He led the NAACP in its brilliant litigation strategy that broke down the barriers of segregation. That effort required a thoughtful understanding of the incremental ways in which the Supreme Court makes doctrine. By litigating cases carefully and bringing them before the Supreme Court in a tactical way, Marshall increased the chances of a successful outcome. Moreover, as an advocate Marshall understood the value of common sense in the court's decision-making process. His advocacy to the court carried special weight because of his own experiences as a black man litigating cases in the South. Marshall thus spoke to the court with an authority of one who had seen and done far more than the justices themselves—and they knew that.

Marshall also practiced what he advocated, giving opportunities to lawyers who might otherwise not have been given the chance because of discrimination. One of the lawyers on his staff at the NAACP Legal Defense Fund was Constance Baker Motley, who argued a number of cases with such skill that one member of the Supreme Court would later write that "the quality of those arguments would place her in the top ten of any group of advocates at the appellate level in this country."[29] In 1966, President Lyndon

---

26. *See* Richard Kluger, *Simple Justice: The History of Brown v. Board of Education and Black America's Struggle for Equality* 672 (1975).

27. *See* Jack Greenberg, *Crusaders in the Courts: How a Dedicated Band of Lawyers Fought for the Civil Rights Revolution* 190 (1994).

28. Incredibly, Marshall was said to have told Jack Greenberg, an NAACP Legal Defense Fund colleague, that during the argument he had "sent a Mason-

ic hand signal—indicating distress—to Justice Jackson, a fellow Mason." Juan Williams, *Thurgood Marshall: American Revolutionary* 223 (1998). Williams does not cite anything for that anecdote, and Greenberg did not see fit to include it in his memoirs. Greenberg did, however, agree that Marshall's performance was "uninspiring." *See* Greenberg, *Crusaders in the Courts,* at 189.

29. Douglas, *The Court Years,* at 185.

Johnson would name Motley to be the first black woman to serve as a federal district judge. At the NAACP Legal Defense Fund, Inc., where she served for 20 years, Motley was involved in many of the most important civil rights cases of the era.

One of those was *Cooper v. Aaron*,[30] in which the court heard argument in a special session convened during its normal recess in the summer of 1958. The case raised issues of surpassing importance involving the integration of the schools in Little Rock, Arkansas. The Arkansas Governor, Orval Faubus, ordered National Guard troops to prevent black children from entering Central High School. President Dwight Eisenhower sent Army troops to escort the black students into the high school. After the school district continued to fight the integration, with consequent violence affecting the black children, litigation ensued over the school board's request to delay integration. As the case came to the Supreme Court, therefore, the protagonists were very much President Eisenhower and Governor Faubus, even though the named parties were a black student (John Aaron) and the white president of the school board (William Cooper). Thurgood Marshall had assembled a team including Motley and Jack Greenberg to develop the facts during lower court proceedings. At the Supreme Court, Marshall took the lead, speaking simply, but powerfully, by turning the school board's argument around and using it to advance his own best affirmative point:

> Education is not the teaching of the three R's. Education is the teaching of the overall citizenship, to learn to live together with fellow citizens, and above all to learn to obey the law.

> And the damage to the education in Arkansas and in Little Rock and in Central High comes about through the order of Judge Lemley which says that not only the school board and the state can and should submit to mob violence and threats of mob violence but that the federal judiciary likewise should do so.

> I don't know of any more horrible destruction of [the] principle of citizenship than to tell young children that, those of you who withdrew, rather than to go to school

---

30. Oral Arg. Tr. of *Cooper v. Aaron*, reprinted in part in *May It Please The Court: The Most Significant Oral Argu-* *ments Made Before the Supreme Court Since 1955*, at 254 (Peter Irons & Stephanie Guitton, eds., 1993).

with Negroes, those of you who were punished last year—the few that the school board did punish: Come back, all is forgiven, you win.

And therefore, I am not worried about the Negro children at this stage. I don't believe they're in this case as such. I worry about the white children in Little Rock who are told, as young people, that the way to get your rights is to violate the law and defy the lawful authorities. I'm worried about their future. I don't worry about those Negro kids' future. They've been struggling with democracy long enough. They know about it.[31]

The court let Marshall speak without interruption in part because he expressed such a forceful moral argument in such reasonable terms.

His opponent Richard Butler, by contrast, committed one of the cardinal sins of Supreme Court advocacy: questioning the court's authority to state what the law is. His colloquy with Chief Justice Earl Warren provides a lesson for all time. It arose in the context of Butler's contention that Governor Faubus's order was entitled to respect by the people of Arkansas:

> MR. BUTLER: The point I'm making is this: that if the governor of any state says that a United States Supreme Court decision is not the law of the land, the people of that State, until it is really resolved, have a doubt in their mind and a right to have a doubt.

> CHIEF JUSTICE WARREN: I have never heard such an argument made in a court of justice before, and I've tried many a case, over many a year. I never heard a lawyer say that the statement of a governor, as to what was legal or illegal, should control the action of any court.[32]

The Supreme Court's unanimous opinion, coming a mere two weeks after the argument, was noteworthy in that all nine justices individually signed the opinion, a rarity in any era of the court's history.[33]

Three years after the Supreme Court decided *Cooper v. Aaron*, Archibald Cox became the Solicitor General. Cox had prior experi-

---

31. *Id.* at 253.   **33.** *Id.*
32. *Id.*

ence arguing before the Supreme Court as an Assistant to the Solicitor General, and was considered one of the greatest oral advocates of his era. In *Heart of Atlanta Motel, Inc. v. United States*,[34] Cox brilliantly defended the constitutionality of the Civil Rights Act of 1964. The case concerned whether a federal law could prohibit a proprietor of a motel from refusing to rent rooms to black travelers. Congress had based the Civil Rights Act of 1964, in part, on its power to regulate interstate commerce. Chapter Six of this book will describe how the best advocates turn a hostile question into an opportunity to make an affirmative point by seguing from the answer in a seamless way into the next point they want to make.[35] Here is how Cox did that when he was asked whether people are commerce:

> GENERAL COX: I say that the movement of people from state to state is a movement in commerce, yes. I hesitate a little to say that the people *are* commerce, but it's certainly movement in commerce.
>
> We think there was ample evidence on which Congress could conclude that the racial practices in hotels and motels and like places did have a very substantial effect upon the movement of people in interstate commerce and that therefore this statute as applied to them is a measure adapted to freeing interstate commerce from restraints and burdens.
>
> The fact that Congress has prohibited hotels and motels from discriminating against all guests rather than against interstate guests does not invalidate the statute. To require a traveler to carry a cachet to show that he is interstate would itself be a burden on commerce. Furthermore, to require the Negro interstate traveler to prove that he was traveling in interstate commerce would itself be a form of discrimination.[36]

Cox's successful defense of the Civil Rights Act of 1964 had obvious and major ramifications for the development of American society. The final point he made in his argument, well-rehearsed and considered, elevated his argument to oratory: "We shall solve

34. *Heart of Atlanta Motel, Inc. v. United States*, 379 U.S. 241, 85 S.Ct. 348 (1964).

35. *See* § 6.3.

36. Oral Arg. Tr. of *Heart of Atlanta Motel, Inc. v. United States*, reprinted in part in *May it Please the Court* at 269.

the problems as one people, and thus escape the consequences of the sins of the past, only if we act in the spirit of Lincoln's Second Inaugural: without malice, with charity, and perhaps above all, without that spirit of false self-righteousness that enables men who are not themselves without fault to point the finger at their fellows."[37]

Cox's opponent, by contrast, took the low road. Moreton Rolleston, Jr., represented the motel owner's right to discriminate against blacks under the guise of exercising personal liberty. His approach to dismissing Cox's argument about commerce occurred during his rebuttal, in which he violated a number of the lessons to be discussed in Chapter Eight:

> In my opinion, the argument of counsel of the Government that this is done to relieve a burden on interstate commerce is so much hogwash * * *. I didn't come here to talk about commerce. I didn't come here to argue the question of whether or not this motel has an effect on commerce. * * * This Court, under the Constitution, is the last bulwark of personal liberty. Where else can a man go to defend personal liberty?[38]

An appeal to the Supreme Court—after ten years of contentious litigation to enforce *Brown v. Board of Education*—that persons should be free to discriminate against blacks, was the most ineffective possible rejoinder to Cox's argument. Two months after the argument, the court unanimously upheld the constitutionality of the Civil Rights Act of 1964.

By 1970, arguments of 30 minutes per side had long become the norm in more than 80 percent of the cases argued in the Supreme Court. The court achieved that control over its docket by designating cases deemed to be of lesser importance for the "summary calendar."[39] (According to one estimate, excluding the multiple cases that were consolidated for argument and multi-party cases, more than 90 percent of the cases were put on the "summary" calendar for 30-minute arguments per side.) In 1970, the court changed the rules to conform to that practical reality. Under those new rules, each case would be allotted 30 minutes per side for

37. *Id.* at 270.

38. *Id.*

39. *See* 49 F.R.D. 689–90 (1970).

argument, although in exceptional cases a party could request additional time. That schedule has persisted to the present day.[40]

The compression of time in Supreme Court arguments has invariably heightened the pressure on counsel to make their points succinctly and precisely. Since the 1970s, the trend increasingly has been for arguments to be marked by the quick thrust and parry of question-and-answer that so fundamentally has changed the nature of advocacy in the Supreme Court, and has filtered down to practice in the courts of appeals.

§ 2.5   Dynamics of Change in Oral Argument Practice

Several historical dynamics, therefore, have contributed to substantial changes in how oral argument is conducted in the Supreme Court. The two most important dynamics have occurred in tandem, as the Supreme Court abandoned the oral tradition of appellate advocacy it had originally adopted from the British experience in favor of a written tradition requiring advocates to submit voluminous briefs and to use oral arguments for further refinement and synthesis of the parties' positions. For the first half-century of practice in the court, the norm was for counsel to engage in extended readings of authorities while in the courtroom, thereby causing arguments in cases to go on for days. For well over a century, the court has relied on written briefs to become familiar with a case. Although the space allotted to written briefs has gradually decreased, with the norm now being 50 pages per side except by leave of court, parties typically have little difficulty framing the issues for decision in their written submissions. That latter development, in turn, has been facilitated by the work of the courts of appeals in winnowing the issues to be decided by the Supreme Court. But the role of the written brief is now so critical that the Rules of the Supreme Court provide that "[o]ral argument will not be allowed on behalf of any party for whom a brief has not been filed."[1]

As the court's reliance on briefs increased, the time allotted for argument declined, which has been a second dynamic that has affected the nature of Supreme Court advocacy. In the twentieth century, the time set for oral argument has decreased from two

---

40. SUP. CT. R. 28.3 (effective May 3, 1999).

1. *See* SUP. CT. R. 28.6 (effective May 3, 1999).

hours per side to one-half hour per side, save for exceptional cases. That compression in time has put a premium on the preparation of counsel, the need to respond to questions with succinct answers, and an understanding of how to shift quickly from point to point within the case. It takes far longer to prepare an argument that must respond to the vicissitudes of intense questioning from the justices than a statement an attorney can deliver uninterrupted.

The development of the Office of the Solicitor General—a third dynamic to affect oral argument—unquestionably has had a profound influence on the nature and quality of advocacy in the Supreme Court. As the regular advocates before the Supreme Court, the Solicitor General and his staff have to be scrupulous in their representations or the government loses credibility with the court. Each new Solicitor General must win the court's confidence. As repeat performers and students of the court, the attorneys in the Office of the Solicitor General are routinely among the best Supreme Court advocates, and are acknowledged by Supreme Court justices and court staff as such. It is therefore not surprising that the leaders in the private Supreme Court bar are often alumni of the Solicitor General's Office and that even non-alumni will routinely emulate advocacy techniques employed by the lawyers in the Solicitor General's Office.

A fourth dynamic affecting the nature of oral argument has been the composition of the court. Beginning in the New Deal era, when President Roosevelt put such former law professors as Felix Frankfurter on the court, the degree of contentiousness at oral argument has often been a function of how inquisitive the justices tend to be. Prior to Justice Frankfurter's appointment, Justices Stone, Butler, Benjamin Cardozo, and Louis Brandeis were active questioners. When former Solicitor General Robert Jackson joined the Supreme Court in 1942, the level of questioning at oral argument increased still further. Even so, the Rehnquist Court may top all previous Supreme Courts for the extent to which its individual members interpose questions to counsel. With the exception of Justice Clarence Thomas, who rarely asks questions at oral argument, the other eight justices tend to be quite active. That activity, in turn, feeds on itself. As a justice from one perspective makes inroads on an advocate's position, the tendency increasingly has been for a different justice to come to that advocate's "rescue" with a friendly question or to attack an advocate's case from another perspective.

Those contextual dynamics thus put a high premium on the advocate's nimbleness and mental agility in maintaining focus on the main points to present and in fending off hostile questions that threaten to undermine the case. Unlike the set-piece orations of the nineteenth century, in which advocates droned on for days about their case, oral argument in the twenty-first century very much mirrors the society: argument often seems as though it is a series of sound bytes, strung together amid frequent interruptions from the bench. The intensity level of a typical Supreme Court or court of appeals argument is great, which makes preparation for the experience all the more challenging.

*

Part II

PREPARATION FOR ORAL ARGUMENT

Chapter Three

BEGINNING THE PREPARATION PROCESS

Analysis

Any great lawyer will say that the key to an effective presentation in the law is total preparation. That is as true for a successful oral argument as for a cross-examination. There is simply no substitute for knowing the record, the case law, the arguments on both sides, and the answers to the hard questions invariably raised by both sides' positions. General William Suter, the current Clerk of the Supreme Court of the United States, goes so far as to say that "there are three secrets for arguing well in the Supreme Court: preparation, preparation, and still more preparation."[1] His words apply equally well to oral advocacy in the federal courts of appeals and state appellate courts.

§ 3.1 Writing the Brief

Preparation for oral argument starts with the writing of the brief. Whoever argues the case should participate in writing the

---

1. Interview with General William K. Washington, D.C. (Aug. 31, 2001).
Suter, Clerk of the Supreme Court, in

brief because that is one of the best ways to learn a case.[1] Occasionally, an attorney who did not write the brief being defended makes a superlative argument, but it is extremely rare, requires far more work in the weeks leading up to the argument, and typically rests on significant experience arguing before an appellate tribunal. Moreover, a brief writer can "write around" problems that simply cannot be avoided in answering questions at oral argument. In tackling those issues or problems in the brief, the advocate should be conscious of how questions on that topic might arise at oral argument. Avoiding an answer in the brief may simply be a stalling technique until a better answer can be developed, or it may be the best means of protecting the client's interests.

An arguing counsel not deeply involved in writing the brief must find a way to internalize all of the briefs filed in the case as quickly as possible. Some advocates take the approach of Solicitor General Theodore Olson by surrounding themselves with all of the cases, statutes, and other materials cited in the briefs. They then slowly work their way through each brief, stopping to read the cited statutory language, legislative history, regulations, or cases. They take notes, start to prepare an opening statement, and begin to generate a list of questions. That approach forces the advocate to confront the cited material and to learn the arguments—both in support and against—in their full context as presented in the briefs. It might take several days to work through the briefs in this way, but that time can be rewarding. By reading and thinking about the cited materials in the briefs, the advocate can better understand the theory of the case within the prevailing statutory, regulatory, and doctrinal framework.

§ 3.2   Determining the Scope of What to Prepare

Because ordinarily some weeks or months elapse between the writing of the brief and the oral argument, the advocate's first challenge is to figure out which materials to review in preparing for argument. Consider that the typical Supreme Court case involves a 30–page petition for a writ of certiorari; an appendix to the petition typically running another 30–50 pages (or more) that includes administrative opinions and orders, state court opinions and orders, and federal district court and court of appeals opinions and orders; a 30–page brief in opposition to certiorari; a 10–page reply brief; a

---

§ 3.1

1. For a fine article on brief writing, see Andrew L. Frey & Roy T. Englert,

Jr., "How to Write A Good Appellate Brief," 20 LITIGATION 6 (Winter 1994).

50–page opening merits brief; a 50–page respondent's merits brief; a 20–page reply brief; and at least a few 30–page briefs filed by friends of the court, *amici curiae*. The parties also ordinarily prepare a joint appendix of several hundred pages consisting of record materials, such as hearing transcripts and key documents.

All told, the typical Supreme Court case requires mastery of as many as 250 pages of legal briefs and perhaps the same number of pages of joint appendix material. In those briefs, the parties will cite scores of authorities, including cases, statutes, regulations, treatises, and law review articles. An extreme example is *United States* v. *Locke*,[1] which involved nearly 1,000 pages of briefs, more than 1,000 pages of statutes, regulations, and international treaty provisions filling four 3–inch binders, and dozens of cited cases.

In certain types of cases, preparation for oral argument in a court of appeals can be even more daunting. When a court of appeals case involves review of a trial or administrative record, the amount of material the advocate is expected to master can be staggering, running to thousands of pages (or more) of factual material. The greater the disagreement between the parties on key facts, the greater the need for the advocate to know the record well so that questions about the facts can be addressed at argument in the most efficient possible manner. And even when the lack of factual disagreement is not especially high, circuit judges may nonetheless probe to find support in the record for a particular legal theory they think would best resolve the case.

It is impossible to gain complete mastery over thousands of pages of material. The trick, therefore, becomes learning what is and what is not necessary to know for oral argument. The best advocates also identify early in their preparation which statements in the record and other materials will most likely be the sources of questions or an opponent's arguments. In their note-taking and annotations, they mark those parts or create a shorthand index that enables them to identify the relevant part of the record, if needed.

§ 3.3   Developing a Preparation Schedule

Because oral advocacy is an art form, there is no one right way either to present an argument or to prepare for one. Every person

1. *United States* v. *Locke*, 529 U.S. 89, 120 S.Ct. 1135 (2000).

who excels at oral advocacy has a slightly different way of preparing. Notwithstanding those differences, preparation—scrupulous preparation—is the common denominator of great appellate advocacy. In undertaking that preparation, an advocate must be disciplined in developing a schedule for preparation and in mastering the materials of the case.

Because of the press of other matters, most lawyers in the Solicitor General's Office have only 10 to 12 days to devote exclusively to preparing for oral argument in the Supreme Court. In more complex cases, as much as two weeks might be set aside. Some seasoned attorneys in private practice start well before then, as much as five weeks before the argument, with the substantial portion of their time during that period devoted to argument preparation. When asked whether clients always paid for that much preparation, the answer of former Deputy Solicitor General John G. Roberts, Jr., was telling for the pride he put in his craft: "Sometimes I have to write down bills. But I long ago decided that telling the court, 'I don't know because the answer to that question wasn't in the budget,' was not what I wanted to say."[1]

Counsel should put together a comprehensive to-do list at the outset of the preparation process and update that list as needed. Some advocates also devise a schedule of when they plan to accomplish each task.[2] If a period of time has elapsed between completing the briefing and beginning preparation for oral argument, counsel should first reread the briefs. While doing so, the advocate should keep a pad handy and write out questions the court might ask, questions that will enrich the advocate's understanding of the case, and questions the advocate should simply know how to answer. In addition to writing around problems in the brief, a well-written brief says just enough on a subject without going so far that it commits the party to a position to which it will be held accountable in this or subsequent litigation. When rereading the brief with a colder eye, those issues seem to leap off the page, becoming fodder for further analysis and reflection. Some advocates use a recorder to dictate questions that occur while rereading briefs, the record, and cases. In addition to being an efficient method for compiling

---

§ 3.3

1. Interview with John G. Roberts, Jr., in Washington, D.C. (Sept. 6, 2001).

2. Sample preparation schedules and to-do lists are set forth in Appendix A.

Appendix A also contains a suggested list of items an advocate should master before a Supreme Court or court of appeals argument.

such questions, dictating also helps the advocate practice the oral articulation of concepts in the case.

Many advocates start their preparation by reviewing a binder of cases after having reread the briefs. That can be arduous and not especially gratifying. The advocate should have a binder prepared that contains a copy of every case cited in the briefs. Depending on the case, the advocate might start reading the cases from A to Z or begin with the cases at the center of the case and work outward. The advocate should generally reread every case, even if it was cited in the briefs for only a tangential proposition, although the least important ones may get only a quick skim.

Some advocates dictate or type summaries of the key cases, which they then compile for insertion in their argument podium binder. In most appellate cases, the court's resolution of the issue presented turns on whether a key case should be extended or a series of cases synthesized in a particular way to craft a new rule. Thus, knowing the key cases becomes imperative. It is not unusual for counsel to reread key Supreme Court or court of appeals cases five or six times before an argument. Significant passages get highlighted, summaries prepared, and every nuance of the cases internalized. In some cases, an advocate may need to double-check a quotation or reference in a case during the argument, so the cases binder should be taken to court.

The advocate must give considerable thought to how key contrary cases can be distinguished and important precedents highlighted. Those distinctions and analogies should be reduced to bullet-point form so that they can be articulated in the cleanest, simplest terms possible. The set of distinctions has to be ironclad: much time should be spent considering those distinctions, because the court has to be convinced in a sentence or two why a particular doctrinal rule should be extended or limited in a certain way. While reading the cases, the advocate should also keep a list of questions handy and take note of unresolved aspects of cases the judges or justices themselves will likely be reading prior to the argument. Those "open" issues may be a source of hypothetical questions to the advocate.

The process of reviewing cases may take two or three days. Particularly after days and weeks of meetings, phone calls, and other professional engagements, there can be something monastic about starting preparation by immersion in the case law. This kind of reading tends to have an unfocused quality to it, and requires diligence and self-discipline. Understanding and remembering cases is an area that many advocates have to work hard to master.

It bears noting that some parts of the oral argument process will come easily to an advocate and some will be more difficult. There is no way around confronting the more difficult aspects and taking additional time to prepare for them well. Oral argument is not like some exercises that enable a person to shield weaknesses and play to strengths. Rather, the advocate must accept that skills which need cultivation simply require more work.

Once the advocate has reviewed and mastered the cases, he should have a long list of questions (generally with no answers yet), a binder of highlighted cases, and a document with case summaries. The advocate should also prepare summaries of key statutes and regulations to put in the podium binder. At that point, the advocate might have a week or more before the argument. It is often useful to create a chronology, with appropriate citations to the joint appendix, statutes, cases, or other materials. Sometimes the chronology consists of key events or facts that are important in the case. Other times it consists of statutory and regulatory developments. And still other times a chronology of Supreme Court holdings may help the advocate learn more completely how the case law has developed. Preparing such chronologies may help to build up the advocate's confidence in his mastery of the key events in the case. The advocate might also include the chronology in the podium binder, so that it is available for reference in the days leading up to the argument.

In the Solicitor General's Office, the norm is to conduct an informal moot court approximately one week before the argument and then a formal moot court two or three days later. Chapter Five addresses moot courts, the reasons for conducting them, and strategies for maximizing their benefits. For now, it is sufficient simply to know that, for most advocates, a principal focus of the last week's preparation centers around the moot courts. Other advocates will begin holding moot courts as many as four weeks before argument, with another practice session two weeks before, and the final moot court one week before argument. Such a schedule provides ample time to track down answers to questions, to master the material, and to lower the level of stress in the week immediately prior to the argument.

Importantly, every advocate will need to determine how much time to allot to preparation. Beginning advocates typically need more time than experienced advocates. And more complex cases obviously take more time than straightforward ones. It is easy to underestimate the time needed, which even an experienced appellate advocate making a maiden argument in the Supreme Court can be prone to do. Moreover, an advocate should generally devote much more time to prepare for a Supreme Court appearance than for a court of appeals argument. The fact that some of the best oral advocates take a month or more to prepare for a Supreme Court argument highlights the difficulty of doing an argument in that court well.

§ 3.4 The Opening

Before the first moot court, the advocate should write an "opening"—a one-page statement of what he hopes to say if the court gives him the chance without interrupting to ask questions. Some advocates start working on the opening at the beginning of the preparation—sometimes as much as five weeks before the argument—on the theory that the sooner the advocate starts thinking about it, the better it will be. The timing of when the advocate begins to work on the opening, however, is a matter of individual comfort. The more time spent with a case, the better the advocate will understand it. Importantly, while the advocate should begin to think about the opening from the very beginning of preparation and may even start drafting ideas, he should be reluctant to finalize the first few sentences until having sufficiently synthesized the case. Nor should the rest of the written opening become "final" until the advocate is completely comfortable with the case. So, although there is general agreement that preparing a written opening is critical to a successful argument, great advocates will vary on when during the preparation process they will start to write it.

Many advocates also write at the top of that statement the traditional opening to the court: "Mr. Chief Justice and may it please the Court." To the inexperienced advocate, that notation may seem unduly lacking in confidence and memory, but the reminder can be useful. In several arguments—including those made by very experienced attorneys—the advocate forgot to begin with that simple phrase. On one of those occasions, there was a slightly audible gasp from a few lawyers in the bar section, and even the justices noticed. (The attorney's opening did not have the introductory words written down at the top.)

For court of appeals cases, practice will vary from court to court. If an advocate does not appear regularly in that court, he should make inquiries to determine the applicable conve; federal courts of appeals still follow the custom of a๛ ๛ starting the argument with "May it please the Court." In some circuits, counsel will introduce himself and his client, perhaps identify in the courtroom other members of the legal team that worked on the briefs, and note (if appellant's counsel) a request to reserve a certain amount of time for rebuttal. In other circuits, those conventions are obviated. In the District of Columbia Circuit, for example, many advocates do not introduce themselves (as in the Supreme Court) because the court has before it identifying information noting which counsel is representing the parties. In the Eleventh Circuit, appellant's counsel does not need to make special mention about reserving rebuttal time because the clerk of court will work out that detail in advance of the argument and the clock will be set accordingly.

Chapter Seven explores in more depth how the opening will vary depending on the advocate's role at the argument: petitioner/appellant, respondent/appellee, *amicus*, or a second party participating in the argument. In general, an opening should begin with a sentence stating that party's position or placing the issue presented by the case into context. The advocate should generally try to condense an argument into a discrete number of points. After an introductory sentence, the opening should signpost for the court the two to four points the advocate hopes to make, using phrases the advocate hopes will be memorable to the court. The signposting sentences should contain certain "mantra" phrases—those phrases that encapsulate in sound-byte form the points the advocate will try to make during the argument. The elaboration of those succinct points then takes up the remaining sentences of the opening.

It is extremely rare for an advocate to get an opportunity to give the entire opening in a Supreme Court or court of appeals argument. But, in breaking down the opening into the introductory position-stating sentence, the summary mantra of the key points, and the more elaborate articulation of those points, the advocate accomplishes a number of important objectives.

First, the attorney builds credibility with the court by showing thoughtfulness and experience. In a complicated case, it is critical to simplify the points into short, understandable sentences. An advocate whose opening does not immediately add value to the court's understanding of the case will very quickly lose the court's attention. Attorneys who begin with sentences like, "This case is very important to my client," cause judges and justices to tune out.

More so than in almost any other public speaking presentation, the first two sentences are absolutely critical to a successful Supreme Court argument. Indeed, they may be the only prepared sentences the advocate gets to state before the onslaught of questioning begins. In most court of appeals cases, the court generally will afford counsel more time to develop the argument before interrupting with questions, although some circuits, like the United States Court of Appeals for the District of Columbia Circuit, can be as vigorous in their questioning as the Supreme Court. Even so, because most federal courts of appeals limit argument to 10 or 15 minutes per side, an advocate who does not carefully prepare an opening can waste valuable minutes. And, as in a Supreme Court argument, an opening that signals to the circuit judges where the advocate seeks to go with the argument can be helpful.

Second, even if the court interrupts the advocate before he can complete his opening, it is not uncommon for a member of the court, upon hearing initially that the attorney has three points to make, to ask later in the argument what the other points are. A sympathetic jurist, in particular, wants the advocate to have the opportunity to advance his argument. Signaling to the court that the advocate has a purpose in stressing particular points will build respect that may be rewarded when a judge or justice prods the advocate to state the other points. And even if the advocate never gets another chance to make a point highlighted in the opening, it may prompt the court to review that part of the advocate's brief prior to the conference in which the justices vote on the case—or, in the case of a court of appeals argument, soon thereafter during the opinion-writing phase.

Third, the construction of the opening focuses the advocate on developing an overarching theme to the argument and on summarizing the principal affirmative points to emphasize during the argument. Those affirmative points are the keys to a successful argument because they represent the strongest points of the advocate's case and the last, best synthesis of the case for the court. Having them internalized enables the attorney to answer a question and then to segue back to those affirmative points. Occasionally, an advocate will face a question that calls for the statement of a point right out of the opening. A thoughtful construction of the opening enables the advocate to respond with the most precisely worded, well-considered response possible. Even when the question itself will not ask point-blank for a statement out of the opening, the advocate may find opportunities to use answers to transition back to points articulated in that prepared statement.

One attorney who routinely crafts excellent opening statements is Deputy Solicitor General Michael R. Dreeben. He is one of the few advocates in recent years that Supreme Court justices have permitted to give his complete opening with any regularity, and he gets to deliver it about half the time. The Supreme Court gives Dreeben that leeway out of respect for his ability to answer their difficult questions and because the court knows that its patience will be rewarded with a succinct expression of the points the government wants to make.

Here is one of Dreeben's openings, in the case of *United States v. Ursery*[1]:

Mr. Chief Justice and may it please the Court: From the earliest years of this Nation, Congress has authorized the Government to seek parallel *in rem* civil forfeiture actions and criminal prosecutions based on the same underlying events. Until recently, the pursuit of such parallel actions was deemed to raise no question under the Double Jeopardy Clause. Two recent decisions of this Court, however, *United States* v. *Halper*[2] and *Austin* v. *United States*,[3] prompted the courts of appeals in these two cases to conclude that the cumulative remedies of *in rem* civil forfeiture and criminal prosecution violated the multiple punishments doctrine under the Fifth Amendment.

These holdings are incompatible with the long tradition and practice in this country, and are incorrect for four reasons. First, civil forfeiture is not categorically punitive within the meaning of the Fifth Amendment, and the forfeitures in this case were not punishment. Second, an *in rem* forfeiture action is not a jeopardy that can give rise to the protection of the Fifth Amendment when the Government seeks to prosecute the owner of the forfeited property for a criminal violation. Third, civil forfeiture of property under 21 U.S.C. 881 is not the same offense as the criminal prosecution of the owner of the property for having violated the narcotics laws and, finally, parallel contemporaneous civil forfeiture actions and criminal prosecutions shall be deemed to constitute a single proceeding

---

1. *United States v. Ursery*, 518 U.S. 267, 116 S.Ct. 2135 (1996).

2. *United States v. Halper*, 490 U.S. 435, 109 S.Ct. 1892 (1989).

3. *Austin v. United States*, 509 U.S. 602, 113 S.Ct. 2801 (1993).

within the meaning of the Fifth Amendment and therefore not to violate the Double Jeopardy Clause.

Now, the overriding question that is presented in both of these cases and in many others that are being litigated in the lower courts is whether *in rem* civil forfeiture should be deemed to be punishment. Both of the courts below adopted a categorical rule that the forfeiture that is accomplished by application of section 881 should be categorically deemed punishment.[4]

It is extraordinary for any advocate to be given that much time to deliver an opening in a Supreme Court case, but the court appreciates Dreeben's economical and substantive style. Dreeben's initial sentences placed the issue in historical context and stressed that, until the Supreme Court's recent decisions in *Halper* and *Austin*, the law had not been in doubt. He then launched into a succinct statement of the reasons why the court of appeals had erred in ruling against the government. Each of those reasons was distinctively, yet simply, worded. An opening should strive to be rich in content, simple in mode of expression, and worded as economically as possible. Chapter Seven contains more openings used in Supreme Court cases by both petitioners and respondents,[5] but Dreeben's opening in *Ursery* is a useful model to emulate no matter when the advocate appears in the argument. Appendices B and C set out a number of other openings for petitioner and respondent—both good and bad—to illustrate various approaches an advocate might take.

A well-worded opening will answer many questions about the party's position and not raise questions unnecessarily by vague wording. Admittedly, it is impossible to state in four or five sentences a legal argument without raising a number of questions, but the opening nonetheless should provide a frame of reference for the court's consideration of the issues. If done well, it can bring a clarity to the argument that will be sharpened still further by the advocate's compelling answers to questions.

§ 3.5 Developing a Plan for Addressing Questions

In any modern appellate court argument, the advocate must effectively answer the court's questions. Failure to do so can spell

---

4. *United States v. Ursery*, Nos. 95–345 & 95–346, 1996 WL 195163 at *4–*5 (Apr. 17, 1996).

5. *See* §§ 7.1 and 7.2.

the difference between winning and losing. From the beginning of preparation, the advocate must focus on developing the best possible answers to questions. Obviously, the first step in that process is to anticipate as many questions as possible. That is why virtually every great advocate will devote a substantial portion of time to thinking of as many questions as possible about the record, the parties' positions, the opponent's arguments, the cases, the statutory and regulatory context, and the policies underlying the advocated rule. This part of the preparation process is so critical that Chapter Four focuses exclusively on the types of questions commonly asked in oral arguments. The remainder of this section addresses how the advocate should get organized in grappling with that aspect of preparation.

The point at which the advocate shifts from raising questions to developing answers is a matter of individual preference. For some advocates, the time between the informal and formal moot courts is best utilized focusing almost exclusively on devising answers to as many questions as possible. Between the advocate's self-prepared list of questions and those generated at the first moot court, he will typically have a bumper crop that covers most of the questions likely to arise at the oral argument. Invariably, questions come up at the first moot court that had not occurred to the advocate; some may require refinement of the particular mantra phrases that help to articulate the theory of the case. The advocate must also be prepared to conduct legal research to deal with other questions. Some advocates try to research and develop their own answers. That individual attention helps the advocate retain the answers and to find information that may assist in answering questions around the periphery of the one anticipated. Depending on the nature of the question, though, it may be more economical or efficient for others to do that legal research.

It can be a satisfying experience, though fraught with some danger, to answer a question at oral argument with a citation to a case not referenced in the briefs. Dangerous because it invites the court to inquire why that case was not cited in the briefs. Some judges—more in the courts of appeals than in the Supreme Court— also look askance at attorneys citing cases for the first time at argument without giving the opposing counsel a chance to rebut them. Frankly, that objection is silly, self-defeating, and unfair. Silly because it is impossible for an attorney to guess which questions will be asked at oral argument, so how could he possibly alert opposing counsel? Self-defeating because the point of oral argument is to help judges decide cases and, if a case not cited in the briefs but subsequently discovered helps the court to do that, why should they object? The objection is unfair because a lawyer arguing a case is presumed to know the decisions of that court, just as a judge of that court is. This is a difficult presumption, because it is impossible for any human being to attain it. If a court really were to think an advocate's citation of a case at argument was unfair, it could invite short post-argument briefs to be filed on the subject. The best course, therefore, is for the advocate to have the cases available, cite them, and be ready to advise the court that it was not so certain that the court would ask the question as to depart from the normal custom that attorneys are on their own for oral argument. In courts where the time allotted to the parties is less formally observed than in the Supreme Court, being ready to hand opposing counsel a copy of the case when it is cited gives counsel at least some opportunity to comment on its applicability.

The formal moot court may also raise questions not previously considered. It certainly should provide an opportunity to test out certain answers. After that moot court session, the advocate obviously must satisfy himself that he has adequately addressed and researched questions that emerged. Because the formal moot court will typically occur three or four days before argument, the advocate can then use the remaining days to polish the opening, develop a compelling answer to every conceivable question, learn the record cold, mark any places in the briefs or records that can be referred to at argument, and prepare the argument podium binder.

§ 3.6 Argument Podium Binder

A few extremely confident attorneys take no notes with them to the podium when they argue in the Supreme Court or court of appeals. Those attorneys do not argue any better (and frequently worse) than lawyers who take some notes with them. Most advocates are like E. Barrett Prettyman, Jr., who always took notes with him to the podium even though he rarely looked at them.

What notes should counsel have at the podium? This, of course, is completely a matter of personal taste. The critical factor in deciding which notes to take to the podium turns on what is useful without being a distraction. Michael Dreeben generally takes two sheets of paper. On one is his opening; on the other his affirmative points. But he has the experience of more than 50 arguments in the Supreme Court upon which to draw. Deputy Solicitor General Edwin S. Kneedler also takes minimal notes to the podium. He has argued in excess of 75 cases in the Supreme Court. Several skilled advocates, such as Assistant to the Solicitor General Jeffrey A. Lamkin, write all of their notes on an open file folder to maximize the notes on one sheet so that they do not have to turn pages back and forth. Some experienced advocates take to the podium a huge, thick binder with dozens of tabs, but that tends to be too much material to be deployed usefully during the argument. Many advocates in the Solicitor General's Office put together a small, one-inch binder of materials. Organizing the materials for the binder can be the best way of making the information stick in the advocate's head—indeed, given how much time may be spent putting together a podium binder, it may come as something of a surprise that an advocate who engages in such meticulous preparation will almost never need to look at it during an argument. The process of putting together those materials will cause them to be internalized by the advocate.

Another useful practice is to tape the opening to the left-hand side of the binder, so that when the advocate opens the binder that written statement will not be obscured by anything else. In one argument, an attorney had failed to tape his opening. He opened his binder as he approached the podium and the piece of paper with his prepared argument fell to the floor. As he bent down to pick it up, all eyes in the courtroom focused on him. That was not the way to make a great first impression with the Supreme Court.

The open-faced first page of the binder contains a list of affirmative points, generally in all-caps and bold face type so that they are easier to see. Next to those points the advocate should include citations in short form in case they are needed. The worst nightmare question for an ill-prepared advocate is, "Where's that in the record?" or "What's the support for that?" An advocate needs to be ready to cite support for every affirmative point. Solicitor General Theodore Olson creates a document with a shortened form of the part of the record he needs, with a notation of where in the record that reference can be found. Thus, he might pull out a sheet of paper with a quotation from the district court, but advise the justices that the quotation is from page 52 of the joint appendix.

Citing the page in the record at the beginning of such a recitation serves several important functions. Many judges will open to the cited page to read the language being cited. The law clerks sitting in the wings of the courtroom almost certainly will take notes and go back to look at those pages later in formulating their own advice to their judge or justice. By citing the page, the advocate ensures that it will be in the transcript of the oral argument, which members of the court may sometimes review during the opinion-writing phase. Finally, citing the page avoids the inevitable interruption from a member of the court who wants to read along during the argument.

Some advocates prepare their podium binders so that pages are taped or stapled together to create double-sided pages. This greatly reduces the number of page turns counsel must make and it thickens the pages so they are easier to turn. Those four pages— one turn of the page—should be a constant in virtually all podium binders. The process of compiling those notes can be an excellent way for an advocate to synthesize the material in very precise terms and to ensure that the advocate can readily find a citation if needed.

With the first page turn, therefore, the advocate comes to argument "blocks" or "modules." Those argument blocks can provide a ready synthesis of the key positions the advocate wants to articulate. Using the column feature of a word processor, the advocate can create two columns with fairly narrow margins. Each column can contain two or three modules on topics, with key points in bullet-point form added underneath. One page can thus summarize all of the advocate's affirmative points. The facing page can contain the responsive arguments to the other side's affirmative points. If synthesized properly, the advocate should be able to put the bulk of the relevant arguments in the case on those two pages, complete with citations of authority, supporting record material, or references to the briefs.

To illustrate, the following are two of the argument blocks used by government counsel in his argument podium binder in *United States* v. *Locke*,[1] which concerned whether Titles I and II of the Ports and Waterways Safety Act preempted rules promulgated by the State of Washington regulating international oil tankers. From the notes, it should be apparent that the United States's position was that subjects falling under Title II were automatically preempted because Congress mandated that the federal government "shall establish" rules, and the needs of uniformity for the design and operation of vessels would be hindered if the federal government's rules were exceeded or superseded by those of the states. With respect to Title I rules, on the other hand, the United States's

<hr/>

§ 3.6

1. *United States v. Locke*, 529 U.S. 89, 120 S.Ct. 1135 (2000).

position was that Congress left some room for state rules, because its directive to the federal government was for permissive, and not mandatory, regulations. As the court had held in *Ray* v. *Atlantic Richfield Co.*,[2] if the State had a rule special to the peculiarities of its waterways, such a rule would not be preempted, provided the Coast Guard had not supplanted it by a federal rule.

TITLE II PREEMPTION INDICATORS
1) Use of "shall establish" **US Br. 24**
2) Regs deemed "necessary" **US Br. 24**
3) Facilitates uniformity ***Ray*, 435 US at 166** Also, Tank Vessel Act of '36 (***Ray*, at 166**)
4) Licenses/Certificates of Compliance ***Ray*, at 163–164**
5) ***Ray***—design and construction—no basis in text for differentiating subjects

TITLE I PREEMPTION INDICATORS
1) Permissive, not mandatory regulations "may," not "shall" **US Br. 26–27**
2) ***Ray*** said "peculiarities of local waters that call for for special precautionary measures," relevant inquiry is whether Secy. issues regs. **435 US at 171–172**
3) ***Ray***: Savings clause of Tit. I allows higher state regs for "structures only" **435 US at 170, 174**
4) Legis. Hist. of PWSA Tit. I to make "absolutely clear that the Coast Guard regulation of vessels preempts state action in the field" **Reply Br. 12**

Those notes may seem somewhat cryptic, but reprinting them illustrates that an advocate can simplify the notes while maintaining the substance and focus of the points to be made. The argument modules can be organized by the affirmative points the advocate hopes to make, responses to the affirmative points the advocate expects the other side to make, and a set of responsive points to key questions the advocate anticipates the court will ask.

After the argument blocks, the podium binder might have several sections separated by marked tabs so that the advocate can quickly find material in those sections. For example, the podium binder might have separate tabbed sections entitled, "Chronology," "Key Statutes," "Regulations," "Case Summaries," and "Ques-

---

2. *Ray v. Atlantic Richfield Co.*, 435 U.S. 151, 98 S.Ct. 988 (1978).

tions and Answers." Occasionally, those tabbed materials come in handy during an argument. But even if the lawyer never looks at them, the process of developing and reviewing them prior to the argument can improve the advocate's memorization of key facts and legal materials.

The rest of the podium binder may include materials that help the advocate prepare, rather than notes he might necessarily expect to use in the argument itself. The advocate should include in the podium binder a photocopy of the key cases (rarely more than two), excerpts of pertinent statutory or regulatory language, and summaries of the cited cases. In the week before the argument, the argument binder is a useful tool for the final stages of preparation, as the advocate can find the most critical materials compiled in one place. At the argument itself, the binder looks far more professional for counsel to use in referring to notes than if the advocate shuffles loose papers, which invariably get out of order. Labeling the tabs on both sides also enables the advocate to easily flip in both directions if needed to find material to answer a question. An advocate should strive not to have too many tabs—say, no more than five or six—so that the tabs are in only a single row down the outside margin.

Another important preparation task is to mark relevant pages in the briefs and record. Some advocates feel the need to put dozens of tabs or post-it notes on their briefs and appendices. That tends to be counter-productive. If left to the end of the preparation process, the marking of record pages with tabs will feature only those few places where an advocate can make an affirmative point out of something in the record or where the court will likely ask a question. The moot courts help the advocate identify which record-based affirmative points will be persuasive, as well as which places in the record have drawn questions by moot court participants. Just as the binder should not be cluttered, so too the tabbed references to the briefs and appendices should be no more than a handful, all easily visible from the podium or counsel table.

The exercise of making an argument podium binder is obviously very detail-oriented. But the point of going through it is to master the material and to be able to access it readily at oral argument. Precious seconds can be wasted hunting through briefs for that one useful reference. An advocate who has anticipated the question and marked the relevant page is more likely to have devised a dispositive answer and be able to then shift back to an affirmative point. Simply as a matter of persuasion, an attorney who has a ready ability to retrieve the materials will be taken more seriously by the court than one who does not.

§ 3.7   Synthesis and Practice

As this method of compiling materials suggests, the process of preparing for oral argument is one of winnowing from numerous pages of briefs, cases, and other sources the key sentences and phrases to be stated at oral argument. It is a process of enormous, and complicated, synthesis. But that synthesis is crucial for simplifying a case for the court.

Charles Alan Wright, the great legal scholar who argued 14 cases in the Supreme Court and countless others in the federal courts of appeals, once said that he had his non-lawyer wife read every brief he wrote. His theory was that if his wife understood his arguments, surely the judges and justices would, too. Professor Wright was being neither facetious nor disrespectful in saying that. His point conveyed numerous truths about the Supreme Court and the courts of appeals. One is that those courts are extremely busy. The simpler and more accessibly the attorney can frame the arguments, the more likely those arguments are to be persuasive. A second insight in Professor Wright's approach is that judges and justices themselves recognize that their legitimacy in part stems from the ability of the courts to render judgments that resonate with the sensibilities of the public. Indeed, Justice Stephen Breyer has stated publicly that the reason he does not use footnotes in his opinions is that he wants the public to be able to read his opinions and understand what he has written.[1]

Test-driving arguments with a lay person is an excellent way to gauge the likely success of the argument. Many advocates practice articulating their arguments to their family or friends. The aim is to explain orally what the client's position is and why it should prevail. Every advocate making an oral argument should incorporate this practice into the preparation process. A thoughtful lay person often will be troubled by the very same aspects of a case as a Supreme Court justice or circuit judge, and ask similar questions to

---

§ 3.7

1. *See, e.g.,* Tony Mauro, "Justices Cool to Curbs on Lawyer's Pitches," LEGAL TIMES, Jan. 16, 1995, at 8 (noting Justice Breyer's "longstanding distaste for footnotes in judicial opinions"); Tony Mauro, "Winds of Change Blow At Clerk's Office," LEGAL TIMES, Aug. 7, 1995, at 8 (noting that Justice Arthur Goldberg had advised him not to use footnotes in judicial opinions).

address those concerns. If an advocate can articulate the position in simple enough terms to a lay person, then he really does understand the case and can explain it in court. A few highly seasoned advocates believe that an advocate who cannot explain to a lay person in five minutes why he should win his case does not understand it well enough himself.

§ 3.8 Speaking Style

Speaking styles vary widely. The most important principle is to speak to be understood. Justice Robert Jackson used the phrase "professional sincerity" to convey the proper attitude an advocate should have in court.[1] That does not mean that an advocate should "orate." Rather, the advocate should try to make a connection to the court that can often best be done simply with eye contact and a conversational tone of voice. No one likes to be talked at, and judges are no exception. Judges typically look directly at the advocate and expect eye contact in return.

Some trial attorneys memorize their opening and closing arguments so that they will not lose the jury's attention by breaking eye contact to look at notes. Some very fine appellate advocates also memorize their openings, but only those who can then present the argument in a natural and conversational tone come across as persuasive. If reading to the court is taboo, so, too, is reciting a memorized opening in a stilted, inflexible manner.

Rather than memorizing the opening and delivering it by rote, an advocate should try writing out the opening and then speaking it extemporaneously over and over. There are fundamental differences in the syntax of written versus oral communication. Winston Churchill is said to have practiced his speeches and rewritten them frequently so that they sounded compelling. Although not striving for Churchillian rhetoric in an appellate argument, a good advocate will nonetheless be conscious of the phrasing, the syntax, and the rhythm of spoken words, especially those in the prepared opening. Because argument is an oral art form, the advocate must focus on practicing the spoken articulation of the points. That will vary slightly each time, as a phrase may come out awkwardly or seem unnatural when spoken. Chapters Eight and Nine will address

---

§ 3.8

1. Robert H. Jackson, "Advocacy Before the Supreme Court: Suggestions for Effective Case Presentations," 37 A.B.A. J. 801, 863 (1951).

matters of stylistic presentation, but for now it suffices to say that a natural, conversational delivery of the opening tends to be the most effective.

Other elements of a persuasive speaking style are also important in Supreme Court and appellate advocacy. The lawyer should stand tall and straight, use gestures in an effective way to punctuate the points made with the spoken word, and be wary of irritating mannerisms. The number of attorneys who hold a pen or pencil while speaking is shockingly high, as is the number who shuffle their papers on the podium and shift uncomfortably from one foot to the other. As discussed in Chapter Five on moot courts, a benefit of videotaping practice sessions is to enable the advocate to become his own harshest critic of those mannerisms that detract from a persuasive presentation.

§ 3.9   Emotional Ups and Downs

No court experience is similar to the intensity of a modern Supreme Court argument. As Justice Jackson well-described it, "When he rises to speak at the bar, the advocate stands intellectually naked and alone. * * * What an advocate gives to a case is himself; he can bring to the bar only what is within him."[1] For most attorneys, this experience is a singular event—the most memorable moment of their career. Adequate preparation is and should be an intense experience, even in court of appeals cases, which tend not to be as demanding as Supreme Court arguments. In virtually all cases, if the attorney does not experience abject fear at least several times during the preparation period, he probably is not fully applying himself to the task. That fear properly stems from a deep appreciation of the opponent's position and a realization that the issues are complex and nuanced. As the advocate develops answers to difficult questions and becomes more facile with the material, that fear recedes and transforms into confidence that the advocate's position is, in fact, correct and that the court should uphold it.

The very best advocates appreciate that some cases simply cannot be won, no matter how skilled the advocate. They steel themselves in a special way emotionally when they know they are

§ 3.9

1. Robert H. Jackson, "Advocacy Before the Supreme Court: Suggestions for Effective Case Presentations," 37 A.B.A. J. 801, 863 (1951).

arguing a position that no member of the court is likely to accept. In such cases, the advocate's objectives become having a reasonable answer to every possible question and not crossing the line where personal credibility becomes sacrificed unnecessarily in a futile advocacy effort. For clients in the private sector, where winning has a higher priority, the advocate has a responsibility to manage the client's expectations. No advocate should go to court without a full belief in the correctness of his client's position, even one tempered by the realization that it may not persuade the court. But thorough preparation and a realistic set of achievable goals can help to focus the preparation and relieve the advocate of the felt need to win at all costs.

A Supreme Court argument is an extremely stressful experience, even for a seasoned advocate. The justices can (and will) ask anything at any time. Before hundreds of spectators, including family and friends, the advocate will have the most profound opportunities for public embarrassment. For the vast majority of lawyers, the most dreaded answer to any jurist's question is, "I don't know." No advocate wants to have that colloquy, particularly with a press that is quick to print the worst moments in oral arguments. If it happens, the attorney should try to handle the moment with grace and humility.

Friends and family can never fully appreciate what the lawyer goes through in preparing a case for argument, as well as the emotional highs and lows of the argument itself and the post-argument letdown. Some of these patterns are common to many advocates, and bear brief mention so that the advocate's family and friends can understand what the advocate endures to prepare for an important appellate argument.

For many advocates, the unease begins in the initial days of preparation, as the attorney realizes just how many conceivable questions he might face but does not yet know how to answer. That fear spurs the first serious, intensive wave of preparation. Increasing the attorney's level of physical exercise can be a useful way to relieve the stress caused by such feelings. In some ways, preparing for an oral argument is like what champion chess masters go through before a chess tournament. The best go into a period of intensive study, pay particular attention to their diet, and maintain a regular program of exercise.

A second wave of apprehension usually occurs after the first moot court when thoughtful colleagues have asked many incisive questions that the advocate—who thought he was prepared—does not know how to answer. While having all of those questions out on the table should become a source of great reassurance, nothing can quite match the feeling of helplessness that arises when question after question comes hurtling in without a coherent legal response. That wave then usually produces a serious emotional trough, as the weaknesses of the advocate's side of the argument appear glaringly obvious and the strengths of the other side's theory much more apparent than when the briefs were filed. If the advocate does not go through at least one of these emotional troughs during the preparation process, he probably is not applying a sufficiently objective analysis to his own case.

Every case in the Supreme Court has two sides in the most meaningful sense, because the court likely did not grant certiorari unless federal courts of appeals or state supreme courts were divided on the question presented. Indeed, most court of appeals cases where the court hears argument have the same dynamic because, if the case could be disposed of by applying clear-cut precedent, the court would have decided it on the briefs. The advocate must, through diligent preparation and force of determination, will himself into a state of absolute conviction by the time he stands up to address the court. But before getting to that point, he must take the other side's position so seriously as to think through the very best ways to articulate its weaknesses. In this respect, an advocate must attempt to understand and reformulate his opponent's position in an even more persuasive manner than opposing counsel may have done. If the advocate can do that—and is still able to rebut those points convincingly—then the advocate is nearing the point of preparation that results in a successful argument.

Every advocate must also prepare emotionally for the distinct possibility that the court will not be persuaded by the brief. The advocate's family and friends have to be prepared to provide support when the crowning moment of the advocate's career does not play out in an ideal fashion. The advocate cannot help but "replay" in his mind key colloquies in the argument even days after the fact.

Indeed, even after what by all accounts was a successful argument, the advocate will go through at least two more discernible emotional cycles. One is the self-doubt that invariably creeps in when the advocate realizes that there were, in fact, better answers to the questions posed from the bench. Even as that self-doubt recedes with the advocate's appreciation that the argument is past and nothing can now improve on it, the emotional letdown of the entire experience takes hold. The adrenaline rush and stress of intense preparation give way to fatigue and exhaustion. After the most intense Supreme Court or appellate arguments, it may take several days to start returning to a more-or-less normal mode of work. However loving family members can be, they rarely understand this emotional journey. Spouses and children do not understand the long absences for work, the distracted disinterest in otherwise important family matters, and the nature of the stress the advocate experiences.

Perhaps because of that stress, few feelings can match the emotional high of getting a hard question from the court and persuading it that the advocate's position is compelling. Or of being so agile of mind as to give succinct and persuasive answers to a series of questions. The reason a Supreme Court argument is the pinnacle of a lawyer's career is not just the singularity of arguing before the nation's highest court, but also the intensity of the experience.

Chapter Four

TYPES OF QUESTIONS COMMONLY ASKED

Analysis

The ability to field questions from the bench is one of the most important skills of an oral advocate. The greater the intensity of the questioning and the fewer the minutes the advocate has to speak, the more important becomes the task of answering questions in the most succinct and precise manner possible. Questions from the bench frequently reveal the thought processes and concerns of the court. Sometimes the question seeks to expose a party's position to create a record the judge will use to persuade another member of the bench. Sometimes the court will express its skepticism about a party's contention and afford the advocate an opportunity to bolster the position with another argument. And sometimes the purpose of the question will be less clear, challenging the advocate to proceed carefully through a potential land mine in crafting the answer.

In modern oral arguments, the advocate must be prepared to answer a range of questions, from those seeking to make the record clear to questions that explore the outer limits of a party's theory of the case. Although a badly conceived opening only rarely loses a case, a badly formulated answer to a question can cause an argument to degenerate and convince the court to reject the advocate's position. Notwithstanding that risk, the very best advocates affirmatively invite questions, because once exposed, the concerns of the court with the lawyer's argument can be addressed and the advocate can seize the opportunity to persuade the court. It is common, however, to observe oral arguments in which the advocate did not anticipate and prepare for questions that appear even to a lay observer to be based on a common sense understanding of the case.

This chapter describes the types of questions frequently asked at oral arguments and offers suggestions for how to address them. The types of questions are arranged in four general categories: questions about the background and context of the issues presented; questions that explore the nature and scope of the rule under review; questions about the implications of the rule being pressed by the advocate; and questions reflecting the personal styles of the members of the court. The advocate who can prepare for questions across the range of these categories and deliver succinct, thoughtful answers will measurably improve her chances of a successful oral argument.

§ 4.1 Background Questions

Questions that address background matters often serve to educate the court about the general subject matter of the case or the context in which the legal issues arise. Preparing for background questions can be quite time-consuming, because the potential variety of such questions is so broad.

§ 4.1.a   Questions About the Parties Involved

It is axiomatic that counsel should have as deep an understanding of the parties involved in the case as possible before oral argument. A failure to know basic answers can throw the advocate off-stride and cause considerable damage to her credibility with the court. Here is an example of how even an experienced advocate can stumble by not knowing the answer to a question that should have been anticipated. In *Lee v. Weisman*,[1] the Supreme Court considered the constitutionality of including clergy in the offering of prayers at the official public school graduation ceremonies of junior high school and high school students. The advocate for the school district seeking to have the prayers upheld under the Establishment Clause, Charles Cooper, had barely begun his argument when Justice Harry A. Blackmun interrupted him:

MR. COOPER: Mr. Chief Justice, and may it please the Court:

At the 1989 graduation ceremony of the Nathan Bishop Middle School in Providence, Rhode Island, Rabbi Leslie Gutterman opened the exercise with an invocation—one characterized by the district court as an example of elegant simplicity, thoughtful content, and sincere citizenship.

QUESTION: How old were these youngsters, Mr. Cooper?

MR. COOPER: I beg your pardon, Justice—

QUESTION: How old were these youngsters graduating?

MR. COOPER: Your Honor, the graduates themselves, were graduating from middle school and into high school. So they were just completing their eighth grade.

QUESTION: Well, how old were they is my question. You haven't answered me.

MR. COOPER: Your Honor, I think—

QUESTION: About 13 or 14, aren't they?

MR. COOPER: Yes, Your Honor.

§ 4.1

1. *Lee v. Weisman*, 505 U.S. 577, 112 S.Ct. 2649 (1992).

QUESTION: Are we getting so—

MR. COOPER: I'm sorry, I could not hear you.

QUESTION: Never mind, go ahead.[2]

It was an inauspicious start to Cooper's argument. Justice Blackmun's aim obviously was to show that the middle school students, in particular, were young and impressionable, so young that they would be heavily influenced by the state's decision to include clergy of a particular faith and denomination in the commencement exercises. It is difficult to say for certain whether Cooper's stumbling at the beginning of the argument contributed to the Supreme Court's 5–4 ruling that the inclusion of such clergy is unconstitutional, but the opening paragraphs of Justice Anthony M. Kennedy's opinion for the court noted that Deborah Weisman "was about 14 years old" when she graduated from Nathan Bishop Middle School.[3]

§ 4.1.b   Questions About the Opinion Under Review

Another obvious source of questions concerns the opinion explaining the judgment being appealed. At the court of appeals level, in particular, a panel might inquire at length about the meaning of a particular sentence in the district court's opinion. That kind of interrogation can also happen in the Supreme Court, especially if a sentence or two is the fulcrum of the court of appeals' opinion. In *Toyota Motor Manufacturing v. Williams*,[4] just such a colloquy occurred between John Roberts (who represented Toyota) and the justices. The questioning concerned a court of appeals decision holding that the company violated the Americans with Disabilities Act of 1990 ("ADA") by not accommodating a worker's allegation of a substantial disability based on her inability to perform certain manual tasks in connection with her assembly line job, such as gripping a sponge and wiping down cars:

QUESTION: Mr. Roberts, may I just stop you on something you just said? I thought the Sixth Circuit said in its opinion that it had considered recreation, household

---

2. *Lee v. Weisman*, No. 90–1014, 1991 WL 636285 at *3–*4 (Nov. 6, 1991).

3. *Lee v. Weisman*, 505 U.S. at 581, 112 S.Ct. at 2652.

4. *Toyota Motor Mfg. v. Williams*, 534 U.S. 184, 122 S.Ct. 681 (2002).

chores, living generally, as well as the work-related impairments.

MR. ROBERTS: A very important sentence that I think has to be read carefully. In the first place, it doesn't say that we've looked at the record and considered those. It was a generic assumption. The assumption is, well, if she can't do this assembly line work, that must affect other areas, recreation and household chores.

A generic assumption like that is wrong, first, because the ADA specifies you have to look at the individual impacts; second, because the impairments we're talking about, myotendinitis and that sort of thing, affect different people in widely different ways. You can't assume, just because someone cannot do the repetitive work for an extended period of time, that that's going to have an effect.[5]

In this fashion, Roberts sought to focus the justices on the specific sentence in the opinion that best exemplified the error in the court of appeals' decision. Roberts' answer cast doubt on the correctness of the sentence both on its own terms—a failure to be based on any facts in the record—and on its broader error in relying on erroneous statutory and factual considerations.

§ 4.1.c Questions About Views of Different Courts to Address the Same Issue

It is rare for an attorney to argue a case of completely first impression. In most instances, an advocate will be making arguments that seek to distinguish or rest upon existing precedents from the district courts or courts of appeals when arguing in those courts. An advocate must be ready to address how different courts have handled the same issue and articulated the governing rule. That, in turn, may require an explication of the principal authorities on which those courts relied, how the facts presented may have caused the court to veer in one direction or the other, and whether any dissenting judges made arguments that were inadequately treated by the majority. In *Dusenbery v. United States*,[6] Jeffrey P. Minear represented the United States in the Supreme Court, arguing that the government did not need to give any additional special

---

5. *Toyota Motor Mfg. v. Williams*, No. 00–1089, 2001 WL 1453954 at *9–*10 (Nov. 7, 2001).

6. *Dusenbery v. United States*, 534 U.S. 161, 122 S.Ct. 694 (2002).

notice to a prisoner prior to bringing an action for the forfeiture of the prisoner's property. The existence of a conflict among the circuits had caused the Supreme Court to grant the petition for a writ of certiorari.

In the argument, the justices asked Minear about the different positions taken by the courts of appeals that had produced the circuit conflict and how much litigation occurs on the question the court had to address:

> QUESTION: How do you think the Sixth Circuit standard differs from the Third Circuit's and the Fourth's?
>
> MR. MINEAR: I think as a practical matter, Your Honor, there's primarily a question of the burden of proof. Under the Sixth Circuit's standard, we are simply—if we are challenged, if there's a challenge to whether mail was—was received or not, it's the obligation of that party who's raising the challenge to prove the lack of reasonableness.
>
> QUESTION: Well, but here the Government is seeking to forfeit property from someone. Maybe it's not unreasonable to think that the Government has the burden of proving that notice was given or reasonably calculated to be given.
>
> MR. MINEAR: Well, the Government met that burden in this case, but again, we don't think that that should be the test. Rather, we think that it's the obligation of the party to show that—what defects are necessary. And in this case, the only defect—the only proof of inadequacy that petitioner showed was his claim that he did not receive the notice, and we in return indicated there were procedures in place that would have ascertained the mail.
>
> Now, because the issue is joined, it's likely the Government would be required or would find it necessary or useful to put forward information about procedures. But the problem with the Third Circuit standard is it requires that we, *ex ante*, at the very beginning of the process, go through and determine what procedures are in various prisons. And that doesn't seem particularly—that seems particularly inappropriate with regard to State prisons where we think it's reasonable for us to send—to mail the receipts to the prisons with the expectation that those State prisons will forward the mail appropriately.

QUESTION: Mr. Minear, we have a smattering of courts of appeals cases addressing the issue that we've got today, but beyond that, I don't know how much litigation there is about this. Do we have any indication of how much time in forfeiture cases is spent litigating the question of notice?

MR. MINEAR: I don't know the answer to that, Your Honor. As we point out in the brief, in the year 2000, the Government, the DEA and the FBI, sent out roughly 9,000 notices of forfeiture to their incarcerated prisoners. Now, how many of those are contested, I don't know the answer to that, but certainly there is the possibility of a substantial clog on the courts, particularly over claims of nonreceipt which are so easily made.[7]

Such questions give an advocate an opportunity to highlight persuasive authority and to criticize weaker analyses. In either the Supreme Court or the courts of appeals, an advocate who invokes such authority should add the further explanation for why those courts correctly decided the issue.

§ 4.1.d   *Questions About the Record*

On appeal, judges frequently seek clarification about various parts of the record—whether the court below had made particular fact findings, whether it had entered a particular order, or whether the parties had advanced an argument. Sometimes those questions merely provide the context for an appeal, but sometimes they can be dispositive of the issue before the court. It is critical for the advocate to know the record. In *Lawyer v. Department of Justice*,[8] Richard G. Taranto represented the State of Florida in a suit in which a challenge was brought to the configuration of a state senate district under the Voting Rights Act after a settlement had been reached. His argument demonstrated a facility with the record:

QUESTION: Did the court below ever enter an order saying, and I hereby give 60 days or 90 days or something in which the legislature can act, or did he just accept somebody's statement that the legislature wasn't going to be called into special session?

---

7. *Dusenbery v. United States*, No. 00–6567, 2001 WL 1398611 at *29–*31 (October 29, 2001).

8. *Lawyer v. Department of Justice*, 521 U.S. 567, 117 S.Ct. 2186 (1997).

MR. TARANTO: I think it's a combination of those. In July of 1995, after this Court decided *Miller*, there was a status conference at which everyone recognized this claim had now become substantially more risky than it had been before. Part of what the district court did was to enter an order directing the State parties every 30 days to file a piece of paper in the court saying whether the State legislature would be convened to address what was now recognized to be a serious Federal claim. That—

QUESTION: What had not yet been adjudicated to be an unconstitutional district.[9]

The court ruled that the state could elect to be represented by its attorney general in district court proceedings and that this objecting party could not block the settlement.

§ 4.1.e   *Questions About Context*

Questions concerning the context of a legal issue can take a variety of forms. They can address a similar type of problem under a companion statutory provision or the types of situations that commonly raise the issue. For factual contexts, questions may concern how a particular device at issue works or the methods law enforcement officers use in analogous circumstances. An advocate preparing for questions about the context of the issue should seek to read broadly in the area of law at issue, learn about the industry implicated in the case, and anticipate how the court's decision might affect others similarly situated.

In *Rubin v. Coors Brewing Company*,[10] Bruce Ennis represented Coors in its First Amendment challenge to a federal statute prohibiting the statement of alcohol content on the labels of malt beverages. During the argument, Justice Scalia suddenly put to Ennis the following question, which tested Ennis's knowledge of his client's products:

---

9. *Lawyer v. Department of Justice*, No. 95-2024, 1997 WL 78440 at *31–*32 (Feb. 19, 1997).

10. *Rubin v. Coors Brewing Company*, 514 U.S. 476, 115 S.Ct. 1585 (1995). Between the argument and the court's decision, Robert Rubin replaced Lloyd Bentsen as Secretary of the Treasury, which caused a change in the styling of the case. For consistency with the cited materials, references to the argument transcript use Bentsen as the petitioner, and references to the court's decision use Rubin as the petitioner.

QUESTION: What is ale? What's the difference between ale and beer?

MR. ENNIS: Well, to the best of my knowledge, Justice Scalia, ale is a malt beverage, but it is produced quite differently from beer. Beer is what's called a bottom fermentation process, and ale is a top fermentation process.

QUESTION: Ah, that explains it.

(Laughter.)

MR. ENNIS: Well, * * * I think it's something like milk in the old days before it was homogenized. The cream on the top of the milk would be the equivalent of the ale, and the rest of the milk would be the equivalent of the beer.[11]

Ennis then went on to explain that another difference between ale and beer is the alcohol content of the two beverages. He noted that Coors wanted to be able to advertise that its light beer product contained 4.1 percent alcohol, but was precluded from doing so by the labeling ban imposed by the government. The Chief Justice then engaged Ennis in a colloquy on the subject of light beer:

QUESTION: Well, light beer * * * has nothing to do with alcoholic content.

MR. ENNIS: It does have a great deal to do with alcoholic content, Chief Justice Rehnquist. It's not one-to-one, but there is a [close to] one-to-one correlation between calories and alcohol, and light beer is supposed to be lower in calories, as it is, and in order to do that, it's necessary to make it lower in alcohol content as well.

QUESTION: So your typical light beer will have less alcohol content?

MR. ENNIS: Your typical light beer will have less alcohol content. There is a range of alcohol contents in light beers, however, and that's what Coors wanted consumers to know.[12]

Although it is hard to say whether Ennis's knowledge of the answers to those questions had any bearing on the Supreme

---

11. *Bentsen v. Coors Brewing Company*, No. 93–1631, 1994 WL 714632 at *15 (Nov. 30, 1994).

12. *Id.* at *16.

Court's decision invalidating the statute under the First Amendment, Ennis successfully educated the court about his client's products while simultaneously weaving in an explanation that bolstered an affirmative point he wanted to make about why it was important to Coors to have the alcohol content information on its beer labels. This mastery of detail also gave the justices high confidence that Ennis's other answers were carefully thought-through.

§ 4.1.f Questions About Why the Supreme Court is Hearing the Case

Courts whose jurisdiction is substantially discretionary, as with the Supreme Court of the United States, will make a decision well in advance of the argument whether to review the case at all. Because a vote of only four justices is sufficient for the Supreme Court to hear the case and that vote occurs many months before the argument, from time to time questions will arise at oral argument about the court's decision to accept jurisdiction. Taranto confronted that line of questioning in *Keene Corporation v. United States*,[13] a case concerning the construction of 28 U.S.C. § 1500, which provides that the Court of Federal Claims shall not have jurisdiction of any claim if the plaintiff has a pending action in any other court. The purpose behind the statute is to ensure that a plaintiff unhappy about the pace or prospects of litigation in another court will not file a complaint in the Court of Federal Claims simply as a means of forum shopping.

Because appeals from Court of Federal Claims decisions are made exclusively to the United States Court of Appeals for the Federal Circuit, a ruling from that court on a question of claims court jurisdiction ordinarily would not create a conflict among the federal courts of appeals, which is the primary basis for getting the Supreme Court to grant a petition for a writ of certiorari. Taranto thus faced questions about why the Supreme Court was hearing the case (presumably from justices somewhat skeptical about why certiorari had been granted in the first place):

> QUESTION: On what general principle of law do you base this argument, Mr. Taranto? I mean, we don't ordinarily review Court of Claims or Federal circuit precedent.

---

13. *Keene Corp. v. United States*, 508 U.S. 200, 113 S.Ct. 2035 (1993).

MR. TARANTO: No, I think that—well, stare decisis in its strict terms perhaps applies only to this Court's review of its own precedent. Nevertheless, because stare decisis is a policy-based doctrine the same—

QUESTION: We wouldn't take a case here, I don't think, to hear it argued that the Ninth Circuit had failed to follow stare decisis in connection with a Ninth Circuit precedent.

MR. TARANTO: No, I think that's right, but this, I think, presents two unique circumstances. One is that the issue of [section] 1500's interpretation is unique to the Federal circuit. There can't be a lower court conflict, and as a consequence, all of the relian[ce] interest both of litigants like Keene and of Congress in legislating in the area, must necessarily look to established law in that circuit to guide litigants and guide Congress, and it's for that reason that we think that cases like the *Casman*[14] line of cases demand special respect.

QUESTION: But I—you would still say that even if there hadn't been a precedent until this one, that the court of appeals just had it wrong.

MR. TARANTO: Yes, I think that's right. The principle—

QUESTION: And since it would be the only court to construe that statute, you couldn't wait for a conflict.

MR. TARANTO: That's right. The reading that the Court of Claims and the Federal circuit gave to the statute for a quarter of a century in fact we think reflects the most natural reading of 1500's language.[15]

This colloquy serves also as a useful reminder that, even though the Supreme Court has granted certiorari and the briefing on the merits likely will take counsel far afield of the reasons why the court is hearing the case, the advocate may be asked to remind the justices of the conflicts among the circuits on the rule of law at issue or the importance of the case. These types of questions may arise in only a handful of cases per term, but they are a sufficiently

---

14. *Casman v. United States*, 135 Ct. Cl. 647 (1956).

15. *Keene Corp. v. United States*, No. 92–166, 1993 WL 754949 at *5–*6 (Mar. 23, 1993).

regular part of the dynamic of a Supreme Court argument that counsel should not overlook them in preparing.

§ 4.2 Questions About the Scope of the Rule Being Advocated

The advocate's mission is to persuade the court to adopt the rule her client seeks. Because the rule of law at issue is the most important focus of the proceedings, the court is likely to ask questions seeking a better understanding of the contours of the rule (as explicated in the party's position), the origins or legal basis of the rule (precedent, statutory text, legislative history, etc.), and what policies support the imposition and application of the rule in the factual situation presented.

§ 4.2.a Questions About the Party's Position

No matter how well the brief is written or clearly articulates the party's position, a court typically will seek to obtain a more refined or nuanced explanation of the party's position at oral argument. In *PGA Tour, Inc. v. Martin*,[1] the Supreme Court considered whether the PGA Tour was obligated to allow Casey Martin to use a cart in PGA competitive events. Martin challenged the Tour's refusal to let him ride in a cart between shots on the ground that the ADA prohibits discrimination on the basis of a person's disability. Martin suffers from a permanent disability that makes walking the entire course during a round of golf extremely painful. Representing the PGA, H. Bartow Farr, III, articulated his position from the opening sentences of his argument:

> MR. FARR: Mr. Chief Justice and may it please the Court: The Ninth Circuit in our view made two critical mistakes in applying the Disabilities Act to this type of claim by a professional athlete. First, it failed to recognize that Title III of the Act, the public accommodations provision, appl[ies] only to claims by persons seeking to obtain inputs of a place of public accommodation, that is seeking to enjoy its goods or services, not to claims by persons seeking to supply inputs as employees or independent contractors.

§ 4.2

1. *PGA Tour, Inc. v. Martin*, 532 U.S. 661, 121 S.Ct. 1879 (2001).

Second, the Ninth Circuit never took account of just what a top-level professional sport really is, nothing more or less than a competition that tests excellence in performing what its rules require. Any attempt to adjust the rules to compensate for an individual player's physical condition fundamentally alters the nature of that competition.[2]

Notwithstanding the clarity and care with which Farr constructed that opening, it obviously did not—and could not—answer all questions about the Tour's position. Justice John Paul Stevens, whom Farr could expect to be hostile to his position, engaged him with this exchange:

> QUESTION: Mr. Farr, can I just identify your theory a little better? Are you contending that when the golf course is being used for a PGA tournament, it is not a place of public accommodation because of the limited number of people that can play on that day or are you contending that even though it's a place of public accommodation, the contestants are not individuals within the meaning of the Act?
>
> MR. FARR: It is a modified version of the second, Justice Stevens. It is that they are not individuals seeking full and equal enjoyment of goods, services, privilege and accommodations, as those terms are properly interpreted.
>
> QUESTION: But you are assuming that the golf course, even though for a specific purpose, continues to be a place of public accommodation?
>
> MR. FARR: That the area generally. There is a difficulty. I mean, one of the questions that one has is, is every piece of the property a place of public accommodation or is the— are the ropes, for example, dividing a place of public accommodation from a place that isn't? That is one way to look at it. In our view, the simpler way to look at it is the second way that you have which is to say, you have to be asking in this question, is the person an individual receiving the kind of goods, services and privileges that are covered?[3]

---

2. *PGA Tour, Inc. v. Martin*, No. 00–24, 2000 WL 41011 at *3 (Jan. 17, 2001).   **3.** *Id.* at *10.

Ultimately, Farr did not convince a majority to accept his position, but he skillfully articulated his position without the kind of ambiguity that often marks appellate arguments and causes confusion.

As the foregoing example illustrates, even the best advocates will at times be asked to clarify their clients' position. In *United States v. Vonn*,[4] for example, Deputy Solicitor General Michael Dreeben had outlined the three points he sought to make during his argument. Not long into his argument, a justice commented that "I'm not sure how your points two and three quite fit together. Your point two is that you look at—to see the outcome of the proceeding, would it have been different? But then your point three is that you should confine yourself just to the record * * *. [I]f your point two is whether or not you know all the circumstances * * * it seems to me you might be going outside the record in order to determine that."[5] Dreeben responded in this way:

> MR. DREEBEN: Our second argument is that the proper inquiry into whether an error affects substantial rights is whether there is an effect on the outcome of the proceeding. And in this case, the relevant proceeding to look to is the guilty plea itself. Now, a court of appeals, in determining whether that standard is met, must of course look at the record.
>
> The difference between the position of the United States and the position of the court of appeals is that the court of appeals says the only record that's relevant is the rule 11 guilty plea colloquy itself. Nothing else matters.
>
> QUESTION: That—that I understand. But if you're going to—if your—if your test under two is whether or not he would have entered the plea, it seems to me that that's a difficult inquiry to make if you confine yourself just to the record even if it's the whole record and not just the rule 11 colloquy plea itself.
>
> MR. DREEBEN: Well, it is—it's a difficult inquiry to make if there is no information in the record that sheds light on it, and in that instance, the party that bears the burden of proof will probably lose, which is why it matters whether the standard is plain error review, in which the defendant

4. *United States v. Vonn*, 122 S.Ct. 1043 (2002).

5. *United States v. Vonn*, No. 00–973, 2001 WL 1412134 at *5 (Nov. 6, 2001).

bears the burden of proof, or harmless error review, in which case the Government bears the burden of proof.

But in this case, the claim of the rule 11 error is that the defendant didn't get, at his guilty plea colloquy, information that he had the right to counsel at every stage of the proceeding. Since the record shows that the defendant, in fact, got that information, not once but at least twice, at earlier stages of the proceeding, and he had counsel by his side when he pleaded guilty, not once but twice, it is untenable on this record to suggest that the guilty plea would have come out any differently if the judge had complied with rule 11 in every relevant respect.

QUESTION: Mr. Dreeben, if we answer what is your second question in your petition, not as outlined this morning, the second question being, do you look to the entire record or just the rule 11 colloquy, if we answer that question in your favor, look to the entire record, is it necessary to get into the two anterior questions that you outline, that is plain error versus harmless error, and this one that troubled Justice Kennedy that you don't list as a question in your cert petition?

MR. DREEBEN: Justice Ginsburg, I believe the Court can reverse the judgment based solely on a favorable resolution for the Government of the third question presented it; that is, if the Court does look to the entire record in this case, then I believe that the Ninth Circuit's judgment is incorrect even if it were correct on the other two points that I've outlined.

But there is a conflict in the circuits over the question of whether harmless error review or plain error review does apply in these circumstances, and the Government sought review on that issue in order to have this Court resolve the conflict.[6]

The court ultimately ruled in the government's favor, holding that an unobjected-to error in a trial court's guilty plea colloquy was reversible only upon a showing of plain error and an effect on the defendant's substantial rights, and that the court of appeals could

---

6. *Id.* at *5–*8.

look to the entire record when determining whether a defendant's substantial rights had been affected.

Sometimes the colloquy can be short and direct: the court asks for clarification and the advocate responds with an answer that goes right to the point. Here is how Jeffrey Minear fielded a question about the government's position in the *Dusenbery* case concerning whether a prisoner had received adequate notice of a forfeiture proceeding of his property when the government used certified mail:

> QUESTION: Let me make sure I understand your position on one point. Is it your view that even if you had not used certified mail in this case, but just used regular mail and an affidavit by the Secretary that it was mailed and so forth, that that would be constitutionally sufficient?

> MR. MINEAR: Yes. It's our view that that would be constitutionally sufficient. The procedures that we use, with regard to certified mail, are something that we do beyond constitutional requirements in order to—primarily to ensure that we can disprove false claims of nonreceipt.[7]

That kind of clear and crisp articulation of a party's position requires thought and practice. But it is critical for an advocate to be able to leave no question about her position.

§ 4.2.b   Case–Dispositive Questions

To narrow the focus of an argument, the court will sometimes put questions in the most direct of fashions. The most blatant of this formulation of the case-dispositive question arises when the court asks simply, "If we think _____, do you lose?" In *Federal Maritime Commission v. South Carolina State Ports Authority*,[8] respondent's counsel, Warren Dean, was defending the proposition that a state was entitled to sovereign immunity as conferred under the Eleventh Amendment from a private suit brought before a federal administrative tribunal. He responded to one question about the relevance of the Eleventh Amendment because that constitutional provision is concerned with the exercise of "judicial power" and an executive branch action cannot be "judicial power."

---

7. *Dusenbery v. United States*, 2001 WL 1398611 at *44.

8. Federal Maritime Comm. v. South Carolina State Ports Auth., 122 S.Ct. 1864 (2002).

Dean argued that the Eleventh Amendment is also concerned with the sovereign immunity of states. That drew this colloquy:

> QUESTION: Let me ask you a slightly different question. If we assume for the sake of argument that it is not the judicial power that's being exercised here, do you lose?
>
> MR. DEAN: No.
>
> QUESTION: Why don't you lose? Why don't you lose?
>
> MR. DEAN: The court below said it was irrelevant.
>
> QUESTION: Pardon me?
>
> MR. DEAN: The court below said it was irrelevant, and I agree with that proposition.
>
> QUESTION: And it's irrelevant because?
>
> MR. DEAN: Because sovereign immunity—
>
> QUESTION: Sovereign immunity—in other words, you've got a sovereign immunity argument which is at least distinct from the Eleventh Amendment argument?
>
> MR. DEAN: Absolutely.
>
> QUESTION: Okay.[9]

Although Dean eventually cleared up the question, he could easily have short-circuited the colloquy by going more directly to the heart of his argument and explaining his sovereign immunity position rather than dismissing the question as "irrelevant." In appellate advocacy, it is important to give a succinct explanation or reason for the answer along with the conclusion. A failure to do so can waste precious time.

Sometimes the case-dispositive question will be veiled somewhat, so the unsuspecting advocate does not fully appreciate that the court is laying a trap. That is what happened in *City of Chicago v. Morales*,[10] a case in which the Supreme Court held as unconstitutionally vague an ordinance authorizing police, who observed a person thought to be a gang member loitering in any public place with one or more other persons, to cite those persons if they failed to disperse:

---

9. *Federal Maritime Comm. v. South Carolina State Ports Auth.*, No. 01–46, 2002 WL 272547 at *28 (Feb. 25, 2002).

10. *City of Chicago v. Morales*, 527 U.S. 41, 119 S.Ct. 1849 (1999).

QUESTION: Assume that there's fair notice for purposes of my question. I want you to get back to where you were going, what you call substantive, or maybe it's procedural. I'm not sure what kind of due process, but think of not the category of gang members—gangs mean people who engage in very serious crimes—but people who are not members of the gang.

The ordinance seems to say on its face that all the people who are not members of the gangs in this ordinance can't use the public streets to stand in when a gang member is present. Now, that I have to say, to me anyway, is of some concern.

MR. ROSENTHAL: Well, they can stand there until a police order is given, when—

QUESTION: Well, it says the police shall order them to disperse, so if you read this statute it says that the people who are not gang members who are standing on a public street and want to talk to a member of the gang, or he's one of the group, that they can't stand on that street because if a policeman comes along he shall order them to disperse.

MR. ROSENTHAL: And under those circumstances the legislature could rationally conclude that hypothetical is unlikely, because they heard from the citizens, who are scared to use the public—

QUESTION: Oh, no, no, there are some gang members and some non-gang members. I take it a lot of people stand around on the street. I doubt that there's evidence here that says the only people who stand on the street, even in the worst neighborhood problem areas, are just gang members.

MR. ROSENTHAL: There is certainly ample testimony that law-abiding people are afraid to stand with gang members, who are going to be dealing drugs and don't—

QUESTION: Can a city council pass an ordinance that says, we've had some gang problems in a certain area. Therefore, no one can stand on the street. No one.

MR. ROSENTHAL: Certainly, nothing vague about that law—

QUESTION: No, nothing vague about it. I'm asking you if—

(Laughter.)

QUESTION: I agree. That's right. So can they do it?

MR. ROSENTHAL: If rational, given the legislative record, and here, we of course confine our argument to the evidence and the findings of the city council. We do think that would be rational.[11]

This colloquy helped to convince the court that Chicago's ordinance against loitering was unconstitutional. Rosenthal's theory of the case—as exposed in answers to Justice Stevens's questions—showed the absence of a reasonable limiting position. A general prohibition on all persons standing on a street corner was simply not one a majority of the court could accept. If that was the logical implication of adopting Chicago's position, the court simply was not going to be persuaded.

§ 4.2.c   *Questions About Precedent*

The importance of questions about precedent will depend greatly on the issue and the court. Issues addressing statutory construction or regulatory decisions invariably raise fewer questions about precedent than constitutional cases. And some constitutional questions, like those involving Fourth Amendment search and seizure, tend to invite more doctrinal questions than those concerning structural constitutional issues, such as separation of powers. Precedent becomes less important as the case moves from the court of appeals to the Supreme Court, where the advocate is less likely to face questions raising distinctions or nuances of doctrine. In the Supreme Court, for example, oral arguments rarely turn on debates or colloquies involving precedent. The justices will have read the key cases and decided for themselves how applicable they find those precedents to the case. That said, even in Supreme Court cases counsel must have a scrupulous command of the cases.

In a court of appeals argument, precedent typically takes on a far more important role. Many cases turn on the applicability of a Supreme Court case or whether other court of appeals decisions are

---

11. *City of Chicago v. Morales,* No. 97–1121, 1998 WL 873033 at *23–*25 (Dec. 9, 1998).

binding or persuasive authority. An advocate also tends to need to master many more cases in the typical court of appeals argument than in most Supreme Court cases, because an appellate case typically raises more issues than the ordinary Supreme Court case, and, on each issue presented, cases from other circuits may be persuasive authority.

In *New Jersey v. New York*,[12] the Supreme Court heard a case under its original jurisdiction about which state had jurisdiction over Ellis Island. Jeffrey Minear, who represented the United States as *amicus curiae* in support of New Jersey, was explaining that "the historic boundary should be fixed by the original contours of the island, because that's what Congress and the parties intended by virtue of the Compact of 1834," when he was interrupted with a question about the applicability of *Washington v. Oregon*,[13] which held that the boundary between the two states was the center of the north channel of the Columbia River, subject to change only through accretions.

QUESTION: I'm just suggesting that there's a little space between the *Washington v. Oregon* case and this one.

MR. MINEAR: That might be, but we think ultimately the general principle at stake in *Washington v. Oregon* does control here, which is that this Court should respect the power of the political branches to determine boundaries and draw those boundaries and, in fact, the Constitution provides for adjustments of boundaries if need be. There is a Compact Clause of the Constitution that does allow the States to agree, with Congress' consent, to the alteration of the boundary, and that's in fact what actually happened in *Washington v. Oregon*. That is how that dispute was ultimately settled, was by virtue of a compact between the two States to alter the boundary.[14]

It is not unusual in any Supreme Court or appellate argument for a member of the court to ask the advocate for authority for a proposition. In preparing for argument, the advocate should be mindful that such requests often come when the advocate makes

---

12. *New Jersey v. New York*, 523 U.S. 767, 118 S.Ct. 1726 (1998).

13. *Washington v. Oregon*, 211 U.S. 127, 29 S.Ct. 47 (1908).

14. *New Jersey v. New York*, No. 120 Orig., 1998 WL 15118 at *24–*25 (Jan. 12, 1998).

statements that push the outer limits of the reasonableness of her position.

§ 4.2.d   Questions About Distinctions in the Case Law

Just as judges often ask questions requesting a precedent, so too do they frequently ask questions that invoke distinctions of applicable precedents. In Fourth Amendment cases, questions about precedent can often be springboards into distinctions or hypotheticals that highlight differences between cases. In *Kyllo v. United States*,[15] the Supreme Court addressed the constitutionality of police using thermal imaging to determine whether excessive heat usage in a house might be related to illicit drug production. Justice David H. Souter raised questions of Deputy Solicitor General Michael Dreeben about how analogous the Supreme Court's decision in *Katz v. United States*[16] was to this case of thermal imaging. In *Katz*, the court had held that officers needed a search warrant before they could place a listening and recording device in a telephone booth. This is how Dreeben dealt with those questions:

> QUESTION: But, you know, all of that could have been said but for a change of senses about *Katz*. What the bug in *Katz* was measuring was the effective sound on the exterior wall of the phone booth. When people talk in phone booths, frequently people can stand outside and hear what's going on inside, and it seems to me that what we've got in this case is a situation in which we are either going to say *Katz* is going to be the paradigm on which we decide this or *Place* is going to be the paradigm, the dog sniffing. Isn't that our choice? Because isn't everything you're saying something that you could have said but for a change of the sense organ in *Katz*?

> MR. DREEBEN: Justice Souter, I think that *Katz* is fundamentally different in the respect that what the bug picked up in *Katz* was sound waves, which is what we hear with, and it amplified them and exactly reproduced what Mr. Katz was saying inside the booth.

> QUESTION: Yeah, but it was the wave after it got through the phone booth, just as what infrared is picking up is the wave after it gets through the roof or the window.

---

15. *Kyllo v. United States*, 533 U.S. 27, 121 S.Ct. 2038 (2001).

16. *Katz v. United States*, 389 U.S. 347, 88 S.Ct. 507 (1967).

MR. DREEBEN: No, I think what the infrared imager is picking up, and the record in this case again corroborates this, is heat leaving the house. Now, there are a number of sources—

QUESTION: What's the difference between heat leaving the house and the sound wave leaving the phone booth?

MR. DREEBEN: Well, there are a number of sources for the heat that will leave the exterior of the house. There is the heat that it has absorbed during the day. There is heat that—

QUESTION: But so what? The phone booth will, I suppose, reverberate back the noise of a truck going by.

MR. DREEBEN: No, but what is picked up and what is discerned is the exact reproduction of the words that the person is speaking, and that is the invasion of privacy that *Katz* was concerned with. The whole point of *Katz* was not to look at it as a technological invasion or to focus on whether the police actually went inside the phone booth in order to acquire that information. The point was that the information that was acquired was from within the booth, whereas here that's not the case at all. What is acquired—[17]

The court was not persuaded. By a 5–4 vote, the court held that officers' use of sense-enhancing technology to investigate the activities of a suspect in the interior of the home constituted a "search" within the meaning of the Fourth Amendment.

§ 4.2.e *Questions About Statutory Text*

If a case turns on the text of a statute, the court will often use the argument to explore specific textual phrases or words that determine the outcome of the case. The advocate must be ready to defend her interpretation against attack grounded in the plain meaning of the words, a parallel usage by the legislature in related provisions, the context in which the language at issue appears, the structure of the provision, and even the caption that describes the statutory language. If the words or phrases used derive from the

---

17. *Kyllo v. United States,* No. 99–8508, 2001 WL 168056 at *31–*32 (Feb. 20, 2001).

common law, the advocate must be prepared to address the common law origins or meanings of the terms. And, if the statutory provision includes some common law terms and other terms that do not derive from the common law, the advocate must be prepared to address the significance of those differences.

§ 4.2.f Questions About Legislative History

Until Justice Antonin Scalia took his seat on the Supreme Court, it was quite common for an advocate to invoke the legislative history of a federal statute to support his position. Justice Scalia's hostility to legislative history has become well-entrenched, as expressed in his opinions.[18] Justice Scalia's antipathy for legislative history, grounded in a view that the entire Congress has not passed or offered support for a House or Senate committee report, has spread to court of appeals' judges, many of whom take a similar view. Notwithstanding that hostility, other justices and judges will continue to be interested in whether the legislative history offers any guidance in the resolution of the issue, even if that guidance is not necessarily definitive. For the most part, that material will be cited in the parties' briefs, but oral argument may nonetheless raise questions about legislative history that are not directly answered in the briefs. In *Great-West Life & Annuity Insurance Co. v. Knudson*,[19] Richard G. Taranto was appointed as *amicus curiae* to defend the judgment of the court of appeals, which the government as respondent had refused to do. In his argument Taranto received the following questions about legislative history, which are quite typical of the form most justices and judges will pose:

QUESTION: Is there any legislative history indicating why Congress limited the relief which it permitted in this section to equitable relief?

MR. TARANTO: I'm not aware of any. * * * I have reviewed the * * * legislative history, the collective three-volume legislative history, and as I think some of this Court's decisions * * * have indicated, some of the earlier bills contained broader relief provisions, legal or equitable

---

18. *See, e.g., Wisconsin Pub. Intervenor v. Mortier*, 501 U.S. 597, 622, 111 S.Ct. 2476, 2490 (1991) (Scalia, J., concurring in the judgment) (noting his objection to the practice of "utilizing legislative history for the purpose of giving authoritative content to the meaning of a statutory text").

19. *Great–West Life & Annuity Ins. Co. v. Knudson*, 534 U.S. 204, 122 S.Ct. 708 (2002).

relief, and that was cut back for reasons that at least I don't recall having seen.

In * * * the one reference * * * cited in * * * my brief I think at page 27—in one of the Senate reports that discusses the immediate predecessor of this provision, there's no general reference to any kind of relief that's necessary to—to make plans [to] protect all of their rights or vice versa. It's been principally a beneficiary protection statute.

And there's also no general reference to restitution in the abstract. There's a reference to injunctions and specifically to constructive trusts. So, even there, there isn't a general idea that anytime we're talking about what sometimes are called direct damages or general damages or contractual damages, and therefore making the whole the loser of a particular sum of money that's been promised, that that action would somehow be transformed into an equitable action when historically it very plainly wasn't.[20]

When asked about legislative history, an advocate should try to identify for the court the most on-point reference possible and to direct the court to the applicable House or Senate report, as well as where in the briefs that document was cited.

§ 4.2.g *Questions About the Policies Underlying the Rule*

Many judges also seek to better understand the parameters of the rule by asking about the policies underlying that rule. Having a solid grasp of the policies behind a rule can assist the advocate in several ways. First, it gives a coherence to the law: the advocate can explain that the rule was adopted for a reason, and that reason is both sound and supported on the facts of this case. Second, if the outer reaches of a rule extend beyond its policy rationale, a court may be reluctant to accept that rule even if ordinary principles of textual construction or common law precedent would otherwise dictate its adoption.

In *Atkins v. Virginia*,[21] the Supreme Court considered a defendant's claim that it would be cruel and unusual punishment to

---

20. *Great–West Life & Annuity Ins. Co. v. Knudson*, No. 99–1786, 2001 WL 1182732 at *39–*40 (Oct. 1, 2001).

21. *Atkins v. Virginia*, 122 S.Ct. 2242 (2002).

execute him for a capital crime because he was mentally retarded. Society's views had shifted in the prior two decades, and a colloquy ensued over the reasons for those changing attitudes:

> QUESTION: And what is—what is the reason? I mean, you—you—in responding to Justice Scalia's question, you point out, well, these people pass the test of comprehension, which is a condition of culpability for execution. What test don't they pass? What is the reason for this emerging consensus?

> MR. ELLIS: The principal reason—and it has changed a little bit as * * * the process has gone on. The original and continuing principal reason is that people, as expressed through the legislature, have reached a judgment that someone whose intellect is at this level and who has grown up with that limitation on their ability to learn—because age of onset is part of the definition of mental retardation as well—are not individuals for whom death is an appropriate punishment.

> QUESTION: No. I realize that that's the judgment they're reaching, and you want us to recognize that judgment as now having constitutional significance. What I want to know is why are they reaching that judgment? What is the reason that elevates that judgment to one of constitutional significance?

> I guess the * * * converse of my question is we're not here simply to add up numbers and say, oh, when it gets to 37, the result is different. You're * * * asking us to * * * draw a different kind of conclusion. And what I want to know is what is it behind the judgment of these emerging States as a reason that should recommend itself to us?

> MR. ELLIS: And—and as I said, the principal focus is on the understanding of people of what the limitations imposed on people with mental retardation are and how it affects their comprehension—[22]

Although Ellis did not deliver especially persuasive answers to those questions, the Court nonetheless held 6–3 that the execution

---

22. *Atkins v. Virginia*, No. 00–8452, 2002 WL 341765 at *19–*20 (Feb. 20, 2002).

of a mentally retarded criminal constitutes cruel and unusual punishment forbidden by the Eighth Amendment.

By contrast, in a federal labor law case involving the right of federal unionized workers to raise collective bargaining issues prior to the conclusion of the term of the collective bargaining agreement, Irving Gornstein represented agency management in succinctly responding to a question about the policy implications of a rule. His colloquy with Justice Scalia led to this exchange, which reflected Gornstein's experience, gracious directness with the court, and ability to capture in a few words the heart of his message:

QUESTION: The big difference, as I understand your position, is that there is no disincentive here to raise [the new issue] midterm, as there is in the private sector.

In the private sector, if you come to an impasse midterm and you want to make something of it, you have to call a strike. After you've gone through a big collective bargaining agreement you're usually not going to get your union members to be willing to do that.

Whereas here, if you raise it midterm and you go to an impasse, it's cost-free. You go to an arbitrator. Maybe he'll rule for you. I mean, it's, you know, heads I win, tails you lose.

MR. GORNSTEIN: Justice Scalia, I was going to make that point first but I thought the text would go first better.

QUESTION: For me of all people. Yes.

QUESTION: He's basically a policy—

(Laughter.)

QUESTION: Basically a policy wonk, you're right.

MR. GORNSTEIN: But that is—yes, Justice Scalia, that's absolutely correct.

That was the second enormous difference that Congress faced when it was looking at this Act as it compared to the private sector experience. The kind of incentives that would be in play for midterm bargaining are just completely different, and when you can take every issue to impasse, you have the incentive to raise any issue of any concern to any Federal employee—[23]

---

23. *National Fed'n of Fed. Employees, Local 1309 v. Department of Interior,* No. 97–1184 & 97–1243, 1998 WL 792045 at *52–*53 (Nov. 9, 1998).

Although this case resulted in a 5–4 loss for the government,[24] it was not through any want of advocacy on Gornstein's part.

§ 4.2.h   Questions Seeking Concessions

One of the most difficult categories of questions to handle well is when a member of the court seeks a concession of the party. An advocate has to proceed with extreme care, because too-expansive a concession can entirely unravel the advocate's case. A skillfully made concession, on the other hand, can make the advocate more credible to the court by demonstrating the reasonableness of the advocate's position. In determining just how much an advocate can concede and still win, the advocate must be conscious of how best to draw the lines around her position and how to express the limiting principles that cabin the proposed rule in a manner that most accurately conveys how the court should articulate its ruling.

§ 4.3   Questions About the Implications of the Rule Being Advocated

One of the most challenging aspects of Supreme Court and appellate advocacy is to address the implications of the rule being advocated. A lawyer's focus throughout litigation is on how to persuade the court to adopt the position that best serves her client's needs. Typically, in district court litigation (and even to a great extent in the courts of appeals), that challenge is best met by arguments tailored to a showing of how the facts of the case fit within a well-established legal framework. In Supreme Court and many appellate cases, however, a critical dimension to the court's decision-making process is understanding the likely consequences that will flow from its ruling. As a result, in many Supreme Court and court of appeals cases, the court will ask questions geared toward an understanding of what the next case in the doctrinal line will look like and how the court should rule in that case. Typically, those questions raise much more difficult scenarios than the one presently before the court, but that is precisely why members of the court will pose those questions to counsel. This section deals with the two most common types of questions that go to the heart of understanding the implications of a rule: hypothetical questions and questions raising analogies.

---

24. *National Fed'n of Fed. Employees, Local 1309 v. Department of Interior,* 526 U.S. 86, 119 S.Ct. 1003 (1999).

§ 4.3.a   Hypothetical Questions

Supreme Court arguments are notable for the frequent, and creative, use of hypothetical questions posed by the justices. This is not a new phenomenon. Writing nearly 20 years ago, E. Barrett Prettyman, Jr., devoted an entire law review article to the subject.[1] The inexperienced advocate too often responds to a hypothetical with, "That's not this case," which has to rank among the most insulting answers possible to a question from the bench. The questioner knows the hypothetical is not this case, but nonetheless wants to know how a case farther from the core of the rule suggested by a party would come out under that party's theory.

An advocate should keep at least three points in mind when preparing for hypothetical questions. First, the hypothetical can be most soundly answered in almost all cases by having a well-considered theory of the case. The theory of the case will provide an ordering frame of reference that gives a coherent explanation of what happened factually and how those facts relate to the applicable legal principle being advanced. It also provides the reference point through which many difficult hypotheticals may be answered.

Second, if possible, the advocate should try to answer a hypothetical question with a "yes" or "no" and then explain the answer. In court, an observer can see the way members of the court lean forward in anticipation of getting the answer to a hypothetical and then lean back when the advocate answers, "Yes, because _____." Alternatively, when an advocate begins with the explanation rather than the simple answer, members of the court tend to become frustrated. They lean forward even more and become more prone to interrupt.

Third, if the advocate plans to distinguish the hypothetical to the case under submission, she should give that distinction *after* directly answering the question. A question may well seek a concession about the limits of the advocate's theory of the case. The advocate should recognize that motivation, give the concession against interest, articulate the necessary distinction, and transition back to an affirmative point.

---

1. *See* E. Barrett Prettyman, Jr., "The Supreme Court's Use of Hypothet-   ical Questions at Oral Argument," 33 Catholic U. L. Rev. 555 (1984).

Examples from arguments in the Supreme Court help to illustrate those points. One of the most commented-upon hypotheticals[2] in recent years was in *California v. Deep Sea Research, Inc.*,[3] which raised three issues involving a historic shipwreck that sank off the coast of California in 1865 with a shipment alleged to contain $2 million in gold and an army payroll of $250,000. One of the issues was whether the shipwreck had been abandoned. Under the Abandoned Shipwreck Act of 1987, Congress provided that abandoned historic shipwrecks in the coastal waters of the United States belong to the states in whose coastal waters they are embedded. In enacting that statute, however, Congress did not define what constitutes "abandonment." Under normal principles of lost property, if the property has been abandoned, whoever finds it gets to keep it. If the vessel is not abandoned, the owner may assert ownership rights and the treasure salvor is only entitled to an award for salvage services rather than a claim of complete title. Thus, establishing the legal standard for abandonment is critical in determining how ownership claims will be resolved in the burgeoning number of shipwrecks being discovered through new technology.

The United States had put forward a standard for inferring abandonment under traditional principles of maritime law that took into account the passage of time and the owner's efforts to salvage the wreck. The government argued that Congress intended for that maritime law approach to apply under the Abandoned Shipwreck Act by using the word "abandon" without defining it in the Act. Under maritime law, an object is considered "abandoned" if a long period of time has elapsed and the owner has not taken steps to recover the property. The advocate's objective, therefore, was to support that theory of the case when Justice Scalia asked the following hypothetical:

> Suppose I drop a silver dollar down a grate, and I try to bring it up with a piece of gum on a stick, and I can't do it, and I shrug my shoulders and walk off because I have not gotten it, and then somebody comes up and lifts up the grate and gets my silver dollar. Is that his silver dollar? Have I abandoned it just because I could not get it? I still

2. *See, e.g.,* Joan Biskupic, "Masters of the Hypothetical," Wash. Post, Jan. 3, 2000, at A17.

3. *California v. Deep Sea Research, Inc.,* 523 U.S. 491, 118 S.Ct. 1464, 1998 AMC 1521 (1998).

think it's my silver dollar. I haven't said, you know, I don't want it any more.[4]

That hypothetical, which is quite far afield from the case and seemed to belittle the significance of the issue presented, put the advocate in an awkward position. It could have aroused a sense of indignation in the advocate or an attempt to ridicule it as absurd. Instead, the government lawyer treated the question on its own terms and answered by invoking the government's theory of the case: "Justice Scalia, if you waited 130 years without attempting * * * to get your silver dollar, it might be appropriate to infer that you have abandoned it."[5]

Sometimes the hypotheticals can come in rapid-fire succession, as members of the court attempt to get concessions or clarifications about the limits of an advocate's position. In *Wilson v. Arkansas*,[6] the state argued broadly that officers' methods of entering a dwelling have no bearing on the Fourth Amendment reasonableness inquiry, meaning that officers are not constitutionally required to knock and announce their presence before gaining entry to execute a warrant. That sweeping position elicited sharp questions to Arkansas Attorney General J. Winston Bryant:

> GENERAL BRYANT: * * * The State's primary or first position is that knock and announce is not required categorically.
>
> QUESTION: No, but my question is, is it a relevant consideration in determining whether a search is reasonable or not? May they consider the fact that there either was a knock and announce, or there was not a knock and announce?
>
> GENERAL BRYANT: No, Your Honor, in that instance the case is—the State's first argument is that it is not relevant in the consideration.
>
> QUESTION: So then under your view the State routinely could use a battering ram to knock down every door.

---

4. *California v. Deep Sea Research, Inc.*, No. 96–1400, 1997 WL 751917 at *30–*31 (Dec. 1, 1997).

5. *Id* at *31. In its opinion, the court did not provide a direct answer to this question, holding that abandonment should be determined based on general principles of maritime law without a definitive statement of what those principles provided.

6. *Wilson v. Arkansas*, 514 U.S. 927, 115 S.Ct. 1914 (1995).

GENERAL BRYANT: No, Your Honor. The use—

QUESTION: So then the way entry is [e]ffected is a component of reasonableness.

GENERAL BRYANT: In the case of a battering ram, Your Honor, that would be subject to the reasonableness clause.

QUESTION: How about kicking?

GENERAL BRYANT: It might be necessary in some instances, Your Honor, where that was the means by which officers had to enter.

QUESTION: How about using a skeleton key?

GENERAL BRYANT: That would be—

QUESTION: All of this is without knocking, obviously. * * * All of these hypotheticals I've given to you constitute reasonable entry in all cases?[7]

This broad approach did not win any adherents on the bench, and, after an additional series of hostile questions, Bryant was forced into this memorable colloquy at the end of his argument:

QUESTION: And there's a very long tradition here that has to be taken into account, and the fact that the officers don't knock and announce certainly at a minimum ought to be a factor in what's reasonable.

GENERAL BRYANT: That is essentially the U.S. Government's position, and that is the State's fall back position, that if this Court does not see fit to announce a categorical rule to protect the police officers in this instance, that a reasonable fall back would be the position by the Solicitor [General], in that knock and announce would be part of the reasonableness test under the Fourth Amendment.

QUESTION: Time to fall back, General Bryant, I think.[8]

Sometimes the hypothetical will be so close to the facts presented in the case that the advocate must proceed with extreme caution (or self-confidence) in offering an answer. In *United States v. Vonn*, the Supreme Court addressed whether a guilty plea should be set aside on the ground that the district court failed to advise the defendant of his right to counsel during the guilty plea colloquy

---

7. *Wilson v. Arkansas*, No. 94–5707, 1995 WL 243487 at *32–*33 (Mar. 28, 1995).

8. *Id.* at *42–*43.

despite the fact that the defendant had earlier been advised of his right to counsel at all stages of the proceedings. The government contended that if the defendant had received such advice prior to the guilty plea colloquy, the failure to give the advice at that time should be reviewed under the more stringent plain error standard, rather than for harmless error. That position led to this colloquy with government counsel:

> QUESTION: Mr. Dreeben, one of the advantages—I don't know if it's a sufficient advantage of Judge Kozinski's position is a simple—very simple job for the court of appeals: either they got the advice or they didn't during the hearing. How does the Government say the court of appeals should dispose of a case in which the record shows that an arraignment 3 or 4 months before the guilty plea colloquy, the defendant's lawyer says I've advised him about his right to counsel at trial? He tells him that at the arraignment. The record shows that. And then that's all it shows. Then you have the guilty plea colloquy. And—and the judge fails to comply with the rule. What should you do with that case?

> MR. DREEBEN: The court of appeals should affirm because there is ample evidence that the defendant had knowledge of the particular right in question that he claims was not given to him at the rule 11 colloquy.

> QUESTION: There's an irrebuttable presumption that he fully understood it three months later.

> MR. DREEBEN: No. There's not an irrebuttable presumption. If there were something in the record that indicated—

> QUESTION: No, nothing else in the record.

> MR.DREEBEN: If there is nothing else in the record, then I think that there's nothing to rebut the presumption. This Court has indicated in a number of contexts that information that a defendant has been given at one stage of a proceeding—give[s] rise to a presumption that the defendant has knowledge of it. For example, the defendant is indicted and read the indictment at an arraignment. This Court made clear in *Bousley v. United States*[9] that there's

---

9. *Bousley v. United States*, 523 U.S. 614, 118 S.Ct. 1604 (1998).

a presumption that the defendant has been given adequate notice of the charge. Now, that presumption can be overcome later in the proceedings if the judge gives the defendant misinformation about the charge or if the defendant otherwise can show from the record that he didn't have an adequate understanding of the charge.[10]

As these examples illustrate, the advocate has to be prepared to address hypotheticals with a theory of the case that bears up to close scrutiny.

§ 4.3.b Questions About Analogous Legal Contexts

More common at the appellate level than at the trial court level will be questions concerning analogous legal contexts. Like hypotheticals, questions raising analogies seek to broaden the court's understanding of whether other legal situations apply a similar rule or whether the rule being requested may also extend the law in an analogous context. One purpose of such questions is to provide comfort to the court that the rule being requested in the factual and legal situation before it is not too great a stretch. Another purpose is to anticipate how arguments similar to those being raised in the case would apply in a case under that other legal regime. In an argument involving the Americans with Disabilities Act, for example, a justice asked one of the advocates: "Under the Longshore Harbor Workers and Compensation Act, the courts routinely look at what jobs are in the community that this person is eligible for after they've suffered an injury. Is that about the same approach that we should use in this case—in these kinds of cases"?[11]

In *Kyllo*, Michael Dreeben faced questions about other analogous legal regimes for searches and seizures:

QUESTION: Mr. Dreeben, the Ninth Circuit seemed to rely on a theory of it's like garbage thrown out, that when the homeowner has waste heat, it's somehow discarded, and there's no privacy interest left in it. Do you support that analogy? I thought—

MR. DREEBEN: I don't think that's—

---

10. *United States v. Vonn*, No. 00–973, 2001 WL 1412134 at *4 (Nov. 6, 2001).

11. *Toyota Motor Mfg.*, 2001 WL 1453954 at *22.

QUESTION:—that was a little hard to understand.

MR. DREEBEN: Well, I don't think it's the strongest analogy, although there are cases where I think the analogy would fit. The theory of the garbage cases is that by voluntarily abandoning—

QUESTION: Abandonment.

MR. DREEBEN: Correct.

QUESTION: It's hard to say the homeowner had abandoned this heat information.

MR. DREEBEN: Well, I think that there are cases in which the analogy would fit better; for example, where there is a very active ventilation system that is specifically attempting to draw the heat out of the house in order to provide a suitable climate for growing the plants that are inside, but the primary rationale that the Ninth Circuit used which is similar to the rationale that I'm articulating here is that the thermal imager doesn't pick up any intimate details or particularly private details about what is going on inside of the house.[12]

In like fashion, *Atkins v. Virginia* gave rise to questions concerning the analogous situation of imposing the death penalty on a person not adjudged to have mental retardation but rather a lesser form of mental illness:

QUESTION: Should the test be the same as for executing someone with a mental illness? We—we have dealt with that, and—and with the level of comprehension that someone must have in order to be eligible for the death penalty who has mental illness. Should the test be the same?

MR. ELLIS: Your Honor, I believe you're discussing the *Ford*[13] issue with regard to competence to be executed? I read the *Ford* case as suggesting that whether the individual had mental illness or mental retardation, if—if that individual lacked the understanding as execution became imminent, that they—that the State would be precluded from executing. This—

---

12. *Kyllo,* 2001 WL 168056 at *47–
*48.

13. *Ford v. Wainwright,* 477 U.S. 399, 106 S.Ct. 2595 (1986).

QUESTION: So, is that test not adequate here in your view?[14]

Because it is quite difficult to prepare for questions concerning analogies, an advocate should take the time to consult colleagues knowledgeable in other areas of law and to test how far an analogy might reasonably extend.

§ 4.4 Questions Reflecting Judicial Idiosyncracies

The more familiar an advocate is with the court conducting the argument, the easier it is to anticipate the kinds of questions a particular member of the court might ask, as well as the manner in which that jurist will ask the question. Each judge will bring a distinctive style to the bench at oral argument, and the advocate's challenge is to be familiar enough with those tendencies to anticipate (where possible) how that judge will react to the case with questions. That said, because there are as many judicial questioning tendencies as there are judges, the purpose of this section is to suggest a few general categories of questions and modes of interrogating that may spark similar analysis by the advocate for the court hearing the argument.

§ 4.4.a Questions Stemming From the Prior Professional Experience of the Judge

It is common for a judge to fall back on personal knowledge or experience in asking questions, even if those questions may strike the advocate as beside the point. Any decision maker will want a comfortable frame of reference through which to view the case. That desire to find comfort, therefore, may produce some surprising colloquies. Justice Clarence Thomas, for example, has said that the reason he does not often ask questions at oral argument is because he wants to hear from counsel and because the other justices jump in to ask the questions he wants to have answered, so there is no need for him also to be active at oral argument. When the other justices do not ask questions, however, Justice Thomas will put his questions to counsel. In *NASA v. FLRA*,[1] for example, Justice

---

14. *Atkins*, 2002 WL 341765 at *16.

§ **4.4**

1. *National Aeronautics & Space Admin. v. Federal Labor Relations Auth.*, 527 U.S. 229, 119 S.Ct. 1979 (1999).

Thomas produced what is his longest recorded, uninterrupted colloquy with counsel in over 10 years as a member of the Supreme Court. It lasted nearly 10 minutes, and may well have been occasioned by the lack of experience of any other justice as the head of an executive branch agency that had to deal with an Inspector General under the Inspector General Act of 1978, as had Justice Thomas when he chaired the U.S. Equal Employment Opportunity Commission.

The case involved the independence of an Inspector General in conducting an investigation into wrongdoing by a unionized federal employee who sought to have a union representative at the interview conducted by an Inspector General special agent. Counsel for NASA had been asked a large number of hostile questions, reflecting the court's discomfort with the position that an Inspector General ought to have the authority to conduct an interview free of the requirement allowing an interviewee to have a union representative present at the interview. The Solicitor of the Federal Labor Relations Authority, David Smith, defended the FLRA's requirement that a union representative be allowed to attend an Inspector General interview. After taking very few questions, he was about to finish his argument after only roughly half of his allotted 20 minutes when Justice Thomas interceded with a long series of questions:

QUESTION: Mr. Smith, I'd like to revisit with you. You said there is a trend away from or toward Inspector Generals investigating these types of cases.

MR. SMITH: Yes, sir.

QUESTION: Now, isn't that only a part of the story? Wasn't there a trend some years ago away from internal auditors in agencies?

MR. SMITH: Prior to the passage of the Inspector General?

QUESTION: That's right.

MR. SMITH: It might get before my time, but I'll have to take your word for it.

QUESTION: Well, not all before your time. For the independent regulatory agencies, wasn't that during the '80's?

MR. SMITH: Well, the Inspector Generals Act was passed in 1978.

QUESTION: Well, there's a separate Inspector Generals act for the smaller agencies. Wasn't there then an attitude in Congress that the investigation should not be controlled by the agency heads?

MR. SMITH: I'm not aware of that particular attitude, Your Honor. I can't—

QUESTION: Well, that was the attitude.

MR. SMITH: I can't dispute your point. I'll certainly accept it.

QUESTION: The point was, I don't think you can have it both ways. You can't say that the Inspector General is under the agency head when we know that the purpose was to do just the opposite and to get the investigations from under the agency heads. And let me ask you this question. Do you agree that in the old days that the head of the agency could actually direct the auditor's investigation of these matters?

MR. SMITH: Yes.

QUESTION: Do you agree that the head of the agency cannot direct the investigation by the IG?

MR. SMITH: The—the legislative history says that if an agency head requested an Inspector General to undertake an audit or an investigation—

QUESTION: No, that's not what I'm talking about.

MR. SMITH:—it is assumed that they would do so.

QUESTION: No, that's not what I'm talking about. If the IG said, I want to investigate this matter—

MR. SMITH: Yes.

QUESTION:—can the agency head say, no, you can't?

MR. SMITH: They cannot do so.

QUESTION: If the IG said, I want to investigate this matter in this manner, can the agency head say, you cannot?

MR. SMITH: I think so. I think the agency head—

QUESTION: The agency head can tell them that?

MR. SMITH: Yes. I think the agency head can say to the Inspector General—

QUESTION: By what authority?

* * *

MR. SMITH: Well, the—the premise of your question is that it is the agency head that is imposing this requirement on the Inspector General.

QUESTION: That's right.

MR. SMITH: We think that's incorrect. It is the Congress that imposes this requirement on the agency, any representative of the agency conducting the—

QUESTION: But your argument is that this IG reports to the Administrator, and if the Administrator can't direct the IG to do precisely what you think the IG should be doing, then I don't know how you can say that the IG reports to the Administrator.

MR. SMITH: Well, I don't want to—I don't want to butt heads with you. We think Inspector Generals are not free agents in conducting their investigations—

QUESTION: I bet you the agency head does.

(Laughter.)

MR. SMITH: In conducting their investigations, they have to comply with the law. This is but one law.[2]

Notwithstanding his personal experience in dealing with an independent Inspector General, Justice Thomas could not garner a fifth vote for his view that the federal labor law did not compel a requirement of a union representative at certain Inspector General investigative interviews. The colloquy demonstrated, however, that even in the most unlikely of circumstances, an advocate has to be prepared to respond to questions stemming from the prior professional experience of the judge.

§ 4.4.b *Questions From the Judge's Personal Knowledge*

Some judges cannot help asking questions based on their own knowledge of the factual situation. Chief Justice William H. Rehn-

---

2. *National Aeronautics & Space Ad-min. v. Federal Labor Relations Auth.,* No. 98–369, 1999 WL 183821 at *36–*43 (Mar. 23, 1999).

quist, for example, loves geography and history and will often ask questions reflecting these interests. In *Clinton v. Goldsmith*,[3] for example, the Supreme Court heard argument on whether the Court of Appeals for the Armed Forces properly declared unconstitutional the President's authority to drop from the rolls an officer who had been convicted in a court-martial proceeding. When a question arose about the role of the Board of Correction of Military Records, the body that hears appeals of service members aggrieved in these personnel actions, the Chief Justice interrupted to ask whether that was the same entity that was deciding an appeal brought by descendants of Dr. Samuel Mudd, who had been convicted by a military tribunal of conspiracy to assassinate President Abraham Lincoln.[4]

In *R.A.V. v. St. Paul*,[5] a case involving a hate crimes ordinance in St. Paul, Minnesota, Justice Blackmun, a native Minnesotan, could not resist asking the county attorney for St. Paul about the local conditions near the site of where the incident had occurred.

QUESTION: Mr. Foley, before you get started, let me ask a couple of questions. You are the county attorney, aren't you?

MR. FOLEY: Yes, I am, Justice Blackmun.

QUESTION: And yet the city is the respondent here.

MR. FOLEY: Yes, under Minnesota law, Justice Blackmun, the county attorney handles all matters involving juveniles and this matter was a prosecution of a juvenile, so we represent any activity, whether the matter is under a city ordinance or State ordinance or a Federal crime.

QUESTION: And this is why the city is a party to one of the amicus briefs as well as being the respondent in the case.

MR. FOLEY: That's correct, Justice Blackmun.

QUESTION: A little unusual, I suppose.

MR. FOLEY: It is an unusual—

3. *Clinton v. Goldsmith*, No. 98–347, 1999 WL 183817 at *8 (Mar. 22, 1999).

4. *Clinton v. Goldsmith*, 526 U.S. 529, 119 S.Ct. 1538 (1999).

5. *R.A.V. v. St. Paul*, 505 U.S. 377, 112 S.Ct. 2538 (1992).

QUESTION: Let me ask one other trivial question. The cross burning took place on Earl Street, didn't it?

MR. FOLEY: Yes, it did.

QUESTION: Whereabouts on Earl Street? That is a long street, it runs from Mounds Park to Finland Park.

(Laughter.)

MR. FOLEY: 290 Earl Street.

QUESTION: Hm?

MR. FOLEY: 290 Earl Street.

QUESTION: I know that, but where is 290? What is the cross street?

MR. FOLEY: I don't have the cross street, Justice Blackmun.

QUESTION: You don't know—

(Laughter.)

QUESTION: It is near Mounds Park or is it near Finland Park?

MR. FOLEY: It's near Mounds Park.

QUESTION: I was up there last June with some U.S. Marshals who had never been there. And I think it's one of the most beautiful views in the City of St. Paul. But the grass was so high you couldn't see the view. Have your maintenance man cut the grass.

(Laughter.)

MR. FOLEY: Justice, under our Constitution everyone is presumed innocent until they've had a trial.

(Laughter.)

QUESTION: Mr. Foley, if you're going to make all these concessions you might as well sit down now.

(Laughter.)[6]

---

6. *R.A.V. v. St. Paul,* 1991 WL 636263 at *24–*26 (Dec. 4, 1991).

It was a light-hearted moment, which can be welcome in any oral argument, but it did not contribute to the court's understanding of the issues. Nonetheless, when a member of the court chooses to use up the advocate's time in that manner, there is not much an advocate can do except to respond with the grace of the St. Paul county attorney in that case.

§ 4.4.c Questions Based on Judicial Philosophy or Constitutional Approach

Lawyers must be mindful when they are arguing cases that judges may view the case through a certain lens. If the case is statutory, some judges may be more or less inclined to adopt a strictly textual approach to construing the language; others may be more inclined to examine legislative history materials in an effort to glean Congress's intent. Still others may be more concerned with the policies behind the enactment. Constitutional cases pose a particular challenge, because the range in viewpoints cannot always be easily categorized. Some advocates attempt to tailor their arguments for a particular set of judges whose philosophies are well known. Although that approach is not always a mistake, a better course is to use the preparation process to anticipate questions from the full range of judicial philosophies, because even a strict constructionist may ask a question about the purpose behind a law, just as a judge generally unsympathetic to states' rights may nonetheless pose questions about how far Congress may encroach on fundamental state responsibilities. An advocate must be sufficiently conversant with the full gamut of how analytical approaches to judging cases may be reflected in questions. Regardless of which judge may convey a particular judicial philosophy through questions, the well-prepared advocate will have anticipated such questions irrespective of their actual source at the argument.

§ 4.4.d Styles of Asking Questions

Just as each judge will bring to court a distinctive personal and professional background and judicial philosophy, so, too, will a judge have a unique personal style or manner in asking questions. An advocate must be as attuned to the manner in which a judge asks a question as to the judicial philosophy espoused by that jurist. Judge David Sentelle of the U.S. Court of Appeals for the District of Columbia Circuit, for example, is quite firm in wanting counsel to give a "yes" or "no" answer to a question that calls for that response. Justice Stephen Breyer is well known for asking complicated questions that contain multiple parts. Justice Ruth Bader

Ginsburg asks very precisely worded questions that rarely leave any doubt or ambiguity as to her meaning, but that require special attentiveness in argument. Justice Souter often invokes history in his colloquies with counsel, while also seeking concessions. Here is an example of a colloquy with Justice Souter that contains those various elements. He was questioning petitioner's counsel in *Atkins v. Virginia*,[7] the case concerning execution of mentally retarded defendants.

> QUESTION: Do you believe there is—there is any role at all in—in the—in Eighth Amendment jurisprudence, death penalty jurisprudence I guess, for—for general rules to the effect that, yes, there may in some instances, let's say, of retardation be—be proof of—that would at least be enough to get to a jury on premeditation and—and deliberation and so on, but that the very fact of—of retardation makes it unlikely in most cases that this can be proven and makes the evidence at least highly debatable, even in those cases that get to a jury? And therefore, the sensible thing to do in order to avoid a high risk either of wrong conviction or in the case of—of the penalty phase a high risk of—of unsound judgments imposing the death penalty, there ought to be a cutoff point of some sort. There ought to be a cutoff of the high risk cases from the general rules of proof. Do you—do you take the position that there is no place in—in death penalty jurisprudence for that kind of a—we'll say a high risk cutoff rule?
>
> MS. RUMPZ: A high risk cutoff rule of? I'm sorry. I didn't follow exactly what you were saying.
>
> QUESTION: Well, I'm—I'm assuming that, sure, there are cases of borderline retardation and so on in which the—there would be enough evidence to get to a jury on the various mental elements for a—for a capital sentencing. I'm also assuming that in cases of retardation, including retardation near the borderline, that that evidence is—is highly debatable in most cases, and it is sufficiently uncertain, it is sufficiently debatable that there's a high risk that a jury is going to come to the wrong conclusion. It's going to say, oh, yes, this person really is the worst of the

---

7. *Atkins v. Virginia* 122 S.Ct. 2242 (2002).

worst and sentence him in—in a case in which that really is not so.

And the reason for having a rule saying, we're going to have a—a retardation cutoff—a person who is retarded will be ineligible for the death penalty—is to avoid those high risk cases and avoid the risk, in effect, of wrong imposition of the death penalty. That's why we would have such a rule, quite apart from moral judgments or anything else. I'm just talking about this practical risk judgment.

And my question to you is, do you say that our death penalty jurisprudence should have no place for such a—a risk assessment rule?

MS. RUMPZ: That's what individualized sentencing is. That is the risk assessment rule. That's what juries—

QUESTION: Well, it's—its very clear that within the category of those who ought to be subject to the death penalty, there should be individual assessment. I'm asking whether you believe that in risky cases there ought to be rules to eliminate the risk. And I take it your answer is yes, but I don't want to say that if—if I'm being unfair to—to your position here.

MS. RUMPZ: You know, I don't want to play dumb here, Justice Souter, but I'm afraid I'm not understanding what—what you're asking me. I think that the risk assessments that you're talking about play into the—the concepts of individualized sentencing under the Eighth Amendment. The juries make those assessments. The juries determine whether someone is sufficiently culpable for the death penalty and they determine whether his mental retardation is a mitigating factor sufficient to outweigh giving the—the defendant the death penalty.[8]

Through a process of frequent arguments and even more frequent observations of the court, the most skilled advocates will gain insights into the questioning styles of the members of the court they will face at oral argument. When an advocate faces a judge who asks complicated questions with many subparts, it can be challenging to listen carefully to the question and to respond to what appears to be the heart of the question. An answer around the

---

8. *Atkins v. Virginia*, 2002 WL 341765 at *30–*33.

periphery of a complex question will frustrate the court and not advance the advocate's cause with the questioning judge.

* * *

One of the advocate's most important tasks is to prepare well for the types of questions she likely will face at oral argument. It is extremely difficult sometimes for an advocate to appreciate that oral argument is designed for the court to ask the questions the advocate would prefer not to have to answer. An advocate can faithfully prepare answers to as many questions as possible, but still be unprepared for oral argument if the answers are not on the tip of her tongue. Because the skillful answering of questions can make the difference between winning and losing a case, the next chapter addresses a way of practicing for an oral argument: moot courts.

Chapter Five

MOOT COURTS

Analysis

A moot court is a practice session that attempts to simulate the experience of arguing in court, with colleagues who have read the briefs putting questions to the advocate and responding to the arguments the advocate attempts to make. Some very fine advocates maintain that they never hold a moot court before arguing a case in the Supreme Court or a court of appeals. One of them, Charles Alan Wright, was one of the most distinguished legal scholars and appellate advocates of the twentieth century. But for every Professor Wright there are easily thousands of attorneys who need the extra preparation a moot court can provide. Indeed, Wright may have been an even greater oral advocate had he conducted moot courts. This chapter addresses how moot courts can benefit the advocate, how to gain the most out of a moot court, and how to use moot courts to address those difficult types of questions raised in Chapter Four.

§ 5.1 Why Do Moot Courts?

The best answer to that question was given by Justice Byron White to legions of his law clerks in a slightly different context: "Two good minds are better than one." Simply put, a moot court enables the advocate to obtain the assistance of other good attorneys in preparing the case for argument. Most moot courts provide a number of benefits.

First, a moot court gives the advocate an opportunity to prepare for the quick thrust and parry of arguing in court. That is particularly important if the advocate has not recently had an appellate argument. It is easy to get rusty in articulating arguments and answering questions with precision. Consequently, the first moot court after a layoff of a few months can be much harder, even for an experienced advocate, for the questions seem to interrupt the advocate more abruptly and make more difficult the formulation of fluent answers. The process is akin to what many great athletes experience in the first days of training camp. Pitched baseballs seem faster and legs feel heavier. Timing is a problem. Getting the hands and eyes to work in sync becomes a critical function of training camp. The same is true for moot courts. The brain's ability to discern the problem in a question and to formulate a coherent answer will improve with practice. When an advocate is well prepared for questions from the bench, the process almost seems to occur in slow motion. Experience in the trial court helps only so much. The process of giving an extemporaneous speech to a jury or examining a witness is far different from facing the questions of a panel of jurists. A benefit of the moot court, therefore, is to condition the advocate's brain to the speed of questions from a Supreme Court justice or circuit judge.

A second benefit is that, when properly done, moot courts raise the questions members of the court are most likely to ask. Most cases will have a dozen or so questions that *will* definitely be asked in the actual argument, a dozen or so that *might* come up, and many others that conceivably *could* be asked. The most experienced advocates will anticipate on their own many of the questions in those three categories, but even the best will rarely anticipate all of them. The moot courts thus improve the odds that all of the questions the advocate will face surface before the argument, giving the advocate a fair chance to develop effective answers.

Third, there is simply no substitute for practice. It is inconceivable that Yitzhak Perlman would perform at Carnegie Hall without rehearsing, or that Michael Jordan would skip practice before the seventh game of the NBA championship series. Why then would any advocate not practice before arguing a case in the Supreme Court of the United States? Yet in many cases advocates have done just that. "Practice" means honing particular skills: how to listen to the question carefully; how to remain patient and respectful in the face of hostile questions; how to deal with abrupt questioners who try to throw the advocate off stride; how to transition back to an affirmative point; how to answer questions directly by saying "yes" or "no" and then giving the explanation; how to make eye contact with the questioner; and how to speak fluently without lots of "ums" and "uhs."

A fourth reason to hold moot courts is that the participants will not know the case as well as the advocate. To persuade them, the advocate will have to find ways to simplify the legal concepts and arguments and to explain why his side of the case is correct. The process of simplifying the case is extremely difficult, but it is crucial to effective oral advocacy. Any simplification of a difficult concept necessarily entails some distortion, so the attorney must find ways to make the argument more understandable to someone less immersed in it while maintaining the legal precision of the argument. Good moot court panelists will be excellent sounding boards for how to simplify the arguments in the case. They also will help to identify the best and most persuasive arguments to make and the arguments not to press. It is not unusual for an inexperienced advocate to want to stress a point that a seasoned moot court panel finds unpersuasive. The advocate should not be so stubborn in the face of such advice that he takes the client down, too! The converse can also be true. An argument that has surface appeal to a moot court panelist may not bear up to closer scrutiny. The attorney must be careful not to rest the case on an argument that can be debunked during oral argument or that a law clerk can easily refute after the case is submitted.

§ 5.2   How to Do Moot Courts

When he was Solicitor General from 1989 to 1993, Kenneth Starr formalized the practice of moot courts for government lawyers arguing in the Supreme Court. Many of the appellate sections in the Department of Justice followed suit. It is extremely rare, therefore, for a lawyer representing the United States government in a major case in the Supreme Court or courts of appeals not to have had at least one moot court prior to the argument. For less significant cases handled by United States Attorney's Offices, practices vary widely. The central point, however, is that government lawyers readily perceive the benefits of moot courts and use them as part of their preparation.

In the past decade, the Solicitor General's Office has developed a fairly standard method for conducting moot courts. That method is a useful starting point from which the advocate with more experience may depart. Members of the Solicitor General's Office typically hold two moot courts before arguing a case in the Supreme Court—an informal and a formal moot court. In particularly momentous cases, the advocate might hold three moot courts. The informal moot court occurs first, typically one week or so before the argument. The purpose of the informal moot court is to begin refining the preparation process. It is "informal" in the sense that the advocate can "stop" the moot court when a question arises to which he does not know the answer and ask for help in formulating a response. The "formal" moot court is videotaped and the attorney strives to make it through the questioning without breaking out of role. This moot court typically occurs two or three days after the informal moot court, and two or three days before the argument. The aim of the formal moot court is to simulate as closely as possible the argument experience.

Before describing the differences between informal and formal moot courts, it is necessary to explain the basic process of a moot court. The idea is simple: the advocate stands before colleagues who have read the briefs and prepared questions, and delivers his argument as though he is in court. The moot court panelists interrupt to ask questions and probe the advocate more deeply when he gives an answer that they deem satisfactory. If done well, a typical moot court in a Supreme Court or court of appeals case may take between one and two hours. The length will be determined by the complexity of the case and the level of preparation of the panelists and the advocate.

Preparation, however, is the key to conducting a successful moot court. The more prepared the advocate, the more he will be able to focus on using the moot court not only as a way of handling questions, but also of turning those questions into opportunities to advance his affirmative case. A successful moot court requires a high level of preparation and experience from the panelists, too. They should come armed with as many questions as they can think of—questions they themselves are curious about and want to have answered, as well as questions they think the court might likely ask.

In some cases where the stakes are extremely high, a party will conduct a moot court by retaining special outside counsel (sometimes former circuit judges) to serve as moot court panelists and sometimes even an outside appellate specialist to prepare an argument for that party's opponent. Such elaborate measures are warranted only in cases with enormous stakes. But the benefits can also be measurable. An outside counsel arguing a case that he did not brief will bring new insights to the case, and may be skilled in asking the types of questions that expose a weakness in the party's position that the opponent's brief did not uncover. This type of moot court—expensive as it is in consuming resources of time, money, and energy—can nonetheless give an important added dimension to the advocate's preparation.

§ 5.3   The Informal Moot Court

Some advocates try to differentiate as little as possible in the form of how the informal and formal moot courts are conducted. They generally start each moot court by reading the prepared opening and eliciting comments from each participant. The purpose of the opening will vary somewhat depending on whether the advocate is representing petitioner/appellant, respondent/appellee, a second party, or an *amicus curiae*. For an opening argument by petitioner/appellant, the Supreme Court and courts of appeals generally permit the advocate a sentence or two to state the issue in the case or otherwise to set the context and then a few sentences to put forward the party's position. A respondent/appellee generally gets somewhat less latitude for giving an opening because the court has heard 30 minutes of argument and is therefore well into the case. Occasionally, the court is so anxious to hear from respondent's counsel that he does not even have an opportunity to say, "May it please the Court," before the first question is asked. The best advocates representing respondents tend to take that dynamic into account in their moot court preparation. Rather than waste participants' time on an opening that will likely never be stated in full, they ask for comments to be given later orally or in writing after the moot court ends. Even when the advocate has no realistic expectation of delivering the opening, those comments can prove to be extremely valuable, not only in how to begin an argument but in what themes to develop during the argument. A discussion of the opening also gives moot court panelists an opportunity to say what they think the best arguments are, as well as how to word them in a clear and unambiguous way.

After that discussion, the best practice is to maximize time for questions and answers. An informal moot court likely will raise a number of questions the advocate has not considered. This moot court gives the advocate an opportunity to try out proposed answers or to simply say "I don't know" and move on to another area of questioning. The latter approach can often be a more efficient way to run the moot court than giving answers that are simply guesses and leading the questioners far afield into areas the advocate is not yet prepared to handle. The court will respect the advocate who acknowledges not knowing the answer, but an attorney can lose a case by being led down a path he is unprepared to defend and making concessions or giving ill-considered answers that make acceptance of his client's position less likely. Although some discourage that practice and seek instead to simulate in all of the moot courts the actual dynamic of an argument, leaving room for flexibility often produces a better management of the moot court. That said, sometimes an advocate can benefit from giving a speculative answer when a moot court panelist is prepared to expose the weakness of the advocate's position. That kind of experience can be extremely valuable in forcing a refinement of the argument.

A critical aspect of conducting a moot court is to choose the participants with special care. Nice people who rarely ask questions do not make for very helpful moot court participants. The advocate wants the toughest, most incisive, and quickest questioners available. Because the aim of the moot court is to raise as many questions as possible, the participants must actually ask them and not sit idly by without actively participating. The best advocates recruit the most experienced lawyers they can for moot courts and encourage as many questions as the panelists have the stamina to ask. Those lawyers recognize that it is far better to face the intense questioning of friends and colleagues than to appear unprepared in a public argument in the Supreme Court or the court of appeals. In this respect, it may be instructive to note that Seth Waxman, when he was Solicitor General, would fill his moot court panels with a dozen or more attorneys and let them fire questions at him for hours. It was not uncommon for Waxman to have moot courts that lasted three and four hours—even for a 15–minute Supreme Court argument.

The advocate should also set some ground rules for the moot court participants. Those ground rules enable the advocate to get the maximum benefit from the session. If the advocate wants to enlist help on his written opening, for example, he should invite comments before moving to questions and answers, while the text is fresh in the minds of the panelists. If he wants the questioning to focus in a more structured way on each of the issues in the case, he should encourage the participants to exhaust all of their questions on an issue before moving to the next one. And if the advocate wants to ensure that the questioning actually covers a topic, he should make that intention known or recruit a participant who will perform that role.

Some moot court panelists develop a reputation for the thorough manner in which they prepare, devising questions that address each aspect of the case. Roy McLeese, Deputy Chief of the Appellate Section in the U.S. Attorney's Office and former Assistant to the Solicitor General, for example, would prepare for moot courts in such a meticulous way. He would ask questions covering the wide range of issues raised in a case, not just those that advanced his own understanding of the issues. And McLeese's knowledge of criminal law was so vast that he could readily perceive comparisons, analogies, and the implications of a case.

An advocate should insist that the participants provide a full and fair opportunity for an answer before interrupting with the next question. If, after a sentence or two, the advocate has not adequately answered the question, then a follow-up question is fair game. But the cardinal rule for a moot court is that it is for the *advocate*'s benefit and not the sporting entertainment of the panelists. The advocate should insist that panelists not question so aggressively that the advocate does not get a reasonable opportunity to answer the questions.

Another useful rule for moot courts, both informal and formal, is to dispense with time limits or time signals. On occasion, there may be some benefit to the advocate knowing that he was unable to make the point he especially wanted to make in a moot court in the time officially allotted. But on the theory that a moot court is like batting practice—the advocate wants to size up the ball and groove his swing—the principal purpose of the session is to raise questions that the advocate must be able to handle. Those questions can come at any time in a moot court, so the advocate has to practice articulating answers. For that reason as well, the advocate may want to focus less in the informal moot court on developing transitions back to affirmative points. After a discussion of the opening, the focus should be on answering as many questions as the participants can ask.

§ 5.4   The Formal Moot Court

A "formal" moot court differs from an "informal" moot court in that it strives to simulate even more precisely the actual experience of conducting the argument. "Formal" means just that. The advocate should wear formal business attire, use a podium, have the argument binder prepared and briefs marked, have the moot court videotaped, and try to stay in role for the entire session. Most of the best advocates have at least one moot court before an argument. For those who also hold an informal moot court, a formal moot court serves to sharpen and refine the practice experience in the same way that a dress rehearsal puts actors through their final paces before opening night of a play. Holding a formal moot court two or three days before the argument leaves ample time to research any questions that arise in the moot court while still allowing time for the advocate to become fluent in speaking extemporaneously about the case. Some choose to hold their last moot court farther in advance of argument, with the last moot court no sooner than one week before the argument. In deciding on a moot court schedule, a number of competing considerations come into play: the need for additional time to develop answers to questions that arise in the moot court, the need for a final review of the materials in the case, the need to give the material a chance to sift and re-synthesize in the advocate's mind, and the need to hone the opening and mantra in order to get the argument off on the right foot.

In the days between the informal and formal moot courts, the advocate is focusing on three concerns: revising the opening, developing answers to questions that came up at the informal moot court, and refining the argument modules for the key points that will likely arise at argument. Depending on which party the advocate is representing, he may handle the opening in a comparable way to the informal moot court, reading it and taking comments if representing petitioner/appellant and reading it without discussion (but inviting comments after the moot court) if presenting respondent/appellee's case. The justification for that difference is that the court is much more likely to let petitioner/appellant's counsel state a few sentences without interruption than it is respondent/appellee's attorney. The precise wording of petitioner/appellant's opening, therefore, is much more critical.

The advocate should try to recruit even more vigorous questioners for the formal moot court panel than for the informal moot court, if possible. Optimally, the lawyer will have heard every question in a moot court, so that when the judge or justice asks the same or similar questions, the advocate will be ready with a considered response. The advocate needs to discover how treacherous certain areas can be, and the only way to do that is to be put on the spot by good moot court panelists. This also helps the advocate identify when the court may be heading down a similar path. In addition, hearing the answers—even if they simply represent informed speculation by the advocate rather than considered analysis—will enable the panelists to help the advocate refine the argument. This process often provides the best means of fully internalizing the theory of the case, especially if the panelists ask difficult hypotheticals.

Videotaping the moot court is also very valuable. It enables the advocate to critically evaluate all aspects of the moot court performance, from the substance of the answers to matters of speaking style. The videotape will also refresh the advocate's memory of when certain questions were posed, and the relationship of some questions to others. In some cases, the answers to questions naturally lead to other questions. That sequencing can be especially helpful when the advocate is considering how to prepare segues, a subject addressed in Chapter Six.[1]

§ 5.5   How Not to Do Moot Courts

Just as there are ways an advocate can maximize the benefits of a moot court, so, too, are there ways the moot court can be run in a less helpful manner. The most common mistake is for the advocate to lose control of the moot court to over-aggressive questioners who do not allow the advocate to give an answer before the next question is asked. An advocate needs to experience the rapid rat-a-tat of questions, because many appellate arguments degenerate in that way. But the *reason* why those arguments deteriorate— and correspondingly the reason why a moot court simulating that kind of questioning can be of limited utility—is that the answers to the questions were lousy. Weak answers beget more questions, and if the answers do not improve, even more aggressive questions follow. The only way to break that cycle is to give good answers that satisfy, or at least mollify, the questioner. Thus, it is far more important at a moot court for the questioners to give the advocate a chance to test an answer than to fire off the next question before hearing the rest of an answer that might be satisfactory. Indeed, sometimes it takes the advocate three or four sentences to articulate an answer that the questioner finds persuasive. But if the questioners do not give the advocate a chance to try out various answers, no one will ever know what might have been the best way to reorder or reword the answer.

1. *See* § 6.3.

A second common mistake—paradoxically the reverse of the one just mentioned—is for the advocate to break out of role so often that the panelists lose confidence in the advocate's level of preparation. A moot court is of limited utility for all but the most experienced and talented of advocates if the attorney is insufficiently prepared to address the most obvious questions. A moot court is a rehearsal, yet the attorney does not want to be in the position of rehearsing "I don't know" too many times. For that reason, most advocates should spend ample time preparing on their own before attempting to present their case to moot court judges.

A third mistake is to simulate too closely the actual time the advocate will have in the argument. Some moot courts outside the Solicitor General's Office last barely 30 minutes, because that is the amount of time allotted to that advocate's argument. In the zeal to give the advocate a sense of the shortness of time in an argument, such a moot court fails to take advantage of the time spent by the panelists in preparing for the moot court. Particularly if the advocate plans to call on those same panelists again, he should not show disrespect for them by failing to give them a full opportunity to pose their questions.

Advocates also err in not giving panelists an opportunity to critique their performance. After an hour-and-a-half or two-hour moot court, the advocate is understandably tired and ready to end the ordeal. But the panelists at that time will have the best recollections of muffed answers or missed opportunities. A short post-mortem can pay huge dividends, particularly if the moot court is not videotaped so that the attorney can see for himself the questions that were mishandled.

The advocate should also follow up with the panelists to try out alternative formulations of answers to their questions. After reviewing the videotape of the formal moot court, the advocate can go back to moot court panelists for additional perspectives, better informed about the nuances of the panelist's questions and the way the advocate tried to answer them. Some of the best suggestions from moot court panelists may come the day after a moot court when, at the coffee machine or during an office visit, the advocate and the panelist discuss whether an alternate formulation works.

Finally, a common mistake of moot courts is a failure by the advocate to take the many questions asked by panelists (who will anticipate the vast majority of questions from the bench) and devise ways to simplify answers. A moot court that may take two hours can translate well into a 30–minute argument if the advocate does the necessary synthesis work in shortening and fine-tuning answers. That synthesis is an absolutely critical reason for holding moot courts and an important missed opportunity when not accomplished. In many moot courts, the advocate's first response may address a procedural element—such as standard of review or sufficiency of the evidence—rather than the substance of the question. One reason for letting the advocate "wind up" to the substantive answer without interruption is to hear the full answer. Once that answer has been articulated, the advocate and panelists alike are in the best position to figure out ways of re-ordering the elements of the answer to get the most persuasive points out first.

§ 5.6   Articulating a Theory of the Case

Moot courts can be especially helpful in affording an advocate the opportunity to articulate and refine a theory of the case that provides a unifying theme for the argument. Without a theory of the case, an advocate can get quickly tangled up in a series of questions that seem to point in reasonable, if inconsistent, directions. If done skillfully, the moot court panelists can expose weaknesses in the advocate's articulation of the theory of the case by pressing the boundaries of the rule of law proposed by counsel to the point at which the underlying guiding principle no longer seems reasonable.

A key part of the theory of the case is a recognition of what limiting principles cabin the application of the rule being advocated. Judges and justices frequently want to know whether an advocate's position has a limiting principle. In *Evans v. United States*,[1] for example, the government took the position that the phrase, "under color of official right" in the Hobbs Act, in effect, codified the common law crime of official extortion. Deputy Solicitor General William C. Bryson engaged in this colloquy:

> MR. BRYSON: Well, the statute uses a term of art, and our position is that term of art is not—it has to be read in light of its origins, which were in New York law and the common law. And its origins make quite clear that we are talking about compensation in excess of that which you are permitted.

§ 5.6
1. *Evans v. United States*, 504 U.S. 255, 112 S.Ct. 1881 (1992).

QUESTION: But you will admit that on its face it has no limiting principle?

MR. BRYSON: Well, I think, yes, I think that the words under color of official right on their face do not answer the question of how broad the statute it. That's true of many common law terms that show up in criminal statutes. [T]he word mayhem in and of itself does not strike one as having a particular meaning, but you look at the common law for the meaning of a term like that when it shows up in a statute.[2]

The government was thus prepared to accept whatever limitations the common law imposed on the application of the phrase "under color of official right" as an element of the crime.

An advocate must be ready to articulate a limiting principle to a position, especially if the proposed rule is susceptible to a broad application. In *United States v. Ramirez*,[3] the government asked the Supreme Court to rule that law enforcement officers must have only reasonable suspicion (and not a higher level of suspicion, such as probable cause) if they damage property when making a no-knock entry into a dwelling to execute a search or arrest warrant. Under the Fourth Amendment, as established in *Wilson v. Arkansas*,[4] officers must knock and announce their presence when executing a warrant unless they have a reasonable basis for believing that the persons inside pose a risk of danger to the officers, of flight from them, or of destroying evidence from the advance warning provided by the knock and announcement. *Ramirez* posed the question whether, when officers have the requisite reasonable belief to dispense with the knock-and-announce requirement because the person they sought to apprehend is an escaped convict, they may damage property to effectuate the entry.

The government's argument was that, if officers had a reasonable suspicion to forego the knock-and-announce requirement, they could cause damage to property reasonably necessary to make the entry. The breadth of that position was not lost on anyone, including the justices. But the government's limiting principle was that an unreasonable destruction of property would give rise to a sepa-

---

2. *Evans v. United States*, No. 90–6105, 1991 WL 636267 at *45 (Dec. 9, 1991).

3. *United States v. Ramirez*, 523 U.S. 65, 118 S.Ct. 992 (1998).

4. *Wilson v. Arkansas*, 514 U.S. 927, 115 S.Ct. 1914 (1995).

rate civil action for damages. That limiting principle was crafted both to assure the justices that officers would not have an incentive to engage willy-nilly in the destruction of property and to prevent the exclusionary rule from applying if officers damaged property unreasonably in making a no-knock entry to search the premises or make an arrest.

At the argument, the court asked questions to elicit that limiting principle:

> [Y]ou said that there could be a Fourth Amendment control of excessive force. What would be the implementation of that? Suppose the agents here had come in like gangbusters and destroyed everything in their path, and also picked up some incriminating evidence, what would be the consequences? You said the Fourth Amendment is involved, how? Do we exclude the evidence that would be garnered in such an unreasonable search?[5]

The government's counsel responded by making a distinction between whether officers had destroyed property in making a reasonable entry into the dwelling, which would be constitutional even if the damage was extensive, as opposed to a situation in which the officers used excessive force and caused significant property damage, which would give rise to a cause of action for civil damages, but would not lead to application of the exclusionary rule to suppress the admissibility of the evidence.[6]

As the foregoing illustration demonstrates, defining the parameters of a party's limiting principle may involve questions of policy. For private litigants, the policy implications of a rule may not be as important, save for those instances in which a private party seeks to vindicate a right that is also subject to government enforcement. Sometimes, such as in the example from *Evans* noted above, the limiting principle may flow out of the legal theory itself: the incorporation of the common law into the statute.

---

5. *United States v. Ramirez*, No. 96–1469, 1998 WL 15476 at *6 (Jan. 13, 1998).

6. *Id.* at *7. The Chief Justice's opinion for the court contained this sentence, which essentially ratified the government's position: "Excessive or un- necessary destruction of property in the course of a search may violate the Fourth Amendment, even though the entry itself is lawful and the fruits of the search are not subject to suppression." *United States v. Ramirez*, 523 U.S. at 71, 118 S.Ct. at 996.

Moot courts can be particularly valuable for raising hypotheticals that members of the court might pose, especially if the participants themselves have significant Supreme Court and appellate experience.[7] An advocate should strive to stock the moot court panel with seasoned counsel who can most closely simulate that aspect of the oral argument experience.

§ 5.7 Perfecting Answers

Modern appellate practice has moved so far away from set-piece oratory that the advocate's ability to answer questions is the fulcrum to a successful argument. There are a number of different ways of perfecting the answers to difficult questions.[1]

From the beginning of the advocate's last ten-day run-up to an argument, the list of questions that need to be answered should never be far away. The advocate has to assume that the court's members will read the briefs, the decisions below, the joint appendix materials, and the key cases cited by the parties. It is not uncommon for many of the questions on that list to stem from reviewing important Supreme Court or court of appeals decisions. That is perfectly natural. Doctrinal uncertainties give rise to subsequent litigation (of which the case currently pending may be the latest in the line). Because judges and justices cannot anticipate where creative litigants will take doctrine, they will use oral argument to probe counsel for analysis of the logical reach, as well as limits, of prior decisions.

Hypotheticals pose an obvious source of questions requiring careful thought and preparation. Questions also may arise about the fact findings of the district court, the procedural posture of the case, and the statutes that may be implicated. Some justices, like Chief Justice Rehnquist, for example, will frequently ask for the legal authority underlying the position advanced by counsel. "What is your authority for that proposition, counsel?" is a question every advocate should be asking throughout the preparation process. (Having that question run through the advocate's mind during preparation also has a temporizing influence on the rhetorical excesses an advocate might be tempted to employ. As soon as the mind's ear hears a sentence that has a bit too much of an edge to it, the advocate should be thinking, "What's the authority for that?")

---

7. *See* § 4.3.a.   § 5.7

1. *See generally* Chapter Four.

Other justices, like Justice Stephen Breyer, will be very interested in the policy ramifications of a rule and in a statute's legislative history. Justice Antonin Scalia might be particularly interested in the textual basis for a statutory rule. Justices David Souter and Ruth Bader Ginsburg will often inquire into the historical origins of a rule. And Justice John Paul Stevens has a way of asking a case-dispositive hypothetical with a precision that can be treacherous for the unprepared advocate.

In dealing with the array of questions, the advocate must develop a process that leads him comfortably to internalize the answers. Research assistance is often needed. If provided in written form, the advocate can go back to review the legal authorities the research produced. On the other hand, for many other types of questions, the advocate may reasonably decide *not* to write out the answers. Instead, the advocate can use the list of questions to practice extemporaneously speaking the answers in the days leading up to oral argument. Those oral answers always come out of the mouth less precisely worded and focused than the proposed written answers. But that is what a Supreme Court or court of appeals argument is—an oral demonstration of facility with the law and of skill at succinctly articulating answers to the hardest questions. No matter how perfectly expressed those answers might be on paper, a failure to verbalize them orally at the argument is still a failure to accomplish the objective.

Some advocates memorize carefully scripted answers to questions. That approach requires a phenomenal memory and runs the risk of appearing canned and unnatural. However one internalizes the answers to questions, the advocate should strive for a natural delivery in the courtroom.

§ 5.8   Use of Analogies

Because Supreme Court judging is heavily based on drawing analogies, the advocate should anticipate questions that seek to elicit comparisons with and distinctions to other areas of law. One of the best advocates in this respect is Edwin Kneedler who, for nearly a quarter of a century, has represented the United States in the Supreme Court, first as an Assistant to the Solicitor General and then as a Deputy Solicitor General. Kneedler's ability to perceive both offensive and defensive uses of analogies is uncanny. In *Vermont Agency of Natural Resources v. United States ex rel.*

Stevens,[1] Kneedler was on the short end of a decision that ultimately rejected the federal government's position that the False Claims Act authorized suits by relators against states, notwithstanding the Eleventh Amendment. In starting with the question of whether the court had jurisdiction under Article III of the Constitution to decide the case, Kneedler responded to Vermont's argument by invoking an analogy in the law of assignment: "[T]he United States was * * * allegedly injured by the violation of the False Claims Act. So, there was an injury in fact, and the False Claims Act operates, in effect, as an assignment or in the nature of an assignment. And under * * * Vermont's theory, no assigned claim could be brought under Article III because the assignor was the injured party, but the person bringing the suit was not. But it is commonplace under our system of justice for claims to be able to be assigned."[2]

At a later point in the argument, Kneedler drew this analogy to the United States' relationship to a relator in a *qui tam* action, by which a person seeks to claim a violation of the False Claims Act on behalf of the United States and, pursuant to statute, receives a portion of the recovery: "[T]here is a single, unitary judgment out of which the * * * United States and the relator in that way could be looked at as joint tenants, and * * * a joint tenant is typically empowered to protect the interests on behalf of both tenants."[3]

Analogies to other principles of law can be an effective way to demonstrate to the court that the rule being proposed is not a frolic and a detour. In a similar way, analogies to real-life common sense situations can also be powerful during oral argument. The advocate who best employs this rhetorical device is John Roberts, who spends considerable time in the preparation process thinking of analogies to use at oral argument. Roberts' purposes in devising such analogies are twofold: first, he believes an argument can be more effective if the advocate brings something new to the argument; and second, that analogy should not be a new argument per se, but rather a new way to look at the advocate's position. Roberts recognizes the high risk involved in raising new analogies at oral argument, which is why he tests them on colleagues and gives careful thought to whether they work. He tends to eschew the kinds of legal analogies that Kneedler uses because he regards them as riskier and less prone to be perfect fits.

---

§ 5.8

1. *Vermont Agency of Natural Resources v. United States ex rel. Stevens*, 529 U.S. 765, 120 S.Ct. 1858 (2000).

2. *Vermont Agency of Natural Resources v. United States ex rel. Stevens*,

No. 98–1828, 1999 WL 1134650 at *38 (Nov. 29, 1999).

3. *Id.* at *47–*48.

Part of his argument in *Bray v. Alexandria Women's Health Clinic*[4] illustrates how he uses real-world analogies to cast a new light on his legal argument. In that case, the United States participated in the case as *amicus curiae*, taking the position that the petitioners' tortious interference with the access of women to an abortion clinic did not satisfy the requisites of 28 U.S.C. 1985(3), which makes it a violation if two or more persons conspire to violate a person's right to, among other things, equal protection of the law. As Roberts began his argument, he launched right into his first analogy:

> If a group of conspirators assault someone carrying a picket sign because they don't believe there should be a First Amendment right to picket, they certainly are guilty of a tort and they interfere with that individual's exercise of constitutionally protected rights, but in no sense do they deprive him of equal protection or equal privileges and immunities simply because they assault him and not everyone else. But if the conspirators come upon a picketer and assault him because he's black and they don't believe that blacks should have equal First Amendment rights, then they satisfy the class-based invidiously animus requirement. That is not what is going on here. Petitioners do not interfere with respondents' rights because respondents are women. Petitioners do what they do because they're opposed to an activity, the activity of abortion. They target their conspirators not because of who they are, but because of what they are doing.[5]

In this argument, Roberts had the luxury of making his points without any interruption from the court until he was about to sit down. He invoked other factual analogies to attack the logic of the respondents' position:

> Respondents' answer to this argument is that only women can exercise the right to an abortion, and therefore petitioners' anti-abortion activities have a discriminatory impact on women. People intend the natural consequences of their acts, and therefore respondents argue, you can infer

4. *Bray v. Alexandria Women's Health Clinic*, 506 U.S. 263, 113 S.Ct. 753 (1993).

5. *Bray v. Alexandria Women's Health Clinic*, No. 90–985, 1992 WL 687912 at *11–12 (Oct. 6, 1992).

from the discriminatory impact that petitioners have a discriminatory purpose.

A few examples will show that the logic of that doesn't hold up. Consider, for example, an Indian tribe with exclusive fishing rights in a particular river. A group of ecologists get together who are opposed to fishing in the river, because they think it disturbs the ecology. They interfere with the Indians' rights. The impact of their conspiracy is on a particular Indian group, but it would be quite illogical to infer from that that they have any animus against Indians. They're opposed to fishing in the river, not Indians, even though only Indians can fish in the river. Petitioners are opposed to abortion, not women, even though only women can exercise the right to an abortion.

Another example. Suppose a group of men and women get together who are opposed to the draft and they interfere with registration. The direct impact of their conspiracy will be felt only by men, since only men are eligible for the draft. But, again, it would be quite wrong to infer from that impact that the conspirators have any animus against men. They're opposed to the draft, not men, even though only men are eligible for the draft.[6]

The Supreme Court's opinion agreed that a violation of Section 1985(3) had not been made out on these facts.[7] Although the court did not use the analogies suggested by Roberts, it was persuaded by his approach, and used other fact-based analogies to explain its decision.[8]

The foregoing examples show how analogies can be used offensively to advance an affirmative point, as well as defensively to respond to a question that challenges the basic premise of the advocate's position. In preparing for argument, the advocate must also be mindful that the justices themselves will be thinking of similar kinds of factual or legal analogies. These can be very difficult to address on the fly at oral argument. It is therefore useful for the advocate himself to have a breadth of knowledge in the law as well as the assistance of colleagues with such knowledge.

6. *Id.* at *12–*13.

7. *Bray v. Alexandria Women's Health Clinic,* 506 U.S. at 269–70, 113 S. Ct. at 759–60.

8. 506 U.S. at 270, 113 S.Ct. at 760 (contrasting the abortion protesters' actions with the example that "[a] tax on wearing yarmulkes is a tax on Jews").

§ 5.9 Preparing Defensively, Arguing Offensively

This concept can be extremely difficult to put into practice. Preparing defensively, but arguing offensively, is an affirmative decision to approach the moot courts from a defensive frame of mind. Seen in this light, the purpose of the moot courts is not to give the advocate a chance to try out all of his affirmative points on colleagues, but rather to give the moot court panelists the maximum opportunity to pose their hard questions and to give the advocate an opportunity to refine the answers.

Thus, instead of practicing transitions and affirmative points per se, one approach is to prepare "defensively," by trying (at least in the first moot court) simply to give the best and most satisfactory answer to the questions possible. This process allows moot court participants to freely ask their questions, and to turn the moot court more into a free-flowing question-and-answer session than an actual argument. This approach also gives the advocate the chance to evaluate more critically where the expected lines of attack are likely to occur at the argument and to be more "offensive" during the argument in making a segue back to an affirmative point. By focusing the preparation on those questions that are designed to put the advocate on the defensive, the skilled advocate will find a way by the time of the argument to transform that hostile question into an opportunity to persuade the court.

This method of "preparing defensively, arguing offensively" also produces a certain freshness in the courtroom. Particularly in short 10– or 15–minute arguments, the advocate must approach the lectern with a recognition that time is limited and an urgency to make the right affirmative points. If the attorney has thoroughly canvassed all of the questions that put him on the defensive, he is better positioned to seize an opportunity to go on the offensive at the argument.

The advocate, nonetheless, must not get stale. Over–rehearsal and unnatural memorization are noticed and not appreciated. Professor Charles Alan Wright used to say that he wanted simply to have a conversation with the court, which is one reason why he never did moot courts. He wanted that conversation to be fresh and spontaneous. Candidly, Wright would have been even better had he come to the court with a more distinctly affirmative agenda. He assumed that his brief would be sufficient to set forth his position and that his role at argument was simply to answer questions. Unfortunately, that type of professorial approach only works for the greatest of the professor–advocates, among whom Wright was distinctive. Most advocates benefit greatly from having a clear set of points they want the court to hear at the oral argument. Sometimes a question from the bench is not immediately forthcoming. There are few things worse than the awkward silences created by an advocate's failure to use that time to move from an answer back into a new affirmative point.

Nevertheless, when the advocate is comfortable giving appellate arguments, the first moot court might be used for defensive preparation and the second moot court for practice going on the offensive. Experience and the dictates of the case will affect how the advocate prepares and executes an argument. But there is a real benefit to thinking through the defensive and offensive aspects of an argument. A judge or justice more commonly votes *for* a side rather than *against* a position. An advocate ought to prepare to give at least one reason why the court should rule in his favor and at least one reason why the court should rule against his opponent. The moot courts provide an invaluable opportunity to try out those arguments. At the hearing itself, the advocate must find an opportunity to articulate them.

Chapter Six

AFTER THE MOOT COURTS: THE FINAL FEW DAYS

Analysis

After the formal moot court, the advocate should allow at least two or three days for refining the preparation before the argument itself. In too many instances, advocates do not use those final days to best advantage. Having survived the moot courts, the attorney gets too tired to summon the necessary energy to initiate a kick through the finish line. An advocate who maximizes the time spent in the last few days before the argument will focus attention on three facets of a successful argument: the mantra, affirmative points, and segues. This chapter addresses those points, and describes a visualization exercise that helps the advocate internalize those features of the argument. Finally, it discusses the use of visual aids and makes suggestions for how the advocate should handle the morning of the argument.

§ 6.1   The Mantra

In the best arguments, the advocate will have a "mantra"—a phrase or sentence to repeat several times so that it becomes the theme of the argument. In this respect, an appellate argument shares a similarity with a political campaign. In 1992, Bill Clinton's campaign theme, "It's the economy, stupid," became one of the most famous political mantras of all time. In like fashion, in 2000, George W. Bush's campaign used "compassionate conservative" as a mantra. Both candidates (and their surrogates) repeated those phrases over and over as a way to focus their campaign messages.

In a successful Supreme Court or court of appeals argument, the mantra will serve as the advocate's unifying theme. It is a way to boil the entire case down to one simple phrase or sentence. In recent years, one of the best examples of using a mantra in the Supreme Court was by John Nields, a Washington lawyer and former law clerk to Justice Byron White, in his argument in *United States* v. *Hubbell*.[1] Nields represented Webster Hubbell, who had been implicated in Independent Counsel Kenneth Starr's investigation of real estate transactions in Arkansas involving President and First Lady Clinton prior to Clinton's election as president. In this case, the Office of the Independent Counsel indicted Hubbell on the basis of documents he had provided under what he thought was a grant of immunity from prosecution. Nields cleverly used the fact of Hubbell's honesty in complying with the document request as having formed the evidentiary basis for the Independent Counsel's assertion that he had committed tax fraud. Thus, as Nields framed the case from the opening sentence of his argument, the issue was whether Hubbell could be indicted for being honest: "My client was indicted in this case at least in part as a result of the fact that under immunity he told the truth."[2] In his third sentence, Nields stressed: "If [Hubbell] had been untruthful and withheld those documents, the independent counsel wouldn't have had them, but instead he told the truth, turned them over, and the independent counsel used those documents to bring this case."[3] That was a devastating formulation for the Independent Counsel's position. When asked later in the argument what legal standard he was proposing, Nields stated: "[T]he principle is whether you're relying on the truth-telling of the witness to find out that the document exists. That's the principle. Are you relying on the truth-telling of the—that's testimony. That's Fifth Amendment language: testimony, truth-telling. That's the issue. And if you are, if you're compelling a person to tell the truth with the consequence that he loses

---

§ 6.1

1. *United States v. Hubbell*, 530 U.S. 27, 120 S.Ct. 2037 (2000).

2. *United States v. Hubbell*, No. 99–166, 2000 WL 230520 at *23 (Feb. 22, 2000).

3. *Id.*

his liberty, you have a Fifth Amendment problem."[4] Throughout his 30–minute argument, Nields reiterated the mantra or worked it into his substantive responses to questions about the applicable legal standard at least a dozen times. Had he repeated it one more time it would have been excessive, but his frequent use of that mantra framed the case in a powerful way that made the government's argument difficult to advance.

In the Solicitor General's Office, Irving Gornstein also effectively formulates a mantra and successfully delivers it in a high percentage of his Supreme Court arguments. In *Florida v. J.L.*,[5] Gornstein argued for 10 minutes as an *amicus curiae* in support of the state's position that it was constitutional for officers who received an anonymous tip that a teenager was illegally carrying a gun to stop and frisk persons who met the general description given by the tipster. The facts were quite weak for the government—the anonymous tipster had said that a young person wearing a plaid shirt on a particular street corner was believed to be carrying an illegal firearm. The issue was whether, under those facts, the officer had reasonable suspicion to stop and frisk all three youths on that street corner.

At argument, Gornstein's mission was to try to persuade the court that a totality-of-the-circumstances test should be applied to the reasonable-suspicion inquiry—as opposed to a *per se* rule not allowing such frisks except on stronger facts—and to convince the court that, if the tipster had given an anonymous warning of a bomb, the officers would have been justified in frisking the suspects. Thus, from his opening sentence, Gornstein set out to convince the justices to apply the totality-of-the-circumstances inquiry: "An officer may conduct a stop and frisk when, under the totality of the circumstances, there is reasonable suspicion that a crime is occurring and that the suspect is armed and dangerous."[6] He then worked the totality-of-the-circumstances formulation into numerous answers, including one in which he was able to posit his theory that the circumstances might require somewhat less externally verifiable observable facts if the tip concerned a more serious weapon than a gun: "If the tip is about somebody at a courthouse with a bomb, or somebody at a school with an automatic weapon, a reasonable and prudent person is going to operate on somewhat

---

4. *Id*. at *28.

5. *Florida v. J.L.*, 529 U.S. 266, 120 S.Ct. 1375 (2000).

6. *Florida v. J.L.*, No. 98–1993, 2000 WL 268550 at *13–*14 (Feb. 29, 2000).

less suspicion than otherwise in deciding whether to make a stop and frisk."[7] Gornstein's persistence in pressing the totality-of-the-circumstances mantra was rewarded to a degree by the court's opinion. The court pointedly stated that "[w]e do not say, for example, that a report of a person carrying a bomb need bear the indicia of reliability we demand for a report of a person carrying a firearm before the police can constitutionally conduct a frisk."[8]

§ 6.2   Affirmative Points

If the mantra is the catch phrase that serves as the unifying theme of the argument, the affirmative points are those critical points that provide the substance underlying the mantra. Without the affirmative points, the advocate has no case, however clever the mantra. The discussion of the opening in Chapter Three emphasized that an advocate should signpost for the court at least three or four points she hopes to make in the argument.[1] Those are the most important of the advocate's affirmative points, but they should not be exclusive.

An affirmative point, simply defined, is any positive reason why the court should adopt the advocate's position, as contrasted with reasons not to accept the opponent's submission. Even if it may not be one of the central themes the advocate hopes to stress, an argument is an affirmative point if it helps to prove the correctness of the advocate's case. Although occasionally affirmative points will include policy reasons for why the rule of law being pressed has advantages, for this particular era of Supreme Court and appellate advocacy, the best affirmative points tend to be focused on indisputable legal principles. As Deputy Solicitor General Michael Dreeben advises attorneys arguing for the government, "Stick to black-letter law." What he means is that the advocate will more likely have a smooth argument by stressing that the holding being advocated follows inexorably from several sources of law, as opposed to policy rationales or abstract notions of fairness.

If the case is statutory, for example, the affirmative points might focus on distinctive features of a statute. In *Carter v. United States*,[2] for example, the issue was whether bank larceny is a lesser-

---

7. *Id.* at *17–*18.

8. *Florida v. J.L.*, 529 U.S. 266, 120 S.Ct. 1375 (2000).

§ 6.2

1. *See* § 3.3.

2. *Carter v. United States*, 530 U.S. 255, 120 S.Ct. 2159 (2000).

included offense of bank robbery under the federal criminal code. Neither side contested that the Supreme Court had already decided in a prior case that the elements of the crime framed the analysis of whether one offense was a "lesser-included" offense of another.[3] Thus, if all of the elements of the putatively lesser crime are included in the greater crime, then it meets the Supreme Court's test. What made *Carter* such an interesting test of legal advocacy was that, at common law, the crime of larceny *was* a lesser-included offense of robbery. Indeed, many jurisdictions defined robbery as larceny (the taking of the property of another with the intent to steal) while using force. When Congress wrote the bank larceny and bank robbery crimes, however, it did not strictly codify the common law. Rather, it borrowed some common-law terms and included others that were not used in the common-law definitions of those crimes. This enactment occurred, however, during a period in which the common law understanding that larceny was a lesser-included offense of robbery was still commonly accepted. In arguing that Congress intended *not* to codify the common law (even though it did not say specifically that it intended that result), the government focused on the three distinctive elements found in bank larceny, but not in bank robbery: a specific intent element (bank property must be taken "with an intent to steal"); an asportation element (the property must be "carried away" after being taken); and a monetary valuation element (the property must have a value in excess of $1,000 for felony bank larceny).

Thus, the mantra became, "Congress did not intend to codify the common law," and the principal affirmative points became the three distinctive elements of bank larceny not found in the bank robbery statute. The court's 5–4 decision closely adhered to those themes. Justice Thomas's majority opinion stressed that the canon of statutory construction to impute common law ideas is limited to specific terms in a statute: "[A] 'cluster of ideas' from the common law should be imported into statutory text only when Congress employs a common-law *term*, and not when, as here, Congress simply describes an offense analogous to a common-law crime without using common-law terms."[4]

The harder part of the argument was providing a theory for why Congress would have enacted a crime analogous to the common law without incorporating common law terms. The govern-

---

3. *See Schmuck v. United States*, 489 U.S. 705, 109 S.Ct. 1443 (1989).

4. *Carter*, 530 U.S. at 265, 120 S. Ct. at 2166.

ment's theory, pressed in its brief and at oral argument, was that robbery was a crime against a person using force, whereas larceny was a crime against property using stealth. Congress was attacking different social wrongs when it enacted these crimes. Interestingly, neither the majority nor the dissent addressed that explanation: both opinions focused on the legal arguments presented. But part of the government's theory of the case had to be that Congress's action was rational—that a logic could be imputed to Congress's decision not to incorporate the common law in crafting this statute.

In this respect, the affirmative points should encompass not only the actual legal arguments in headline form, *i.e.*, the statute says *x* or *y*. They should also advance a theory or explanation for the advocate's position. Thus, affirmative points might include arguments about the statutory text, a holding of a key case, language in the legislative history, a policy argument, a description of the history behind a particular rule, or an explanatory theory behind the rule or interpretation being argued.

The number of affirmative points an advocate can hope to make in an argument will vary depending on the length of the argument. In a 30–minute argument, an advocate might realistically hope to make, at most, 5 or 6 affirmative points. In a 10–or 15–minute argument, which is common for *amicus* arguments in the Supreme Court and for arguments generally in the courts of appeals, an advocate will be fortunate to make 3 affirmative points.

§ 6.3 Thinking Through Segues

In the last few days before the argument as the advocate is refining the mantra and the affirmative points, the defensive aspect of argument cannot be neglected. As Chapter Five explains, the moot courts prepare the advocate for the hostile questions to be expected from the bench. The challenge, therefore, is to anticipate opportunities for the advocate to segue from questions designed to probe weak points in the case back to affirmative points that persuade the court of the soundness of the position being pressed. This is the most difficult aspect of oral argument. When done seamlessly, it is inspiring to watch and is what elevates oral argument to an art form.

In *United States* v. *Ursery*,[1] Dreeben demonstrated in a thoughtful way how an advocate can take a hostile question,

---

§ 6.3

1. *United States v. Ursery*, 518 U.S. 267, 116 S.Ct. 2135 (1996).

answer it, and then segue back to an affirmative point. The government's position was that the Double Jeopardy Clause is not offended by the government seeking parallel in rem civil forfeiture actions and criminal prosecutions based on the same underlying events. One of Dreeben's affirmative points was that, until recently, such parallel proceedings had been thought constitutional. Representing petitioner, Dreeben's mission was to cast doubt on the validity of the court of appeals' approach. Dreeben had just conceded that civil forfeiture could be punitive for purposes of the Excessive Fines Clause and still not be considered multiple punishment within the meaning of the Double Jeopardy Clause. Here is how he dealt with a skeptical question about that position from Justice Scalia, and then, after a follow-up question by Justice Scalia, segued into a critique of the court of appeals' decision:

QUESTION: Why? I can't understand why somebody who would write a Constitution would think that a punishment is a punishment for one purpose but not another. I mean, if it's punishment enough that you can't make it excessive, why isn't it punishment enough that you shouldn't get it twice? What policy reason is there?

MR. DREEBEN: The answer to that question goes in part back to the roots and origins of the Double Jeopardy Clause itself. That clause was an embodiment of common law protections that were accorded to finality in a criminal judgment in very specific contexts that this Court has developed over time in a series of rather intricate and complicated rules. It has never been the case, though, that the pursuit of an *in rem* action against property and the criminal prosecution of the owner of the property for separate violations would be deemed to constitute an impermissible multiple punishment.

* * *

QUESTION: I say, I suggest that's only because it was never applied to multiple punishments, period, of any sort. I mean, greater includes the lesser, to be sure, but once we are on the track that double punishment, as opposed to double jeopardy, is covered by the Double Jeopardy Clause, I don't see why all punishment deemed punishment by the Constitution shouldn't qualify.

MR. DREEBEN: Well, I think the answer, Justice Scalia, is that to the extent that there is protection against multiple punishments that has been recognized in this Court's cases as subsumed by the Fifth Amendment, that protection has been limited and defined in very specific contexts, and has never been a freestanding doctrine that would invalidate any and all simultaneous or contemporaneous pursuit of two actions that had some punitive component to it. And what the courts below did, I think, is to take to the absolute logical limits the principle that was in part reflected in *Halper*,[2] recognizing a prohibition against multiple punishments, and have taken that principle and extended it so that it overrides very familiar common law practices that were well known to the Framers and that have been reflected throughout the history of this country—[3]

Although all observers in the courtroom—including the justices themselves—might perceive no preparation in a segue as seamless as the one just highlighted from Dreeben's argument in *Ursery*, in fact much time can and should be spent thinking about how to make a transition from the answer to a hostile question into an affirmative point. John Roberts has a useful exercise for practicing segues. He puts on note cards the six or seven key points he wants to try to make during an argument. In the days before the argument, he shuffles the note cards and practices making those points in a different order each time. Thus, his practice argument might transition from the statutory text to doctrine to legislative history to policy in one practice run-through. In the next, the practice argument might proceed from policy to doctrine to statutory text to legislative history. The idea behind this drill is that a question from the bench may spark an answer that calls for articulating one of those themes. If the advocate has practiced moving from that particular topic to another affirmative point, the segue in the courtroom will appear seamless.

A reason for saving the best thinking about segues until the last few days before the argument is that the advocate will have had the benefit of the moot courts to hear the most difficult questions probing the weaknesses in her case. Anticipating that a

---

2. *United States v. Halper*, 490 U.S. 435, 109 S.Ct. 1892 (1989).

3. *United States v. Ursery*, Nos. 95–345 & 95–346, 1996 WL 195163 at *7–*9 (Apr. 17, 1996).

member of the court will ask many of those same questions, the advocate can then devote time and care to planning how to transition from those areas of weakness back to topics of rhetorical strength. Sometimes it will not be until the second moot court that an advocate can fully appreciate that a particular line of questioning will almost certainly be asked: if the topic comes up early in both moot courts, it is also likely to be asked by a judge. This process of thinking through segues can be critical to maintaining the court's attention and focus at the argument itself and to ensuring that the advocate creates opportunities to articulate to the court the reasons why it should rule in her client's favor.

§ 6.4   Final Preparation of Materials

After the formal moot court, a key task is to ensure that the advocate has all needed materials for court and that those materials contain every necessary marking for ready identification. It is not unusual, for instance, to save the placement of tabs or other markings on the briefs or joint appendix until the last few days before the argument. That sequencing may strike most readers as counterintuitive: highlighting passages and placing markers on them is what many advocates do throughout the preparation process. Some of the best advocates have found, however, that such markings and tabs clutter up the materials they use in the courtroom. To avoid that problem, they remove most of the tabs or do not put on any tabs at all until the final days of preparation. In that way, the markings are placed only on those pages of the record the advocate either affirmatively wants to use in court if given the chance or feels reasonably certain a judge will ask about during the argument. Every other marking is unnecessary and detracts from the advocate's ability to find the source quickly while in court.

A similar culling or refining process is helpful for the podium binder or materials. The advocate should purge all unnecessary notes or references, or at least cut and paste them to the back of the binder. At the same time, the advocate must ensure that the podium notes contain all necessary references to the briefs, cases, or record, including those being discovered in researching answers to questions just prior to the argument.

One of the last tasks many advocates perform the day before the argument is a final reread of the key documents in the case: lower court opinions, the parties' briefs, any key *amicus* briefs, and the principal case or two implicated in the case. Occasionally that review will bring to light a point or reference that helps to crystallize the case and thus warrants mentioning at the argument.

§ 6.5   A Visualization Exercise

In the final days leading up to the oral argument, some advocates engage in various forms of rehearsal. Some go for walks in the woods and practice, some do chores around the house and rehearse, and still others bend the ears of their loved ones while going over their arguments. A few highly skilled advocates use a visualization exercise not unlike what world-class skiers do before the beginning of a race. Before racing a slalom or downhill course, skiers will stand at the top of the mountain, close their eyes, and visualize what the course looks like. They have done the run enough times that, in their mind's eye, they can see every switchback, flag pole, turn, and dip in the snow. Their final "rehearsal" is to run the race in their mind before they leave the starting gate. The idea of the visualization exercise before an oral argument is similar. By visualizing in advance what will happen before and during an oral argument, the advocate will adapt more quickly to the situation during the actual argument. The aim of the exercise is to create an extra degree of comfort for the advocate in the courtroom.

Here is how it works: the advocate finds a quiet place and sits with eyes closed. The exercise starts with the advocate visualizing her entrance into the courtroom, what she will be wearing, what she will be carrying, even who she might see (such as family or friends) in the audience while making her way to counsel table. The advocate then visualizes sitting quietly in the courtroom just before court is announced, standing as the members of the court enter, listening attentively as the presiding judge announces the orders, approaching the lectern, and addressing the court. If the advocate is tall, she might visualize making an appropriate adjustment to the lectern. In the Supreme Court, the lectern is manually adjusted and requires a turn of the handle toward the body in a counterclockwise motion to raise the lectern. In some courts of appeals, such as the D.C. Circuit, the lectern raises and lowers electronically with the push of a button. (Nothing tips off the court faster that the advocate is inexperienced than fumbling with the lectern.) The next part of the visualization exercise is the most important—and more difficult. The advocate visualizes the opening, "May it please the Court," with eye contact starting with the presiding judge and then sweeping across to the other members of the court. Then the advocate visualizes the beginning of the opening. Because in the vast majority of cases the advocate will be interrupted with questions, she should try to visualize who will interrupt at what point in the opening and with what questions.

This exercise forces a hypersensitivity to the precise wording of sentences and answers. With each phrase that misstates the advocate's position or overstates the applicable legal authority, the advocate can imagine an interruption from the bench with a request for clarification or authority. The Chief Justice, in particular, listens with extreme care and will be quick to interrupt at even the slightest misstatement. In *Alexander v. United States*,[1] which was Kenneth Starr's last argument before the Supreme Court as Solicitor General, Starr was making a point and paused to say, "[I]f I may, let me share with you a bit of the record in the case."[2] While there is nothing objectionable *per se* about that phrasing, the Chief Justice nonetheless interrupted to say, "Why don't you just tell us about the record, rather than share it with us."[3] To his credit and without any hesitation, Starr immediately said, "The record tells us, Mr. Chief Justice,"[4] and then went on to describe it. But interruptions like that are common in Supreme Court and appellate cases; an advocate must employ scrupulously precise language when making an argument.

If done well, the visualization exercise creates an additional sensitivity to the reasonableness of each sentence stated and of each answer to the questions naturally sparked by the point just made. This exercise also gives the advocate an opportunity to gauge how quickly and in which directions the prepared argument is likely to break down. That, in turn, provides a means of planning and trying out various segues and other opportunities to make affirmative points. It is also a final way of eliciting questions that may require last-minute research.

An additional benefit of the visualization exercise is simply the extra practice it provides the advocate in articulating arguments. Even if the attorney has difficulty visualizing the scene, the extemporaneous speaking practice will increase the odds that she will speak fluently and succinctly in the argument itself.

§ 6.5

1. *Alexander v. United States*, 509 U.S. 544, 113 S.Ct. 2766 (1993).

2. *Alexander v. United States*, No. 91–1256, 1993 WL 751735 at *32 (Jan. 12, 1993).

3. *Id.*

4. *Id.*

§ 6.6   What to Bring to Court

Although at some level making a checklist of what to bring to court may strike some readers as unnecessarily attentive to detail, many advocates invariably forget something important that they should have had with them in the courtroom. A checklist of items to take to court can help the advocate be assured that nothing necessary is left behind. Some of the items are fairly self-evident. Here's a sample list:

Briefs

Binder of cases

Podium binder

Federal Rules (Criminal, Civil, etc.)

Pad of paper

Pens

Post-its

Highlighters

Pocket Constitution

Aspirin

Extra contact lenses, solution, and case

Reading glasses

Throat lozenges

A few of these items might bear special mention. The briefs, podium binder, and case binder are obviously a must, as are the general procedural rules: questions about them arise at the most unexpected moments. (Indeed, in a surprising number of cases, a reference in the courtroom to the rules of procedure has proved to be helpful.) Sometimes the needs of a case will dictate taking something extra—a volume of the Code of Federal Regulations, the pertinent volume of the United States Code, or a frequently cited book. The checklist lets the advocate worry about what to say rather than whether she has omitted bringing something important to court.

Once at the court, the advocate has to be mindful to keep track of her material. An advocate in the second case in the Supreme Court once suddenly ran out of the courtroom just as his case was about to be called. He came rushing back into the courtroom a few moments later clutching his podium binder. Apparently when the first case ended, this attorney—who was petitioner's counsel in the second case—placed his podium binder on the lectern in anticipation of his case being called. Counsel from the just-argued case was busy packing up to depart the courtroom. In the hurried moments trying to clear out, counsel in the first case saw the binder on the podium and grabbed it, thinking he had left it there by mistake. Panic must have set in for petitioner's counsel in the second case upon discovering that his podium binder was gone! Fortunately he got it back in time, but undoubtedly began his argument in a flustered state.

§ 6.7   Visual Aids

Although Supreme Court and appellate advocacy is intensely law-based and, therefore, not readily susceptible to the use of visual aids, such aids can at times be an important part of the advocate's presentation at oral argument. In the Supreme Court, visual aids are rarely used and affirmatively discouraged. At times, however, they can be devastatingly effective. In *Shaw v. Reno*,[1] for example, the Supreme Court considered whether the North Carolina legislature had drawn a congressional district in a manner that comported with the Voting Rights Act and constitutional standards. Counsel for Shaw, who was challenging the district as impermissible, brought to court a large map of North Carolina, with the district at issue denoted in bright red. The district stretched for nearly 160 miles long, "and [was], for much of its length, no wider than the I—85 corridor."[2] The visual representation of the district highlighted what a majority would describe as its "bizarre" quality—lacking the normal community contiguity that typifies most congressional districts, the mere shape of the district gave rise to questions about whether the state legislature had taken race into account by creating a district that essentially snaked its way up Interstate 85 to maximize the number of cities and towns with a predominance of black residents.[3]

In the courts of appeals, the use of visual aids is far more common than in the Supreme Court, a function perhaps of appellate courts' greater informality and the tendency of trial lawyers

---

§ 6.7

1. *Shaw v. Reno*, 509 U.S. 630, 113 S.Ct. 2816 (1993).

2. 509 U.S. at 635, 113 S. Ct. at 2820.

3. 509 U.S. at 644, 113 S. Ct. at 2825.

accustomed to using visual aids arguing their cases in the courts of appeals. In an argument sitting in the Eleventh Circuit in March 2002, for example, counsel in five of six cases argued that day came to court with poster-sized charts. Not all ended up using those visual aids, but they were prepared to do so if the need arose.

If an advocate considers using a visual aid in a court of appeals argument, a few rules of thumb should be observed. First, counsel must check the court's rules to determine whether and how such aids will be permitted. Showing the poster itself to the clerk or marshal present in the courtroom in advance of the hearing is advisable. Some courts of appeals will want to know whether opposing counsel objects to the use of the visual aid. Second, the visual aid must be sufficiently legible from a position that may be 15 or 20 feet away from the judges. A sloppy or illegible visual aid obviously detracts from the advocate's presentation. Third, the aid should portray an exhibit or other information in a simple way so that the advocate's point is immediately grasped. Making the court work too hard to get the point is self-defeating. Finally, the advocate should have someone in court to assist with the visual aid. The advocate has enough to worry about without also fumbling with a large poster-board.

§ 6.8   The Morning of Argument

Writing a few words about what to do and think about the morning of a Supreme Court or court of appeals argument is difficult. Each person must face this test in the way best suited to her or her own personality. The reason for thinking about this routine is to reduce stress and complications. The advocate's focus should be on getting to the courthouse in the most positive frame of mind possible. A few experienced advocates have shared their typical routines.

Most advocates generally get a poor night's sleep the night before an argument. That tendency, by the way, puts a premium on the advocate's getting a good night's sleep two nights before the argument. Adrenaline will get the advocate through court even without much sleep the night before; performance may be impaired, however, by two consecutive sleepless nights. Many advocates also share having experienced bad dreams about arriving late to court or having an upset stomach, both of which put a premium on planning to arrive early and on eating a suitable breakfast.

In the Supreme Court, the Clerk's Office is uncommonly courteous in all manner of last-minute emergencies. A member of the

Solicitor General's Office once tore a seam shortly before argument—the Clerk's Office promptly produced a seamstress to fix up the hole. (The Clerk of the Court, William Suter, has also told of providing aspirin and other medicines to advocates the morning of argument.)

In the courts of appeals, the levels of helpfulness and professionalism of the Clerk's office can vary widely from court to court. An advocate inexperienced arguing in that circuit should make inquiries of the Clerk's office in advance of the argument to get acquainted with special procedures. Because of the frequency of oral arguments in the courts of appeals and the volume of cases those courts handle, it is imperative for counsel to check and double check the scheduling of cases for oral argument. Some circuits will shuffle cases at the last moment—even the morning of argument—and some cases will be removed from the docket because of a settlement or mediation.

Advocates should dress traditionally in suitable business attire. Appearance matters. Judge Thomas M. Reavley of the U.S. Court of Appeals for the Fifth Circuit emphasized dress in the law school seminar he taught on appellate advocacy. "Dress immaculately," he preached, "the best clothes you have." The advocates who wear bolo ties and cowboy boots in the well of the Supreme Court simply draw attention to themselves for all the wrong reasons. As Justice Jackson dryly noted more than a half-century ago, "You will not be stopped from arguing if you wear a race-track suit or sport a rainbow necktie. You will just create a first impression that you have strayed in at the wrong bar."[1] The advocate wants spectators and court personnel talking about the quality of the argument, not the goofy attire thoughtlessly worn to court.

Before arriving at court, the advocate might relax by sitting quietly and listening to music or do one last visualization exercise. Each person will have a preference for how to spend those last moments before heading to the courthouse. But more than any other external source, music can put the advocate in the right frame of mind to confidently address what awaits and to calm any unsteady nerves. One advocate tells of listening to John Phillip Sousa marches on the way to court to feel that extra element of confidence; still others have a favorite opera or symphony they

§ 6.8

1. Robert H. Jackson, "Advocacy Before the Supreme Court: Suggestions for Effective Case Presentations," 37 A.B.A. J. 801, 862 (Nov. 1951).

always listen to the morning of argument. Before leaving for court, the advocate should make one final check of the contents of the carrying case and argument binder.

The advocate should arrive comfortably on time. (Read: a little early.) Arriving late adds to stress and throws off the advocate's concentration. Professor Wright always hired a car and driver to take him to court. He never wanted to risk the vagaries of cab service or the idiosyncracies of their driving style when he was arguing a case. If one chooses not to incur that expense, at least be sure not to press for time.

§ 6.9   At The Supreme Court

Well in advance, the advocate should read the guide for counsel written and compiled by the Clerk of the Court.[1] This small booklet contains an enormous amount of helpful information. Once at the court the advocate is in the capable hands of the Clerk's and Marshal's Offices. The personnel of both are exemplary in their professionalism. Notwithstanding that they see as many arguments as the justices themselves, they appreciate the difficulty of the advocate's task and treat arguing counsel with unfailing courtesy.

The Clerk requests that arguing counsel arrive at the court by 9:00 a.m., even if the case is the second or third on the docket. Counsel will report to the Lawyer's Lounge on the first floor, where they are briefed on basic courtroom procedures and etiquette. The Lawyer's Lounge also has speakers where arguments may be heard.

Once inside the courtroom, petitioner's counsel for the first case will proceed to the table immediately to the left of the podium. Respondent's counsel takes the right-hand table. The exception to that general rule is when petitioner is supported by the United States as *amicus curiae* or the federal government is a party to the case. In those situations, petitioner's counsel sits on the right-hand side of the podium. When only one counsel is representing a side, two co-counsel are permitted to sit at counsel table. When two counsel for a side are arguing, such as when multiple parties are granted argument time or an *amicus* is participating, only one co-counsel is permitted to sit with each arguing attorney at counsel table.

---

§ 6.9

1. *See* William K. Suter, *Guide for Counsel in Cases to be Argued Before the* *Supreme Court of the United States* (October Term 2002).

Counsel arguing the second case sit at the tables immediately behind the tables in the well of the court. Sometimes counsel refer to those as the "backup" tables. Counsel for the third case to be argued that day will typically arrive in the courtroom at some point after the first argument has begun. They sit in the bar section until the first case ends and counsel depart, then counsel for the second case leave the backup tables and take their places on either side of the podium. At that point arguing counsel for the next case move to sit at the backup table.

For counsel arguing the third case (it has been rare in recent years for the court to calendar a fourth case in a day for oral argument, although that was common in the 1980s), it is important to be ready to argue before the lunch break. The court recesses at 12:00 p.m. and resumes at 1:00 p.m. But, if the first two cases end early, the Chief Justice will call the third case and begin the argument before lunch. Only occasionally can petitioner's counsel make an entire argument in such circumstances, so she should be prepared for the Chief Justice to interrupt and advise that the argument will resume after lunch. Many advocates choose not to eat lunch before an afternoon argument, but the cafeteria is quite good (by government standards) and court personnel will escort the attorneys to the cafeteria so that they receive priority in the line. Some very experienced attorneys bring a brownbag lunch for arguments when they are third on the docket.

In the courtroom itself, the court places quill pens on counsel tables for the advocates to take as a memento of their Supreme Court experience. Water, pencils, and paper are also available for the use of counsel. Until 2000, an advocate at counsel table could request a book from the library. That privilege ended when one attorney apparently abused it by bringing undue attention to himself with such a request and causing a distraction to the justices. Shortly thereafter, the library request forms were simply removed from counsel table.

Prior to the first case being called, the court may conduct certain business, such as the announcement of decisions and/or the admission of attorneys to the bar. Petitioner's counsel thus should not assume being able to prepare the podium prior to the argument. Rather, once admissions to the bar have been completed, the Chief Justice will call the case and petitioner's counsel will begin the argument.

An advocate scheduled to argue a case in the Supreme Court should come to see other cases being argued in advance of her own argument. Much can be learned by watching other counsel, seeing the court in action, and getting a feel for the procedures and protocols practiced in that courtroom. Such a scouting mission also helps an advocate who attempts the visualization exercise. Indeed, merely visiting the courtroom and seeing another argument can help to demystify the experience so the advocate can focus on dealing with the features of Supreme Court practice that differ from the advocate's typical courtroom experiences. Counsel should coordinate with the Clerk's Office in advance to obtain seating.

6.10   At The Court of Appeals

The time counsel is required to report to the Clerk's office for a court of appeals argument will vary depending on the circuit. The Clerk's Office will send instructions to counsel in the weeks before the argument. Once at the Clerk's Office, counsel may be asked to confirm how much time should be reserved for rebuttal (if representing appellant) and be briefed on other procedures, such as on which side of the podium appellant's counsel should sit. (In some courts of appeals, the court is indifferent to this practice, so counsel is well-advised to check with the Clerk before making any unwarranted assumptions.)

In the courtroom itself, most courts of appeals follow an informal practice whereby counsel in cases after the first argued case may sit anywhere in the courtroom until their case is called. The timing procedures for court of appeals arguments can also vary, with some courts stricter in their adherence to time limits than others. However permissive the circuit is, counsel shows respect for the court by asking for permission before going beyond the time limit.

* * *

Each aspect of the morning's schedule suggested here is to achieve the demeanor of calm professionalism the advocate wants to project. From the moment the advocate arrives at court—and especially once inside the courtroom—she should assume that all eyes are on her. Even before the argument begins, she wants everyone in the courtroom to think, "That lawyer knows what she's doing." Judges and justices are human, too, and when the advocate is totally prepared and projects a self-assured (but not cocky) confidence, they will treat her with respect.

Having said that, the most important aspect of this morning-of-the-argument preparation is for the advocate to know herself, gauge her own needs, and arrive at the podium carrying a psychological shield and a quiver full of arrows. Each great advocate will have an approach individually tailored to her personality. One Supreme Court advocate, Maureen Mahoney, can be seen at counsel table writing furiously on a yellow pad just prior to the opening of court. Those notes constitute her last, best synthesis of her case. Most advocates could never approach court that way, but her skill and record cannot be disputed.

In closing, it is difficult to improve upon the advice of Robert Jackson, a former Solicitor General and Supreme Court Justice who was one of the great advocates of the twentieth century: "When the day arrives, shut out every influence that might distract your mind. * * * Friends who bear bad news may unintentionally distract your poise. Hear nothing but your case, see nothing but your case, talk nothing but your case. If making an argument is not a great day in your life, don't make it; and if it is, give it everything in you."[1]

§ 6.10

1. Robert H. Jackson, "Advocacy Before the United States Supreme Court," 37 CORNELL L.Q. 1–16 (Fall 1951).

*

Part III
PRESENTATION OF ORAL ARGUMENT

Chapter Seven

BASIC APPROACHES TO ORAL ARGUMENT

Analysis

Individuality and inspiration-in-the-moment mark the greatest argument performances. But an advocate cannot realistically expect lightning to strike at the appropriate moment. So much of what goes into a great oral argument is the product of careful preparation. This chapter sets forth basic approaches to argument for petitioner/appellant, respondent/appellee, rebuttal, *amicus curiae*, multiple-parties, and arguments where the government is participating on the advocate's side. By considering various alternatives, an advocate can best tailor his approach to the case.

§ 7.1 Petitioner's Argument[1]

The opening lines of petitioner's argument can make a critical difference in the success of an argument. Except in the rarest of cases, the modern Supreme Court typically allows petitioner's coun-

---

§ 7.1

1. To simplify use of nomenclature, an argument as appellant, movant, or petitioner—all of which represent the party seeking review of a decision below—is referred to generically in this chapter as "petitioner," as the topside party is referred to in a typical Supreme Court case. For most court of appeals cases, the topside party most often will be denominated "appellant," but the advocacy principles are the same.

sel some latitude to deliver a few sentences before the questioning begins. The more helpful those sentences are to the court, the more likely the justices are to let the advocate continue without interruption and, thereafter, to proceed in giving fuller answers to questions. In the courts of appeals, counsel can typically count on opening for at least several minutes before interruption, except in the most unusual of cases. In planning not only those opening sentences but also the general thrust of the case petitioner hopes to make throughout the argument, a few considerations should be borne in mind.

First, the petitioner's job is to get the decision below reversed or vacated. The natural instinct is to attack—attack the court of appeals, district court, or state supreme court—or attack the other side. Notwithstanding the intensity of the questioning, argument in the Supreme Court does not lend itself comfortably to that kind of advocacy approach. Rather, petitioner has to build a case for reversal by stressing the correctness of the legal position he is advancing. Advocacy is far more effective in the Supreme Court when petitioner's counsel first makes a case that a certain legal rule is correct rather than that the court of appeals' approach is incorrect. In that sense, the "affirmative points" give the justices something positive to vote for, while criticisms of the decision below only work to persuade them what to reject. The same is true in the courts of appeals. In both forums, judges tend to approach review of the lower court's decision with a view that it is likely correct, so the pressure on petitioner's counsel to make affirmative points can be even greater than it is on respondent's counsel.[2]

Second, notwithstanding the magisterial words "Equal Justice Under Law" etched in the marble facade of the Supreme Court building, that court typically is more concerned with articulating the proper rule than trying to achieve justice for the particular parties. If the law is right, then the Supreme Court's general presumption is that justice will follow from the proper application of the law. For that reason, stressing the injustice of the court of appeals' decision without the reinforcement of a sound legal theory is not likely to win votes.

---

2. For the year ending September 30, 2001, for example, the courts of appeals reversed in only 9.1 percent of criminal cases and 10.7 percent of civil cases. Administrative Office of U.S. Courts, *Judicial Business of the United States Courts 2001*, Table B.

Third, petitioner's counsel must try to identify the single most persuasive point for his side and seize an opportunity to make that point. Although that advice may seem obvious, many Supreme Court arguments proceed without either side advancing a real affirmative point. Court of appeals arguments—as short as they are—tend to be even less impressive in that regard. Petitioner's counsel must internalize the affirmative points and seize any appropriate opportunity to make them.

Fourth, petitioner's counsel must be able to articulate why the case matters to his client and why the issue presented is of broad significance. Ordinarily, that topic is well covered in the petition for a writ of certiorari but, as a rhetorical matter, the justices sometimes need to be reminded why they granted review in the case and why the outcome will be important (and to whom). An argument can break down if an advocate fails to give a satisfactory explanation for why the case is important.

In *Idaho v. United States*,[3] for example, the court of appeals had held that the United States owned the submerged lands underneath Coeur d'Alene Lake in trust for the Coeur d'Alene Indian Tribe and that those lands had not passed automatically to Idaho when it became a state in 1890. The state's counsel was asked repeatedly why the case was important, what its practical consequences were, and what difference a decision one way or the other would make. The response he gave to Justice O'Connor's second attempt to get an answer was: "We care because the majority of the users on the lake are not Indians and because of that we have a significant interest in protecting their safety, for example, citing people who are boa[t]ing in an unsafe manner or i[n] citing somebody who doesn't have the requisite amount of life vests on board for small children."[4] That answer caused Justice Breyer to pounce: "[A]ll this is about is whether or not the state wants to have a policeman in a boat cite someone for not wearing a life vest and the tribe just won't agree to figuring out some method so that people boat safely? It sounds like is that all that's at stake and you can't work it out with the tribe?"[5]

---

3. *Idaho v. United States*, 533 U.S. 262, 121 S.Ct. 2135 (2001).

4. *Idaho v. United States*, No. 00–189, 2001 WL 436234 at *4 (Apr. 23, 2001).

5. *Id.* at *5.

By contrast, here is how Jeffrey P. Minear addressed similar questions about what was at stake in *New Jersey v. New York*,[6] the case that determined which state had jurisdiction over Ellis Island. Minear argued as *amicus curiae* on behalf of the United States in support of New Jersey:

> QUESTION: I can't think of an original action since I've been here in which the issue is not who owns the land but where one state is simply suing, claiming that the other state has no jurisdiction over a particular action over a particular thing. Usually that issue comes up in the context of a private party defending against the asserted jurisdiction by one state or the other.

> MR. MINEAR: That is correct, and that's—this case is unusual insofar as the United States owns title to all of the land in question here.

* * *

> QUESTION: So Mr. Minear, in view of that, what practically is at stake? I mean, you said the United States has been there since it was a fort, and now, and it's continuing, so the states want the boundary set, but what consequence does that have as long as the United States owns and exercises jurisdiction over the island?

> MR. MINEAR: Oh, there are some modest consequences with regard to certain activity, such as the collection of tax revenues and the like. Even if the United States has exclusive jurisdiction over the entire island, which is not something that we're asserting, but even if it did, under the Buck Act the states can still collect certain types of taxes from activities that take place on the land.

> QUESTION: For example?

> MR. MINEAR: Sales taxes from concessions on the island would be one example. Both States would have no doubt claimed some interest in the renovation of the southern portion of the island here, but ultimately we think that Congress will make those determinations, taking into account the concerns and considerations of both States.[7]

---

6. *New Jersey v. New York*, 523 U.S. 767, 118 S.Ct. 1726 (1998).

7. *New Jersey v. New York*, No. 120 Orig., 1998 WL 15118 at *26–*28 (Jan. 12, 1998).

Although counsel should assume that the court is well prepared, many advocates come to court assuming the opposite. They waste precious minutes restating the obvious to the court. Examples abound: "This is a criminal case from the Eighth Circuit." A wholly unnecessary and needless sentence—if the members of the court have not figured out beforehand that this is a criminal case, the process has gone seriously awry. And reminding the court from where the case is being appealed only serves as a pejorative, in that some courts are statistically more likely to be reversed than others. There simply is no need for the opening sentence from petitioner's counsel to tell the members of the court something they can discern from the cover of a brief. Yet in past years even fine Supreme Court advocates have suggested such openings.[8]

Another common approach is to open petitioner's argument with a statement of the issue presented, particularly when the wording of the issue is important for the court's decision: "The issue in this case is whether the Double Jeopardy Clause bars successive prosecutions for contempt of court and substantive criminal offenses which are based on the same underlying conduct."[9] That case, *United States v. Dixon*,[10] was argued by William C. Bryson, who immediately followed the statement of the issue with a statement of the government's position: "Our position is that the Double Jeopardy Clause does not bar such successive prosecutions because crimes such as assault with intent to kill or drug trafficking are not the same offense as contempt of court."[11] The approach taken by Bryson in *Dixon* has the benefit of giving the court a

---

8. In his otherwise useful article on Supreme Court advocacy, Stephen Shapiro offered the following as a model opening: "Thank you Mr. Chief Justice, and may it please the court. This case is here on the State of Illinois' petition for certiorari to the Illinois Supreme Court. The State contends that the court below erred when it required suppression of relevant evidence. After briefly summarizing the facts, I would like to explain why the court below misconceived this Court's decisions in the *Aguilar* and *Spinelli* cases, and then explain why, in any event, the evidence should be admitted in view of the good faith of the arresting officers." Stephen M. Shapiro, "Oral Argument in the Supreme Court of the United States," 33 Catholic U. L. Rev. 529, 536 (1984). Whether that type of approach was optimal in the 1980s, it certainly does not work in the twenty-first century. None of the sentences advances a clear position or generally applicable rule. And although it nicely signposts where the advocate would like to take the argument, it does not articulate the points in an especially memorable or positive way that gives the court something affirmative to vote for.

9. *United States v. Dixon*, No. 91–1231, 1992 WL 687919 at *3 (Dec. 2, 1992).

10. *United States v. Dixon*, 509 U.S. 688, 113 S.Ct. 2849 (1993).

11. *See* 1992 WL 687919 at *3.

moment to recall the issue in the case—which can be particularly valuable if it is the second or third case being argued that day—but it does not advance the petitioner's position. Unless very carefully executed, this approach also runs the risk that petitioner's counsel will state the issue in a slightly different way than it had been presented in the brief, so counsel must be absolutely scrupulous in stating the issue if opening the argument in that manner. The Chief Justice, in particular, pays very close attention to such articulations. Not infrequently, he will interrupt counsel when the attorney frames the issue differently from how it was written in the petition for a writ of certiorari.

A better approach involves using the opening sentences to describe the overarching theme of petitioner's position in a memorable way, or to cast the case in a manner that augments the approach taken in the briefs. To illustrate these approaches, here are a few of the best openings in recent Supreme Court arguments.

In *United States v. Scheffer*,[12] Michael Dreeben argued for the government in seeking reversal of a decision by the United States Court of Appeals for the Armed Forces which held that an accused in a court-martial had a constitutional right to introduce exculpatory polygraph evidence. The case drew enormous attention given the widespread use of polygraphs as "lie detectors" in various investigative settings. The military had adopted a rule of evidence that made polygraph results inadmissible, but the court of appeals held that rule unconstitutional. The government was thus in the somewhat awkward position of advocating that polygraph results should be inadmissible as trial evidence in a court-martial, even though the government conducts tens of thousands of polygraphs for various purposes every year, including to deny people jobs or security clearances. Dreeben opened the argument as follows:

> Mr. Chief Justice, and may it please the Court: Polygraph evidence is opinion evidence about credibility. Based on inherent doubts about the reliability of polygraph evidence and the burdens of litigating about polygraph results, it has long been banned from courtrooms in a majority of the states. In 1991, the President adopted the same rule for

---

12. *United States v. Scheffer*, 523 U.S. 303, 118 S.Ct. 1261 (1998).

military courts martial. Exercising delegat[ed] authority from Congress, the President promulgated Rule 707, which makes polygraph evidence per se inadmissible in military courts martial[]. That determination is constitutionally valid for three main reasons. First, the reliability of the polygraph remains unproven. Second, polygraph evidence is not necessary to help the trier of fact perform its core function of determining credibility of witnesses, and third, the costs of litigating about the reliability of polygraph evidence on a case-by-case basis outweigh any limited probative value that the polygraph may have.[13]

At that point, the Chief Justice interrupted Dreeben with a question about whether the consequences of the court of appeals' decision would result in the validity of polygraph evidence being tested on a case-by-case basis.

Dreeben's opening did so many things well it is worth analyzing in depth. First, his initial sentence succinctly cast doubt on the probative value of polygraph evidence, but did so without using any pejorative language: "Polygraph evidence is opinion evidence about credibility." The justices thus had to confront from the outset that the evidence the military defendant sought to introduce was the opinion of a witness about the accused's credibility. Credibility determinations ordinarily are made by the trier of fact and not an expert commenting on the credibility of a person generally. Dreeben's second sentence placed the issue presented by the case in the larger context of the American legal system, and in so doing gave a rationale for why the general rule has been that polygraphs are not admitted as evidence: "Based on inherent doubts about the reliability of polygraph evidence and the burdens of litigating about polygraph results, it has long been banned from courtrooms in a majority of the states." That sentence also accomplished several other important advocacy objectives. It reassured the court that the rule being pressed in military courts-martial was well within the mainstream in American law for civilian criminal trials. And it gave the court two concrete reasons—"inherent doubts about the reliability of polygraph evidence and the burdens of litigating about polygraph results"—why it should not adopt a contrary rule for the military.

---

13.   *United States v. Scheffer*, No. 96–1133, 1997 WL 689299 at *3–*4 (Nov. 3, 1997).

Dreeben's next two sentences succinctly explained that the President had merely followed the majority rule in the states in promulgating a rule of evidence for military courts-martial. In addition to describing the rule at issue in the case, the sentences contained a subtle advocacy sub-text: the court of appeals had intruded on the President's power as commander in chief to set the rules for the armed forces. Thus, even if the court were not persuaded that the general rule in civilian criminal trials made sense, Dreeben was underscoring that the military was special. Traditionally, the Supreme Court has broadly upheld exercises of the President's constitutional authority as commander in chief with respect to decisions about the military. Dreeben was reminding the justices in a subtle way of those cases, without challenging the Supreme Court's supremacy to interpret the meaning of the Constitution. Dreeben then launched into his three reasons for adopting the rule the government sought to obtain from the court. Those reasons, simply expressed, distinctively and clearly signaled to the court the affirmative points Dreeben hoped to make during the argument. Instead of giving reasons why the court of appeals had erred in striking down the rule as unconstitutional, Dreeben focused on points that affirmatively supported the constitutionality of the military rule.

As an opening, Dreeben's statement was a tour de force. It set the context of the case, put the theme of polygraph unreliability front and center in the argument, and gave the court three reasons why the Constitution does not require polygraph evidence to be admissible in a military trial. He obviously put a great deal of care into constructing that opening. And the justices afforded Dreeben great respect by allowing him to deliver it without interruption until after he had summarized the three points he hoped to make during the argument.

The questioning continued for some time before Dreeben was asked whether the government's position was inconsistent with the rule announced by the court in *Daubert v. Merrell Dow Pharmaceuticals, Inc.*,[14] on the uses of expert witness testimony under Federal Rule of Evidence 702. Dreeben's answer effectively transitioned back to the three points he had outlined for the court in his opening:

---

14. *Daubert v. Merrell Dow Pharmaceuticals, Inc.*, 509 U.S. 579, 113 S.Ct. 2786 (1993).

I don't think there is any inconsistency. The point of *Daubert* was to drop the strict rule of general acceptance in the scientific community as a prerequisite for scientific evidence to be admitted. *Daubert* did not do away with the rest of the evidentiary considerations that may bear on whether particular evidence may be admitted. Prominent among those are the requirement in Rule 702 itself that evidence in the form of expert testimony must assist the trier of fact, and furthermore that [its] benefits, its probative value must not be significantly outweighed by the waste of time, confusion, or redundancy of other evidence that might be admitted. Those type[s] of considerations amply justify exclusion of polygraph evidence.[15]

After Dreeben answered the question on the inconsistency with *Daubert* and then seamlessly shifted back to his opening point that the costs of admitting polygraph were outweighed by the burdens their admissibility imposed on courts and litigants, one might have expected a justice to interrupt with another question. But Dreeben's use of reasonable language and his ability to explain the relationship of his answer while simultaneously moving back into his affirmative case was a masterful demonstration of how to make that transition without uttering a statement that raises another question.

When Dreeben ended the above-quoted sentence and did not receive another question, he then shifted back to one of his affirmative points in this way: "Polygraph evidence is very different from most other kinds of scientific evidence that comes into the courtroom. It represents in essence the opinion of the polygraph examiner that, based on an examination of the particular subject, he was deceptive or not deceptive on one particular occasion."[16] Note the care with which Dreeben worded these sentences. He cast doubt on the reliability of the polygraph by characterizing it as "the opinion of the polygraph examiner." That was the first affirmative point he had outlined for the court in his opening. He alluded to his second affirmative point—the polygrapher's substitution for the trier of fact in making credibility determinations—by characterizing the polygrapher's role in deciding whether the person "was deceptive or not deceptive on one particular occasion." Dreeben made those points during the transition in an answer to a question designed to

---

15. *See* 1997 WL 689299 at *6.   **16.** *Id.* at *6–*7.

put him on the defensive: whether the government's approach was inconsistent with the court's holding in *Daubert*. Dreeben's argument in *Scheffer*, therefore, presented in a straightforward manner a solid affirmative case for the position he was advocating.

Another approach is for petitioner's counsel to use the opening moments of an oral argument to recast the case in a way that the briefs may not have advanced or that the court may not have considered. One of the best illustrations of that approach was by Professor Laurence Tribe when *Cipollone v. Liggett Group*[17] was reargued. The case presented the question of whether the federal Cigarette Labelling Act preempted state common law tort claims against cigarette manufacturers for failure to warn, fraud, deception, and misrepresentation. *Cipollone* was the case that opened up the tobacco companies to significant liability in the 1990s. It was first argued on October 8, 1991,[18] before Clarence Thomas took his seat on the Supreme Court, but shortly after the argument, an order issued setting the case for reargument on January 13, 1992.[19] Observers reasonably suspected that the vote in conference by the justices had resulted in a 4–4 tie and that Justice Thomas would cast the deciding vote.

Professor Tribe did not participate in the first argument and had not been involved in writing the petitioner's briefs. The reargument order did not allow for the parties to write supplemental briefs, so he was stuck arguing a brief he had not written or helped to craft. His opening was a provocative bid for Justice Thomas's vote by recasting the case to appeal to the new justice's conservative philosophy:

> Mr. Chief Justice and may it please the Court: Although the substance of this case focuses on fair warning to consumers, at a structural level the case is really about fair warning to the 50 States. The premise of their ability to defend their interests in the national legislative process is, of course, that they be, clearly, warned of what they are about to lose as Congress considers a new statute. The Cigarette Labeling Act undoubtedly warned the states that with respect to three specific areas—cigarette package labels, cigarette advertisements, and cigarette pro-

---

17. *Cipollone v. Liggett Group, Inc.*, 505 U.S. 504, 112 S.Ct. 2608 (1992).

18. *Cipollone v. Liggett Group, Inc.*, No. 90–1038, 1991 WL 636252 (Oct. 8, 1991).

19. *Cipollone v. Liggett Group, Inc.*, 502 U.S. 923, 112 S.Ct. 335 (1991).

motions—the states were about to lose the authority to tell the cigarette companies what health messages they must include, once those companies had put the Surgeon General's warning on their package labels.

But if the Third Circuit is upheld and respondents prevail here, the states will end up having lost considerably more than that, because affixing the Surgeon General's warning to a cigarette compan[y's] packages would absolve that company, prospectively, of any legally enforceable duty, regardless of how longstanding or broadly applicable that duty might be, in the context of that company's communications with the public about smoking and health.[20]

That opening boldly sought to take the high ground asserted by conservatives—that the Federal Government should not encroach on the rights of states to determine public welfare rules. By recharacterizing the case from a simple preemption case of whether a person injured by smoking could sue a tobacco company under state law for damages into a "structural" case about "fair warning to the 50 States," Tribe was attempting to make his client's position the one most consonant with a core tenet of conservative political philosophy. Ultimately, the Supreme Court's fractured decision upheld the right of injured persons to sue tobacco companies for injuries under several different theories. A majority concluded that the federal statute requiring warning labels on cigarette packages did not preempt state damages actions generally but preempted only positive enactments of law by state rulemaking bodies. A plurality concluded that certain common law claims were preempted, but others were not.

As those illustrations suggest, petitioner's counsel has numerous critical choices to make in how to frame the argument. Some of the factors that go into the decision include: how complicated the issues presented are; when in the session the case is argued (first in the morning or later in the session); whether the case presents more than one issue; whether the case needs to have a fresh reconceptualization; the extent to which the reply brief simplified the issues; and whether petitioner's time is shared with an *amicus curiae*. Those factors affect such dynamics as how much time the advocate has to work with, how immediately focused the court may

---

20. *Cipollone v. Liggett Group, Inc.*, No. 90–1038, 1992 WL 687857 at *3 (Jan. 13, 1992).

be on the case (typically, members of the court take slightly more time before asking questions in cases argued later in a particular day's session than in the earliest cases), and whether the participation of another arguing counsel can produce some pre-arranged sharing of affirmative points.

§ 7.2   Respondent's Argument

The advocate representing respondent or appellee obviously seeks to win an affirmance, though obtaining a rule that can be won on remand should not be overlooked as a reasonable objective. Just as petitioner should not be engaging in a pointed attack on the court below, so, too, respondent should be presenting an affirmative case for the correctness of the holding he is defending.

Bruce J. Ennis was one of the finest advocates before the Supreme Court in the last two decades of the 20th century.[1] He argued 16 cases in the Supreme Court, many in important First Amendment cases for which he was principally known. Ennis made his points with short, declarative sentences that contained no excess verbiage. His argument defending the issuance of a preliminary injunction against enforcement of the Communications Decency Act ("CDA") in *Reno v. ACLU*[2] provided a textbook illustration of one approach to how a respondent can begin an argument. Here is his opening:

> Mr. Chief Justice and may it please the Court: There are four reasons why the preliminary injunction should be affirmed. The CDA bans speech. It will not be effective. There are less-restrictive alternatives that would be much more effective. And the combination of an imprecise standard, coupled with the threat of severe criminal sanctions, will chill much speech that would not be indecent.

Note how his approach differed from that taken by Dreeben in the *Scheffer* case. Dreeben made a few general statements before launching into his affirmative points. Ennis did not need to do that because he had just witnessed Seth Waxman, then the Principal Deputy Solicitor General, skillfully defend the constitutionality of the CDA for nearly 30 minutes, during which the context of the

§ 7.2

1. *See* Tony Mauro, "Bruce Ennis: An Appreciation," LEGAL TIMES, Aug. 7, 2000, at 8.

2. *Reno v. ACLU*, 521 U.S. 844, 117 S.Ct. 2329 (1997).

case had been more than amply set. Ennis could get right to the point without any wasted time.

The succinctness with which he summarized his affirmative points may have caught the court somewhat off-guard, because, after summarizing his fourth point, Ennis was not interrupted. He therefore did exactly what he should have done: he went back to his first point and provided a more elaborate explanation. This is how he proceeded from his summary of outline points into his argument:

> First, the District Court found as fact that the CDA completely bans a vast amount of speech, all of which is constitutionally protected for adults, from all of the unique means of communication in cyberspace except the World Wide Web, and effectively bans that speech from most of the Web as well. Virtually all speech that is displayed on the Internet in a manner that would be available to adults would also be available to minors.[3]

At that point, Justice Scalia interrupted Ennis with the first of many questions he would receive, but Ennis had succeeded in making the points that would figure in the court's opinion affirming the judgment that the CDA was unconstitutional.[4] The court's opinion put special emphasis on the vagueness of the CDA's content-based regulations on speech.[5]

William C. Bryson, a former Deputy Solicitor General and now a circuit judge on the U.S. Court of Appeals for the Federal Circuit, was similarly skillful at choosing the right opening as respondent. In *Nichols v. United States*,[6] he delivered an ideally structured and focused opening, much in the same style as that of Ennis just described:

> Mr. Chief Justice and may it please the Court: Our position in this case is that a valid uncounseled misdemeanor conviction can be used for sentence enhancement even if it could not support a sentence of imprisonment in its own right. And we base this contention on three positions. First, a particular factor does not need to be sufficient to support a criminal conviction and imprisonment in order

---

3. *Reno v. ACLU*, No. 96–511, 1997 WL 136253 at *33–*34 (Mar. 19, 1997).

4. *Reno v. ACLU*, 521 U.S. 844, 117 S.Ct. 2329 (1997).

5. *See* 521 U.S. at 871–72, 117 S.Ct. at 2345.

6. *Nichols v. United States*, 511 U.S. 738, 114 S.Ct. 1921 (1994).

to be used at sentencing. Second, there is nothing so inherently unreliable about a valid uncounseled misdemeanor conviction that would bar its use in a later sentencing proceeding. And third, an enhanced sentence for a second offense is not simply an additional sentence for a first offense. Instead, it's a sentence for the second offense that is imposed on a person who has a criminal record, that takes into account of the fact that the person has a criminal record.

Now, let me address each of these three points in more detail. First, it's a well-settled principle of sentencing law that this Court has reiterated again and again, that the court in sentencing may consider a very broad range of factors. Just because a particular factor would not have supported, in itself, a sentence of imprisonment, doesn't mean it can't be used at sentencing. And this—[7]

At that point, Bryson was interrupted by his first question. Note how succinctly he articulated the government's position. He stated the three points he wished to make during the argument and then, having not yet been interrupted, he proceeded to launch into an elaboration of those points.

Bryson often utilized that type of approach when arguing as respondent. This is how he opened his respondent's argument in *Evans v. United States*[8]: "Our position in this case is that the under color of official right portion of the Hobbs Act codifies, in effect, the old common law crime of official extortion, which was taken directly from New York law, which in turn had this crime of official extortion."[9] He was then interrupted by a question. But there was no ambiguity about the government's position in the case. His statement of position included both the legal theory on which the government's position rested—the incorporation of common law for the phrase "under color of official right" in the Hobbs Act—as well as the outcome in this particular case: that the crime of official extortion was encompassed within that phrase. Bryson's use of the "statement of position" opening approach was an indication that he was often interrupted with questions from the court and that it was

---

7. *Nichols v. United States*, No. 92–8556, 1994 WL 663472 at *29 (Jan. 10, 1994).

8. *Evans v. United States*, 504 U.S. 255, 112 S.Ct. 1881 (1992).

9. *Evans v. United States*, No. 90–6105, 1991 WL 636267 at *29 (Dec. 9, 1991).

useful to articulate in a simple way the government's position before that happened.

Of a piece with Bryson's style was this opening by Assistant to the Solicitor General Lisa S. Blatt, arguing for the respondent in *Bates v. United States*[10]: "Mr. Chief Justice and may it please the Court: The decision below is correct, because both the text and structure of Section 1097 [of Title 20 of the United States Code] compel the conclusion that an intent to injure or defraud is not an element of the misapplication offense."[11] It is hard to improve upon that opening.

Advocates like Bryson and Blatt recognize that much can happen in petitioner's opening argument that affects how to open an argument on behalf of the respondent. That recognition is something the best advocates appreciate. John Roberts has jokingly suggested that respondent's first duty in an argument is to demonstrate having been awake during the questioning of petitioner's counsel. His point is that, no matter what he planned to say, respondent's counsel should try to pick right up where the thread of the court's questioning has led. In *Posters 'N' Things v. United States*,[12] Bryson did just that: he ditched his prepared opening to address the issues that seemed to be of greatest concern to the court during petitioner's argument:

> MR. BRYSON: Thank you, Mr. Chief Justice, and may it please the Court: A great deal of the discussion this morning has been over the instructions. And while I recognize that isn't the principal issue that the court has before it, I would very briefly, just as a predicate to my argument, like to review the portions of the instructions that did specifically address the question.
>
> QUESTION: And, of course, I suppose you're doing it because the Government changed its theory * * * after the case was granted, didn't it?
>
> *   *   *
>
> MR. BRYSON: Well, I think we certainly changed our approach to the case in this respect, in that in the lower

---

10. *Bates v. United States*, 522 U.S. 23, 118 S.Ct. 285 (1997).

11. *Bates v. United States*, No. 96–7185, 1997 WL 632965 at *22 (Oct. 7, 1997).

12. *Posters 'N' Things v. United States*, 511 U.S. 513, 114 S.Ct. 1747 (1994).

courts the thrust of the argument being made by the defendants was that a subjective intent was required. That is—and this was the basis for the objections that were made in the district court—that the defendant herself had to have designed or intended the drug use. And we said that was not so, and the district judge agreed with us.

So the question of where the intent, where the knowledge lay, and so forth, was really not the focus of the district court proceeding. In the court of appeals, the argument was made—the principal argument made by the defendants was that this statute has no scienter requirement at all and therefore is unconstitutional. So, again, as the court of appeals pointed out, they did not argue for a particular scienter requirement. They didn't press the issue of knowledge. They were looking for a constitutional ruling based on an assumption of no scienter. So we are addressing the case as it now comes to the court, and addressing in particular the question that's raised in the petition.[13]

Through this opening, Bryson sought to reassure the court that the government's putative change of position was reasonable, in light of the manner in which petitioner had brought the case before it. Bryson's approach succeeded: the Supreme Court affirmed, holding that the intent requirement of the offense of using the mail to sell drug paraphernalia should be determined by objective standards for what constitutes such paraphernalia, rather than the subjective intent of the recipient.[14]

In keeping with the notion that respondent's mission is to win an affirmance of the judgment below, and not necessarily to defend every aspect of the lower court's reasoning, respondent's counsel should be mindful that the court is in the business of drawing lines and his job is to keep his client within those lines. In *United States v. Hubbell*,[15] John Nields defended the judgment of the court of appeals, which had remanded for a determination of whether the government had a reasonably particular knowledge of the existence of the documents it had subpoenaed, to which his client Webster

13. *Posters 'N' Things v. United States*, No. 92–903, 1993 WL 757642 at *28 (Oct. 5, 1993).

14. *See* 511 U.S. at 517–18, 114 S.Ct. 1751–52.

15. *United States v. Hubbell*, 530 U.S. 27, 120 S.Ct. 2037 (2000). For additional discussion of this argument, *see* § 6.1.

Hubbell had objected because of "the Fifth Amendment's protection against the government probing the mind of an accused in order to ascertain evidence it can use to convict him."[16] As the case was argued in the Supreme Court, the issue arose over a difference in standards to apply. Nields neatly sidestepped that problem in this way:

> [T]his isn't the case to lay down the exact standards, only to say that the analysis has to be are you relying on the witness' truth-telling to get the document. And if you do, it's testimony and the Fifth Amendment applies. And if you only got an incriminating document because the witness told the truth and you got it under immunity, you [have] got to hold the witness harmless. You have to leave him—as *Kastigar*[17] said, as emphatically as *Kastigar* could say, you must leave him after immunity in just as good a position as he would have been if he had been left to his Fifth Amendment privilege. And under *Doe*,[18] Mr. Hubbell had a Fifth Amendment privilege not to tell whether he had any of these documents.[19]

As the colloquy ended, it was clear that the court did not need to choose between two alternative tests to rule for Hubbell—Nields had accomplished his objective of giving the court an easier way to rule for his client.

Another facet of respondent's argument that can be very difficult to manage is to end on a strong point. When petitioner has managed to save time for rebuttal, respondent will not get the last word in the argument. It is important, therefore, for respondent to try to make a powerful point at the very end of the argument. Indeed, if respondent can end the argument by setting out a challenge to petitioner that can continue to seize the agenda during petitioner's rebuttal, he should try to do so. This is so much easier said than done, because the time is ticking away, the court is asking questions, and the point has to be made in a sufficiently succinct way that it is not obliterated when the time expires. But it is something that, with planning, can be quite effective. The idea is to

---

16. *United States v. Hubbell*, 167 F.3d 552, 585 (D.C.Cir.1999) (per curiam), cert. granted, 528 U.S. 926, 120 S.Ct. 320 (1999).

17. *Kastigar v. United States*, 406 U.S. 441, 92 S.Ct. 1653 (1972).

18. *Doe v. United States*, 487 U.S. 201, 108 S.Ct. 2341 (1988).

19. *United States v. Hubbell*, No. 99–166, 2000 WL 230520 at *40 (Feb. 22, 2000).

end on a point that puts the onus on petitioner in rebuttal to confront an issue other than the one petitioner may have intended to address. If petitioner ignores respondent's challenge, the omission is telling. If petitioner speaks to that point, respondent has seized control of the rhetorical agenda.

In *Bush v. Gore*,[20] David Boies was peppered with so many questions that he ran out of time just as he was being asked a lengthy question. Perhaps because of the historic nature of the case, the Chief Justice granted an extraordinary extension of time—giving Boies an additional two minutes. In the last 10 years of Chief Justice Rehnquist's presiding over the Supreme Court, he apparently had done that only a few times before in cases.[21] On another occasion, he had announced—at the beginning of the argument—that each side would get an additional five minutes. That was in the *Reno v. ACLU* case argued by Seth Waxman and Bruce Ennis.[22] But in *Bush v. Gore*, Boies had not been able to make his best arguments until after the Chief Justice extended his time. He was barely into his additional minutes when he was asked to concede that having a single judge at the end of the process of examining contested ballots would not, in fact, cure the equal protection/due process problems of having different standards apply to the interpretation of ballots that had been suggested by Bush and by several justices in earlier questions. Here is how Boies ended the argument:

> No, I think it is an answer. I think there are two answers to it. First, I think that the answer that they did it differently, different people interpreting the general standard differently, would not raise a problem even in the absence of judicial review of that. Second, even if that would have raised a constitutional problem, I think the judicial review that provides the standardization would solve that problem. The third thing that I was saying is that any differences as to how this standard is interpreted have a lot less significance in terms of what votes are counted or not counted than simply the differences in machines that exist throughout the counties of Florida.

20. *Bush v. Gore*, 531 U.S. 98, 121 S.Ct. 525 (2000) (per curiam).

21. Interview with General William K. Suter, Clerk of the Supreme Court, in Washington, D.C. (Aug. 31, 2001).

22. *See* Tony Mauro, "Extra Time, Extraordinary Argument," LEGAL TIMES, Mar. 24, 1997, at 8.

There are five times as many undervotes in punch card ballot counties than in optical ballot counties. Now, for whatever reason that is, whether it's voter error or machine problems, that statistic, you know, makes clear that there is some difference in how votes are being treated county by county. That difference is much greater than the difference in how many votes are recovered in Palm Beach or Broward or Volusia or Miami–Dade, so that the differences of interpretation of the standard, the general standard are resulting in far fewer differences among counties than simply the differences in the machines that they have.[23]

In other words, if the court was going to find an equal protection violation for interpretations of the ballots among counties, the entire electoral system of the country would pose an equal protection problem, because, throughout the country, election districts vary in usage of punch card versus optical scan devices. It was one of Boies' best arguments. However, but for the Chief Justice's grace in extending his time by two minutes, he would not have been able to make it. Yet that very point figured in the dissenting opinions of Justices John Paul Stevens and Ruth Bader Ginsburg.[24]

§ 7.3   Rebuttal Argument

Rebuttal is the hardest argument to make in any court. In the Supreme Court and in most courts of appeals, petitioner has to work hard to save any time at all for rebuttal. In the Supreme Court, rebuttal time comes directly out of the 30 minutes allotted to petitioner's side and, if the justices keep asking questions that use up petitioner's time, the case is submitted without rebuttal. Many courts of appeals permit counsel to reserve time for rebuttal, either through the clerk in advance of the argument or at the beginning of the argument itself. It is the rare court of appeals panel that does not permit counsel at least one minute of rebuttal, even when counsel's time has expired. Between the questions petitioner has received that require further amplification or clarification and the questions put to respondent's counsel that merit some comment by petitioner, invariably some important decisions

---

23. *Bush v. Gore*, No. 00–949, 2000 WL 1804429 at *72–*73 (Dec. 11, 2000).

24. *Bush v. Gore*, 531 U.S. 98, 123, 121 S.Ct. 525, 539–41 (2000) (Stevens,

J., dissenting); 531 U.S. at 135, 121 S.Ct. at 550 (Ginsburg, J., dissenting).

must be made by petitioner's counsel about what to stress in as little as a few minutes. Each case will require a different emphasis, but if ever there was a time to "go for the jugular vein," as John W. Davis put it, rebuttal is the last chance.[1] A great rebuttal can materially assist the court and help win a case; a weak rebuttal reinforces the perception that there are insufficient reasons to reverse the decision of the court below.

John Roberts' approach to rebuttal can be summarized in this way: only go for home runs. Singles, doubles, and triples are not good enough.[2] He takes this approach even so far as to suggest that the advocate only go for home runs on slightly less important issues in the case. In other words, if the advocate only has a somewhat persuasive argument to make on an issue critical to the case, Roberts suggests bypassing that argument in favor of a clear winning argument on a lesser point. His theory is that the advocate wants the members of the court to leave the courtroom thinking the very last point the advocate made was absolutely correct. In his view, that is more important than revealing weakness by stressing a point to which there is a ready answer, even if that point may be on an issue critical to petitioner's case. Although that approach has many virtues, it is not immune from criticism. In particularly close and hard-fought cases, rebuttal can sometimes be used to pick off that crucial fifth vote. In those situations, hitting a single or double may score the winning run.

In addition to his effective opening argument in the *Scheffer* case, Michael Dreeben also delivered an excellent rebuttal. His argument was a model demonstration of how to use rebuttal to make one last affirmative point that had not been made during the opening argument. During her argument, respondent's counsel, Kim Sheffield, stressed a range of points. She had made substantial inroads on Dreeben's argument that polygraphs were unreliable by stressing the fact that the military had more stringent standards for conducting polygraphs and evidently found them sufficiently reliable for use in national security classifications and employment decisions.

The one argument the government had made in the briefs but Dreeben had not been able to articulate orally concerned the

---

§ 7.3
1. John W. Davis, "The Argument of an Appeal," 20 A.B.A. J. 895, 897 (1940).

2. Interview with John G. Roberts, Jr., in Washington, D.C. (Sept. 6, 2001).

countermeasures that a person can take to fool the polygraph examiner. Without making any effort to respond to the numerous points made by Sheffield or in the justices' questions to her, Dreeben sought to make only one point in rebuttal: the last of his affirmative points that had not been made during his opening argument. To use Roberts' analogy, this was not just a home run, it was a grand slam. This is Dreeben's rebuttal argument in its entirety:

> The fundamental unreliability of polygraph evidence is underscored not only for the reasons that Justice Breyer adverted to, but also because of the possibility that countermeasures can defeat any test. Any individual who wants to can go on the Internet and download a book called "Beat the Box: The Insider's Guide to Outwitting the Lie Detector." And studies have shown that with about a half an hour of education in how to outwit the lie detector test, a suspect can do that by provoking physiological responses that fool the examiner by measures as easily as pressing his toes against the ground or biting his tongue when asked particular questions. Those kinds of ways of skewing any reliability that polygraph might otherwise have make it clear that the examiner can never be confident to the level that should be required before this form of evidence is admitted in a criminal trial. If the court has no further questions, thank you.[3]

Dreeben did not feel any need to respond point-by-point to respondent's arguments, nor to elaborate on any other point he had tried to make in his opening. Rather, with a brief description of countermeasures, he had significantly bolstered the government's principal point that polygraph evidence is inherently unreliable and injected great uncertainty into the uses of polygraphs for evidentiary purposes because of the ways the subject can manipulate the tests. This was a textbook example of how to use rebuttal to make one devastating point that goes to the core of the case but has not been made in the opening presentation.

At the opposite end of that spectrum are the rebuttal arguments in complicated cases that require more of an effort to assist the court in clearing up enough small points so that the central thrust of the case will not be lost. In such cases, petitioner's counsel

---

3. *United States v. Scheffer,* 1997 WL 689299 at *53.

must use rebuttal to give the court a roadmap of where to find material in the briefs or record to dispose of respondent's best arguments. Counsel can quickly and effectively use rebuttal to argue, "In response to counsel's argument [or a question from the court] that _____, I would direct the court's attention to page ___ of our brief/joint appendix/record excerpts." If the advocate has time for a one-sentence explanation of what the court will find when it consults those pages, that can be very helpful.

§ 7.4   *Amicus Curiae* Argument

Presenting an argument as *amicus curiae* involves significant advocacy challenges. Typically, an *amicus* in the Supreme Court will only have 10 minutes in which to present argument, whereas the party whom the *amicus* is supporting gets 20. (Occasionally, when the *amicus* straddles both sides of the case, the court will take five minutes per side for the *amicus*.) In the courts of appeals, an *amicus* may only have five minutes. In addition to the shorter amount of time in which to present argument, the *amicus* has to be ever mindful of the nuances in the party's argument, while not being unfailingly obeisant to them. That need for professional independence in some cases can create diplomatic challenges, because the *amicus* may be making a different argument (though one that supports the proposed disposition of the party). Finally, if the court has granted the motion for divided argument to permit the participation of *amicus*, it typically reflects confidence that the *amicus* will help the court. But the *amicus* is always batting clean-up: if a less experienced advocate representing a party has made case-damaging mistakes, an *amicus* will have special challenges in getting the case back on track.

An *amicus* should go to court with fairly limited and discrete objectives. Unlike a 30–minute argument in which the advocate might hope to make as many as 6 to 10 points, in a 10–minute *amicus* argument, counsel should try to make no more than 3. Those points must be chosen with care, because they must be arguments that can completely dispose of the case if possible. Non-governmental *amici* will sometimes use their time to press their distinctive interests or reasons for participation. Almost always, that is a mistake. The brief should say all that needs to be said on those subjects. The argument is the forum for resolving the legal issues in the case. Because the *amicus* will speak after the party, that advocate will be able to gauge the problems the court is having.

There are at least four distinctive approaches to an *amicus* argument. First, an *amicus* with a legal position slightly different from the party should consider beginning by articulating the *amicus'* position. In *National Collegiate Athletic Association v. Smith,*[1] for example, the United States participated in the case as an *amicus curiae* in support of respondent in part. But Deputy Solicitor General Edwin S. Kneedler's opening sentences made it clear that the government also agreed in part with petitioner: "The Third Circuit decided this case, at least as petitioner understands it, on a theory that someone in the position of the NCAA can be subject to suit under Title IX solely on the ground that it is a mere beneficiary of the program and on that ground alone. We agree with petitioner that that reading—if that is what the Third Circuit meant to hold—that that is incorrect, and that that is inconsistent with the decision in *Paralyzed Veterans*.[2]"[3]

A second objective of an *amicus* can be to help the court see the superstructure, or overarching themes, of the case to facilitate its resolution. In *Maryland v. Wilson,*[4] Attorney General Janet Reno brought the court back to a principled structure for deciding whether officers should have per se authority to order passengers to get out of vehicles that are stopped for normal traffic violations. Her opening refocused the court on the problems officers face in these situations:

> Mr. Chief Justice and may it please the Court: Traffic stops present special dangers to police officers. They're faced with an unknown situation, an unknown area, they're faced with little knowledge, if any knowledge of the occupants of the car, and they are vulnerable to attack not just from the driver but from the passenger. In *Mimms,*[5] this Court found that these safety concerns justify a *per se* rule that an officer in a valid traffic stop can order the driver to exit the vehicle. We submit that *Mimms* should be applied to passengers for three reasons * * *.

---

§ 7.4

1. *NCAA v. Smith*, 525 U.S. 459, 119 S.Ct. 924 (1999).

2. *U.S. Department of Transp. v. Paralyzed Veterans*, 477 U.S. 597, 106 S.Ct. 2705 (1986).

3. *National Collegiate Athletic Ass'n v. Smith*, No. 98–84, 1999 WL 32847 at *46–47 (Jan. 20, 1999).

4. *Maryland v. Wilson*, 519 U.S. 408, 117 S.Ct. 882 (1997).

5. *Pennsylvania v. Mimms*, 434 U.S. 106, 98 S.Ct. 330 (1977) (per curiam).

First, the driver—the officer has to focus on the driver in implementing the traffic stop and in securing the information with respect to a license or to the vehicle. He cannot monitor the passenger's conduct at the same time. The focus in *Mimms* was on the inordinate risk, and the court made specific reference to the inordinate risk as an officer approaches a person seated in the car, and the court specifically said that the officer had no reason in *Mimms* to believe that the officer [suspected] foul play, so it was the focus on a person seated in the car that created the danger.[6]

Reno was then interrupted by questions about the reasonableness of the government's position, in light of the many possible situations where officers might encounter danger when making a traffic stop. Her answer stressed the theme of her argument: "[T]he justification that I'm advancing is that that officer should have the ability to immediately size up the situation, determine if there is any reasonable suspicion to believe that a person is armed, and then advance to *Terry*[7] frisk if that is appropriate, but that he should have the opportunity to control the situation if he is the single officer on the scene before the backup comes, to keep them in the car so that he doesn't have a person moving here, here, and here, or to get them out of the car if there are circumstances that dictate that they should be out of the car."[8] Reno's use of simple, clear language to convey the threats posed to officers provided valuable *amicus* support for the court and contributed to the government's victory in the case.

A third objective of an *amicus* argument is to seal off as quickly as possible a line of questioning that the party was not answering adequately. This is the "triage" approach to *amicus* arguments, where the advocate's role is to stop the bleeding. Like a respondent's argument in which the advocate goes right to the troublesome question, an *amicus* argument must do the same by taking the questions that the party stumbled on and give a compelling answer right away. In some arguments, the party's argument broke down because it was based on too broad a theory. The *amicus*

---

6. *Maryland v. Wilson*, No. 95–1268, 1996 WL 721111 at *20 (Dec. 11, 1996).

7. *Terry v. Ohio*, 392 U.S. 1, 88 S.Ct. 1868 (1968).

8. *Maryland v. Wilson*, 1996 WL 721111 at *23–*24.

advocate's role, however, is to put forth an argument the majority of the court will accept.

A fourth approach for an *amicus*, therefore, is to shift the court's focus from the legal theory being advocated by the party to a narrower theory that achieves the same disposition but is more acceptable to the court. In *Wilson v. Arkansas*,[9] for example, after the state's Attorney General was told by a justice that it was "time to fall back"[10] because he had not persuaded any of the justices of the state's broad Fourth Amendment theory, the lawyer for the United States followed with an *amicus curiae* argument that articulated a narrower position on behalf of the federal government.[11]

Amicus counsel must make quick decisions about what to say in the opening moments of an argument. Their judgments often can implicate conflicting considerations. On the one hand, the advocate has to assess the need for stating the position clearly and providing a frame of reference to the argument that may have been missing by the party the *amicus curiae* is supporting. On the other hand, the advocate must weigh the tactical considerations of addressing concerns expressed during earlier parts of the argument by members of the court who may be swing votes. *Amicus* counsel also has to be mindful of attempting to argue the affirmative points that the party the *amicus* is supporting may not have been able to articulate.

In that last regard, it is advisable for the *amicus* and the party to work closely together to coordinate their arguments. If possible, they should attend each other's moot courts, trade ideas about which affirmative points to try to make, and discuss problematic questions and answers.

§ 7.5   Multiple–Party Arguments

Many of the same principles for *amicus* arguments apply as well to multiple-party arguments. A party should be clear when it is presenting a position that differs from another party on the same side of the case. In *California v. Deep Sea Research, Inc.*,[1] the

---

9. *Wilson v. Arkansas*, 514 U.S. 927, 115 S.Ct. 1914 (1995).

10. *See* § 4.3.a.

11. *Wilson v. Arkansas*, No. 94–5707, 1995 WL 243487 at *43 (Mar. 28, 1995).

§ 7.5

1. *California v. Deep Sea Research, Inc.*, 523 U.S. 491, 118 S.Ct. 1464 (1998).

United States was a respondent supporting petitioner in part. Of the three issues, the federal government agreed with respondent on the first, petitioner on the second, and neither party on the third. The Solicitor General's motion for divided argument sought and obtained five minutes from each side. Thus, the opening sentence by the United States' counsel sought to make clear the federal government's position: "Although we agree with petitioners that the courts below misconstrued the Abandoned Shipwreck Act, we disagree with them that the Eleventh Amendment applies because this is not a suit against the state."[2]

It is not always so easy to get an opportunity to state the party's position. In *Dickerson v. United States*,[3] for example, the United States was in the unusual position of agreeing with the criminal defendant that the rule in *Miranda v. Arizona*[4] was a constitutional rule that could not be modified by an enactment of Congress. Solicitor General Seth Waxman gamely attempted to get the position of the United States on the record at the outset. He began his argument this way: "Mr. Chief Justice and may it please the Court: The position of the United States is based on three propositions, and I'd like simply to state them. First, as this court's repeated application of *Miranda* to the states reveals, its rule is a constitutional one. Second—." He was then cut off by a question from Justice Sandra Day O'Connor.[5]

As with *amicus* arguments, a party arguing second on one side of the case has an obligation to go to the hardest problem and attempt to address it. In *National Credit Union Administration v. First National Bank & Trust Co*,[6] John Roberts represented the private petitioners, the AT&T Federal Credit Union. The case concerned whether the National Credit Union Administration ("NCUA") had properly construed the National Credit Union Act's requirement that a credit union be composed of "groups having a common bond" by allowing a multiple group credit union so long as each group had its own common bond even if the bond was not common to all of the participating groups. In the Supreme Court, the case boiled down to two issues—whether banks had standing to

2. *California v. Deep Sea Research, Inc.*, No. 96–1400, 1997 WL 751917 at *24 (Dec. 1, 1997).

3. *Dickerson v. United States*, 530 U.S. 428, 120 S.Ct. 2326 (2000).

4. *Miranda v. Arizona*, 384 U.S. 436, 86 S.Ct. 1602 (1966).

5. *Dickerson v. United States*, No. 99–5525, 2000 WL 486733 at *10 (Apr. 19, 2000).

6. *National Credit Union Admin. v. First Nat'l Bank & Trust Co.*, 522 U.S. 479, 118 S.Ct. 927 (1998).

sue the NCUA claiming that its interpretation of the statute was flawed and whether the NCUA had correctly construed the Act.

Roberts spoke for 10 minutes after Seth Waxman opened the argument on behalf of the NCUA. Roberts opened this way: " * * * * I would like to pick up with Justice [Anthony M.] Kennedy's question: If the banks had known about this interpretation, they would have objected. First of all, that's beside the point. You don't get standing under the zone of interest test simply because you objected. Congress may not have accepted your objections."[7] At that point, Justice Kennedy sought to rehabilitate his concern: "Well, I–I don't know that it's beside the point, because the way you're arguing, it's something of—of a trap. Let's assume that the most plausible interpretation of this regulation is the interpretation that the banks now advance."[8] In retrospect, it might not have been possible to get Justice Kennedy's vote, which turned out to be crucial in the court's 5–4 decision. But Roberts' statement that Justice Kennedy's concern was "beside the point"—while correct under the law of standing—might have been worded more artfully to have avoided alienating the justice. Roberts may have calculated that he could obtain the fifth vote from another source by exposing the fallacy of Justice Kennedy's suggestion. Such a calculation would not have been wholly unwarranted because Justice O'Connor agreed with Roberts' contention that the banks lacked standing to challenge the agency's interpretation.

Unless there are extraordinary reasons for multiple-party oral arguments, parties should have only one advocate argue per side, as is the normal case under the rules. Supreme Court and court of appeals arguments are simply too short for multiple advocates to effectively represent a side. This concern is particularly marked when the multiple parties are petitioners, because it is difficult to reserve time for rebuttal when the normal 30 minutes is cut down to 20 because the other party has been ceded 10 minutes of time.

A problem that often arises in multiple-party arguments is whether trial counsel should be one of the arguing counsel on appeal. The point is often made that trial counsel knows the record and may therefore be of assistance to the court at the argument. That concern rarely bears out in practice. More often, the putative

---

7. *National Credit Union Admin. v. First Nat'l Bank & Trust Co.*, Nos. 96–843 & 96–847, 1997 WL 611828 at *18 (Oct. 6, 1997).

8. *Id.*

value of trial counsel's participation is outweighed by the problems at argument caused by his lack of experience in arguing in the court of appeals or, especially, the Supreme Court. Records can be mastered, but experience in Supreme Court and appellate advocacy can be won only through actually arguing cases in those courts. As the principles described in this book seek to demonstrate, the skills of effective Supreme Court and appellate advocacy are different from those needed to master trial practice.

§ 7.6   Arguing on the Same Side as the United States

Throughout the 1990s and into the twenty-first century, the Solicitor General was participating in approximately two-thirds of all arguments in the Supreme Court. In the 2001 Term, the United States participated in 65 of 78 oral arguments, or 87 percent.[1] In virtually all of those cases, an attorney from the Office of the Solicitor General represented the United States as a party or an *amicus curiae* in support of one of the parties in a divided argument. In the courts of appeals, the United States is a party to thousands of cases and a participating *amicus curiae* or intervening party in many others.

For counsel for the party on the same side as the United States, a few points are important to stress. First, no matter how experienced the advocate, substantial benefits accrue to the advocate from working closely with the member of the Solicitor General's Office who is arguing the case in the Supreme Court, or the appellate attorney from the Department of Justice or administrative agency arguing in the court of appeals. That lawyer frequently will have significant experience as a Supreme Court or appellate advocate and will also have access to a wealth of agency knowledge about the particular area of law. Moreover, the moot courts conducted by the Solicitor General's Office or the appellate staffs invariably raise points the advocate for the party would be well-advised to consider. The advocate should try to attend moot courts held by the government attorney in the case.

Notwithstanding the experience the government attorney might have, that lawyer typically will have far less time to prepare than private counsel. The press of cases handled by most govern-

§ 7.6

1. This data was provided by the Office of the Solicitor General. The author is grateful to Emily C. Spadoni for her assistance in providing this information.

ment attorneys is simply too great. It therefore behooves the private counsel to do what he can to facilitate preparation by the government's lawyer. Inviting that attorney to a moot court, providing copies of an opening and draft affirmative points, and conferring about the case by telephone can assist both attorneys. While these points may seem to be common sense, practice varies widely. Interestingly, the norm seems to be that the more experienced an attorney is in arguing a case in the Supreme Court, the more closely that lawyer seeks to work with the lawyer in the Solicitor General's Office. The same holds true for practitioners experienced before the courts of appeals.

* * *

Each case in the Supreme Court or court of appeals presents a unique advocacy challenge. That challenge becomes more complex as the case proceeds through the argument and as successive advocates add their own unique perspective that alters the dynamic of the argument. Petitioner's challenges differ in key respects from respondent's. By approaching the argument with those basic approaches in mind, the advocate can maximize the opportunities to convince the court.

Chapter Eight

COMMON MISTAKES IN ORAL ARGUMENTS

Analysis

Sec.

8.5.f   Use Intemperate Language

8.5.g   Be Too Informal with the Court

———————

Supreme Court and appellate advocacy requires the highest level of preparation, experience, and skill. Arguing a case on appeal is enormously stressful because there is no margin for error and the scope of difficult questions to address is broad. That combination of elements contributes to the frequent occurrence of mistakes in Supreme Court and court of appeals arguments. Indeed, every lawyer who makes an appellate argument can expect to make mistakes. The best advocates shrug them off and move on; the worst compound their errors with others. Supreme Court and appellate advocacy, like golf, is not a game of perfect.[1] No advocate wants to have her mistakes publicized, particularly by an author who has made his own share. Unfortunately, the best examples of what *not* to do come from actual Supreme Court and court of appeals arguments. Regrettably, many mistakes are fairly common and avoidable. This chapter describes and illustrates such errors in five different categories: speaking style errors, substantive errors (mostly in response to questions), errors of citation, errors in handling the court, and decorum errors. An advocate who minimizes the commission of these errors has a much greater chance of making a successful argument.

§ 8.1   Speaking Style Errors

Notwithstanding its cavernous size, the Supreme Court is actually a very intimate forum in which to argue a case. The advocate is very close to the justices—no more than 15 feet from the Chief Justice. Most court of appeals courtrooms are similar, with the advocate 20 feet or less from the circuit judges. That intimacy facilitates an opportunity to have a conversation with the court. Commonly, however, advocates make the mistake of thinking that they cannot simply converse with the members of the court, but rather must go to greater lengths to press their cause. Those efforts lead to the following speaking style errors.

———————

1. Bob Rotella & Bob Cullen, *Golf is Not a Game of Perfect* (1995). John Roberts suggested this analogy between the inherent imperfections in an oral advocate's performance and a golfer's shot-making in a round of golf.

§ 8.1.a   Speak With Too Much Passion or Rhetoric

Advocates not infrequently come to the Supreme Court or a court of appeals thinking they must be at their most eloquent. They concoct elaborately beautiful phrases and utter them with a kind of nineteenth century pomp. It is all very unnecessary and can be counterproductive. One of the most memorable examples of this error was by respondent's counsel in *Forsyth County v. The Nationalist Movement*,[1] which concerned whether a local ordinance was unconstitutional on its face because it imposed a fee of $1,000 for a parade permit. The county's attorney competently marched through his arguments, with few persons in the courtroom having an inkling of what was to come. Respondent Nationalist Movement was an extremist group that had sought the parade permit. Its counsel, Richard Barrett, began with the most extraordinary opening lines heard in recent years in the Supreme Court:

MR. BARRETT: Mr. Chief Justice, if it please the Court:

If the right of the people to peacefully assemble to petition the Government becomes only a privilege then the county becomes a kingdom. The courthouse is a castle and the citizen is a subject. The moat around this castle, if you will, is the $1,000 permit fee for those seeking to assemble on the steps, and there is no drawbridge for either the poor who have no fee to pay for the steps, or for the free, who refuse to kneel upon the steps.

Here is the battering ram against the palace of privilege, it is the inalienable and universal rights of man, and here is the crossbow against the ramparts of tyranny. It is the First Amendment. And here are the keys to the kingdom: 1943, *Murdock*.[2] There can be no charge for the enjoyment of a right guaranteed by the Federal Constitution. 1944, *Follett*.[3] There may not even be a $1.00 per day fee to exercise rights under the First Amendment.[4]

At that point, the irritation among the justices was evident in the curt colloquy that interrupted Barrett's oratory:

§ 8.1

1. *Forsyth County v. The Nationalist Movement*, 505 U.S. 123, 112 S.Ct. 2395 (1992).

2. *Murdock v. Pennsylvania*, 319 U.S. 105, 63 S.Ct. 870 (1943).

3. *Follett v. Town of McCormick*, 321 U.S. 573, 64 S.Ct. 717 (1944).

4. *Forsyth County v. The Nationalist Movement*, No. 91–538, 1992 WL 687825 at *27 (Mar. 31, 1992).

QUESTION: Mr. Barrett, do you think those cases over-ruled *Cox*?[5]

MR. BARRETT: *Cox* was adopted, Your Honor, at a time—

QUESTION: Will you answer my question?[6]

Barrett continued in that vein throughout his argument. Not long thereafter, he committed another sin of advocacy in the Supreme Court—getting too emotional. After he went on another rhetorical tear, he drew the ire of the Chief Justice:

> MR. BARRETT: * * * Since the county has already said in its brief that they regard this speech as deficient and they say that the only reason for the permit fee in their brief is to rid the public forum of unwelcome harassment, well, then this speech must be so nauseating that they would have to charge for more toilets for the public that is going to vomit at the assembly that is wanting to be put on.
>
> QUESTION: Mr. Barrett, I think you better calm down a little and address the issues. I think we have heard enough rhetoric.
>
> MR. BARRETT: It's an emotional issue based on humanity, Your Honor.
>
> QUESTION: I suggest you try to keep your emotions under control and try to discuss the merits of the case.[7]

Most counsel rebuked in that way by the Chief Justice would proceed meekly. Barrett, however, gamely pressed on. Toward the end of his argument, another colloquy made clear that the justices had abandoned any hope that he might help them figure out how best to decide the case. Instead, when an opportunity arose to have fun at Barrett's expense, a justice took it. The colloquy started, however, with a perfectly serious question:

> QUESTION: But the facial challenge to the statute is it is invalid because it would require somebody to give a name to get a permit, that makes the whole thing bad, doesn't it?

---

5. *Cox v. New Hampshire*, 312 U.S. 569, 61 S.Ct. 762 (1941).

6. *See* 1992 WL 687825 at *27.

7. *Id.* at *37–*38.

MR. BARRETT: If there is a valid exception where the confidentiality could be respected, Your Honor, then there would be no challenge. * * * But [the parade fee] is a tax, Your Honor, and I simply draw the court's attention in what meager abilities I have to Forsyth County or any county and ask what do we see here when this assembly takes place, and how valuable is that to America? I see Americana and I see the stump speech. I can't put a price on it, but I see the furrowed brow of labor listening. I see the tender graces of motherhood feeling. I hear the assertion of youth speaking out.

QUESTION: I see the mother paying out in municipal taxes what she might be buying food for her child with.

(Laughter.)

MR. BARRETT: Balance that if you will, Your Honor, between perhaps the sharpening right there of democracy's rusty instruments. Can I speak of the spoken word and the sparks that come from it? Can I speak of reason and the glitter that lightens our minds? Can I speak of the shiny sword of reason that ousts tyranny from among us? Your Honor, they have spoken of money. May I speak of freedom? They have spoken of convenience. May I speak of happiness? Someone asked if I would pay a fee. Your Honor, write this epitaph, if you will, on my tomb: The road not taken, but not the speech not given. * * *

QUESTION: How about the argument not made?

(Laughter.)[8]

Notwithstanding Barrett's performance, the Supreme Court held by a 5–4 vote that the county's ordinance permitting the administrator to vary the parade permit fee based on the estimated costs of maintaining public order was facially unconstitutional because it was not drawn in a sufficiently narrow manner and did not provide reasonably definite standards to guide how much should be charged as the fee.

§ 8.1.b   *Speak Too Loudly or Rapidly*

It is not surprising that nerves will show in an advocate's argument in the Supreme Court or court of appeals. A common

---

8. *Id.* at *47–*49.

manifestation of nervousness is for an attorney to speak too loudly or too quickly when addressing the court. In one argument, the Chief Justice said, "[Counsel], we have a good amplifying system. I think we could hear you even if you didn't speak quite as loud."[9] It is a good sound system. But on numerous occasions counsel have boomed their argument into the microphone, even though the Clerk's Office advises counsel to "[a]void emotional oration and loud, impassioned pleas."[10] There is also a sound technician in attendance who will adjust the volume on the microphone. To be sure, the acoustics in the Supreme Court are not ideal. Spectators will often complain of difficulty hearing counsel's argument or the justices' questions. But, in the well of the court and to the justices themselves, the speakers provide more than ample assistance without the advocate using her loudest voice.

In the courts of appeals, acoustics vary widely. Some courtrooms, such as in the Eleventh Circuit and the ceremonial courtroom where the D.C. Circuit hears cases en banc, have ineffective sound systems. In any court of appeals argument, counsel should become familiar with the courtroom and its acoustics. An advocate must make adjustments, even if that means speaking directly into the microphone and being less animated than usual.

In like fashion, nervous attorneys also routinely speak too rapidly. Few sound systems in the United States courts—including in the Supreme Court—are so good that an advocate can speak quickly and be understood. Most judges and justices are quite extraordinary listeners, but if counsel goes too fast, the court will not follow the arguments. During one Supreme Court argument, Stephen McAllister, Dean of the University of Kansas Law School and an experienced appellate advocate, saw that his opponent was speaking too rapidly. He wrote on a pad of paper, "SLOW DOWN." The recipient of that helpful advice was one of McAllister's former students, who no doubt appreciated McAllister's grace in the heat of the moment and who responded by slowing down and making a more effective argument.[11] Counsel should adopt a conversational volume but a slightly slower than conversational cadence. In addi-

---

9. *Lewis v. Brunswick Corp.*, No. 97–288, 1998 WL 106133 at *3 (Mar. 2, 1998).

10. William K. Suter, Clerk of the Court, *Guide for Counsel in Cases to be*

Argued Before the Supreme Court of the United States 9 (October Term 2002).

11. Tony Mauro, "Anthrax Scare Still Takes a Toll," Legal Times, Dec. 10, 2001, at 9.

tion to being easier to follow and understand, a slower pace also adds a certain gravitas to the presentation.

§ 8.1.c   Read to the Court

Premier advocates for decades have advised against reading in appellate arguments.[12] Decades ago, or at least in the nineteenth century, it was much more common for the attorney to read the argument. That process must have been stultifying for all concerned. In today's argument environment, it is extremely rare for counsel to be given the opportunity to speak long enough without interruption to engage in any reading of prepared remarks. And even if presented with the opportunity, the advocate should not plan on taking it. A failure to make eye contact through obvious reading by the advocate will lead a judge to interrupt simply to break up the monotony of the presentation.

In *United States v. Microsoft Corporation*,[13] one of the attorneys for the company launched into a prepared written argument that was delivered in a manner that made it obvious that he was reading to the court. Judge Sentelle interrupted to say to counsel, "[Y]ou might recall that our rules recommend against, really speak against, reading your arguments to the Court, Counsel."[14] Notwithstanding that admonition, the Microsoft attorney continued to read his argument, even as the court visibly appeared to be tuning him out.

At the beginning of arguments, particularly with a prepared opening, it is a tempting crutch to look down at the written page for help. As important as those opening lines are, the advocate should try to have them memorized. With the first spoken sentences, the advocate is trying to build credibility with a court that is at its most attentive. When an advocate completes, "May it please the Court," and then puts her head down to read the beginning lines of the opening, a natural reaction by any listener (and judges are no exception) is to lose interest in what the advocate is saying.

---

12. *See, e.g.*, Robert H. Jackson, "Advocacy Before the Supreme Court: Suggestions for Effective Case Presentations," 37 A.B.A. J. 801, 865 (Nov. 1951); John W. Davis, "The Argument of an Appeal," 26 A.B.A. J. 895, 898 (Dec. 1940).

13. *United States v. Microsoft Corp.*, 253 F.3d 34 (D.C.Cir.) (en banc) (per curiam), cert. denied, 122 S.Ct. 350 (2001).

14. Oral Arg. Tr., *United States v. Microsoft Corp.*, Nos. 00–5212 & 00–5213 at *239–40 (Feb. 27, 2001).

Reading to a court is a sign of insecurity and inexperience. It makes good eye contact impossible. It interferes with real communication with the court and prevents an attorney from making the most of what she perceives in the court, such as elaborating on an answer when an initial stab is greeted with the furrowed brow of incomprehension. An advocate making eye contact may also better accommodate a judge whose posture makes clear a desire to ask a question. An advocate may also use a sweeping eye contact with the court to move away from a judge who appears to be engaging in a one-on-one question-and-answer session that does not facilitate the advocate's development of her affirmative points. Those techniques are not available to the advocate whose head is stuck in a binder.

Even without reading, an advocate should try to look down at notes as infrequently as possible. Unless a question requires the advocate to scan notes or briefs for an answer, counsel should try to maintain focus on the questioner for several reasons. First, it is easy to lose the train of a question when the advocate is not looking the questioner in the eye. It is also rude to be asked a question and immediately to look away. Thus, even when the advocate knows she will have to look down, she should try to keep her focus on the questioner for as long as possible before doing so. One technique to avoid unnecessarily looking down is to set the tabs on the podium binder so that the advocate can simply feel for the tabs and know exactly where the answer to the question will be without having to look down until the last moment.

§ 8.1.d Fail to Maintain a Professional Posture While Arguing

The Supreme Court is both a comfortable and an uncomfortable place in which to argue. The seats at counsel table are comfortable and the podium is adjustable to the height of the advocate. Most of the discomfort is occasioned not by the physical surroundings but simply by the intimidating atmosphere that exists there. Some attorneys have raised a few eyebrows among spectators by leaning over the lectern, kicking their feet back with their toe stubbing the floor, or bobbing back and forth like a metronome. One attorney was admonished to speak into the microphone because he tended to walk toward the justice who was asking him a question. When Justice Ginsburg asked a question, he left the podium to take a few steps to his left; when Justice Breyer chimed in, he moved a few steps to his right. It looked like a daytime talk show, with the host roaming the audience looking for volunteers. But it was irritating to the court because it made the amplification of his voice all but impossible when he kept moving away from the microphone.

In a similar vein, a newspaper columnist once commented (with some disfavor) that, in one of his early arguments as Solicitor General, Seth Waxman at one point in the argument had his hands in his trouser pockets.[15] Of all the "sins" on which to comment this one seemed a small one. Tellingly, Waxman rarely, if ever again, put his hands in his pockets during an argument. The one time it happened may have been completely unconscious, but he was far too elegant an advocate to do anything twice that would receive that kind of public comment.

Except when gesturing, an advocate should generally try to keep her hands on the podium. Because the advocate can adjust the podium before beginning, the podium can be at a comfortable position for both seeing notes and placing folded hands. It is hard for some people to stand erect for 30 minutes while arguing. Long-time Assistant to the Solicitor General Jeffrey P. Minear is invariably impressive for (among other reasons) the professionalism of his posture. He stands straight and tall to argue, always uses natural gestures, and never moves his body to communicate anything other than that he is a first-class advocate. Some lawyers arguing in the court will bend a leg and fidget with their foot. Some will hold a pen or pencil. Some will unbutton and button their jacket. Some will flip the pages back and forth in their podium binders. Some will riffle through loose-leaf papers. All of these mannerisms distract attention away from what the lawyer is saying.

§ 8.2 Substantive Errors

This category of errors refers to broadly comparable errors affecting the substance of the argument and not to those types of case-specific mistakes from which one obviously cannot generalize.

§ 8.2.a Avoid Direct Answers to Questions

Few things irritate a judge or justice more than an answer that does not directly address the question. If a question calls for a "yes" or "no" answer, the court expects the answer to begin with

15. Tony Mauro, "Waxman Scores Rare Double Play," LEGAL TIMES, Dec. 8, 1997, at 7.

one of those words. There are two common errors counsel make when confronted with a "yes" or "no" question. The first is answering the question with the explanation before getting to the "yes" or "no" part of the answer. The second is viewing the question as a trap from which the perceived successful escape is avoidance and obfuscation. Both approaches create far more problems than they solve. Indeed, the best advocates will begin their answers "yes, because _____" or "no, because _____." A judge wanting a straight answer will be more willing to give the advocate an opportunity to explain the answer if it begins along the lines of, "Yes, except in certain circumstances."

In *Reno v. Condon*,[1] South Carolina Attorney General Charles Condon argued pro se on behalf of the respondent in a suit testing the constitutionality of the Driver's Privacy Protection Act, a law enacted by Congress under the Commerce Clause to ensure that states in receipt of driver's license information do not sell or otherwise transfer that information except in certain circumstances. Condon quickly found himself on the defensive. One colloquy illustrated—to the amusement of the courtroom spectators—the hazards of not directly answering a question:

QUESTION: Do you agree that the wage and hour law, therefore, has got to be struck down in its application to the States?

GENERAL CONDON: This Court has said that was a law of general applicability.

QUESTION: But it has administrative burdens, so—

GENERAL CONDON: And my point about administrative burdens is to get to the heart—

QUESTION:—they're okay if they're distributed to States and to private entities? No matter what the administrative burden, it's okay as long as private entities also have administrative burdens?

GENERAL CONDON: Again, in terms of trying to answer your question directly—

QUESTION: Well, that would be yes or no.

§ 8.2

1. *Reno v. Condon*, 528 U.S. 141, 120 S.Ct. 666 (2000).

(Laughter.)[2]

Obviously, an advocate aspires not to have the court poke fun at an answer. The line to draw between answering the question directly and getting an opportunity to give an adequate explanation can be a very fine one. It takes a great deal of preparation, self-assurance, and wherewithal to answer a question "yes" or "no," particularly when it involves a hypothetical. But an advocate who can get right to the point in answering the question and then offer an explanation will, far more often than not, avoid wasting time and frustrating the court.

§ 8.2.b　Use Ill-Considered Metaphors

The argument in *Reno v. Condon* also illustrated the hazards of answering a question with a poorly conceived metaphor. At one point, a justice asked Condon a hypothetical about state compliance with other federal directives: "I mean, suppose you sell hot dogs at the State park. Don't you have to comply with the food and drug laws?"[3] Condon's answer first betrayed his inexperience in dealing with hypotheticals. "Justice Breyer, * * * [w]e aren't selling hot dogs here."[4] Justice Breyer was fully aware of that, but graciously moved to a different hypothetical involving state taxation of Internet transactions. But Condon seemed fixated on selling hot dogs. A few minutes later, he brought up on his own the hot dog hypothetical. When Justice Breyer evinced no interest in going back to that example, Condon nonetheless pressed on. After another colloquy, Condon again injected the hot dog hypothetical: "[A]nd again, if I could go back to the hot dog, because I like that one, if I could, we're not selling hot dogs here."[5] The persuasive value of reintroducing a hypothetical in which the justices themselves no longer expressed interest was lost on everyone.

Overuse of metaphors can also spark attempts at humor by the court at the advocate's expense. In *United States v. Salerno*,[6] Michael Tigar used the metaphor of trial counsel "opening the door" to the admission of evidence that might otherwise have been blocked. That metaphor, of course, is well known and was apt for

---

2. *Reno v. Condon*, No. 98–1464, 1999 WL 1075199 at *28 (Nov. 10, 1999).

3. *Id*. at *22.

4. *Id*.

5. *Id*. at *26.

6. *United States v. Salerno*, 505 U.S. 317, 112 S.Ct. 2503 (1992).

the case. But Tigar took it too far, and then abruptly shifted to a different metaphor, which led to this exchange:

QUESTION: Your position, Mr. Tigar, is that the Government opens the door when it begins cross-examination in the grand jury?

MR. TIGAR: No, Justice Kennedy, we do not take that position.

QUESTION: When does this door get opened?

MR. TIGAR: The door is opened, one—and the court of appeals went through this in *Bahadar*,[7] so I'm not making it up as I go along. It's in the record. * * *

QUESTION: But the doctrine about opening the door [is] so that you don't take an inconsistent position before the same trier of fact. The jury never heard this testimony.

MR. TIGAR: The inconsistent position * * * is that the Government indicted these defendants and said, members of the trial jury, there is a conspiracy here to rig bids. Now, at the same time they're telling the jury that, in the back room, they have lit a candle—the candle of the exculpatory testimony of these witnesses. And now they want from this Court the authority to put a basket over that candle so the light doesn't shine in the dark corners. That is—

QUESTION: Well, I'm still having trouble opening the door. I haven't gotten to the candle yet.

(Laughter.)

MR. TIGAR: I apologize for the * * * metaphor, sir.

QUESTION: I just—* * * I'm aware of no doctrine of opening the door other than to avoid taking an inconsistent position before a trier of fact, which confuses the trier of fact. That did not happen here.[8]

As experienced and excellent an advocate as he is, even Tigar appeared to be trying to devise metaphors at the expense of a simple articulation of his position. A metaphor is only powerful if

---

7. *United States v. Bahadar*, 954 F.2d 821 (2d. Cir.1992).

8. *United States v. Salerno*, No. 91–872, 1992 WL 687558 at *31–*33 (Apr. 20, 1992).

the legal position it purports to illustrate is sound. But a metaphor cannot mask a weak argument.

§ 8.2.c   Make up Hypothetical Examples

It is rare for an advocate to effectively introduce his own hypothetical example in a Supreme Court or court of appeals argument. There are two dangers with trying to illustrate a point at oral argument with a hypothetical. First, unless perfectly articulated, it will simply add more confusion than clarity. Second, unless it is well thought out, a member of the court will immediately pick out a distinction between the hypothetical and the actual case before the court.

Notwithstanding that cautionary note, two of the finest Supreme Court advocates, Charles Alan Wright and John Roberts, on occasion used hypotheticals in their arguments to illustrate their points. But those attorneys put considerable care into constructing their hypotheticals before attempting to use them in court. In *Ruhrgas AG v. Marathon Oil Co.*,[9] Professor Wright introduced a hypothetical of his own, but this example worked only because he did it with a self-effacing sense of humor and the justices had such great respect for him that they let him get away with its length and complexity:

> QUESTION: Well, is there not a value to Federalism in deciding subject-matter jurisdiction first in an instance like this, so that in the event it does not exist, the State can address its own long-arm statute?
>
> MR. WRIGHT: I wonder if I could answer that by putting to you a hypothetical.
>
> QUESTION: So long as you answer the hypothetical for me.
>
> (Laughter.)
>
> MR. WRIGHT: I'm surely going to answer the hypothetical. In fact, I think it's self-answering. I hope so. Let us suppose that in this case our only argument for Federal jurisdiction was fraudulent joinder and therefore diversity, an argument that Norge should not have been a party and then there would have been complete diversity, and that

9. *Ruhrgas AG v. Marathon Oil Co.*, 526 U.S. 574, 119 S.Ct. 1563 (1999).

the basis of the argument for fraudulent joinder is that even if there was personal jurisdiction with regard to the claims of Marathon there was not personal jurisdiction with regard to the claims of Norge. And let us suppose that the Federal court says no, you were wrong, there is personal jurisdiction over Norge's claim, therefore Norge is properly a party, therefore there is no diversity, and remands the case to the State court. In my submission we could not then come in and seek to relitigate the issue in State court of whether there was personal jurisdiction of the claims of Norge against us. That would have been an issue determined by Federal court and, under *Baldwin v. Iowa Traveling Man*,[10] we would be barred from ever raising that again. That would mean that the State court would never have had an opportunity to pass on that issue of personal jurisdiction.[11]

After reprinting that colloquy, the advice of professional stuntmen comes to mind when they explain how they jump out of a multistory building and land safely: do not try that one. That is the kind of argument only very few advocates can make in the Supreme Court or court of appeals. No right-thinking advocate without the stature of Wright should come to court expecting to pull that off.

§ 8.2.d   Use Tendentious Propositions

Counsel who make tendentious arguments before an appellate court soon find themselves in trouble. In *C & L Enterprises, Inc. v. Citizen Band Potawatomi Indian Tribe*,[12] the Supreme Court considered whether an Indian tribe had waived sovereign immunity and consented to be sued in a contract with an arbitration clause containing this language: "The award rendered by the arbitrators * * * shall be final and judgment may be entered upon it in accordance with applicable law in any court having jurisdiction thereof."[13] As the argument proceeded, counsel for the Tribe, Michael Minnis, first raised the ire of the court by calling that language "boiler plate" and attributing to it little meaning:

10. *Baldwin v. Iowa State Traveling Men's Ass'n*, 283 U.S. 522, 51 S.Ct. 517 (1931).

11. *Ruhrgas AG v. Marathon Oil Co.*, No. 98–470, 1999 WL 183813 at *5–*6 (Mar. 22, 1999).

12. *C & L Enterprises, Inc. v. Citizen Band Potawatomi Indian Tribe*, 532 U.S. 411, 121 S.Ct. 1589 (2001).

13. *See* 532 U.S. at 415, 121 S.Ct. at 1592–93.

MR. MINNIS: * * * I think this is boiler plate language. It simply made it clear—

QUESTION: What does the fact that it's boiler plate language have anything to do with it?

MR. MINNIS: Well, because it has—what it has to do with is the intention of the parties to waive sovereign immunity. And if it's a contract, it's not a contract tailored any way for a government, or any way for an Indian tribe, you're reading it and it seems like a party—

QUESTION: Then, the answer is, is it not—it isn't a severely specific waiver. I don't see why the fact that it's boiler plate cuts one way or the other.[14]

It turned out that Minnis was arguing for a form of "gotcha": the Tribe had not waived its sovereign immunity, so the reference to an arbitral award being enforced in "any court" was unenforceable. When the justices figured that out, they unloaded on Minnis:

QUESTION: Is it your position that you consent that you waive immunity in Tribal Court?

MR. MINNIS: No.

QUESTION: You don't think it even mean[s] Tribal Court, do you? I didn't understand your answer to Justice Breyer.

MR. MINNIS: Well, I—what I tried to—

QUESTION: You think it means any court that you can get me in without this agreement, which doesn't include any Tribal Court.

MR. MINNIS: That's correct.

QUESTION: Is it a court on the moon? I mean, what is—there are only to my knowledge Tribal Courts, federal courts, state courts, what else is there?

MR. MINNIS: There are any courts that have jurisdiction. It begs the questions which court has—

QUESTION: But, you say no court has jurisdiction because this isn't a waiver of tribal immunity.

---

14. *C & L Enterprises, Inc. v. Citizen Band Potawatomi Indian Tribe*, No. 00– 292, 2001 WL 300633 at *27 (Mar. 19, 2001).

MR. MINNIS: That's correct.

QUESTION: I thought your position was no court had jurisdiction.

MR. MINNIS: That's correct.

QUESTION: You're on the moon.

MR. MINNIS: That's correct.

QUESTION: So, the tribe in effect has asked the contractor to use a term which in fact is totally meaningless, utterly misleading, and apparently an act of intentional bad faith. Isn't that the consequence of your position?

MR. MINNIS: No, Your Honor. The—every—

QUESTION: It means any court having jurisdiction. A-ha, there isn't one of those. Too bad. We didn't mention that. That seems to be the argument.

MR. MINNIS: That is the argument, Your Honor. * * *[15]

Unfortunately, it got worse. Even with that colloquy, some of the justices had not fully grasped the extent of the duplicity in Minnis's position.

QUESTION: I'm asking you what your answer to Justice Ginsburg was, whether you didn't agree whether it was a deceptive contract?

MR. MINNIS: I don't believe it's a deceptive contract as a matter of law because everyone is chargeable with knowledge of the law, which are that Indian tribes have sovereign immunity * * * unless they waive it. And they don't have a clear and unequivocal waiver here and therefore—

QUESTION: So, the tribe brings this contract to the contractor. It says they agree to arbitration in any court having jurisdiction, but it really doesn't grant anything that way.

MR. MINNIS: Absent from something from the tribe, that's correct, Your Honor.[16]

---

15. *Id*. at *31–*33.   **16.** *Id*. at *37.

That is a sure way to lose a case, 9–0, in the Supreme Court.[17] As soon as Minnis conceded that his client's position was based on a bad-faith interpretation of the contract that gave the opposing party to the contract no recourse, he completely lost the court.

§ 8.2.e Lead Off With a Proposition that Generates Questions

The opening moments of any appellate argument are critical for establishing the advocate's credibility before the court. The advocate must articulate the key theme she hopes to develop in the argument and create a bond with the court. The advocate can quickly get off track if the opening sentences of an argument spark questions or raise doubts about whether the court should have confidence in the advocate.

In *Richards v. Wisconsin*,[18] the Supreme Court considered the second case addressing the parameters of the constitutional rule that officers must generally knock and announce their presence before executing a warrant. (The first was *Wilson v. Arkansas*.[19]) In *Richards*, the Wisconsin Supreme Court had held that officers in drug cases did not need to knock and announce their presence because to do so would enable drug dealers inside the premises to destroy evidence. Petitioner's counsel, David Karpe, obviously sought a dramatic way to begin his argument that the Constitution should not permit a blanket exception to the rule announced in *Wilson v. Arkansas* that officers must knock and announce before executing a warrant. But the way he chose to be dramatic was ill-conceived. This excerpt shows just how quickly Karpe's argument degenerated:

> CHIEF JUSTICE REHNQUIST: We'll hear argument next in Number 96–5955, *Steiney Richards v. Wisconsin*. Mr. Karpe, you may proceed whenever you're ready.
>
> MR. KARPE: Mr. Chief Justice, and may it please the Court: This case presents the issue of whether the Fourth Amendment prohibits a blanket exception to the knock-and-announce rule in drug-dealing cases. This case turns on the sanctity of the home, the ultimate private place—

---

17. *See* 532 U.S. at 413, 121 S.Ct. at 1592.

18. *Richards v. Wisconsin*, 520 U.S. 385, 117 S.Ct. 1416 (1997).

19. *Wilson v. Arkansas*, 514 U.S. 927, 115 S.Ct. 1914 (1995). *See* § 4.3.a.

QUESTION: This fellow was actually in a motel room, wasn't he?

MR. KARPE: Mr. Chief Justice, I fully agree, and as one who has been a resident of a hotel room recently I would submit that it is the longstanding doctrine of this Court that a hotel room is a home for the purposes of the Fourth Amendment under *Stoner v. California*[20]—

QUESTION: Is there a case that says a motel room is a home?

MR. KARPE: I believe *Stoner v. California, United States v. Jeffers,*[21] *United States v.*—

QUESTION: I agree with you those cases said that a hotel room is protected by the Fourth Amendment. I don't know that any of them ever said a hotel room is a home.

MR. KARPE: I—Mr. Chief Justice, I believe that those stand for the proposition that the hotel room has the same protection as a home. If it has four walls and a roof, it's a home.

QUESTION: I think that's probably correct, but to say—when you say that a motel room—we're talking here about the sanctity of the home. You're talking about something that is protected under the Four[th] Amendment in the same way that a home is.

MR. KARPE: Yes, Mr. Chief Justice.

QUESTION: The Fourth Amendment doesn't mention homes anyway, does it?

MR. KARPE: It mentions—

QUESTION: The right of people to be secure in their persons, houses, papers, and effects, so I guess the real issue is whether a hotel room is a house. Do you think it's a house?

(Laughter.)

---

20. *Stoner v. California*, 376 U.S. 483, 84 S.Ct. 889 (1964).

21. *United States v. Jeffers*, 342 U.S. 48, 72 S.Ct. 93 (1951).

MR. KARPE: Justice Scalia, I believe that the textual use of house is not referring to the—protecting the structure but rather what occurs inside the house.[22]

In fairness to Karpe, he won the case, with the court holding that there is no blanket exception in drug cases to the general rule that officers must comply with the knock-and-announce rule. But the breakdown of his opening was completely foreseeable and preventable if he had considered how the justices would react to his invoking the "sanctity of the home" in a case involving a drug bust on a person in a motel room. All too often, an advocate's opening words can be so misdirected that the advocate is forced off balance before she barely gets started.

§ 8.2.f *Reargue Facts Decided Adversely Below*

It is axiomatic that the Supreme Court is a court of law, and each year decides only the most important legal issues to come before it. Particularly for trial lawyers who are mired in the facts of their case, the temptation is great to reargue facts to the Supreme Court. An advocate should avoid doing so. Often, the court will be prepared to make assumptions about the record. If the courts below have ruled on the facts or made findings of fact, the Supreme Court is extremely unlikely to revisit those facts. Rather, the justices will decide the case as it comes to them. To reargue the facts in a Supreme Court case risks running up against opposition and, ultimately, to waste time at oral argument.

In a court of appeals case, of course, it may be perfectly appropriate to challenge a trial court's findings of fact as clearly erroneous. But the party seeking to make such a challenge should be clear from the outset of the briefing that it intends to do so. Oral argument is too late to seek to overturn findings of fact without having launched such a challenge in the briefs. In *United States v. Microsoft Corp*,[23] counsel for the company made that mistake:

QUESTION: Let me ask you about and this goes back to Judge Sentelle's original questions to you. The District Court's Finding 228, which you don't challenge, says that

---

22. *Richards v. Wisconsin*, No. 96–5955, 1997 WL 143822 at *3–*4 (Mar. 24, 1997).

23. *United States v. Microsoft Corp.*, 253 F.3d 34 (D.C.Cir.) (en banc) (per curiam), cert. denied, 122 S.Ct. 350 (2001).

the company's restrictions here were not motivated to protect its copyright.

* * * Now, you don't challenge that, frankly.

[COUNSEL]: We have not challenged that finding.

QUESTION: Since your obligation is—since findings of fact are considered binding on us unless demonstrated to be clearly erroneous, I don't see how you can get a reversal on this part of your case.[24]

The court's opinion made clear that Microsoft's challenge was too late: "Microsoft neither points to evidence contradicting the District Court's findings nor alleges that supporting record evidence is insufficient."[25] If the advocate has adequately preserved factual issues, the oral argument has to focus on the key counter facts the advocate hopes to persuade the court to accept. That challenge, however, has to flow from contentions raised in the briefs.

§ 8.2.g Argue About Issues Outside the Questions Presented

An illustration of the foregoing point, as well as this one, occurred in the 1992 case of *United States v. Salerno*.[26] As it came to the Supreme Court on the Solicitor General's petition for a writ of certiorari, the case concerned whether Federal Rule of Evidence 804(b)(1) contained an express "similar motive" requirement, such that former testimony would be admissible if the party against whom the testimony is given has an opportunity and a similar motive to cross-examine the declarant at the time the testimony is given. Respondent's counsel, Michael Tigar, began his presentation with a rather dramatic unveiling of a large stack of documents, but his tactic backfired almost immediately:

MR. TIGAR: Mr. Chief Justice Rehnquist, and may it please the Court:

I hold in my hand nearly 400 pages of grand jury transcript, first released to us after certiorari was granted: 280 pages of Mr. DeMatteis, including 10 separate document

---

24. Oral Arg. Tr., *United States v. Microsoft Corp.*, Nos. 00–5212 & 00–5213 at *239–40 (Feb. 27, 2001).

25. 253 F.3d at 52.

26. *United States v. Salerno*, 505 U.S. 317, 112 S.Ct. 2503 (1992).

requests, with which he complied; and 75 pages of Mr. Bruno, under a subpoena duces tecum. This is the testimony of which the Government said we didn't have a similar motive and, in fact, we didn't develop it. * * *

QUESTION: Mr. Tigar, do I have the question presented wrong? I thought that under the question presented, we are assuming that the Government lacked motive to cross-examine. As I read the question presented, it's whether Federal Rule of Evidence authorizes admissions against the Government of the former testimony of a declarant who has been rendered unavailable by his assertion of his Fifth Amendment privilege, even though the Government lacked any motive to cross-examine, when—

MR. TIGAR: Under the question presented, Justice Scalia, the answer is clearly yes, because the question presented misstates the rule. The rule—

QUESTION: Well, it's an easy case, then. I mean, we took the case to decide the question presented.[27]

The case did prove to be an "easy" case, with the court voting overwhelmingly to reverse,[28] but the argument illustrated the insistence of the court in keeping counsel within the confines of the question presented on the appeal.

§ 8.3   Errors in Citing Materials

Lawyers routinely cite materials in court for the benefit of the judges deciding the case. They refer to record materials, invoke cases, and cite statutes. In drawing upon those sources to support the argument, however, advocates frequently commit a range of errors, which can detract from the substance of the argument and diminish the credibility of the advocate in the eyes of the court.

§ 8.3.a   Cite Authority Incorrectly

When a member of the court requests authority for a proposition that the advocate does not know, the best course is to say, "I don't know" or "I am not prepared on that point." It is completely improper to fake it. The worst sin of all is knowingly to mis-cite authority to a court or to take a snippet in an opinion and

---

27. *United States v. Salerno*, 1992 WL 687558 at *24–*25 (Apr. 20, 1992).   **28.** *See* 505 U.S. at 317, 112 S.Ct. at 2503.

represent that as the holding of the court. By contrast, note how Wright dealt with the Chief Justice when asked about the applicability of a precedent with which Wright was unfamiliar. In *Ruhrgas AG v. Marathon Oil Co.*,[1] the Chief Justice invoked the case of *Treinies v. Sunshine Mining Co.*,[2] for the proposition that a party "could relitigate the issue of jurisdiction if the first court had not had jurisdiction." This is how Wright, the foremost authority on federal procedural law, answered that question: "I'm sorry, * * * I'm not prepared on that case." To his great credit, the Chief Justice then graciously allowed: "Well, I'm not sure that's right, either."[3] As it turned out, the court's unanimous opinion in *Ruhrgas* did not cite *Treinies*.

§ 8.3.b   Cite the Record Incorrectly

Citing the record incorrectly is completely inexcusable in any court proceeding, but to do so in the Supreme Court or court of appeals risks inviting judicial wrath at its most vocal. One of the most regrettable demonstrations of this mistake was in the case of *Shalala v. Whitecotton*.[4] The case concerned an interpretation of two provisions of the Vaccine Injury Act. Counsel for respondent, Robert Thomas Moxley, gave one of the least-prepared performances in recent memory. A reprint of large portions of his colloquy with the court illustrates how tough the questioning can become if counsel is not well prepared and cites portions of the record without being sure those citations are accurate. References to the "table" are to the schedule for payments of benefits to a person under certain criteria:

QUESTION: That's one of your arguments. And alternatively you argue, under the table, that the seizure within 3 days, or whatever the period was, was the first symptom of serious aggravation.

MR. MOXLEY: That is correct, Your Honor.

QUESTION: So you have two alternative arguments.

MR. MOXLEY: That is correct.

§ 8.3

1. *Ruhrgas AG v. Marathon Oil Co.*, 1999 WL 183813 at *9 (1999).

2. *Treinies v. Sunshine Mining Co.*, 309 U.S. 693, 60 S.Ct. 464 (1939).

3. *Ruhrgas AG v. Marathon Oil Co.*, 1999 WL 183813 at *9.

4. *Shalala v. Whitecotton*, 514 U.S. 268, 115 S.Ct. 1477 (1995).

QUESTION: Where did the finder of fact conclude as to that?

MR. MOXLEY: The finder—

QUESTION: I mean, surely that's a factual question.

MR. MOXLEY: The finder of fact found that we technically fit the table, but that maybe Congress did not intend for the table to be literally applied.

QUESTION: Can you point to the words in the finder of fact's findings that say what you've just summarized?

MR. MOXLEY: There is a footnote. One would have to look in the petition for writ, and have to look for the special master's decision. Page 27a of the petition for writ of certiorari.[5]

The problem was, the justices actually looked at page 27a of the petition appendix and did not find counsel's reference. A few minutes later, this colloquy ensued:

QUESTION: Mr. Moxley, may I come back to Justice Ginsburg's question about what the finder of fact had to say about aggravation? You referred us to page 27a, and footnote 4. I have read it now three times, and I find not a word about aggravation. It says nothing about aggravation.

MR. MOXLEY: The special master went into the question of comparing the ultimate condition, consistency of ultimate conditions.

QUESTION: This is the closest you can find to a finding by the special master that this was a significant aggravation—

MR. MOXLEY: No, Your Honor.

QUESTION: Page 27a.

MR. MOXLEY: No, Your Honor.

QUESTION: Well, give me another page.

MR. MOXLEY: That is the—

---

5. *Shalala v. Whitecotton*, No. 94–372, 1995 WL 116213 at *31–*32 (Feb. 28, 1995).

QUESTION: I don't find a mention of aggravation on page 27.

MR. MOXLEY: I agree. I—

QUESTION: Well then, why did you cite that page in response to Justice Ginsburg's question?

MR. MOXLEY: I believe that she was asking me if I was— if I could point out whether or not the court had addressed the issue of a table injury, Your Honor.

QUESTION: I thought it was aggravation.

MR. MOXLEY: I believe that—

QUESTION: Well, I'll ask you. Aggravation. * * * Where did the finder of fact find an aggravation?

MR. MOXLEY: The finder of fact used the *Massoci* test as articulated—as ostensibly argued in my brief, which was to compare the ultimate condition of the speculative—compare the ultimate condition to the outcome from the speculative organic brain syndrome. * * *

QUESTION: I think what you're saying is, not at all.

MR. MOXLEY: Not at all, properly. That is correct, Your Honor.

QUESTION: Not at all, that the finder of fact did not find any aggravation.

MR. MOXLEY: No. He addressed aggravation at page 36a.[6]

Moxley's citation to page 27a might have been forgivable as an inadvertent error or misstatement. The problem was, aggravation was not addressed on page 36a, either:

QUESTION: Where on 36a does the special master talk factually about aggravation?

MR. MOXLEY: I don't believe the special master did. * * *

QUESTION: Did the special master anywhere make any factual finding that there was an aggravation? Yes or no.

MR. MOXLEY: No. He found that there was no aggravation. * * *[7]

---

6. *Id.* at *37–*38.   **7.** *Id.* at *38–*39.

That colloquy exasperated the entire court. This exchange followed, which produced one of the harshest statements made in open court by a justice to an advocate:

QUESTION: Mr. Moxley, we've been questioning you several times about findings of aggravation. You answered me just a moment ago that the special master made no finding. Now Justice Ginsburg points out that he made a very express finding. How can you stand up there at the rostrum and give these totally inconsistent answers?

MR MOXLEY: I'm sorry, Your Honor. * * *

QUESTION: Well, you should be.

MR. MOXLEY: I don't mean to confuse the court.

QUESTION: Well, you—perhaps you haven't confused us so much as just made us gravely wonder, you know, how well-prepared you are for this argument.

MR. MOXLEY: Your Honor, it is our assertion that the onset of a residual seizure disorder in table time is a significant—

QUESTION: Your time has expired.[8]

No counsel ever wants to have that kind of tongue-lashing from any court, much less the Supreme Court of the United States. But an attorney certainly faces that risk by incorrectly citing the record, giving inconsistent answers, and demonstrating a complete lack of preparation.

§ 8.3.c   Cite Record Materials the Court Cannot Easily Find

Because the exchanges between the court and counsel in an oral argument can be very rapid, counsel must be prepared to refer quickly to supporting materials in the record to justify a particular argument or position. When doing so, an advocate must be extremely careful that a member of the court interested in looking at that reference can easily find it, as the colloquy from *Shalala* just demonstrated. In *Glickman v. Wileman Brothers & Elliott, Inc.*,[9] the Supreme Court considered whether the Department of Agricul-

---

8. *Id.* at *39–*40.

9. *Glickman v. Wileman Bros. & Elliott, Inc.*, 521 U.S. 457, 117 S.Ct. 2130 (1997).

ture could require agricultural producers of peaches, plums, and nectarines to provide funds to conduct an advertising campaign of generic fruit. Thomas Campagne, counsel for the agricultural producers, immediately got off on the wrong foot with the court by referring to a document in the administrative record:

> MR. CAMPAGNE: * * * We sue before an ALJ employed by the Secretary of Agriculture. She gave the Government every opportunity possible—as a matter of fact, they stipulated that Exhibit 297, and they made that stipulation at Stipulation Number 57—I'm sorry, 59, that that was the exclusive rulemaking record. When the district court relied on—
>
> QUESTION: Just a minute, Mr. Campagne.
>
> MR. CAMPAGNE: Yes.
>
> QUESTION: That isn't terribly helpful to simply hold up a brief and say that Stipulation Number 59—we don't know what—if you want to make a point, make it so that we can all understand it.[10]

Words to live by. Except that in Campagne's very next statement he asserted that the government relied on Exhibit 297, which caused one justice to ask, "Where is that?" and another to chime in immediately, "Can we find it in something that we have before us?"[11] Only then did Campagne state that the exhibit was on page 134a of an appendix to the brief in opposition to certiorari. But valuable time had been lost and Campagne's credibility before the court was damaged.

§ 8.3.d   *Rely on Citations of Material Not Found in the Brief*

Chapter Three suggests that the advocate doing the oral argument be involved in the writing of the brief. Occasionally, an advocate appears to walk away from positions taken in the briefs. The distinct impression is left with the court that the advocate was not involved in writing the brief or did not think carefully about the arguments when preparing the briefs. Not only are such impressions embarrassing to all concerned, they detract attention

---

10. *Glickman v. Wileman Bros. & Elliott, Inc.,* No. 95–1184, 1996 WL 700569 at *30 (Dec. 2, 1996).

11. *Id.*

from the advocate's position and lead the court to question the strength of the party's contentions. In *Freightliner Corporation v. Myrick*,[12] former Solicitor General Charles Fried represented petitioner in arguing that respondents could not bring state tort actions claiming design defects against vehicle manufacturers that had not incorporated antilock devices in their airbrake systems. Soon after beginning his argument, Fried cited a page of a regulation that had been lodged with the Clerk, prompting a justice to ask, "Where do we find that?"[13] A moment later, Fried cited another item, which drew this rebuke from the court:

> QUESTION: I still don't quite understand, Mr. Fried, just following up with—you were interrupted on—you were going to quote something that was in writing that was in place now, that preempts the State—
>
> MR. FRIED: Yes, Your Honor.
>
> QUESTION: Is that what you just referred to?
>
> MR. FRIED: No. I'm going to refer to another provision as well, which I'm frank to say we didn't focus on until late in the game, but the respondents cite it on page 9, footnote 8 of their briefs, and that is Standard S5.5.1 on page 383 of the lodging. Now, that standard—
>
> QUESTION: That is footnote 8 on page 9 of the respondent's brief?
>
> MR. FRIED: That is correct. * * *
>
> QUESTION: I find this quite unsatisfactory, Mr. Fried, that things that seem to be at the core of the case were either lodged or are in the footnote in someone else's brief.
>
> MR. FRIED: I wish it had been otherwise, Mr. Chief Justice.[14]

Although anticipating what materials will be crucial at oral argument is one of the most difficult parts of litigating a case, an advocate ought to be involved in the brief-writing process and

---

12. *Freightliner Corp. v. Myrick*, 514 U.S. 280, 115 S.Ct. 1483 (1995).

13. *Freightliner Corp. v. Myrick*, No. 94–286, 1995 WL 115558 at *7 (Feb. 22, 1995).

14. *Id.* at *8–*9.

should be thinking about what references, if any, may assist the court at the time of oral argument.

§ 8.3.e   Cite Cases Without Explaining Them

In many Supreme Court and court of appeals cases, the judges and justices likely will have read at least the principal opinions on which the case depends. That does not mean that they have anything remotely close to the same facility with the cases as a well-prepared advocate. In too many arguments counsel will reel off a number of case names, offering various distinctions to the cases. That technique rarely succeeds in persuading the court. Members of the court wonder what the argument is, because they cannot readily discern it when the advocate invokes case after case. A better approach is to crystallize the distinctions into a neater synthesis, explaining the argument or distinction before invoking case names.

Alternatively, an advocate *can* effectively put together a string of case holdings to explain a proposition. Rather than invoking case names without stating the holding of the case, the advocate accurately states the holding of the case (and may mention the case name as an aside for reference). Wright employed that tactic in *Rurhgas*, a case involving whether a district court had to decide whether it had subject-matter jurisdiction before it could decide any other non-merits-based issue in the case. As the foremost authority on federal procedure, Wright's advocacy carried special weight with the court in this case and he was given a more expansive opportunity than less-respected advocates to make his points. Wright's argument was that district courts should have the authority to decide issues preliminary to the merits in a manner that promoted judicial efficiency.

> MR. WRIGHT: * * * [T]he rule of law that I believe your cases support is that a Federal court may make a wide variety of decisions prior to determining whether or not it has subject matter jurisdiction of the case, but that it may not decide any issue that relates to the merits of the case. We believe that that is the line that was clearly drawn in *Steele Co.*[15] and a line that has been drawn in many of the other cases. Your cases say that * * * a court can pass on

---

15.   *Steel Co. v. Citizens for a Better Environment*, 523 U.S. 83, 118 S.Ct. 1003 (1998).

the issue of class certification without deciding whether or not it has subject matter jurisdiction, that was *Amchem*,[16] of course, that a court can hold that a lower court properly exercised its discretion in declining to use pendent jurisdiction without deciding whether pendent jurisdiction existed under the circumstances of the case; that a court can order *Younger*[17] abstention, though it hasn't decided whether it has subject matter jurisdiction, that was *Ellis v. Dyson*;[18] that a court can rule on a tag bar to habeas corpus without deciding whether there was a prisoner in custody, whether there is a final—an independent adequate judgment reason that would bar review by any Federal court.[19]

That passage illustrates many of the attributes of great appellate advocacy that will be described at greater length in the following chapter: Wright avoided the common error of confusing the court by citing numerous cases. Instead, he invoked the court's cases by describing the holdings as statements of black-letter law, educating the court about its cases, and analogizing the court's prior holdings to the rule of law being sought by his client.

§ 8.4   Errors in Handling Members of the Court

In far too many cases, an advocate will diminish her personal credibility by interacting with members of the court in an inappropriate manner. Those types of errors are entirely self-inflicted. Although it is more difficult to say that the commission of such errors will change any outcomes, an advocate who errs in handling a judge or justice brings unwanted attention to herself and away from her client's case.

§ 8.4.a   Interrupt the Court

Few things raise the ire of judges more than being interrupted by an advocate. For an inexperienced counsel, the tendency is natural to want to finish her sentence before being interrupted again. But judges jump in anyway and, unless counsel stops talking, the colloquy ends up being much more protracted and ineffectual—frustrating for the advocate, maddening for the court. As Justice Ginsburg has recounted, "[m]ore than occasionally, I have repeated

---

16. *Amchem Products, Inc. v. Windsor*, 521 U.S. 591, 117 S.Ct. 2231 (1997).

17. *Younger v. Harris*, 401 U.S. 37, 91 S.Ct. 746 (1971).

18. *Ellis v. Dyson*, 421 U.S. 426, 95 S.Ct. 1691 (1975).

19. *Ruhrgas AG*, 1999 WL 183813 at *3–*4.

a lawyer's name three times before he gives way to my inquiry."[1] When a judge starts talking, the advocate should stop speaking, whether in mid-sentence or not. The advocate should permit the judge to finish the question and then proceed with the answer. Apart from being simple courtesy, the court will more likely give the advocate an opportunity to answer fully when the advocate has shown the proper respect and deference to the court by remaining silent when being questioned. Here is an example of what happens to an advocate who interrupts a Supreme Court Justice:

> QUESTION: Well, I'm still so confused by your position here. Do you want this Court to just focus on the fact that—
>
> MR. SHAPIRO: No.
>
> QUESTION: Wait a minute. You didn't even hear the question, and you've already answered it. Do you want to hear the question and then answer it?[2]

Although that colloquy put the problem in stark relief, it is not uncommon for advocates to trip over questions from the bench without stopping, listening to what is asked, and offering the best possible answer.

§ 8.4.b Misaddress a Member of the Court

This is rather obvious advice, but it bears mentioning that an advocate can immediately erode her credibility by misaddressing a member of the court. In *Bush v. Gore*,[3] the case that ultimately determined the outcome of the 2000 presidential election, Joseph P. Klock twice misidentified justices during his argument. The first time, he inexplicably referred to Justice Stevens as "Justice Brennan," who had not been on the Supreme Court since 1990. The second time, he called Justice Souter "Justice Breyer," which drew this icy rebuke from Justice Souter, who is consistently among the most polite justices at argument: "I'm Justice Souter—you'd better cut that out." A short while later, Justice Scalia could not resist the impulse. He began a question with these words: "Mr. Klock—I'm

§ 8.4

1. Ruth Bader Ginsburg, "Remarks on Appellate Advocacy," 50 S.C. L. REV. 567, 569 (1999).

2. *Lawyer v. Department of Justice*, No. 95–2024, 1997 WL 78440 at *23–*24 (Feb. 19, 1997).

3. *Bush v. Gore*, 531 U.S. 98, 121 S.Ct. 525 (2000).

Scalia."[4] If the advocate is not absolutely sure about referring to a member of the court—be it in the Supreme Court or any other court, for that matter—the safest course is simply to call that jurist, "Your Honor." It will not offend any of them, and it will avoid the advocate making a public spectacle of herself by misaddressing a member of the court.

§ 8.4.c Misaddress the Chief Justice

Chief Justice William H. Rehnquist can be a very intimidating presence on the bench. An advocate stands no more than 15 feet directly in front of him. He is not shy about showing his displeasure or disagreement with counsel. Few misstatements raise his ire more than calling him "Judge Rehnquist," "Justice Rehnquist," or some other appellation that fails to accord the full measure of respect for his position as Chief Justice of the United States. That became clear in the 1988 argument of *Teague v. Lane*,[5] when the Chief Justice upbraided the lawyer from the state attorney general's office for calling him "judge." "I'm the Chief Justice, not a judge," he admonished.[6]

§ 8.4.d Ask Questions of the Court Except to Clarify the Meaning of a Question

Perhaps because of the relatively greater informality of district court practice, attorneys arguing in the Supreme Court or court of appeals will occasionally phrase their argument in the form of a question or actually put a question directly to the court. That is a mistake. Even when well-considered, a rhetorical question intended for persuasive effect often falls completely flat in a court. An advocate is better advised to state the argument in simple, direct terms without resorting to any questions or other rhetorical flourishes. Occasionally, a question will be sufficiently unclear that it is appropriate to ask for clarification. The advocate obviously must understand the question before she can answer.

Asking questions for their rhetorical effect, however, rarely works. An unsympathetic member of the court is likely to chime in with an answer that may not necessarily assist the advocate, as in

---

4. *Bush v. Gore*, No. 00–949, 2000 WL 1804429 at *33–*35 (Dec. 11, 2000).

5. *Teague v. Lane*, 489 U.S. 288, 109 S.Ct. 1060 (1989).

6. Tony Mauro, "Supreme Court's Highs and Lows," LEGAL TIMES, Dec. 19, 1988, at 21.

this example from respondent's opening presentation in *Glickman v. Wileman Brothers*:

> MR. CAMPAGNE: Mr. Chief Justice and may it please the Court:
>
> I think there's one thing everybody's missing, and that is, what is the problem? What is the problem with peaches, plums, and nectarines in California that's any different than the other 32 States that grow these commodities?
>
> QUESTION: Disorderly markets are the problem.[7]

Before Campagne could make any affirmative points, he had already been knocked off track by his own rhetorical question.

§ 8.4.e *Defer Consideration of Questions*

This may have been a problem in decades past, when the Supreme Court and the courts of appeals interrupted with questions less frequently and established advocates could count on the judges and justices not to embarrass them in public. At the turn of the twenty-first century, courts are much more prone to criticize counsel for not directly answering questions. The notion that counsel could, as John W. Davis did in the *Steel Seizure Case*,[8] defer consideration of a question from a justice, is a relic of a bygone era.[9]

§ 8.5 Decorum Errors

§ 8.5.a *Attack Opposing Counsel*

In every contested litigation, there is a strong impulse to be extremely unhappy with how an opponent has characterized a case or construed the record or purported to represent the other side's position. That impulse leads many advocates to attack right back and accuse that opponent of impropriety. The Supreme Court or a court of appeals is not the place for such advocacy. There are ways of politely disagreeing with counsel's characterizations, and an advocate should strive to employ them. For example, if opposing counsel incorrectly characterizes the other side's position, a proper

---

7. *Glickman v. Wileman Brothers & Elliott, Inc.*, 1996 WL 700569 at *29.

8. *Youngstown Sheet & Tube Co. v. Sawyer*, 343 U.S. 579, 72 S.Ct. 863 (1952).

9. *See* § 2.4.

response might be: "I believe there is some confusion about our position. If I might be permitted to clarify it, our position is _____." If opposing counsel makes an accusation that an advocate has improperly cited the record or misconstrued something in the record, an advocate might say: "An issue arose earlier as to page ___ of the record. We rely on that passage to support our argument in this way. [Explain.]" As E. Barrett Prettyman, Jr., once wrote, attacking an opponent "is a demeaning practice and one that does not sit well with the court."[1]

§ 8.5.b   Use Sarcasm in the Courtroom

In the *Glickman* case mentioned above, respondent's counsel, Joseph Campagne, committed an infamous faux pas in the courtroom, which led to his being removed as counsel for the company and sued for malpractice after the government prevailed, 5–4.[2] He was in the midst of a colloquy concerning whether the federally mandated generic advertising program improperly created the impression that all types of a particular fruit were the same, regardless of quality or their other characteristics.

QUESTION: To what effect? To the effect that the advertising goes primarily or overwhelmingly to support the proposition that all California peaches are desirable?

MR. CAMPAGNE: Are the same.

QUESTION: Are the same?

MR. CAMPAGNE: Yes. * * *

QUESTION: And you object to that. You'd be here even if they weren't pushing the Red Jim or whatever this nectarine is.

MR. CAMPAGNE: Absolutely, because that's not truthful. I want to tell * * * that you ought to buy green plums and give them to your wife, and you're thinking to yourself right now you don't want to give your wife diarrhea, but green plums—

---

§ 8.5

1. E. Barrett Prettyman, Jr., "Supreme Court Advocacy: Random Thoughts in a Day of Time Restrictions," 4 LITIGATION 16, 20 (1978).

2. Tony Mauro, "Calling a Bad Day in Court Malpractice?" LEGAL TIMES, July 20, 1998, at 7.

QUESTION: Green plums? I would never give my wife a green plum.

(Laughter.)[3]

At that point, the argument completely disintegrated. Four justices simultaneously tried to speak. The justices were embarrassed that Campagne would suggest to Justice Scalia that his wife would get diarrhea from eating a green plum. Campagne's inability successfully to press his legal argument may well have contributed to his client's loss of the case, a conclusion supported in part by the court's decision in *United States v. United Foods, Inc.*,[4] which involved a similar program of government-mandated funding of generic advertising for the mushroom industry. The government argued strenuously that the case was indistinguishable from *Glickman*, but a majority (principally composed of the dissenters in *Glickman* plus Justices Stevens and Kennedy) distinguished that case. Thus, *Glickman* may well have been a case that was lost at oral argument.

§ 8.5.c Show Anger or Frustration with the Court

Although it is rare, on occasion counsel will receive so many questions in the Supreme Court or court of appeals that anger or frustration will begin to show. That seems particularly to be the case with advocates representing classes of litigants who view themselves as disadvantaged in the legal system, such as criminal defendants and Indian Tribes. It is always a mistake to lose one's poise in a court. However important the case may be to the client, the advocate must maintain a sufficient detachment as an officer of the court to provide the best possible representation. Before his death, Justice Thurgood Marshall was asked about the many times he was harassed in and out of courtrooms throughout the South and whether that made him so angry he ever lost his temper. In his avuncular way, he said, "Sure. I got mad all the time. It wasn't right. But I tried never to show my anger. If I got mad that would be used as a pretext for harm to myself and my client. I was taught the following rule of advocacy: 'Lose your head and you lose your case.' I've always tried to remember that."[5]

---

3. *Glickman v. Wileman Bros. & Elliott, Inc.*, 1996 WL 700569 at *53 (Dec. 2, 1996).

4. *United States v. United Foods, Inc.*, 533 U.S. 405, 121 S.Ct. 2334 (2001).

5. This story was recounted in a speech in 1991 by Justice Thurgood

§ 8.5.d Use Humor Inappropriately

Using humor in an argument can be quite dangerous. If the humor is contrived, it can backfire. If it is unnatural, it can fall flat. If it is at the expense of a member of the court or an opponent, it can appear unprofessional. In *Quill Corporation v. North Dakota,*[6] Nicholas J. Spaeth, who was the North Dakota Attorney General at the time, argued to defend a state supreme court decision that upheld the right of the state to tax mail order sales. The state supreme court had done so notwithstanding a Supreme Court decision from decades before (*National Bellas Hess, Inc. v. Department of Revenue of Illinois*[7]), which held that states do not have such authority under the Due Process and Commerce Clauses of the United States Constitution. In effect, the state supreme court had held that *National Bellas Hess* was no longer good law, a rather brazen holding for a state court to make. To confused looks by the justices, Spaeth began, "I suppose I ought to begin with a disclaimer. This is not a Buffalo Bills tie."[8] No one had a clue what he was talking about. Presumably, Spaeth assumed the justices were fans of the Washington Redskins, who were slated to play the Buffalo Bills soon thereafter in the Super Bowl. His purpose became evident shortly thereafter, when a justice commented that Justice Byron White was the only present member of the court serving when *National Bellas Hess* was decided, which led Spaeth to say: "Exactly, and that's why I wore this tie today. As you can see, I'm going to use everything I can to sway that last vote. It is a Colorado buffalo."[9] Now, Justice White did frequently wear a college tie from his alma mater, the University of Colorado, a navy blue tie with golden buffaloes on it. But Spaeth's attempt at humor was turned around at his expense when Justice Kennedy jumped in to say: "Do you have any better reasons?"[10] Barely 45 seconds of Spaeth's argument had elapsed when it began to break down at this self-inflicted wound. As it turned out, Justice White's was the only vote Spaeth received—the one justice left on the court who had

---

Marshall attended by the author. The quotation marks in this instance do not denote an exact quotation, but are intended to capture as closely as possible what the justice said.

6. *Quill Corp. v. North Dakota,* 504 U.S. 298, 112 S.Ct. 1904 (1992).

7. *National Bellas Hess, Inc. v. Department of Revenue of Ill.,* 386 U.S. 753, 87 S.Ct. 1389 (1967).

8. *Quill Corp. v. North Dakota,* No. 91–194, 1992 WL 687848 at *24 (Jan. 22, 1992).

9. *Id.*

10. *Id.*

signed on to the majority opinion in *National Bellas Hess* being the only one to overrule it in its entirety.[11]

§ 8.5.e Make Statements the Court Can Easily Ridicule

Akin to misusing humor is when an advocate makes inappropriate statements that invite the court's ridicule. In *Regents of University of California v. Doe*,[12] for example, respondent's counsel started inauspiciously by attempting to argue issues outside the question presented in the petition for a writ of certiorari. Notwithstanding a clear rebuke from the court, counsel continued to inject matters outside the issue the court took the case to resolve, which led to this colloquy:

QUESTION: * * * [W]e're only addressing the indemnity question, or are we supposed to decide the whole case? I'm still a little puzzled about that.

MR. GAYER: Well—

QUESTION: Because this focuses on—everything focuses on point 1 in their five-factor test.

MR. GAYER: That's correct.

QUESTION: Does your opponent agree that it would not be satisfied out of State funds even without the indemnity agreement?

MR. GAYER: I don't think so.

QUESTION: Oh.

MR. GAYER: I don't think so, but Your Honor, to respond to your question, I'm not an expert on this Court's Rule 14.1, but I believe that the general question of the Regents' overall immunity is subsumed within the question presented. If I'm wrong, I'm sure Your Honors will tell me.

QUESTION: Well, subsumed generally means a smaller question included in a larger question. What you're saying is that a larger question is included in a smaller question, which is quite different.

(Laughter.)

---

11. *Quill Corp. v. North Dakota*, 504 U.S. at 321, 112 S.Ct. at 1916 (White, J., concurring in part and dissenting in part).

12. *Regents of University of California v. Doe*, 519 U.S. 425, 117 S.Ct. 900 (1997).

MR. GAYER: Well, as I say, I'm here to please the Court—

(Laughter.)

MR. GAYER:—and if that doesn't do so, I'll just move on.

(Laughter.)

* * *

QUESTION: But did you argue in the court below that even without the indemnity agreement the judgment could not have been satisfied out of State funds?

MR. GAYER: Unfortunately, no. I was, shall we say—I won't use the dirty word, but that was an omission on my part.

QUESTION: Well, * * * it was an understandable omission, inasmuch as the Ninth Circuit had held in a number of cases that the State universities were, indeed, the State for purposes of sovereign immunity, haven't they?

MR. GAYER: But those cases are built, I submit, on a foundation of sand. In those—

QUESTION: I understand, but you didn't want to antagonize the district court and the court of appeals. You were there to please them, just as you're here to please us—

(Laughter.)

QUESTION:—and they wouldn't have been pleased at your calling their whole circuit law into question.

MR. GAYER: Well, the point is there the issue wasn't fully litigated, and one of the cases, the *Jackson v. Hayakawa*,[13] the Regents corporation was not even a party. The other cases, *BV Engineering*,[14] *Armstrong v. Meyers*,[15] and the *Mascheroni*[16] case out of the Tenth Circuit, all those cases simply cited either *Jackson v. Hayakawa*, where the—

QUESTION: Yes, but Mr. Gayer, if you did not call into question—I don't think your job is to please the court.

13. *Jackson v. Hayakawa*, 682 F.2d 1344 (9th Cir.1982).

14. *BV Engineering v. University of California*, 858 F.2d 1394 (9th Cir.1988), cert. denied, 489 U.S. 1090, 109 S.Ct. 1557 (1989).

15. *Armstrong v. Meyers*, 964 F.2d 948 (9th Cir.1992).

16. *Mascheroni v. Board of Regents*, 28 F.3d 1554 (10th Cir.1994).

Your job is to represent your client, and if, on behalf of
your client, you did not challenge a line of authority in the
Ninth Circuit, I'm not sure you can challenge it for the
first time up here, despite everybody else's saying how
important it is to be friendly to the Court.[17]

In that example, the justices had a field day with the advocate's
allusion to the opening lines of an argument, "may it please the
Court," to signal their amusement at his wandering afield of the
issue before the court. But that illustration also demonstrates how
perilous a poor choice of words can be for an advocate.

§ 8.5.f   Use Intemperate Language

Because they hear such a high number of oral arguments,
circuit judges and Supreme Court justices typically listen so closely
at oral argument that an advocate who uses intemperate language
will frequently get called on it. If an advocate says a position is
"outrageous," a judge might jump in with a question about why or
how. Words like "ridiculous" are inappropriate to characterize an
opponent's position or a court decision. The court can make those
characterizations if it so chooses. The single best way to avoid
getting interrupted is to articulate each sentence in as reasonable a
manner as possible, so that an advocate does not provide the rope
with which to hang herself.

That tenet of effective advocacy is particularly important when
the advocate is phrasing the relief sought by her client. In *Bates v.
United States*,[18] petitioner's counsel got tripped up by the Chief
Justice's close attention to the precise words used by the advocate
in framing the remedy he sought from the court:

MR. OREN: * * * So what I'm asking of this Court is to
strictly examine the indictment that was brought before
Mr. Bates—that was brought against Mr. Bates.

QUESTION: When you—you say strictly examine, Mr.
Oren, are you suggesting some extremely skeptical scrutiny of the language of an indictment?

MR. OREN: No, not extremely skeptical, Your Honor. I–I
believe I'm using that in the sense that prior to evidence

---

17. *Regents of University of California v. Doe*, No. 95–1694, 1996 WL
700567 at *36–*40 (Dec. 2, 1996).

18. *Bates v. United States*, 522 U.S.
23, 118 S.Ct. 285 (1997).

being taken, the only thing we have to look at is the indictment. If—if there was dismissal after evidence had been taken, then I think that if there was no prejudice shown, then if the indictment was not sufficient, it would still not really—

QUESTION: So here you're saying all we have to look at is the indictment and nothing more than that?

MR. OREN: That's—that's correct, Mr. Chief Justice.[19]

That interruption in the flow of counsel's argument could have been avoided if he had not overstated his position.

§ 8.5.g Be Too Informal With the Court

Some advocates have a tendency to be more informal in a Supreme Court or court of appeals argument than they should. Such informality may extend not only to their body language and word choice, but also in the way they comport themselves in answers to questions. Edwin S. Kneedler and Jeffrey P. Minear of the Solicitor General's Office are great exemplars of how to avoid that tendency. Notwithstanding that Kneedler has argued more than 75 cases and Minear more than 40 cases before the Supreme Court, neither ever crosses the line of decorum with the justices. Both advocates maintain a completely professional manner and show a respect for the justices that is mirrored by the justices themselves toward those advocates in ways that are clearly evident in the courtroom. No matter how well an advocate may personally know members of the court she is addressing, she should maintain a formal decorum with a respectful distance in interactions with the court.

* * *

As these illustrations demonstrate, errors are common in Supreme Court and appellate advocacy, which is to be expected given the intensity of the experience and the stakes involved. People under stress do and say unusual things. Minimizing those mistakes can greatly help the party's cause. Because those errors are so common, an advocate who can avoid making them will earn respect from the court with each exchange during the argument.

---

19. *Bates v. United States*, No. 96–7185, 1997 WL 632965 at *4–*5 (Oct. 7, 1997).

Chapter Nine

ATTRIBUTES OF THE BEST ADVOCATES

Analysis

In the courtroom at the Supreme Court, a brass railing separates the spectators from the section reserved for members of the bar. Attorneys admitted to practice in the Supreme Court check in at a special desk at the court, obtain a card designating them as a member of the bar, and enjoy the privilege of entering the courtroom in the middle of an argument. It is not uncommon for members of the bar to attend an argument in a case of special interest or historic significance. It is also not uncommon for members of the bar to make a special trip just to observe the very best advocates before the court. For even when a spectator knows nothing about a case, the best advocates have a way of expressing their arguments to make their case intelligible. The dueling between a skilled advocate and the justices can be wonderful to watch, even when the case is otherwise obscure. In so few instances in our government does a live performance with spontaneous give-and-take affect the outcome of the decision. The fact that this exchange involves the leaders of a branch of government gives added gravitas to the proceedings.

The best advocates have common attributes. They are uniformly intelligent, well-spoken, and learned in the law. They have prepared their cases carefully and come to court equipped to handle the most difficult questions the members of the court can pose. They have a command in the courtroom that belies the fact that the court is running the show. The respect they elicit from the members of the court is palpable—in the way they listen carefully to the advocate, take notes if the advocate makes a particularly telling point, and challenge the advocate to help them understand the complexities of the case and the implications of their ruling. This chapter describes the attributes of the best advocates and the moments in oral arguments over the past decade that best illustrate those attributes.

§ 9.1   Substantive Approaches

Oral argument fundamentally is a substantive exercise. There is no room for fluff, puffing, or rhetoric. The court wants an oral presentation geared to the difficult issues presented in the case, but one cognizant of the shortness of time. The advocate must get to the point. This chapter begins with substantive approaches because the court is more tolerant of a less-talented speaker if that advocate is rich in substance.

§ 9.1.a   Have a Mantra

The best advocates will have a simple mantra that reduces the case to its bare essence.[1] In *Ohio* v. *Robinette*,[2] the Supreme Court

---

§ 9.1

1. *See* § 6.1.

of the United States addressed whether, under the Fourth Amendment, an officer must tell a motorist at the end of a routine traffic stop whether she is free to leave and whether, if the officer fails to say so, any cooperation from the motorist is presumed to be involuntary. The Ohio Supreme Court had issued a per se blanket rule that, when an officer fails to tell a motorist she is free to leave, if the motorist answers any further questions or permits a search of the vehicle, such actions are presumed to be involuntary and the evidence obtained therefrom must be suppressed if the officer fails to give *Miranda* warnings. The case had broad implications for how traffic stops are conducted. Interestingly, it also arose the same term as *Maryland v. Wilson*,[3] in which state and federal governments urged the Supreme Court to announce a per se rule that officers could order passengers out of a vehicle during a routine traffic stop to further the aim of officer safety. Thus, in *Robinette*, law enforcement interests wanted a totality-of-the-circumstances test to determine when a person was free to leave the scene of a traffic stop, while in *Wilson* they wanted a per se rule that officers could order passengers to exit the vehicle regardless of the circumstances.

During his *amicus* argument, Assistant to the Solicitor General Irving L. Gornstein kept urging the court to adopt the traditional totality-of-the-circumstances test that marks much Fourth Amendment jurisprudence.[4] From the initial questions put to him after the first sentence of his opening, he sought to drive home his point that whether a person would feel free to leave should be assessed by the totality of the circumstances.

> QUESTION: Supposing we disagree with that holding [that a per se rule applies requiring an officer to inform a motorist that he is free to leave], is it nevertheless true that we might affirm the judgment in this case?

> MR. GORNSTEIN: I think that * * * [i]t is possible, if you concluded that on the totality of the circumstances in this case the respondent would not have felt free to leave in light of the officer's conduct in this case, you could affirm the judgment. We would suggest that you go on and

---

2. *Ohio v. Robinette*, 519 U.S. 33, 117 S.Ct. 417 (1996).

3. *Maryland v. Wilson*, 519 U.S. 408, 117 S.Ct. 882 (1997).

4. *See also* § 6.1.

conclude, based on the totality of the circumstances, that he was free to leave at that point in time.[5]

Gornstein thus neatly took the question, emphasized subtly that the Ohio Supreme Court had applied the wrong test, and argued that, under the correct test, its result was wrong. For the government's interest, getting the court to announce the correct rule—a totality-of-the-circumstances inquiry—was of paramount importance. But Gornstein also perceived that how that test was applied in this case would be important, hence his secondary focus on applying the proper test to these facts.

Gornstein then fielded a question from Justice Ruth Bader Ginsburg about whether it was conceded that the officer had ordered the motorist out of the car "so he could turn on the video tape in the police officer's car and have a video tape of what next transpired?"[6] Gornstein responded: "That is correct, but as I was just saying, Justice Ginsburg, it does not matter under the Fourth Amendment what the officer's subjective motivation was, it is what is a reasonable conduct under the circumstances, and under this Court's decision in *Mimms*,[7] as long as the business of that traffic stop was not completed, a reasonable officer can order a person out of the car to issue the warning."[8]

Gornstein was well over halfway into his argument before he was able to seize an opportunity to return to his opening and summarize his affirmative points. Here is what he said:

> "[T]he Ohio supreme court's *per se* test should be rejected, for three reasons. First, this Court has in a wide variety of contexts decided whether there is a Fourth Amendment seizure based on the totality of the circumstances. The relevant inquiry has always been whether under the totality of the circumstances an officer's conduct would have communicated to a reasonable person that he was not free to leave. That is the test that has been applied in street encounters, in airports, [and] on buses."[9]

At that point, Justice John Paul Stevens asked Gornstein whether a person's testimony that he thought he was free to leave was

---

5. *Ohio v. Robinette*, No. 95–981, 1996 WL 587659 at *20 (Oct. 8, 1996).

6. *Id*. at *23.

7. *Pennsylvania v. Mimms*, 434 U.S. 106, 98 S.Ct. 330 (1977).

8. *Ohio v. Robinette*, 1996 WL 587659 at *23.

9. *Id*. at *25–*26.

irrelevant. Justice Stevens was setting a clever trap, which if Gornstein handled incorrectly would have the effect of conceding away the objectively based totality-of-the-circumstances test on which he had based his theory of the case. He had not long before answered questions to the effect that the officer's subjective intentions were irrelevant to the totality of the circumstances. But here, how could he possibly disagree with the notion that the motorist's subjective intention—his own understanding that he was free to leave—was irrelevant? Here is how Gornstein perceived Justice Stevens' trap, and used his mantra to avoid it:

QUESTION: And under that test, is [the person's] testimony he was free to leave therefore irrelevant?

MR. GORNSTEIN: I don't think it is entirely irrelevant, Justice Stevens. I think in this case an admission—

QUESTION: His subjective motivation is relevant, but the officer's subject motivation is not relevant?

MR. GORNSTEIN: Well, it tends to show whether—it's of some relevance, but then you have to go on from there and examine whether—what a reasonable officer would do. It is not dispositive. Similarly, the cases here, what this particular person thought is of some relevance. You still then have to go and conclude—

QUESTION: Well, similarly, then, is what this particular officer thought of some relevance?

MR. GORNSTEIN: It is of some relevance, but it ends up being—

QUESTION: Not controlling.

MR. GORNSTEIN: Not dispositive, because a reasonable officer could always conclude that it is reasonable to order somebody out of the car when you're going to have interaction and you haven't completed the work of the stop.

QUESTION: Is there any difference between a consensual encounter, where the person has never been under detention, and a case where there has been a detention and then it's asserted that the detention ended and the rest was consensual?

MR. GORNSTEIN: I would say that you apply the same totality of the circumstances test, but of course, in applying that test, you take into account in deciding whether at a later point in time something is consensual or a seizure, that at an earlier point in time there was a seizure. That is a relevant factor in deciding, but it does not change the ultimate inquiry, which is whether on the totality of the circumstances at the later point in time the officer's conduct would have communicated to a reasonable person that he was not free to leave.[10]

Gornstein's use of this mantra—the totality-of-the-circumstances test applies when analyzing whether a person has been "seized" under the Fourth Amendment—helped him steer clear of a potentially case-dispositive concession to Justice Stevens. It also facilitated his ability to work through a subsequent difficult hypothetical and kept the court focused on the proper standard to apply in this case.

§ 9.1.b   Answer Questions Directly

The best advocates understand the relative impatience of the members of a court to get an answer to their questions. Virtually all great advocates answer questions with simple, dispositive answers. If a question calls for a "yes" or "no" answer, they give it. But the great advocates also perceive and appreciate when a member of the court is badgering them into making a "yes" or "no" concession that will be used in an incomplete or distorted way. There are a number of different approaches to dealing with this problem. First, if the advocate has answered a series of questions with a "yes" or a "no," he can realistically expect the court to give him some leeway if he suddenly puts a qualifier in the answer before saying "yes" or "no." Another approach is to say, "Yes, but not in all cases and here is why." Or, "Generally, yes." That method softens the harsh effect that can sometimes be produced with a "yes" or "no" answer.

An advocate who fights too hard to avoid giving the answer sought by the questioner simply wastes time and irritates the court. A few very experienced advocates knowingly violate this "rule," but they do so perhaps not appreciating how much it annoys the court. They can get away with it to a degree—judges tend to stop asking them direct questions—but the court also tends to tune them out. Such advocacy obviously violates the cardinal rule of advocacy that an advocate should not alienate the decision maker.

---

10. *Id*. at *26–*27.

There are several reasons why an advocate will not answer a question directly. One is the lack of an answer. Advocates are not immune from attempting a filibuster if it helps them think through an answer to a question. A second is to avoid directly conceding something harmful to their case. A protracted response that does not get directly to the point can sometimes satisfy a court without necessarily providing a direct answer. A third reason for not responding directly to a question is that it is phrased in a manner that may cause the advocate to answer in a potentially misleading way. A questioner seeking a concession will use the best of cross-examination techniques. The best advocates will know going into the argument who on the court is likely to be sympathetic and who is opposed to their case, so a likely opponent can be expected to ask questions designed to trip up the advocate. Listening carefully to the question and pausing before answering can be crucial in such circumstances, as can seeking a clarification from the questioner.

Unfortunately, the most common reason why an advocate fails to answer directly is simply a lack of confidence that "yes" or "no" is the correct answer. Except when the question is far afield from the case, the best advocates typically do not hesitate to give the direct response sought by the court.

§ 9.1.c *Make Affirmative Points*

The best advocates will arrive at court knowing that their principal objective is to use the scarce time they have to accomplish two objectives: address any questions the court has and articulate the best affirmative points that support their case. The reason why the affirmative points become so important is that they redirect the focus of the courts' questions—which typically probe weaknesses in the advocate's position—back onto the strengths of that position. It is axiomatic that, if the argument dwells only on the weak aspects of a case, members of the court are unlikely to come away from oral argument with any positive reasons to vote for that advocate's side.

In *California Public Employees' Retirement System v. Felzen*,[11] Michael Kellogg represented petitioner (known by its acronym, CALPERS) in attempting to persuade the Supreme Court that it should uphold the right of shareholders who were not parties to a lawsuit to object to a settlement agreement struck between share-

---

11. *California Public Employees' Retirement Sys. v. Felzen*, 525 U.S. 315, 119 S.Ct. 720 (1999).

holder-plaintiffs and the company in a derivative action. As the case came to the court, the legal theory on which CALPERS had advanced its position was not well developed. In the Supreme Court itself, CALPERS and its *amicus curiae*, the United States, had come up with a legal theory to support the right of objecting shareholders to appeal when the district court overruled their objections and entered a settlement.

From the outset, Kellogg stressed three characteristics of when objecting shareholders had earned the right to appeal when their objections had been overruled: when they had received notice in the form of a show cause order why the settlement should not be approved; when they appeared and litigated their objections; and when they were bound by the judgment and thus subject to claim preclusion. During his 20–minute argument (the United States took 10 minutes as *amicus curiae*), Kellogg was interrupted 35 times with questions or statements. He was able to make and elaborate on those affirmative points to bolster his argument in response, or as segues from the answers, to 20 of those questions. It was a highly disciplined performance. Although the decision Kellogg sought to reverse was affirmed by an equally divided Court (Justice O'Connor had recused herself), it was not for any want of advocacy. Kellogg achieved that performance through careful preparation. He had thoughtfully constructed his affirmative points and internalized them. The questions became the vehicles through which he articulated those points.[12]

§ 9.1.d   Fill "Air" Time

In almost every oral argument, after the members of the court have exhausted their questions, a moment will occur when the advocate realizes that he has the floor and must make arguments. The intensity of the questioning can make that moment an awkward one, but the best advocates will plan for how they want to fill this unexpected "air" time. In *Dickerson v. United States*,[13] Solicitor General Seth Waxman argued for the preservation of the rule announced by the court in *Miranda v. Arizona*,[14] which the United States Court of Appeals for the Fourth Circuit had held could be supplanted by a congressional enactment. Waxman faced active

---

12. Three years later, the Supreme Court held that objecting class members have a right to appeal without formally intervening. *Devlin v. Scardelletti*, 122 S.Ct. 2005 (2002).

13. *Dickerson v. United States*, 530 U.S. 428, 120 S.Ct. 2326 (2000).

14. *Miranda v. Arizona*, 384 U.S. 436, 86 S.Ct. 1602 (1966).

questioning for the first 12 minutes of his argument time—so active, in fact, that he had been unable even to outline the three points that he hoped to make from his prepared opening. One of those points was that the case to overrule *Miranda* had not been made. As he stated that point, no member of the court immediately interrupted again. Without hesitating, he launched into this argument, brilliant in its succinctness and persuasive appeal:

> Now, why do I say that in our view, because it is certainly—it may be very unusual, but it would not be improper for the Solicitor General of the United States to ask this Court to reconsider and overrule one of its precedents, although in this case we're talking about 34 years and, as the Chief Justice has mentioned, 50 precedents, but let me just list the four reasons why, in our view, the Court—the case has not been made to overrule *Miranda v. Arizona*. First, we think that stability in the law is important, and it is nowhere more important than in this case, given the Court's extremely unhappy experience with the law of confessions under the totality-of-the-circumstances, and the certainty that this Court has repeatedly recognized that *Miranda* provides.
>
> Second, in our view, *Miranda*, as it has been developed and tailored and refined by this Court, has proven workable, and its benefits to the administration of justice have been repeatedly emphasized by this Court and documented by the Court. Third, in its—all of its post-*Miranda* cases, this Court has reaffirmed *Miranda*'s underlying premise, that is that custodial interrogation creates inherently compelling pressures that require some safeguards. And finally, any reevaluation of *Miranda* must take account of the profoundly unhappy experience of this Court that impelled its adoption. Applying the totality-of-the-circumstances test in 36 cases over 30 years before 1966, the Court was simply unable to articulate manageable rules for the lower courts to apply.[15]

As Waxman made that argument, it became clear to many in the courtroom that the court would not overrule *Miranda*. And it did not.

---

15. *Dickerson v. United States*, No. 99–5525, 2000 WL 486733 at *14–*15 (Apr. 19, 2000).

§ 9.1.e　Educate the Court

The best advocates view argument not just as an opportunity to make the points to sway members of the court, but also to educate them about the issues raised by the case. Although the phrase "educate the court" may seem presumptuous, that is in fact what the best advocates do. The law is so vast and a federal court's docket so varied that each argument provides an opportunity to enrich the court's understanding of an area of law. The best advocates try to find something helpful to the case that creates an opportunity to educate the court. That form of educating, as Waxman demonstrated in *Dickerson*, can come in the context of stating affirmative points. When an advocate enlightens the court while also making affirmative points, he is elevating oral advocacy to an art form.

One of the best illustrations of this attribute was by Miguel Estrada in 1994, when he was an Assistant to the Solicitor General arguing in *United States v. Mezzanatto*.[16] That case concerned whether a criminal defendant may waive the protection of Federal Rule of Evidence 410 and Federal Rule of Criminal Procedure 11(e)(6), both of which provide (in identical terms) that evidence of plea discussions is not admissible against the defendant. Estrada displayed many attributes of the finest advocates in this argument, but what really stood out was his ability to educate the court about how plea bargain discussions between criminal defendants and the federal government take place. A former Assistant United States Attorney who himself had engaged in such discussions, Estrada was well placed for this assignment. But unlike some lawyers who fail to apprehend how to use their trial experience in arguing a Supreme Court case, Estrada completely appreciated how to make the court understand the plea negotiation process and to place that understanding in the context of the rule permitting waiver that he was advocating. His argument covered the range of practical concerns federal prosecutors face on a daily basis: in what circumstances they seek discussions with cooperating witnesses and defendants; how false statements made in the context of plea negotiations impede investigative efforts and should be subject to prosecution for perjury; and the different ways in which a guilty plea may be obtained (in the prosecutor's office and before the judge). He informed the court of those processes, however, while advancing his

---

16. *United States v. Mezzanatto*, 513 U.S. 196, 115 S.Ct. 797 (1995).

legal argument that the rules should be construed to permit a defendant to waive the protections against admissibility.[17]

Former Deputy Solicitor General William Bryson also understood the importance of educating the court. In fact, he was so skilled in this regard and so knowledgeable about criminal law that the justices occasionally asked questions outside the core of the case just to get the benefit of Bryson's knowledge. In *Evans v. United States*,[18] for example, the court considered whether the common law crime of official extortion was incorporated into the Hobbs Act by Congress's use of the words "under color of official right." Near the end of his argument, after he had addressed the justices' question about the core of the case, a justice put to Bryson this question:

> QUESTION: May I ask one other question, just as a matter of information? If we disagreed with your reading of the extortion statute, is there a provision of the criminal code that covers the knowing acceptance of money that the donor expects to be used to pay for a legislative vote or something like that?
>
> MR. BRYSON: I would think you would have to go to the Travel Act, which is the statute that governs interstate travel or transportation, the use of interstate facilities to effect a violation of State bribery or extortion laws. Then you would have to prove, of course, there was some—
>
> QUESTION: But there's no independent, just plain garden variety, like a bribe, that no separate crime other than extortion—Federal crime—for the receipt of a bribe?
>
> MR. BRYSON: Well, except with respect to official—Federal officials, of course. Federal officials would be covered, but with respect to State officials and local officials * * * they would not be covered.[19]

The educating of the court should be respectful and contextual. Lecturing at the court rarely persuades, but when the advocate can provide useful information or perspective within the context of the issues presented, the members of the court are genuinely appreciative.

---

17. *See United States v. Mezzanatto,* No. 93–1340, 1994 WL 757606 (Nov. 2, 1994).

18. *Evans v. United States,* 504 U.S. 255, 112 S.Ct. 1881 (1992).

19. *Evans v. United States,* No. 90–6105, 1991 WL 636267 at *48–49 (Dec. 9, 1991).

§ 9.1.f   Cull Down Distinctions to Problematic Cases

One of the most difficult tasks at oral argument is to distinguish cases. Doctrine is best addressed in written briefs. During the period of reading cases and preparing case summaries, an advocate should spend considerable time thinking through how to articulate distinctions to cases. Those might involve short bullet-point summaries that remind the advocate of those distinctions (sometimes even putting them into argument blocks in the podium binder). An advocate should then test those selected distinctions in moot courts to see how they play with colleagues. Not infrequently, a member of the court will invoke cases—particularly the ones that pose problems for an advocate's position—and ask questions that require the advocate to articulate succinct distinctions. The argument itself is not the time to be offering spontaneously conceived distinctions to cases—members of the court are simply too well-prepared and mentally agile for most advocates to succeed that way. An advocate should not invoke the names of cases in a rapid-fire fashion, because a sling-shotting of case names will often mask the advocate's inability to articulate his argument in simple declarative sentences.

In *Franklin v. Gwinnett County Public Schools*,[20] Joel I. Klein gave one of the finest arguments of the Supreme Court's 1991 October Term. That case involved whether a person who brought a private right of action to enforce Title IX's prohibition on discrimination on the basis of sex could sue for damages. The case arose in a climate of great judicial hostility to the notion of judges inferring rights of action and remedies. Indeed, it was quite doubtful that the court in 1991 would have ruled as it had in 1979 in *Cannon v. University of Chicago*[21] that a cause of action could be implied under Title IX. Given the justices' hostility to the basic proposition that a cause of action even existed under Title IX, it seemed doubtful going into the argument that this conservative court would hold that such an implied right of action could be used to obtain money damages—as opposed to non-monetary relief such as an injunction.

One of the ways Klein so effectively presented his case was by distinguishing carefully among the various decisions that had upheld a right of action under the civil rights laws. His central theme

---

20. *Franklin v. Gwinnett County Pub. Sch.*, 503 U.S. 60, 112 S.Ct. 1028 (1992).

21. *Cannon v. University of Chicago*, 441 U.S. 677, 99 S.Ct. 1946 (1979).

was that the question whether to imply a right of action was distinct from what remedies should be inferred. If the courts could discern an intent by Congress to allow a person to enforce a statute by bringing suit, then the traditional rule should be applied that all available remedies were available, including a damages action.

MR. KLEIN: * * * I'd like to return * * * to the general rule which authorizes damages under an implied right of action unless there is good evidence to suggest that Congress intends otherwise. That rule has been consistently applied by this Court both before and after Title IX was passed, including well into the era when the Court tightened up its criteria for implying a right of action in the first place. In particular, in 1983 and 1984 the Court applied this rule in the *Guardians*[22] and *Darrone*[23] cases to hold that a back-pay remedy is available under both title VI of the 1964 Civil Rights Act and section 504 of the Rehabilitation Act of 1973.

QUESTION: Well, back pay, of course, is not the equivalent of damages.

MR. KLEIN: I agree with that, Mr. Chief Justice, but I think the principle is that in *Guardians* and *Darrone* the reason back pay was found to be available is that once the Court finds an implied right of action it infers the availability of traditional damages. So there is no doubt a difference in remedy, but I think there is not a difference in—

QUESTION: I don't see how you draw upon a case which allowed back pay as saying that therefore damages are available, unless just by a rather distant implication.

MR. KLEIN: Well, I think it is by implication in the sense that I think the reasoning that led the Court to think—to conclude rather—that damages—that back pay is available, that same reasoning applies here. There was, for example, no direct legislative intent that the Court ruled on to say that Title VI would include back pay. I mean, there was no specific or even indirect suggestion. What the Court really concluded is that once we find sufficient indication of a

---

22. *Guardians Ass'n. v. Civil Serv. Comm'n*, 463 U.S. 582, 103 S.Ct. 3221 (1983).

23. *Consolidated Rail Corp. v. Darrone*, 465 U.S. 624, 104 S.Ct. 1248 (1984).

right of action we presume, it's just a natural presumption, that all the remedies are available. We don't pick and choose among them.

QUESTION: This was *Guardians* that you're talking about now?

MR. KLEIN: This is *Guardians*, which I think then was—

QUESTION: I think it's very difficult to draw any very compelling inference from *Guardians*. The Court was split so badly.

MR. KLEIN: I think it is hard to draw it from *Guardians* alone. I agree with that, Mr. Chief Justice. But I think—

QUESTION: What's the other case?

MR. KLEIN: *Darrone. The Consolidated Railway v. Darrone*, which was the year after *Guardians*, where frankly a unanimous Court basically came together, I think, on these principles.

QUESTION: Mr. Klein, I think that our cases in *Touche Ross*[24] and maybe the *Sierra Club*[25] indicate that the Courts won't engraft a remedy on a statute that Congress didn't intend to provide. Do you think that notion has any applicability here?

MR. KLEIN: I don't in the following sense, Justice O'Connor. I think that *Touche Ross* and its progeny stand for the proposition that the Court won't imply a right of action unless it concludes that there is congressional intent to do so.

QUESTION: You think it has nothing to do with scope of the remedy?

MR. KLEIN: I don't, for the following reason. If we agree that once you imply a private right of action that must mean two things. One, Congress intended to allow a judicially enforceable right. That's what a private right, I think, means. It also must mean the fact that it's an implied right is that Congress has left the issue to the courts, because they haven't set it out in the statute or in

---

24. *Touche Ross & Co. v. Redington,* 442 U.S. 560, 99 S.Ct. 2479 (1979).

25. *California v. Sierra Club,* 451 U.S. 287, 101 S.Ct. 1775 (1981).

the legislative history. Now, what I suggest, if you knew that much, which is I think what you know in an implied right of action case, the logical inference is that all remedies are going to be available.[26]

Klein succeeded in persuading a majority of the court—notwithstanding its hostility to the concept of implying rights of action—that, if such a right has been recognized, the traditional rule allows a court to award all appropriate remedies (including damages) to vindicate a person's rights.

§ 9.1.g Understand the Context of the Problem or the Client's Business

Although members of the court principally focus at oral argument on understanding the outer limits of the legal principles that undergird the rationale they are being asked to adopt, not infrequently they will ask questions to better understand the factual context in which the issue arises. Inexperienced counsel, schooled in the notion that a court decides the case based on the record that has been created in the courts below, will often express surprise that judges and justices routinely ask more general questions about the subject matter. The least effective advocates pointedly remind the jurist who deigns to ask such a question that it is, "of course, irrelevant to the decision in the case." Like the hypothetical question that extends well beyond the facts of the case presented, the judge or justice is well aware that the question about context goes beyond the narrow factual situation before the court. And, as with hypotheticals, it is no answer to say, "That's not this case, Your Honor." They know that. But because the decision invariably has broader significance, the court will want to understand better the context in which the issues arise.

Counsel prepared to address that broader context will be in a better position to assist the court. That context may involve the process of taking plea bargains in criminal cases, as in the example of Miguel Estrada arguing in the *Mezzanatto* case.[27] It may be in the broader use of polygraphs, as in Michael Dreeben's argument in the *Scheffer* case.[28] Or it may be in understanding the industry before the court, as in Bruce Ennis' argument in *Rubin v. Coors*

---

26. *Franklin v. Gwinnett County Pub. Sch.*, No. 90–918, 1991 WL 636273 at *5–*8 (Dec. 11, 1991).

27. *See* § 9.1.e.

28. *See* § 7.1.

Brewing Company.[29] A mastery of detail in the broader subject matter of the issue can inspire confidence in the court that the advocate can be trusted and will provide the type of information that will facilitate the court's decision making.

§ 9.1.h   Research Answers to Questions that May Arise

An advocate's understanding of a case deepens with each increment of significant time spent thinking about it. That is true even when the attorney has filed a reply brief and is preparing to argue the case. An advocate should spend time conducting legal research between the filing of the briefs and the oral argument. Sometimes that research runs to ground issues intentionally left open in the brief; sometimes to close holes that did not seem so wide or significant when writing the brief but now seem much more significant. An advocate who can anticipate a question and provide an answer that conveys additional research builds credibility with the court.

§ 9.1.i   Stick to the Black–Letter Law

After all that has been written in this book thus far about addressing hypotheticals and analogies, this attribute may come as a surprise. Although the Supreme Court and the courts of appeals will announce decisions that may have broad policy implications, they generally disdain arguments that focus too heavily on such matters. The best advocates will "stick to the black-letter law," as Deputy Solicitor General Michael Dreeben puts it when advising less experienced advocates in arguing appellate cases. By that he means the advocate should ground the argument in the legal tests announced by the court that are analogous or otherwise applicable in particular settings, the statutory language enacted by Congress to address a particular situation, or case holdings from the court—in short, those principles of settled law to which the advocate hopes the court will draw analogies in announcing its decision.

In *Lujan v. Defenders of Wildlife,*[30] then-Assistant to the Solicitor General Edwin S. Kneedler relentlessly invoked black-letter principles of the law of standing to argue that the organizations lacked standing to challenge regulations promulgated by the Department of the Interior. In nearly every answer he gave, Kneedler

---

29. *See* § 4.1.e.

30. *Lujan v. Defenders of Wildlife,* 504 U.S. 555, 112 S.Ct. 2130 (1992).

returned to a principle of settled law. The second question he fielded concerned whether abridgment of a right conferred by Congress could constitute the kind of injury Congress intended to be redressed by a lawsuit. Kneedler responded by conceding that if a statute "defines a statutory right and then says that a person may sue for a violation * * * then standing would result because Congress has defined the right."[31] But he then contrasted the statute at issue—the Endangered Species Act—by pointing out that "the citizens' suit provision does not define any substantive rights. Just as this Court said in *Valley Forge*,[32] the [Administrative Procedure Act] provision, giving any person aggrieved a right to sue, does not define substantive rights, it simply creates a cause of action. So respondents would be required to look elsewhere in the Endangered Species Act for any substantive rights that they would seek to invoke in this case."[33]

At another point, Kneedler was asked whether "the citizens' suit provision would enable a citizen to sue because * * * a Federal agency had failed to consult?" His response was a perfect illustration of sticking to black-letter law:

> It would confer a right of action. But again, the article III standing requirements would have to be met. And as this Court has made clear, there are three essential standing requirements that, even under a citizens' suit, a plaintiff has to meet. First, the plaintiff must show that he has suffered some actual or threatened injury; second, he must show that that injury is fairly traceable to the challenged action; and third, he must show that that injury—there's a likelihood that that injury will be redressed by a decision in his favor.[34]

Kneedler's focus on settled principles of law—stated with unerring accuracy—proved very powerful.

§ 9.1.j   *End on a Powerful Note*

Controlling the ending of an argument is extremely difficult. But, if possible, an advocate should try to finish on a powerful note.

---

31. *Lujan v. Defenders of Wildlife,* No. 90–1424, 1991 WL 636584 at *5–*6 (Dec. 3, 1991).

32. *Valley Forge Christian College v. Americans United for Separation of* *Church and State, Inc.,* 454 U.S. 464, 102 S.Ct. 752 (1982).

33. *Id.* at *6.

34. *Id.* at *8–*9.

Indeed, the best advocates will think through the very best way to end an argument and focus on how to get to that point as time is expiring. Solicitor General Theodore Olson, for example, will try to transition from the point he is making to the point on which he wants to end when a minute is remaining in his allotted time. In his view, it is far better to end on a strong note than to use up all of his time.

In *INS v. Doherty*,[35] then-Deputy Solicitor General Maureen Mahoney demonstrated this principle. She was seeking to overturn a court of appeals decision holding that the Attorney General had abused his discretion in denying Joseph Doherty's motion to reopen his deportation hearing. Doherty, believed to be a member of the Irish Republican Army, sought asylum in the United States or deportation to some country other than the United Kingdom, where he had been convicted in absentia for murdering a British officer in Northern Ireland. Mahoney sought to paint Doherty as especially dangerous, as contrasted with other aliens whose immigration cases sometimes made their way to the Supreme Court. Thus, she ended her argument in this way:

> MS. MAHONEY: * * * The facts surrounding the May '80 events that Mr. Doherty admitted were that his group hijacked a van, held the driver captive, forcibly seized a private residence in a residential neighborhood, held the family captive, and waged a gun battle with automatic weapons from the family's living room. The Attorney General found that that conduct was precisely the type of conduct that endangered innocent civilians and could not—and had to be regarded as serious nonpolitical offenses. I see my time is up. Thank you.[36]

Mahoney's effectiveness in persuading the court of Doherty's dangerousness was evidenced not only in the court's decision, which ruled that the Attorney General had not abused his discretion in refusing to reopen the deportation proceedings, but also in a colloquy she had a month later in a different immigration case. In *INS v. Elias–Zacarias*,[37] Mahoney urged the Supreme Court to reverse a court of appeals decision holding that an 18–year-old alien's fear that he would be kidnapped by guerrillas to serve in

---

35. *INS v. Doherty*, 502 U.S. 314, 112 S.Ct. 719 (1992).

36. *INS v. Doherty*, No. 90–925, 1991 WL 636238 at *48 (Oct. 16, 1991).

37. *INS v. Elias–Zacarias*, 502 U.S. 478, 112 S.Ct. 812 (1992).

their military in Guatemala made him eligible for asylum. During the argument, Justice Blackmun pointedly asked Mahoney how old Zacarias was.

MS. MAHONEY: Your Honor, I believe he was 18.

QUESTION: He's no [Joe] Do[h]erty, is he?

MS. MAHONEY: No, Your Honor, he is no [Joe] Do[h]erty, and the Government has never said otherwise.[38]

It is extraordinary for a justice to refer in one argument to another pending case, but Justice Blackmun's reference signaled how successfully Mahoney had persuaded the justices of Doherty's dangerousness.

§ 9.2   Speaking Style

Virtually all books and articles about oral advocacy will emphasize the same aspects of a speaker's style. Posture, suitable hand gestures, a clear speaking voice, inflection for emphasis, and a natural delivery are all features of a polished speaking performance. Those elements, however, are much easier to articulate than to execute. Ultimately, a speaker has to be comfortable in his own skin when speaking in public. Two of the best aids to improving a speaker's own consciousness of style are the videotape and the mirror. Until a speaker sees for himself what he looks like when presenting an oral argument, he will tend not to be conscious of attributes that irritate someone watching.

§ 9.2.a   Make Eye Contact

Making eye contact with the members of the court is an important aspect of a persuasive argument. An advocate who avoids making eye contact commits a number of cardinal sins. He misses an opportunity to persuade, because a judge's reaction to a point can be gleaned through a facial reaction; he behaves rudely, because a judge will expect to be treated respectfully and speaking to someone without making eye contact is impolite; and he risks having the court tune out his argument. It is rare to see counsel admonished for not making eye contact, but in at least one case the Chief Justice has chastised a lawyer for looking at his notes when

---

38.   *INS v. Elias–Zacarias*, No. 90–1342, 1991 WL 636277 at *19 (Nov. 4, 1991).

the Chief Justice was asking him a question. Expecting counsel to look him in the eye, the Chief Justice expressed his disdain when the attorney's first motion was to look at his notes. It is not uncommon for judges whose gaze is not returned to look away from counsel in the universal sign of disinterest in what the speaker was saying.

Counsel also should avoid looking at the large clock located high above the justices. Although the court instructs counsel to keep track of time, that clock is too high to be useful in doing so. At the lectern, an advocate seeking to refer to that clock has to crane to see it, which produces an unnatural posture and gives the impression that the lawyer is seeking divine guidance. On at least one occasion, an advocate was admonished by the Chief Justice not to look at that clock.[1]

By contrast, when an advocate makes direct eye contact, a member of the court invariably will lock on to the counsel. The difficulty then can become breaking eye contact with that member to sweep across the bench to communicate to the rest of the court. In a three-judge court of appeals argument, including the entire court within the attorney's eye contact is relatively easy. The Supreme Court bench is so wide and angled on the ends, however, that counsel must be conscious of not turning his back on a justice, as he might when addressing the junior-most justices, who sit at the far left and far right ends of the bench. The best advocates try to make direct eye contact with a justice in the first couple of sentences of answering a question and then, while transitioning back into an affirmative point, begin a visual sweep of the bench. From that sweep the advocate can generally tell whether a justice is leaning forward to ask a question and also whether a point is understood by the justices.

§ 9.2.b Speak in a Conversational Tone, But With Professional Sincerity

Counsel's first instinct arguing in a large courtroom might be to speak in a big voice to fill up the room. That is not necessary. The best advocates maintain a low-key, conversational tone with the justices. Some of them, like Carter Phillips, Richard Taranto,

---

§ 9.2

1. *See* Tony Mauro, "It's Not Over For Ed Lazarus," LEGAL TIMES, May 10, 1999, at 8.

and James Feldman, reassure the court with their conversational tone. They speak in what Robert Jackson, the former Supreme Court justice and Solicitor General, referred to as a conversational tone, with "professional sincerity."[2] As E. Barrett Prettyman, Jr., one of the finest Supreme Court advocates of the last third of the twentieth century, once wrote, "it should be a joy for the Court to hear you, not just its duty."[3] Attorneys who speak too loudly get admonished, as do attorneys who do not talk into the microphone and who mumble. (Yes, there are such attorneys and they do argue in the Supreme Court and the courts of appeals.)

In most appellate forums, and the Supreme Court is no exception, the more animated a speaker becomes, the more foolish he tends to look. A calm and cool demeanor works best in most appellate arguments because the members of the court look at oral argument as an opportunity to have a conversation with counsel to help solve the legal puzzle presented by the case. It is not a place, like the floor of the House of Representatives or Senate, for rhetoric and more impassioned speech. That said, the advocate must demonstrate "professional sincerity." An advocate has to care about the case, the client, and the cause he is arguing. That sincerity gets communicated by a politely insistent tone that conveys a controlled passion about the case. Of course, some cases and legal positions lend themselves more readily to somewhat more passion, and the advocate's tone must adjust to the equities presented by the case. An advocate speaking more passionately to defend sovereign immunity against a victim of a hideous tort may well cause offense; a respectful, but firm, tone that the position is simply required by the law will be much more effective. The nature of the legal issue thus can affect the advocate's tone.

§ 9.2.c   *Speak in Short Sentences*

For most attorneys, reading a transcript of an oral argument is a painful experience. The syntax of spoken speech is never as clearly expressed as a written brief. The common errors of grammar so assiduously corrected by parents and school teachers come back to haunt even the most skilled advocate. The Supreme Court is not as ideal a forum for speaking in short sentences as some other courts, including most courts of appeals, simply because the

---

2. Robert H. Jackson, "Advocacy Before the Supreme Court: Suggestions for Effective Case Presentations," 37 A.B.A. J. 801, 863 (Nov. 1951).

3. E. Barrett Prettyman, Jr., "Supreme Court Advocacy: Random Thoughts In a Day of Time Restrictions," 4 LITIGATION 16, 19 (1978).

justices so frequently interrupt the advocate. The tendency of most experienced advocates is to say as much as possible of substance in the shortest amount of time. That instinct often leads very fine advocates to speak in long, convoluted sentences, a mode of expression that can be difficult to break.

The best advocates speak in short, clear sentences and maintain their connectedness without getting interrupted by questions. Here is a brief excerpt of Jeffrey Minear's argument for the United States in the D. C. Circuit in *United States v. Microsoft Corporation*,[4] in which Minear was explaining that Microsoft feared that Netscape Navigator would become the standard browser and that applications software writers would write programs that interfaced directly with the browser, which in turn could make irrelevant what operating system ran the computer:

> MR. MINEAR: Your Honor, I think that what we indicated at trial, that by becoming the standard browser did not mean that it had to become a monopolist.
>
> QUESTION: That's not what the District Court found. If you look at Finding 378, the District Court found specifically that Netscape or Navigator had become the standard. It's just exactly what Judge Williams said. How do you explain Finding 378?
>
> MR. MINEAR: By becoming the standard, it did not need to become the only browser. Microsoft realized that simply by preventing it from having a sufficiently broad usage level, it could—it would not attract applications development. And usage is key here. I think that's something that's important to understand in terms of the anticompetitive acts that Microsoft took to protect its monopoly. That as Microsoft itself recognized, that it's usage that determines what's important here, not merely distribution; and the fact that numerous copies of Netscape could have been distributed does not answer the question of whether there was sufficient usage that applications writers would be writing to Netscape and Java as platforms.[5]

---

4. *United States v. Microsoft Corp.*, 253 F.3d 34 (D.C.Cir.) (en banc) (per curiam), cert. denied, 122 S.Ct. 350 (2001).

5. *United States v. Microsoft Corp.*, Nos. 00–5212 & 00–5213, Oral Arg. Tr. at 74–75 (Feb. 26, 2001).

Other outstanding advocates have figured out how to modulate their cadence so that they can give a longer explanation before they are interrupted. Malcolm Stewart has no peer in this respect. Over the years, he has earned respect among Supreme Court justices for the rich substance of his arguments. He has a way of articulating his points in a manner that brings to mind what Jimmy Carter is said to have done in the 1976 presidential campaign to extend the time of his sound bites on the evening news. Carter would slow down or pause in the middle of the thought and then accelerate into the next sentence so that the news editors could not conveniently edit his speeches. Stewart uses a similar technique, with great effectiveness. It is extremely difficult to emulate, and may well be innate to Stewart's personality, but as a means of articulating arguments it is a useful tactic that minimizes interruptions.

§ 9.2.d   Be Respectful, But Not Obsequious

An advocate's tone is important in an appellate argument. The best advocates are respectful without being either arrogant on the one extreme or obsequious on the other. Just because it is a court does not justify the kinds of stylistic genuflections some less-experienced attorneys are prone to give. Counsel is there to represent a client who has every right to have the court—even the highest court of the land—hear its case. The court's job is to decide it. Judges will not respect an advocate who is too submissive. An advocate should politely, but firmly, disagree with a proposition put by the court if the advocate disagrees with it. As Justice Jackson once advised, "Be respectful, of course, but also be self-respectful, and neither disparage yourself nor flatter the Justices. We think well enough of ourselves already."[6]

§ 9.2.e   Use Humor in an Appropriate Manner

Using humor can often fail. But the best advocates appreciate that occasional levity can be healthy in the courtroom. The general rule, however, is that humor is for the members of the court and not the advocates. The advocate serves as the setup man for the judge's wit. Never should an advocate say something humorous at the expense of a member of the court. If a judge or justice makes a dig at the advocate, the best course is to maintain a composed, self-deprecating air. Theodore B. Olson, prior to becoming Solicitor General, had earned a reputation as a fine Supreme Court advocate

---

6. Jackson, "Advocacy Before the Supreme Court," 37 A.B.A. J. at 802.

through his thorough preparation and facile mind at argument. In *Rice v. Cayetano*,[7] he also demonstrated a nice self-deprecating wit:

> QUESTION: If that kind of legislation were expanded to allow any group of American Indians to, whether they're tribal or not to run a casino but nobody else.
>
> MR. OLSON: I'm not sure I'm understanding the question. * * *
>
> QUESTION: The question's very easy.
>
> MR. OLSON: It's the answer that's hard, perhaps.
>
> (Laughter.)[8]

Every now and then an advocate can use humor to affirmative advantage. In his argument in *United States v. Scheffer*,[9] Michael Dreeben pulled off a use of humor rarely seen in a Supreme Court case. Dreeben was defending the constitutionality of a military rule of evidence that precluded the admission of polygraph results. He had to deal with the inconsistency between the United States government's use of thousands of polygraphs each year and its desire to keep the results of polygraphs from being admitted into evidence in military courts-martial. Dreeben found an exceedingly clever way to draw a line between the partial utility of polygraphs and the reasons why they could be precluded from admission into evidence:

> MR. DREEBEN: In investigations, the polygraph is an extraordinarily productive interrogation tool. An enormous amount of confessions are given when a suspect either fails a polygraph or believes that a polygraph is about to smoke him out. I have to say that in that sense there are examiners who believe that it is entirely reliable in this respect, and that it's a great interrogation tool because it's accurate. There are other people who will say that, well, it's a great placebo.
>
> There is a story of a police interrogation in a State system where the police put a colander on a suspect's head and wired it up to a Xerox machine, and then pressed a button

---

7. *Rice v. Cayetano*, 528 U.S. 495, 120 S.Ct. 1044 (2000).

8. *Rice v. Cayetano*, No. 98–818, 1999 WL 955376 at *12 (Oct. 6, 1999).

9. *United States v. Scheffer*, 523 U.S. 303, 118 S.Ct. 1261 (1998).

that produced a picture, a little copy that said, you're lying, every time the suspect answered.

(Laughter.)

MR. DREEBEN: The suspect confessed.

(Laughter.)

MR. DREEBEN: So if a suspect believes that the polygraph is accurate and is about to catch him, then it will be very useful to do that.

QUESTION: It's the tainted morsel of the 20th Century.

(Laughter.)[10]

Dreeben's use of that example was exceedingly well thought out. That story was recounted in an article discovered during the research on the case. While considering how and whether it could be fitted into his argument, Dreeben went to the trouble of tracking down the law enforcement officer who had used the colander and photocopying machine. He was not about to use that story unless he was absolutely sure that it was true. In the argument itself, he waited to gauge the pulse of the court. He would not have used that example if the questioning by the justices had been overwhelmingly hostile to the government's position. And he waited until he received a question about the government's investigative uses of the polygraph before attempting to use it. For the humor to work most effectively, the context had to be just right.

§ 9.2.f Maintain a Professional Demeanor

The best advocates comport themselves in the most professional of manners. Their posture is erect; their grooming impeccable; their gestures emphatic without being a distraction. Most importantly, they are unflappable when under a constant grilling. They continue unflinchingly to take question after question without losing either their composure or the thread of their argument. They expect tough questioning and do not appear in the slightest bit fazed when the court pushes very hard to understand the limits of their position.

---

10. *United States v. Scheffer*, No. 96–1133, 1997 WL 689299 at *18 (Nov. 3, 1997).

§ 9.3   Dealing With Members of the Court

Because the Supreme Court and courts of appeals hold such respected places in our national life, it is sometimes easy to forget that judges and justices are human. One occasionally sees a justice rushing toward the courthouse to avoid being late for court the morning of an argument, the Chief Justice strolling around the courthouse with a law clerk discussing a case, or others in similarly public, less-than-judicial situations. It is therefore not surprising that the judges and justices may not always be in top form for an oral argument. They may be prepared for the case in varying states and may be in better or worse moods depending on other concerns. Though rather obvious, this point bears mentioning because the advocate typically is so focused that he will often lose sight of the fact that members of the court may be in shorter temper than usual or not as prepared on certain aspects of the case. How the advocate deals with the court can be an important component of a successful argument.

§ 9.3.a   Demonstrate Flexibility

Few things can be as irritating for an advocate who is on the brink of making an important point as an interruption from the bench. There are times when the advocate wants to make a point, but is precluded from doing so by questions. And a member of the court hostile to a party's position will recognize when the advocate is about to make a persuasive point and interrupt to ask a difficult question. Few advocates have been able to deal with the court as gracefully as Seth Waxman. In his argument as Solicitor General in *Dickerson v. United States*, Waxman announced from his opening sentence that the government's position was based on three principles, but he was able to state only the first before being interrupted by questions. Well into his argument, he took the opportunity of a question to tell the court that his response was going to be the second point he wanted to make. Just as he finished the fragment of that thought, he was interrupted. This colloquy followed:

GENERAL WAXMAN: The second premise I was going to address, which is that—

QUESTION: Before you get into detail on that, tell us the third one and then argue the second.

(Laughter.)

GENERAL WAXMAN: Okay. The third one is that we don't believe that the showing required to overrule *Mi-*

randa has been made. The second, which really does precede the third one, is that Section 3501 [of Title 18 of the United States Code] in our view cannot be reconciled with *Miranda* and therefore could be upheld by this Court only if the Court were to be prepared to overrule *Miranda*.[1]

A skilled advocate will move nimbly from point to point, making the arguments best tailored to the moment. Rather than tell the court to be patient and wait, Waxman went right with the flow of the questioner without missing a beat.

John Roberts is another advocate who demonstrates that type of flexibility. In *National Credit Union Administration v. First National Bank & Trust Co.*,[2] the court addressed both whether banks had standing to challenge the NCUA's administrative regulations and the merits of the agency's implementation of statutory language that defined how credit unions could form their memberships. Virtually all of then-Acting Solicitor General Seth Waxman's argument had addressed standing. Roberts had only 10 minutes, and, when most of his time also was spent on standing, some justices began to chafe that the merits of the case had not yet been addressed. Here is the colloquy that redressed that problem:

QUESTION: Mr. Roberts, I—I know you're still trying to address standing, but, so far, nobody has even talked about the merits.

MR. ROBERTS: Well, I'll turn to that right now, Your Honor. The test is that the banks must show that Congress unambiguously expressed its intent on the precise question at issue. The precise question at issue is, may the multiple groups in a Federal credit union each have their own common bond or must they share a common bond? The language simply says: Federal credit union membership shall be limited to groups having a common bond. There is no way to tell from that, as a matter of common parlance or technical grammar, whether each group must have its own common bond or whether all of the groups in

---

1. *Dickerson v. United States*, 2000 WL 486733 at *14.

2. *National Credit Union Admin. v. First Nat'l Bank & Trust Co.*, 522 U.S. 479, 118 S.Ct. 927 (1998).

a Federal credit union must share the same common bond. It is simply ambiguous language.[3]

Roberts moved from the law of standing to the merits without missing a beat in a few concise sentences that articulated the black-letter law and then applied it to the statutory language at issue. Roberts made no attempt to make one last point on standing. He took the suggestion to move on to the merits and did so without hesitating or losing his train of thought. And when he stated the merits issue, he formulated the points with precision.

§ 9.3.b   Handle Antagonistic Questions

Every great advocate will develop a particular style for dealing with hostile questions from the bench. Depending on the case, and how persuasive they found the position being advocated, any judge will have an urge to put tough, challenging questions to the advocate. Thus, expressing disagreement with the court can be an important skill for an advocate. In the *Coors Brewing Co.* case,[4] Bruce Ennis demonstrated how an advocate can stand up to a Supreme Court justice with a firm, but respectful, disagreement:

> QUESTION: I'm sorry, you think a statute survives judicial attack if Congress makes findings which it would not survive if Congress didn't, so we're telling Congress to legislate in a certain fashion?
>
> MR. ENNIS: No, no, not at all, Justice Scalia.
>
> QUESTION: Don't we assume that the necessary findings sustain any congressional statute? Isn't that the assumption?
>
> MR. ENNIS: No, Justice Scalia, it's not. As this Court pointed out in the *Sable*[5] case, it was precisely the absence of any congressional findings of fact that resulted in the striking down of that law under the First Amendment. The only point I'm trying to make is that in terms of deference—

3. *National Credit Union Admin. v. First Nat'l Bank & Trust Co.*, Nos. 96-843 & 96–847, 1997 WL 611828 at *35–*36 (Oct. 6, 1997).

4. *See* § 4.1.c.

5. *Sable Communications of California, Inc. v. FCC*, 492 U.S. 115, 109 S.Ct. 2829 (1989).

QUESTION: This would be valid if there were findings of fact—

MR. ENNIS: No.

QUESTION:—but since Congress did not make findings of fact it's invalid?

MR. ENNIS: No. If Congress had made findings of fact, then there would be an argument that the courts should show some deference to those congressional findings of fact. It should never—

QUESTION: But otherwise a statute could be valid, could be invalid, we don't assume that the findings were there?

MR. ENNIS: You simply apply the *Central Hudson*[6] test. There's no congressional finding to which the Court should defer.

QUESTION: That's not my understanding. I think every piece of legislation comes to us with a presumption of validity, with a presumption that * * * it's not a conclusive presumption, but certainly we take it that going in, Congress did its job.

MR. ENNIS: That's why statutes are subjected to judicial review under the *Central Hudson* test, and on applying the *Central Hudson* test, the Court [of Appeals] found there was no evidence—no evidence that in fact accurate disclosure of alcohol content on beer labels would result in strength wars. And to return to your question, Chief Justice Rehnquist, those concurrent findings of fact by two lower courts should be binding here. The Government is inappropriately attempting to reargue the very same evidence it argued in the lower courts.[7]

Note how Ennis kept up his disagreement with Justice Scalia, explained the theory behind his disagreement, and then came back to a related point suggested in a question by the Chief Justice as a means of moving to a topic from which he could make an affirmative point.

---

6. *Central Hudson Gas & Elec. Corp. v. Public Serv. Comm'n,* 447 U.S. 557, 100 S.Ct. 2343 (1980).

7. *Bentsen v. Coors Brewing Co.,* No. 93–1631, 1994 WL 714632 at *9–*10 (Nov. 30, 1994).

An antagonistic colloquy can also tend to raise the ire of a justice, causing the justice to speak more loudly, emphatically, and quickly. Richard Seamon, a longtime Assistant to the Solicitor General before becoming a law professor, had a very clever way of dealing with justices who got louder and more animated as their frustration with Seamon's position increased. Rather than matching them decibel for decibel, or increasing the pace of his delivery, he did the opposite: the more exercised a justice got in questioning him, the calmer Seamon got. It was an amazingly effective technique for disarming the court. Seamon had a way of calming the court, showing that he would not be pushed into a corner by the justices, and earning their respect by his professional demeanor.

Antagonistic questioning can also manifest itself in pointed questioning that grows out of that jurist's judicial philosophy. Most law professors will use the cases in a law school course to teach the various justices' judicial philosophies. Longstanding practitioners before the Supreme Court and the courts of appeals are keenly aware of those philosophies. But there are times when the advocate has no recourse but to fly headfirst into the philosophy of a jurist that will conflict with the advocate's position. In *Lewis v. Brunswick Corporation*,[8] Kenneth Geller demonstrated a fortitude and quickness of mind during the argument. Justice Scalia's aversion to relying on the legislative history behind congressional enactments is well known.[9] He made clear early in his tenure on the court that he would not cite or rely on the legislative history of a statute to better understand the meaning of the text.[10] In *Lewis*, the parties argued over the construction of a provision in the Federal Boat Safety Act. Geller was getting pressed by Justice Souter on the need for a provision in the Act saving certain types of state actions from being preempted by the Act. Justice Scalia was not persuaded by the example Geller had just given and jumped into the colloquy:

QUESTION: I don't think you really need it for that. Do you have any other examples?

MR. GELLER: Yes. Well, I think actually, Justice Scalia, that's precisely what the legislative history again says this

---

8. *Lewis v. Brunswick Corporation*, 523 U.S. 1113, 118 S.Ct. 1793 (1998) (order dismissing certiorari).

9. *See* § 4.2.f.

10. *See, e.g., Wisconsin Pub. Intervenor v. Mortier*, 501 U.S. 597, 620–21, 111 S.Ct. 2476, 2490 (1991) (Scalia, J., concurring in the judgment).

was trying to do, because when it discusses the savings clause, which I should say was added at the last minute—

QUESTION: You're talking to me?

(Laughter.)

MR. GELLER: I'm talking to the Court. But it does explain what * * * [Section] 4311(g) is intended to do.[11]

It is impossible to capture in writing the aggressive manner in which Justice Scalia immediately challenged Geller's invocation of the legislative history, as though an advocate is not permitted to cite the most supportive material simply because it does not comport with a justice's judicial philosophy. But Geller was equally quick of mind in reminding Justice Scalia that, when an advocate responds to a question from the bench, he is speaking to the full court, and not just to an individual member.

§ 9.3.c   Correct Misstatements From the Bench

Because of the quick give-and-take at oral arguments, occasionally a judge will misunderstand an advocate's answer and perceive an inconsistency. It is critical for counsel to be as clear as possible in clarifying matters without being intimidated into making a concession. The government's counsel was presented with that situation in *Carter v. United States*,[12] a case concerning whether bank larceny is a lesser-included offense of bank robbery under the federal criminal code. The government's position that bank larceny is not a lesser-included offense turned on the distinctive elements of bank larceny that the prosecution must prove that are not found in the bank robbery provision. One of those elements is an "intent to steal." From the 1930s, when the bank robbery and bank larceny provisions were enacted by Congress, to 1948, when Congress enacted a major revision of the criminal code, the bank robbery provision had included the term "feloniously takes" to describe the action a defendant must be proven to have committed. In the 1948 revision, Congress took out the word "feloniously" but in none of the legislative materials accompanying the law explained why. In *Carter*, that feature of the statute drew a number of questions from the court. Early on, the government counsel had argued that "[t]he Government has consistently charged these as independent provi-

---

11. *Lewis v. Brunswick Corp.*, No. 97–288, 1998 WL 106133 at *44 (Mar. 2, 1998).

12. *Carter v. United States*, 530 U.S. 255, 120 S.Ct. 2159 (2000).

sions, according to their elements, from the time of enactment up until the present day."[13] Justice Ginsburg then asked:

> So, before 1948, if on a bank robbery indictment, which did not include also a count of bank larceny, counsel for the defense had said, judge, I would like you to give a lesser included offense charge pre–1948. The—the proper answer for the judge would have been, no, it's not a lesser included offense.[14]

The government attorney responded in the affirmative by invoking "the two additional reasons that we've highlighted as differences between these two provisions, that there is no carrying away, asportation, requirement in bank robbery and that for a felony bank larceny to be made out, the prosecution must plead and prove that the property is worth more than $1,000."[15]

Later in the argument, the question of the "intent to steal" element came up again, and government counsel urged the court not to read back into the statute an intent element where Congress had expressly omitted one. One justice, who had skeptically questioned the government attorney throughout the argument (and who would subsequently write a dissent in the case expressing disagreement with the court's decision accepting the government's arguments), heard the advocate's answer and followed with this question: "In 1948 is the [deletion of] felonious. But you told me that—nothing turned on that. I had thought that up until '48, bank robbery meant intent to steal. And you told me no."[16] This was a crucial moment in the argument. The advocate had tried to explain earlier why the deletion of "feloniously" in 1948 aided the government's argument but was not dispositive of it, but had evidently not been clear enough. This was the response to that question:

> [In] our previous colloquy, you asked me whether intent to steal was encompassed within the word feloniously. I said it was. You asked me whether or not that meant that before '48 bank larceny was a lesser included offense of robbery, and I said no because of the other two elements.

The court then saw that counsel was referring to the carrying away and monetary valuation elements.[17]

---

13. *Carter v. United States*, No. 99–5716, 2000 WL 489422 at *30 (Apr. 19, 2000).

14. *Id.*

15. *Id.*

16. *Id.* at *42.

17. *Id.*

There are times when the heat of the moment will flare up and the advocate perceives that a misunderstanding by a member of the court can be devastating to the case. It is absolutely critical for the advocate to maintain poise and respond firmly, but politely, to the court's request for clarification of the issue.

§ 9.3.d   End, if Possible, Before Time Expires

The best advocates appreciate what Justice Breyer once said in a speech is "the value of silence."[18] In other words, if the court is not asking questions, the advocate should make the pertinent points and end the argument. Some advocates go so far as to suggest trying to complete the argument before time expires simply as a signal to the court of the strength of the advocate's position. In one of his arguments, Mark L. Evans had such confidence in his argument and his ability to read the court was so good that he ended his opening presentation in a 30–minute argument after just 12 minutes.[19] Just because it is the Supreme Court does not mean that the advocate has to use all of the time allotted. If the advocate has made the most important points, he should sit down. The more the advocate talks when the justices are not asking questions, the more likely the advocate is to say something that will raise questions, which may, in turn, have the effect of weakening his case. In this respect, an advocate's attention to visual cues can be very important: if the members of the court stop asking questions and stop making eye contact, they are probably trying to signal that the advocate need not say anything more. As Justice Jackson nicely put it, "Time has been bestowed upon you, not imposed upon you. It will show confidence in yourself and in your case, and good management of your argument, if you finish before the signal stops you."[20]

§ 9.3.e   Ask for Permission to Speak Beyond the Red Light

Notwithstanding the point just made, on some occasions the questioning will be so vigorous that the argument will extend right

---

18. This quotation is from informal notes taken of Justice Stephen Breyer's remarks to the judicial conference of the United States Court of Appeals for the First Circuit, Summer 2001.

19. *South Central Bell Tel. Co. v. Alabama*, No. 97–2045, 1999 WL 32890 at *3–*13 (Jan. 19, 1999).

20. Jackson, "Advocacy before the Supreme Court," 37 A.B.A. J. at 861.

up to the end. Unlike in many courts of appeals, which police time restrictions with a relaxed attitude, Chief Justice Rehnquist is typically quite scrupulous about ending an argument when the red light comes on. The best advocates appreciate the Chief Justice's control over the argument and stop what they are saying when they see the red light. If an advocate is making a particular point, he might politely inquire whether he may finish the sentence. If the red light comes on during a justice's question, an advocate should ask the Chief Justice for permission to answer. It does not matter whether the advocate is an attorney making his first Supreme Court argument or the Solicitor General of the United States—the best practice is to request an opportunity to continue. Even as Solicitor General, Seth Waxman would stop in mid-sentence when the red light came on and, if he felt the need to continue, would request permission to do so. The last thing an advocate wants to do is to end an otherwise-successful argument on a bad note by violating a basic precept of modern Supreme Court practice.

In the courts of appeals, practice in this respect will vary. Some courts will make their practices clear through their written rules and through the instructions given to counsel by the clerk. Observing the court in action can greatly benefit the advocate, because prior cases provide the best indication of what the court is likely to do in the advocate's case. If the advocate is unclear whether the court will permit argument once time has expired, the polite and respectful practice is simply to stop, ask for permission to continue, and be brief if permission is granted.

§ 9.3.f Maintain Personal Credibility

Every advocate will encounter the situation of having a client ask him to push the outer limit of what is reasonable. Without some challenge to existing law, there would be no advancement or development in the law. But the advocate facing a hostile bench must know the limits of how far he is willing to push an argument without losing personal credibility. An attorney who argues well in the Supreme Court or the courts of appeals enjoys a special reputation in the bar. No case or client is worth endangering that reputation. An advocate must sometimes make concessions or not press arguments that will strike the court as unreasonable. The finest advocates are those who have talked their client out of making losing arguments and who have come to court prepared to make necessary concessions to advance the client's ultimate interests.

* * *

The greatest appellate advocates each have a distinctive style, but each share common characteristics of flexibility, mental agility, preparedness, and toughness in the face of incessant questioning. They recognize that they are in a forum over which they have little real control, but through diligent advanced work and skill in the moment they establish control through the respect they win from the court. The best advocates demonstrate to the court that their command of the case is so comprehensive that the judges can trust the answers given and know that the advocate will actually help them decide the case. Those advocates practice at the highest levels of the legal profession and make a profound contribution to the law and the history of the country.

Part IV
APPENDICES

Analysis

A. Checklists
 1. Basic Chronology of Preparation
 2. Items to Prepare
 3. Items in Argument Podium Binder
 4. Items to Take to Court

B. Openings of Petitioner/Appellant
 1. Model Openings
    i. Michael R. Dreeben in *United States v. Ursery*
    ii. Laurence H. Tribe in *Cipollone v. Liggett Group, Inc.*
    iii. Seth P. Waxman in *Reno v. Condon*
    iv. Edwin S. Kneedler in *Lujan v. Defenders of Wildlife*
    v. Malcolm L. Stewart in *Ohio Forestry Association v. Sierra Club*
 2. Ineffective Openings
    i. David R. Karpe in *Richards v. Wisconsin*
    ii. James W. Ellis in *Atkins v. Virginia*

C. Openings of Respondent/Appellee
 1. Model Openings
    i. Bruce J. Ennis in *Reno v. ACLU*
    ii. Edwin S. Kneedler in *Bennett v. Spear*
    iii. Miguel A. Estrada in *Degen v. United States*
 2. Ineffective Openings
    i. Thomas E. Campagne in *Glickman v. Wileman Bros. & Elliott, Inc.*
    ii. Michael Minnis in *C & L Enterprises, Inc. v. Citizen Band Potawatomi*
    iii. Nicholas J. Spaeth in *Quill Corporation v. North Dakota*
    iv. Richard Gayer in *Regents of University of California v. Doe*

D. Model *Amicus* Openings
 1. Lisa S. Blatt in *Texas v. Cobb*
 2. Seth P. Waxman in *Nixon v. Shrink Missouri Government PAC*
 3. Jeffrey P. Minear in *New Jersey v. New York*
 4. Barbara B. McDowell in *Toyota Motor Manufacturing v. Williams*

E. Examples of Effective Mid–Argument Advocacy Techniques
 1. Use of Precedent
    i. Seth P. Waxman in *Withrow v. Williams*

263

    ii.   Michael R. Dreeben in *Glover v. United States*
    iii.   Irving L. Gornstein in *Mickens v. Taylor*
  2. Segues
    i.   Jeffrey P. Minear in *United States v. Microsoft Corp.*
    ii.   Paul R. Q. Wolfson in *United States v. Beggerly*
  3. Use of Analogies
    i.   John G. Roberts, Jr., in *Bray v. Alexandria Women's Health Clinic*
    ii.   Edward C. DuMont in *Chickasaw Nation v. United States*
  4. Handling Hypothetical Questions
    i.   Malcolm L. Stewart in *Illinois v. Wardlow*
    ii.   Malcolm L. Stewart in *Florida v. White*
    iii.   Irving L. Gornstein in *Pennsylvania Department of Corrections v. Yeskey*
  5. Advancing a Reasonable, Limited Rule
    i.   Jeffrey P. Minear in *Dusenbery v. United States*
  6. Clearly Articulating the Client's Position
    i.   Malcolm L. Stewart in *Illinois v. Wardlow*
    ii.   Irving L. Gornstein in *Village of Willowbrook v. Olech*
  7. Refuting Opposing Counsel's Argument
    i.   Drew S. Days, III, in *Felker v. Turpin*
    ii.   Edwin S. Kneedler in *Unum Life Insurance Co. v. Ward*
    iii.   Robert A. Long, Jr., in *Kay v. Ehrler*
  8. Candor to the Court
    i.   Matthew D. Roberts in *SEC v. Zandford*
    ii.   Edward C. DuMont in *Chickasaw Nation v. United States*
  9. Closing to Argument
    i.   William C. Bryson in *Custis v. United States*
    ii.   Mark C. Hansen in *Conwood v. United States Tobacco Co.*
    iii.   Theodore B. Olson in *Rice v. Cayetano*

F. Model Rebuttals
  1. John G. Roberts, Jr., in *Toyota Motor Manufacturing v. Williams*
  2. Jeffrey A. Lamken in *Department of Army v. Blue Fox, Inc.*
  3. Stephen J. Marzen in *INS v. National Center for Immigrants' Rights*
  4. Seth P. Waxman in *Reno v. Condon*

Appendix A

CHECKLISTS

1. *Basic Chronology of Preparation*

- [ ] Review Briefs
- [ ] Review Record
- [ ] Review Cases Cited in Briefs
- [ ] Draft List of Questions
- [ ] Draft Opening
- [ ] Prepare Argument Blocks
- [ ] Prepare Answers to Questions
- [ ] Conduct Moot Courts
- [ ] Research Answers to Questions
- [ ] Mark Record Materials and Briefs with Tabs
- [ ] Make List of Key Affirmative Points
- [ ] Develop Segues
- [ ] Prepare Argument Binder Materials
- [ ] Memorize Opening
- [ ] Prepare Briefcase Contents
- [ ] Review Argument Binder Materials
- [ ] Review Briefs

2. *Items To Prepare*

- ☐ Record

- ☐ Key Precedents

- ☐ Affirmative Points

- ☐ Responsive Points to Opponent's Arguments

- ☐ Statutory Text

- ☐ Legislative History

- ☐ Applicable Rules of Procedure

- ☐ Policy Rationale for Rule Being Advocated

- ☐ Hypothetical Questions Concerning Case

- ☐ Legal and Factual Analogies Raised by Issue Presented

- ☐ Opening

- ☐ Closing

3. *Items In Argument Podium Binder*

☐ Opening

☐ Affirmative Points

☐ Responsive Points to Opponent's Arguments

☐ Key Statutes

☐ Brief Chronology of Facts and Proceedings

☐ Summaries of Cases

☐ Questions and Answers

☐ Key Case or Cases

4. Items to Take to Court

- [ ] Argument Binder
- [ ] Briefs
- [ ] Binder of Cases
- [ ] Joint Appendix/Record Excerpts
- [ ] Rules of Procedure
- [ ] Pertinent Statutes
- [ ] Pertinent Regulations
- [ ] Pens
- [ ] Pad of Paper
- [ ] Post-its or Tabs
- [ ] Throat Lozenges
- [ ] Band–Aids
- [ ] Glasses
- [ ] Contact Lenses, Case, and Solution
- [ ] Aspirin
- [ ] Chapstick
- [ ] Tissues
- [ ] Hi–Liter
- [ ] Comb or Hair Brush

Appendix B

OPENINGS OF PETITIONER/APPELLANT

1. *Model Openings*

   i. *United States v. Ursery*, Nos. 95–345 & 95–346, 1996 WL 195163 at *4–*8 (Apr. 17, 1996).

   Oral Argument of Michael R. Dreeben on Behalf of the Petitioner

   MR. DREEBEN: Mr. Chief Justice, and may it please the Court:

   From the earliest years of this Nation, Congress has authorized the Government to seek parallel *in rem* civil forfeiture actions and criminal prosecutions based on the same underlying events.

   Until recently, the pursuit of such parallel actions was deemed to raise no question under the Double Jeopardy Clause. Two recent decisions of this Court, however, *United States v. Halper* and *Austin v. United States*, prompted the courts of appeals in these two cases to conclude that the cumulative remedies of *in rem* civil forfeiture and criminal prosecution violated the multiple punishments doctrine under the Fifth Amendment.

   These holdings are incompatible with the long tradition and practice in this country, and are incorrect for four reasons. First, civil forfeiture is not categorically punitive within the meaning of the Fifth Amendment, and the forfeitures in this case were not punishment.

   Second, an *in rem* forfeiture action is not a jeopardy that can give rise to the protection of the Fifth Amendment when the Government seeks to prosecute

269

the owner of the forfeited property for a criminal violation.

Third, civil forfeiture of property under 21 U.S.C. 881 is not the same offense as the criminal prosecution of the owner of the property for having violated the narcotics laws and, finally, parallel contemporaneous civil forfeiture actions and criminal prosecutions shall be deemed to constitute a single proceeding within the meaning of the Fifth Amendment and therefore not to violate the Double Jeopardy Clause.

Now, the overriding question that is presented in both of these cases and in many others that are being litigated in the lower courts is whether *in rem* civil forfeiture should be deemed to be punishment. Both of the courts below adopted a categorical rule that the forfeiture that is accomplished by application of section 881 should be categorically deemed punishment.

QUESTION: Now, do you think, Mr. Dreeben, that the civil forfeiture could be punitive for purposes of the Excessive Fines Clause and yet not multiple punishment within the meaning of double jeopardy?

MR. DREEBEN: Yes, Justice O'Connor, I do. The question that this Court has considered in determining whether civil forfeitures should be subjected to analysis under the Excessive Fines Clause is really an issue of whether it is sufficiently punitive to trigger the threshold applicability of that clause, and this Court held in the *Austin* decision that civil forfeiture does have such a punitive component both historically and in its contemporary applications, but civil forfeiture has never been deemed so punitive when considered in light of its simultaneous remedial aims as to constitute either a prosecution or a punishment under the Double Jeopardy Clause, and we submit that that is the correct analysis here.

In *Halper* itself, the Court applied a case-by-case analysis to determine whether a particular sanction applied in a particular case constituted an impermissible punishment. The Court's conclusion in *Austin* that categorically civil forfeiture warrants analysis under the Eighth Amendment does not dictate that all civil forfeitures applied in all cases at all times should be deemed punishment with the rather radical consequences that were accomplished by the courts below.

QUESTION: So you think *Halper* maybe could be viewed as a multiple prosecution case and not a multiple punishment case.

MR. DREEBEN: I think that *Halper*, analyzed in the terms that the Court analyzed it, was a multiple punishments case, but it is nonetheless true that under *Halper*, there is some confusion about the exact test that the Court adopted in that case due to different formulations.

But our reading of *Halper* is that a sanction that is rationally related and can be explained by reference to underlying remedial purposes is not to be deemed punishment for purpose of the Double Jeopardy Clause even if there may be some element of punishment associated with that sanction.

QUESTION: And even though it's considered such for purposes of Excessive Fines Clause?

MR. DREEBEN: That is correct, Justice Scalia.

QUESTION: Why? I can't understand why somebody who would write a Constitution would think that a punishment is a punishment for one purpose but not another. I mean, if it's punishment enough that you can't make it excessive, why isn't it punishment enough that you shouldn't get it twice? What policy reason is there?

MR. DREEBEN: The answer to that question goes in part back to the roots and origins of the Double Jeopardy Clause itself. That clause was an embodiment of common law protections that were accorded to finality in a criminal judgment, and they were accorded to the criminal judgment in very specific contexts that this Court has developed over time in a series of rather intricate and complicated rules.

It has never been the case, though, that the pursuit of an *in rem* action against property and the criminal prosecution of the owner of the property for separate violations would be deemed to constitute an impermissible multiple punishment.

* * *

ii. **Cipollone v. Liggett Group, Inc.**, No. 90–1038, 1992 WL 687857 at *3–*7 (Jan. 13, 1992).

Oral Argument of Laurence H. Tribe on Behalf of the Petitioner

MR. TRIBE: Mr. Chief Justice, and may it please the Court:

Although the substance of this case focuses on fair warning to consumers, at a structural level the case is really about fair warning to the 50 States.

The premise of their ability to defend their interests in the national legislative process is, of course, that they be, clearly, warned of what they are about to lose as Congress considers a new statute.

The Cigarette Labeling Act undoubtedly warned the states that with respect to three specific areas—cigarette package labels, cigarette advertisements, and cigarette promotions—the States were about to lose the authority to tell the cigarette companies what health messages they must include, once those companies had put the Surgeon General's warning on their package labels.

But if the Third Circuit is upheld and respondents prevail here, the States will end up having lost considerably more than that, because affixing the Surgeon General's warning to a cigarette companies' packages would absolve that company, prospectively, of any legally enforceable duty, regardless of how longstanding or broadly applicable that duty might be, in the context of that company's communications with the public about smoking and health.

Now in that context, the placement of the Surgeon General's warning on all of the company's cigarette packages becomes an iron-clad guarantee that, as far as the 50 States are concerned, the company can do no wrong. That is if it should deliberately lie or break its promises, no State can make that company compensate its victims providing the deception involves smoking and health.

If the company should suddenly discover some new health information that a similarly situated manufacturer of another product would be duly bound under the background law of the States in some way to communicate to its buyers or to bystanders who are at risk, no State can pressure this cigarette company to communicate that information or to make it compensate those who are hurt because it chooses not to.

Now it is, of course, possible but I think quite remarkable for Congress to take quite that much authority away from all 50 States on the basis of a cigarette company's compliance with this one requirement. I do submit that the Surgeon General's warnings are obviously very important and quite effective, but this result, if correct, treats them as though they were almost a magical cure-all. And the issue, certainly, is whether Congress did that. Did it do it in a way that would have alerted any State at the time that so large a part of its basic body of law was being cut away?

Now, let me say very clearly at the outset, the fact that Congress probably—I say probably because I'm no mind reader—was not thinking in terms of preempting damage actions, as such, is not decisive and I do not intend to rely on it. I will not suggest that all State court damage actions are simply beyond the reach of this labeling act just because the act's invocation in the context of a damage action might surprise some of those who drafted it or voted on it.

The only way to tell what the act does is to look carefully at its text. It's on page 3 of our opening brief, and I think it would be helpful if I focused precisely on it to analyze what legally enforceable duties it preempts.

And I would like, if I might, to begin with duties not to deceive and then turn to duties to warn. With respect to deception—broken promises, conspiracy to mislead by neutralizing—the active wrongs as opposed to the omissions—the issue arises, of course, in part because cigarette companies have so many avenues of communication besides just the package. It's rather hard to deceive people on the package, although I suppose it can be done.

They have advertisements, which are subject to the act's warning requirements, including, as of 1984, Congress' own four rotating warnings. And they have promotions, which they have maintained are not subject to the warning requirements. It's a little ambiguous, but that seems to be the current state of the law. They have what they call advertorials, opinion pieces, where they communicate to the public and do not place the warnings.

One thing I should call to the Court's attention, which I think escaped me the first few times I read the statute, is that failure to comply with the Federal warning requirements as to the advertisements is a misdemeanor, a $10,000 fine, but it does not prevent the preemption provision of section 5 from kicking in. That provision is triggered by compliance with the requirements with respect to the package.

So the issue becomes could Congress have meant, could it have said, does this language say, that once you have stamped the proper warning on the package, you are home free with regard to deliberate torts like lying about smoking and health. Well, certainly not in 1965. I think that's clear.

* * *

iii. *Reno v. Condon*, No. 98–1464, 1999 WL 1075199 at *3–*4 (Nov. 10, 1999).

Oral Argument of Seth P. Waxman on Behalf of the Petitioners

GENERAL WAXMAN: Mr. Chief Justice, and may it please the Court:

We live in an age in which data bases of personal information are widely used in the national economy. They are bought and sold, and they're critical to national marketing, yet their dissemination threatens personal privacy and sometimes safety.

The Driver's Privacy Protection Act is one of a series of laws in which Congress has balanced the benefits to commerce of disseminating personal information against the costs of that dissemination to personal security. Beginning with the Privacy Act and the Fair Credit Reporting Act in the early 1970's, up until the Financial Services Act that was enacted just last week, Congress has acted on a sector by sector basis as new uses of personal data and new threats emerge.

In this case, Congress heard testimony that, while motor vehicle data bases are of particular value in commerce, their dissemination poses unique risk to personal safety and privacy.

Once disseminated, motor vehicle data bases are things in commerce, just as surely as are data bases that belong to financial institutions, cable operators, health care providers, and Congress may therefore regulate a State's discharge of data into the national economy just as it restricts a State discharge of pollutants or other State activities that have a substantial effect on interstate commerce, like operating airports, or issuing municipal bonds.

QUESTION: As I understand it, General Waxman, the Government says it's the Commerce Clause authority here, not anything to do with the Fourteenth Amendment.

GENERAL WAXMAN: That is correct. We have not sought this Court's review on the Fourteenth Amendment questions.

QUESTION: And what are the other examples of Congress' choice to regulate States alone, exclusively under the Commerce Clause power, rather than general legislation?

GENERAL WAXMAN: I think Justice O'Connor, that there are few examples of Congress' attempt to regulate States alone directly, as actors as opposed to the traditional preemption doctrine, because ordinarily what States do in interstate commerce is similar to what other people do, and in this case I think it's very important to recognize that this act, the Driver's Privacy Protection Act, is one of a series of laws that stretches from the 1970's until last week, in which of necessity Congress has been dealing with this kind of evolving information age on a sector-by-sector basis.

QUESTION: Well, that could be the case, but I still have my question, if there are other examples—

GENERAL WAXMAN: Well—

QUESTION:—of Congress' choice under the Commerce Clause power to regulate exclusively the States.

GENERAL WAXMAN: Well, I think the best example that I've come up with, and it's in our brief, is, for example, the regulation of the operation of commercial airports. All commercial airports are—I believe they are all operated by State or municipal entities, and yet Congress has the authority and has given the FAA the authority to [regulate].

* * *

iv. *Lujan v. Defenders of Wildlife*, No. 90–1424, 1991 WL 636584 at *3–*5 (Dec. 3, 1991).

Oral Argument of Edwin S. Kneedler on Behalf of the Petitioner

MR. KNEEDLER: Thank you, Mr. Chief Justice, and may it please the Court:

The Eighth Circuit, in this case, invalidated a regulation issued by the Secretary of the Interior in 1986 to interpret the geographic reach of the first sentence of section 7(a)(2) of the Endangered Species Act of 1973.

That sentence provides that each Federal agency, in consultation with the Secretary, shall ensure that any action it authorizes, funds, or carries out, is not likely to have either one of two consequences: first, jeopardize an endangered or threatened species or, second, adversely modify habitat that is determined by the Secretary, after consultation with affected States, to be critical for the species.

The Secretary, from the outset, has construed the portion of section 7(a)(2) that concerns critical habitat of a species not to apply in foreign countries, because the reference to affected States gives it a domestic focus, and because application in foreign countries would present practical difficulties and impose this Nation's environmental laws and land use planning on foreign countries. Neither respondents nor the courts below have challenged that construction.

In the 1986 interpretive regulation at issue here, the Secretary concluded, for similar reasons, that the portion of the same sentence that concerns actions that affect the species themselves likewise does not apply in foreign countries.

The court of appeals invalidated that interpretation, thereby setting aside the uniform interpretation of not only the agencies charged with administering the act, but also the agencies engaged in furnishing assistance to foreign governments for projects in their countries.

The court of appeals erred in two fundamental respects. First, the court should not have even reached the merits of the validity of the regulation, because the respondent organizations do not have standing to challenge it. The respondent organizations wholly failed to carry their burden of showing that any of their members suffered actual or threatened injury as the result of U.S. assistance to a project in a foreign country affecting their ability to view wildlife.

QUESTION: Mr. Kneedler, how does the citizens' suit provisions affect the standing inquiry?

MR. KNEEDLER: In the first place, we think the citizen suit provision is inapplicable in this case because that refers to situations generally where persons [are] alleged to be in violation of the act. The Secretary's interpretive regulation, which he wasn't even required to issue in the first place, in our view, does not fall within the citizens' suit provision.

The provision that addresses the Secretary's enforcement responsibilities, which is what respondents seem to be directing their suit to, does not govern this sort of regulation. It governs a specific category of regulations under section 4 of the act. So in the first place, we think the citizens' suit provision is inapplicable here.

But moreover, the citizens' suit provision, as this Court has made clear in *Sea Clammers* and other cases, cannot extend the standing—the jurisdiction, case or controversy requirement—jurisdiction under the case or controversy requirement beyond that specified in this Court's cases.

v. *Ohio Forestry Ass'n v. Sierra Club*, No. 97–16, 1998 WL 96282 at *3–*5 (Feb. 25, 1998).

Oral Argument of Malcolm L. Stewart on Behalf of the Federal Respondents, Supporting the Petitioner

MR. STEWART: Thank you, Mr. Chief Justice, and may it please the Court:

The National Forest Management Act requires the United States Forest Service to devise forest plans for each of the units within the national forest system. Th[e] plans are to be revised at 10 to 15–year intervals, and they perform two basic functions.

First, they provide general guidance to Forest Service employees in the management of the affected unit and, second, they serve a public informational function by giving the public general information about the likely management activities within the forest and, while the plans vary widely from place to place, all forest plans contain projections concerning anticipated timber harvesting activities within the national forest, and it's that feature of the plan that's at issue here today.

I'd like to start by saying that in our view it would be misleading to frame the question presented in this case as whether forest plans are reviewable. We're not asking for a per se rule in this case and, indeed, we're really not asking for a special rule for forest plans.

What we're saying is that the Court should examine the particular plan provision that is at issue and ask whether the decision or determination reflected in that provision is reviewable under ordinary principles of administrative law and, in our view, the timber harvesting projections at issue in this case don't meet that test.

The harvesting—

QUESTION: Well then, in most cases the plans aren't unified documents?

MR. STEWART: The plans are unified documents. That is, the plan is bound together. It is a single document, but it contains a variety of provisions and some provisions may reflect decisions having immediate on-the-ground impact, others will not, and the question should be whether the particular plan provision at issue in a case has immediate on-the-ground impact, and—

QUESTION: Can you give me an example of a provision that would have immediate impact?

MR. STEWART: One of the cases we had in the Ninth Circuit this past summer and fall was a case in which the Forest Service amended the standards and guidelines contained in a plan that regulated the manner in which timber harvesting activities would be conducted and the document that adopted the plan amendment said, these amended standards and guidelines will not apply to ongoing timber harvesting activities.

And we were sued in that case and the plaintiffs contended that the agency had behaved unlawfully in failing to apply the new standards and guidelines to ongoing projects.

In the end we prevailed on the merits in that case, but we conceded that that was a justiciable controversy, because the decision not to make the standards and guidelines immediately applicable would have immediate on-the-ground impact.

* * *

2. *Ineffective Openings*

i. *Richards v. Wisconsin*, No. 96–5955, 1997 WL 143822 at *3–*4 (Mar. 24, 1997).

Oral Argument of David R. Karpe on Behalf of the Petitioner

MR. KARPE: Mr. Chief Justice, and may it please the Court:

This case presents the issue of whether the Fourth Amendment prohibits a blanket exception to the knock-and-announce rule in drug-dealing cases. This case turns on the sanctity of the home, the ultimate private place—

QUESTION: This fellow was actually in a motel room, wasn't he?

MR. KARPE: Mr. Chief Justice, I fully agree, and as one who has been a resident of a hotel recently I would submit that it is the longstanding doctrine of this Court that a hotel room is a home for the purposes of the Fourth Amendment under *Stoner v. California*—

QUESTION: Is there a case that says a motel room is a home?

MR. KARPE: I believe *Stoner v. California, U.S.— United States v. Jeffers, United States v.*—

QUESTION: I agree with you those cases said that a hotel room is protected by the Fourth Amendment. I don't know that any of them ever said a hotel room is a home.

MR. KARPE: I—Mr. Chief Justice, I believe that those stand for the proposition that the hotel room has the same protection as a home. If it has four walls and a roof, it's a home.

QUESTION: I think that's probably correct, but to say—when you say that a motel room—we're talking here about the sanctity of the home. You're talking about something that is protected under the Fourteenth Amendment in the same way that a home is.

MR. KARPE: Yes, Mr. Chief Justice.

QUESTION: The Fourth Amendment doesn't mention homes anyway, does it?

MR. KARPE: It mentions—

QUESTION: The right of people to be secure in their persons, houses, papers, and effects, so I guess the real issue is whether a hotel room is a house. Do you think it's a house?

(Laughter.)

* * *

ii. ***Atkins v. Virginia***, No. 00–8452, 2002 WL 341765 at
*3–*5 (Feb. 20, 2002).

Oral Argument of James W. Ellis on Behalf of the
Petitioner

MR. ELLIS: Mr. Chief Justice, and may it please the
Court:

In 1989, this Court, surveying the already growing
evidence from a variety of sources that the people of
this country oppose the execution of individuals with
mental retardation, observed that that growing senti-
ment might some day be manifested in legislation,
particularly by the States, which this Court identified
as the sort of evidence upon which it typically can rely
in Eighth Amendment cases.

The evidence is now clear that the American people in
every region of the country have reached a consensus
on that question. By every measurement and through
a course of legislative enactments that is literally
unprecedented in the field of capital punishment—

QUESTION: What is your definition of a consensus,
Mr. Ellis?

MR. ELLIS: Mr. Chief Justice, the—I would define
consensus—and this Court had discussed it in various
terms in the cases, but I would distill from the cases in
which the Court has described it that it is when the
American people have reached a settled judgment
based on a—

QUESTION: Yes, but I—that's—that's a perfectly
sound phrase, but how do we go about figuring out
when that occurs? I mean, how many States must be
on a particular side? Does the population make any
difference? How about those factors?

MR. ELLIS: Your Honor, there—there has never been
a suggestion by this Court that it differentiates among
States with regard to size, and yet obviously logically
if—if a—an—if a collection of statutes only was found

in the smallest of the States or the States of a single particular region, it would cut against the evidence that there was a consensus.

QUESTION: And—and how many States out of the 50 do you need, do you think, for—for a consensus?

MR. ELLIS: This Court has never suggested that there's a particular number in response to that. And when you look at the cases, both that have found a consensus and that have not, they vary.

QUESTION: Well, but you're saying there is a consensus. So, you must have some figure that you're submitting to us.

MR. ELLIS: I'm—I'm not submitting on the basis of a figure, Your Honor. I'm suggesting that read in their entirety, the Court's cases talking about consensus seem closer to us to be a—a totality of the evidence test but with the requirement that that evidence across the board have found expression unambiguously in statutes.

* * *

Appendix C

OPENINGS OF RESPONDENT/APPELLEE

1. *Model Openings*

   i. *Reno v. ACLU*, No. 96–511, 1997 WL 136253 at *33–*36 (Mar. 19, 1997).

   Oral Argument of Bruce J. Ennis on Behalf of the Appellees

   MR. ENNIS: Mr. Chief Justice, and may it please the Court:

   There are four reasons why the preliminary injunction should be affirmed. The CDA bans speech. It will not be effective. There are less-restrictive alternatives that would be much more effective. And the combination of an imprecise standard, coupled with the threat of severe criminal sanctions, will chill much speech that would not be indecent.

   First, the District Court found as fact that the CDA completely bans a vast amount of speech, all of which is constitutionally protected for adults, from all of the unique means of communication in cyberspace except the World Wide Web, and effectively bans that speech from most of the Web as well. Virtually all speech that is displayed on the Internet in a manner that would be available to adults would also be available to minors.

   QUESTION: Excuse me. You say it banned it from other applications but not from the Web. Is it your contention—and there is much of this in the briefs—that every—every facet of—of cyberspace must be open to this kind of communication? I mean what is wrong with saying, well, if you want to use cyberspace, you have to use the Web?

MR. ENNIS: Well, Justice—

QUESTION: You can't get into—into some of the other—

MR. ENNIS: Justice, Scalia, let me try to answer that question this way. There are 40 million speakers who use news groups, listservs and chat rooms. It is not technologically possible in those means of communication to screen for age. The Government's expert conceded that.

There are about 100,000 Web sites in all. And most speakers cannot afford the $1,000 to $10,000 it costs to have their own Web site. Furthermore, there is a much—

QUESTION: But, look. Let's take printed communications. It is certainly lawful—and we have upheld provisions that require pornographic materials to be kept away from minors and not to be sold in such a fashion that minors can obtain them. This effectively excludes the publishers of pornographic publications from vending their material on the streets in vending machines, where minors can get access to them. Do we say it's unconstitutional because they cannot use that manner of communication? I don't think so. We say tough luck, you have to sell it in stores.

MR. ENNIS: Your Honor, in *Southeastern Promotions*, in *Schad*, in *Bolger*, in case after case, the Court has held, both under intermediate scrutiny and under strict scrutiny—particularly under strict scrutiny— that the possibility of a functionally equivalent alternative does not save the Government. Here the alternative is not functionally equivalent. Let me say why.

In news groups, chat rooms and listservs, you are engaging in an interactive dialogue, a conversation, in which you speak and the listeners reply and you can reply to what they say. They can be outraged. They can be offended. They can have a good point to make.

A Web site is static. What the Government is saying is that the 40 million people who can speak in an interactive dialogue in the other modes of communication on the Internet should post a static message on their

Web site. And maybe the people who are in the news group would come to see it, maybe not. But the speaker would not get any feedback. There would be no dialogue.

Second, there are only 100,000 Web sites. But most of those do not have the screening capability that is required to screen for age. Only those Web sites that have what is called CGI Script capability can screen for age. We know from the record that all of the 12 million subscribers to the Internet who gain access through America Online, Compuserve, Prodigy, Microsoft, the major online service providers, those service providers provide Web site to those 12 million subscribers, but not one of those Web sites can have the capacity to screen for age.

So, in effect, there is a minuscule portion of the population that—for which it is technologically possible to screen for age.

* * *

ii. **_Bennett v. Spear_**, No. 95–813, 1996 WL 668337 at *29–*31 (Nov. 13, 1996).

Oral Argument of Edwin S. Kneedler on Behalf of the Respondents

* * *

QUESTION: Very well, Mr. Wilkinson.

Mr. Kneedler, we'll hear from you.

Mr. Kneedler, there are two questions presented in the petition for certiorari. One is whether the standing under the citizen suit provision of the ESA has a zone of interest test, and if it does, is it a one-sided test. I wasn't able to tell from the Government's brief what the Government's response was to either of those questions. I hope you'll tell us during your argument.

Oral Argument of Edwin S. Kneedler on Behalf of the Respondents

MR. KNEEDLER: Yes. Let me answer that from the outset.

The zone of interest test or formulation, as this Court said in the *Clarke* decision, is ultimately traceable as a gloss on the Administrative Procedure Act when there—for determining when there's a cause of action under the Administrative Procedure Act. At least that's where it originated. So, it's ultimately a question of statutory interpretation.

In our view the proper approach to whether there is a cause of action under the Endangered Species Act citizen suit provision in this case is also a question of statutory interpretation, not by reference to unanchored questions of zone of interest, but by reference to the specific text of the citizen suit provision that we have at issue here.

And as to that, we say that there is—the only cognizable claims under the citizen suit provisions are things for violations of the act, and as we explain in our brief, violations of the act refer to on-the-ground activities that could be engaged in by a private person or by a Federal agency with on-the-ground responsibilities equally. In other words, the citizen suit provision for actions against any person, including the United States, includes situations in which the United States, like any person, might be taking on-the-ground activities that would adversely affect a species.

In our view it does not provide an avenue for judicial review of ordinary administrative action of a regulatory nature. It provides for a citizen suit against those who are regulated, not the agency that is regulating. The APA—

QUESTION: But even if that were true, the Administrative Procedure Act would provide for a suit against Government action, action that couldn't be taken by private individuals—

MR. KNEEDLER: That—that's—

QUESTION:—but can be taken by Government so long as the individual is within the zone of interest.

MR. KNEEDLER: That's correct.

QUESTION: And if the statute requires economic considerations to be taken into account, a person who would be favored by taking them into account is certainly within the zone of interests.

MR. KNEEDLER: Yes, but that would be a suit under the APA.

* * *

iii. ***Degen v. United States***, No. 95–173, 1996 WL 204130 at *25–*27 (Apr. 22, 1996).

Oral Argument of Miguel A. Estrada on Behalf of the Respondent

MR. ESTRADA: Thank you, Mr. Chief Justice, and may it please the Court:

It is undisputed that this civil forfeiture action is directly related to a criminal case that is pending in the same district courthouse against Degen, and that Degen refused to appear to stand trial on the criminal charges.

For two reasons, the court of appeals correctly held that a claimant in Degen's situation may be disentitled from contesting the civil forfeiture action. First and foremost a civil claimant's participation in the civil forfeiture action fundamentally threatens the integrity of the criminal case.

Second, the claimant's—

QUESTION: You say the defendant's participation in the civil forfeiture threatens the criminal case?

MR. ESTRADA: Yes, Mr. Chief Justice, and that is, in fact, our principal argument here.

Our argument starts from the premise that courts always have had the inherent authority to protect against the abuse of their processes by a litigant, and that is precisely what the rule at issue here does.

If a civil claimant is allowed to participate in a civil forfeiture action while at the same time he refuses to stand trial on a criminal case that is based on the identical event, he may then use the very broad civil discovery rules that—to circumvent the very well settled and strict restrictions on criminal discovery.

QUESTION: But couldn't that be dealt with by a judge administering the civil discovery rules?

MR. ESTRADA: That is not true, Mr. Chief Justice, with respect, and in order to understand why, it is useful to note why it is that we have limited criminal discovery in our society. Those rules limiting strictly criminal discovery exist because long experience has taught Congress and the courts that early disclosure of the Government's case in a criminal prosecution often leads to contrived defense testimony—

QUESTION: But Mr. Estrada, wouldn't that be possible even if he appeared in the criminal case, that he could use civil discovery in the forfeiture case to find out the same information?

MR. ESTRADA: That is not so, Mr. Justice Stevens, for the following reason. Congress has recognized precisely the danger that we're pointing to in this case, and in section 20—and section 881(i) of title 21 has given the Government the right to go to the district court and get a stay of the civil forfeiture action pending the conclusion of the criminal case.

QUESTION: Well, why couldn't they have done that in this case?

MR. ESTRADA: Well, I take it that if we had done that in this case, Mr. Justice Stevens, the net—the result would have been that we couldn't get any judgment in the civil forfeiture action because the criminal case can't start while Mr. Degen is in Switzerland.

* * *

2. *Ineffective Openings*

  i. *Glickman v. Wileman Bros. & Elliott, Inc.*, No. 95–1184, 1996 WL 700569 at *29–*32 (Dec. 2, 1996).

  Oral Argument of Thomas E. Campagne on Behalf of the Respondents

  MR. CAMPAGNE: Mr. Chief Justice, and may it please the Court:

I think there's one thing everybody's missing, and that is, what is the problem? What is the problem with peaches, plums, and nectarines in California that's any different than the other 32 States that grow these commodities?

QUESTION: Disorderly markets are the problem.

MR. CAMPAGNE: Well, Justice Scalia, the Solicitor, in answering your question in that regard, I believe misspoke. He indicated that there was a finding that there was disorderly markets—

QUESTION: So—

MR. CAMPAGNE:—and he cites the 1954 act, which doesn't deal with that subject whatsoever. The way the promulgation records show here—because we have an unusual situation that Justice O'Connor spoke about in the *Community Nutrition* case, where we file a 15(a) petition. We sue before an ALJ employed by the Secretary of Agriculture.

She gave the Government every opportunity possible—as a matter of fact, they stipulated that Exhibit 297, and they made that stipulation at Stipulation Number 57—I'm sorry, 59, that that was the exclusive rulemaking record. When the district court relied on—

QUESTION: Just a minute, Mr. Campagne.

MR. CAMPAGNE: Yes.

QUESTION: That isn't terribly helpful to simply hold up a brief and say that Stipulation Number 59—we don't know what—if you want to make a point, make it so that we can all understand it.

MR. CAMPAGNE: Very well, Your Honor.

In that stipulation the administrative law judge said, I've got a problem. I don't understand what some of you are expressing in your questions. I want to give you every opportunity to show me that there's disorderly marketing going on in California but not in the other 32 States, and the stipulation that was entered into is that the USDA relies on Exhibit 297.

QUESTION: Where is that?

QUESTION: Can we find it in something that we have before us?

MR. CAMPAGNE: Yes. It's page 134a of our appendix to our opposition to the petition, Your Honor. In there, they actually stipulate that the Government relies solely and exclusively on Exhibit 297, and I'm paraphrasing, as being the entire rulemaking record regarding the implementation of the advertising program.

QUESTION: It doesn't say exclusively in what I'm reading.

MR. CAMPAGNE: It says, as being the entire rulemaking record—

QUESTION: Oh, okay.

MR. CAMPAGNE:—on the third line, your honor, regarding the implementation of the advertising record with respect to peaches, plums, and nectarines which occurred approximately 6 years after the act was amended. The next—

QUESTION: Mr. Campagne, can I ask you a question?

MR. CAMPAGNE: Yes.

QUESTION: We basically have a constitutional question here, and there are an awful lot of details floating around. Would it make any difference, as a matter of constitutional law, if Congress had made a finding that this particular market had particular problems that justified this kind of group advertising program? Would you still have the same constitutional argument?

MR. CAMPAGNE: It would make a huge difference, Your Honor.

QUESTION: You do.

MR. CAMPAGNE: They would have an easier time with *Central Hudson*.

QUESTION: So you're not saying this sort of program is always unconstitutional.

MR. CAMPAGNE: No, Your Honor. Despite what the *Wall Street Journal* said last week, we're not saying that the beef program has to be thrown out or the milk program has to be—

* * *

ii. ***C&L Enterps., Inc. v. Citizen Band Potawatomi Indian Tribe,*** No. 00–292, 2001 WL 300633 at *25–*27 (Mar. 19, 2001).

Oral Argument of Michael Minnis on Behalf of the Respondent

MR. MINNIS: Mr. Chief Justice, and may it please the court:

An arbitration clause is just that, it's an arbitration clause. It is not a waiver of sovereign immunity and it's certainly not one by the standards that this Court has adopted, which is clear and unequivocal.

QUESTION: Isn't there more here than a mere arbitration clause and let me direct you to the language that concerns me. I'm quoting it from page of the blue brief, page six. The relevant—page six on the blue brief. The relevant language in the middle of the block quotes is this "The award rendered by the arbitrators," I'm skipping "shall be final and judgment may be entered upon it in accordance with applicable law in any court having jurisdiction thereof."

That reference to jurisdiction thereof has to mean jurisdiction to enter judgment on an arbitration award. So, it is describing a court by reference to a certain kind of subject matter jurisdiction that that court has.

When they agree that in effect they will be subject to a court, having that subject matter jurisdiction, and when they agree that they are subject to any court having that subject matter jurisdiction, isn't that a pretty clear waiver and doesn't it go beyond certainly merely an agreement to arbitrate? And doesn't it go beyond merely an agreement to be subject to a court with jurisdiction or with competent jurisdiction? Isn't it pretty darn specific in identifying courts by reference to a certain subject matter?

MR. MINNIS: No, Your Honor.

QUESTION: Why?

MR. MINNIS: This language, as we pointed out before, is boiler plate language in an agreement, a standard form agreement between private parties. The language there in the arbitration clause is merely, closes the loop. The first part of the loop is we're waiving in an arbitration clause our right to go in and have a jury trial on the issue of who has got the damages.

Any contract is presumably enforceable in any court having jurisdiction thereof. All this does is close the loop and say once your arbitration agreement, once you have your arbitration award, it can be enforced in a court of, any court having jurisdiction.

QUESTION: But, it does—

MR. MINNIS: Just like the contract could have.

QUESTION: But, it does take it out of the ambit of those cases that are merely considered references to courts of competent jurisdiction in which the reference to the jurisdiction in those cases is far less specific than it is here. Isn't that true?

MR. MINNIS: In the—you mean in the language of the courts in the cases that said any court of competent jurisdiction?

QUESTION: Yeah.

MR. MINNIS: I think it's just the same thing. I think it's said in a different way. I do not agree with the Justice that the language is interpreted. You have to go in and construe it as you did when you announced it.

I think this is boilerplate language. It simply made it clear—

QUESTION: What does the fact that it's boiler plate language have anything to do with it?

* * *

iii. ***Quill Corp. v. North Dakota,*** No. 91–194, 1992 WL 687848 at *23–*24 (Jan. 22, 1992).

Oral Argument of Nicholas J. Spaeth on Behalf of the Respondent

MR. SPAETH: Chief Justice Rehnquist, members of the Court, may it please the Court:

I suppose I ought to begin with a disclaimer. This is not a Buffalo Bills tie. The question presented in this case is whether the Court should abandon the physical presence test set out it in its 25–year-old decision of *National Bellas Hess* in favor a standard that focuses on the economic realities of direct marketing sales transaction.

This case—

QUESTION: Are you asking that *Bellas Hess* be over-ruled?

MR. SPAETH: Yes, I am, Justice Blackmun. This case arose when North Dakota sued Quill when it refused to collect our use tax. Quill, of course—

QUESTION: Of course, of the present members of the Court, I think only Justice White was here at the time, and he was a member of the majority.

MR. SPAETH: Exactly, and that's why I wore this tie today. As you can see, I'm going to use everything I have to sway that last vote. It is a Colorado buffalo.

MR. SPAETH: And as you surmised, our—

QUESTION: Do you have any better reasons?

(Laughter.)

MR. SPAETH: If you give me a minute, Justice Kennedy, I'll think of some.

* * *

iv. ***Regents of Univ. of California v. Doe***, No. 95–1694, 1996 WL 700567 at *21–*23, *39–*40 (Dec. 2, 1996).

Oral Argument of Richard Gayer on Behalf of the Respondents

MR. GAYER: Mr. Chief Justice—excuse me—and may it please the Court:

This is a Federal case involving 100 percent Federal money at a Federal facility, the Lawrence Livermore National Laboratory, which executes a Federal program for an exclusively Federal interest: nuclear weapons research.

The Regents here, Regents' corporation is not managing a university. It's not even running its hospital. What it's doing is managing the Lawrence Livermore National Laboratory as a public service to the Nation, for no loss or gain. That's on page 1 of the contract, which is not part of the joint appendix.

QUESTION: But I didn't think we had taken this case to go into whether, absent the indemnification provision, there is sovereign immunity or not.

You know, there are a million different entities, and each one of them have different considerations, and we normally don't take up each case to decide whether the court of appeals got it right that applying the normal factors this was the State or this wasn't the State.

I thought the only issue before us here was whether, assuming it is otherwise the State, the indemnification feature makes a change. That's a point of law I think we can grapple with that has, you know, permanent significance Nationwide.

MR. GAYER: Focusing on that narrow issue, which I personally believe that the broader issue is subsumed within the question presented—

QUESTION: Well, let's read—

MR. GAYER: Focusing on the—

QUESTION: Let's read the question presented. What—

MR. GAYER: Well, I agree with Your Honor's statement of the question presented, so—

QUESTION: Well—

MR. GAYER: I'd like to focus on that. Here we have something where the university is really some sort of facade or name between the outside world and the Federal Government. The Federal Government has made a solemn, written promise to pay directly—not to indemnify, not to reimburse, but to pay directly any judgment awarded against the name of the university.

QUESTION: Well, if the university is just a facade, Mr. Gayer, perhaps you should sue only the Federal Government, not the university.

* * *

Appendix D

MODEL *AMICUS* OPENINGS

1. *Texas v. Cobb*, No. 99–1702, 2001 WL 55343 at *18–*20 (Jan. 16, 2001).

Oral Argument of Lisa S. Blatt on Behalf of the United States, as Amicus Curiae, Supporting the Petitioner

MS. BLATT: Mr. Chief Justice, and may it please the Court:

Police have a compelling interest in investigating un-charged crimes and in obtaining voluntary confessions from suspects who have been advised of their right to counsel under *Miranda* and are willing to speak to the police about those uncharged crimes. That questioning does not violate the Sixth Amendment right to counsel because that right is offense-specific.

Under that rule, the statements may not be used to prove the charged offense, but the statements are admissible in a trial for the uncharged offenses. It does not matter, under this rule, whether the two crimes are factually related. The test is rather whether the two crimes constitute the same offense.

QUESTION: Why? Why? I mean, you see my problem from what I said before, don't you? I mean, crime is ambiguous as to whether you're describing a set of events in the world, or a legal concept.

Look at the set of events in the world. It would have all been over in 15 seconds, and it could constitute any one of 15 crimes, and the police charge on the basis of that 15 seconds of real-world behavior three crimes, and he gets a lawyer for those three. Why should the police be able, without a lawyer, to interrogate him about what happened in the real world because there are eight other things that weren't charged?

MS. BLATT: Because the Sixth Amendment, the test of the Sixth Amendment only applies to someone who has been accused in a pending prosecution, and the prosecution is limited by the actual offenses that are charged by the State, and it is only at that time that the right to counsel attaches under the Sixth Amendment.

QUESTION: So it's purely formal. Your argument is purely formal.

MS. BLATT: No. This Court has repeatedly recognized that the requirement that there must be a shift from investigation to accusation is more than just a formalism, because the purpose and the essence of the Sixth Amendment is to make sure the defendant has an opportunity to consult with counsel and prepare for a defense against the pending charges.

A suspect has no Sixth Amendment right to counsel, to have a lawyer appointed or assist him in connection with charges that have not been brought by the State, that may never be brought by the State. The suspect has never indicated any unwillingness to talk to the police about those uncharged offenses.

* * *

2. *Nixon v. Shrink Missouri Gov't PAC*, No. 98–963, 1999 WL 813789 at *9–*11 (Oct. 5, 1999).

Oral Argument of Seth P. Waxman on Behalf of the United States, as *Amicus Curiae*, Supporting the Petitioners

GENERAL WAXMAN: Thank you, Mr. Chief Justice, and may it please the Court:

Buckley's validation of the $1,000 contribution limit was based on three holdings, each of which remains as valid today as it was in 1976. First, that a $1,000 limit on contributions imposed only an attenuated burden on First Amendment rights.

Second, that of all forms of political support, large contributions pose the greatest threat to the integrity of the system because the potential for and the appearance of corruption are what this Court deemed inherent in a regime of large financial contributions.

QUESTION: General Waxman, whose First Amendment interests are being burdened?

GENERAL WAXMAN: There are two, Justice O'Connor, and there are three different interests. The contributor has a First Amendment right in expression, and a First Amendment right in association. The candidate has a First Amendment right in amassing sufficient resources in order to produce and project effective advocacy.

Looking at all three of those, either separately and together, the Court in *Buckley* concluded that a $1,000 limit imposed only an incidental burden, or an incidental restriction, or an attenuated burden on the three rights taken together, and for that reason, and this responds to Justice Ginsburg's question, the Court applied a less-than-strict standard of scrutiny that it formally announced and unanimously adopted in another election-related case shortly after, a case called *Burdick v. Takushi*, in which the Court said, in an election context, when First Amendment rights are subjected to severe restrictions, the regulation must be narrowly drawn to advance a governmental interest of compelling importance.

But when an election-related provision imposes only reasonable nondiscriminatory restrictions against First Amendment rights, the Government's important regulatory interests are generally sufficient to justify the restriction, and that—

QUESTION: *Burdick* was a ballot access case, wasn't it?

GENERAL WAXMAN: Yes, it was, and the *Burdick* standard has been—first of all, it was agreed upon as a standard I believe by all members of the Court in *Burdick*, both the majority and the dissent, and it was also affirmed by this Court in *Timmons* and in the *American Constitutional Law Foundation* last term.

QUESTION: But this isn't, strictly speaking, ballot access.

GENERAL WAXMAN: No, that's—

QUESTION: Do we apply the same test?

GENERAL WAXMAN: I think you do, in—the *Burdick* standard has been applied not just in ballot cases, but really in all election-related cases, cases like *Timmons*, for example.

QUESTION: Well, election-related cases where the State has to manage the election. You have to have some rules, and those rules have to be laid down for the state, or you can't have an election. You have to know who the candidates are, how you qualify as a candidate, and so forth and so on, in the nature of things.

In the nature of things, however, the State does not have to control how people who want to be elected go out and convince the people of the United States to vote for them.

GENERAL WAXMAN: That's precisely—

QUESTION: It does not require the State to make one decision or another, and it's quite—with *Buckley* it was quite new that the State should intervene in what previously had been a matter of private First Amendment activity.

GENERAL WAXMAN: Yes, Justice Scalia, and that's why the *Burdick* standard, or what this Court referred to or what Justice O'Connor referred in her concurrence and dissent in *American Constitutional Law Foundation* as the variable standard also applies, as it did in the other *Buckley* case, in a nonballot access case where the Government is restricting what people have to do to get their message out, and in *McIntyre*, and in other campaign finance cases like *California Medical Association* and *Massachusetts Citizens for Life*.

I'm just suggesting that there is not some novel standard that was applied and inappropriately enunciated in *Buckley*, but rather that *Buckley* and these other cases that I've described fall into a rather unbroken line of jurisprudence that this Court has announced where in the election context, where First Amendment rights are involved, particularly where what's being regulated is not speech directly itself, but conduct that includes speech as part of that—

* * *

3. *New Jersey v. New York*, No. 120 Orig., 1998 WL 15118 at
    *20–*22 (Jan. 12, 1998).

Oral Argument of Jeffrey P. Minear on Behalf of the
United States, as *Amicus Curiae*

>   MR. MINEAR: Mr. Chief Justice, and may it please
>   the Court:
>
>   The master correctly rejected New York's contention
>   that Article Second of the Compact of 1834 gives New
>   York sovereignty over the filled areas of Ellis Island.
>   The Compact was written against a back-drop of com-
>   mon law rules respecting coastal boundaries, and
>   those rules recognized that avulsive changes such as
>   the addition of fill did not change the location of the
>   boundary. The Compact does not address fill, and it
>   does not purport to alter the common law rules. As a
>   result, the Compact should be interpreted as following
>   the common law and therefore granting and preserv-
>   ing New Jersey's sovereignty over the filled areas.
>
>   Now, the master was also correct in rejecting New
>   York's contention that the filled portions of Ellis Is-
>   land became territory of New York through the doc-
>   trine of prescription and acquiescence, and we think
>   the single most important consideration on this score
>   is the fact that the United States exercised dominant
>   and virtually exclusive jurisdiction over the island
>   during the relevant time period.
>
>   [T]he United States presence is important for two
>   reasons. First, the United States recognized New Jer-
>   sey's claim to the filled lands by purchasing that area
>   from New Jersey and by indicating in subsequent
>   maps that it was situated in New Jersey.
>
>   Second, the United States' dominant sovereign pres-
>   ence prevented New York from taking those acts of
>   sovereignty that would have established its claim of
>   entitlement to the filled areas, and likewise would
>   have put New Jersey on notice of the fact that New
>   York was making such a claim.

Now, New York also makes a claim that New Jersey is guilty of laches in this case, but that really adds nothing to New York's claim in this case at all. As this Court indicated in *Illinois v. Kentucky*, the equitable defense of laches is subsumed within the doctrine of prescription and acquiescence, so nothing is added by making those types of charges here.

[A]lthough we agree with the Master's determination of the historic boundary on Ellis Island, we disagree with his ultimate remedy, which would reconfigure the boundary based on considerations of practicality and convenience. We think it's important to note at the outset that New Jersey asked this Court to determine the historic boundary line. It did not request that the Court withdraw the boundary. Neither did New York make such a request, as well.

But equally important, the master's proposal would require this Court to exceed its historic role in determining—

* * *

4. *Toyota Motor Manufacturing v. Williams*, No. 00–1089, 2001 WL 1453954 at *18–*20 (Nov. 7, 2001).

Oral Argument of Barbara B. McDowell on Behalf of the United States

MS. McDOWELL: Thank you, Mr. Chief Justice, and may it please the Court:

We agree that the Sixth Circuit applied an incorrect test in determining whether a person is substantially limited in the major life activity of performing manual tasks.

The correct test asks whether a person is significantly restricted relative to the average person in performing those basic manual tasks that are central to everyday life, tasks such as grasping objects, manipulating objects, holding objects. That inquiry is indicated by the statutory focus on substantial limits and major life activities.

The Sixth Circuit's approach, which focuses only on a plaintiff's ability to perform particular manual tasks required by a specific job, seems to us both over-inclusive and under-inclusive.

First, the Sixth Circuit's approach would extend the protections of the act to persons who are substantially limited only in performing a particular job, not in everyday life and not in performing a range of jobs or a class of jobs. That approach would undermine the established test for establishing a substantial limitation based on the major life activity of working. That test, as the Court recognized in *Sutton*, requires the plaintiff to show that she's substantially limited in a class or a range of jobs.

QUESTION: Ms. McDowell, I didn't think that the Sixth Circuit had said we're looking only at one job. I thought they were looking at assembly line work as a broad category of jobs.

MS. McDOWELL: No, we don't think so, Your Honor. And I would refer you to page 4a of the petition appendix where the court is engaging [in] its analysis. It refers to certain types of manual assembly line jobs that require the gripping of tools and repetitive work with hands and arms extended out or above shoulder level for extended periods of time. So, it appears that the Sixth Circuit was focusing on a particular category of assembly line jobs and not assembly line jobs generally.

QUESTION: Types. It uses the plural. So, it wasn't just talking about a particular job, which is what I thought you reduced this to, and I think that is not quite a fair characterization of what the court said.

MS. McDOWELL: That may be correct, Justice Ginsburg. It may be that the Sixth Circuit was thinking about categories of jobs that would require these particular limits. There is no indication in the record, though, of how many other assembly line jobs there are that would—the plaintiff would be disqualified from performing.

QUESTION: It refers to painting, plumbing, and roofing, *et cetera*.

MS. McDOWELL: That's correct. And that appears to be an assumption by the court of appeals. There does not appear, at least from our examination of what record has been presented to this Court, any specific discussion of building trades, plumbing, roofing, *et cetera* in the record.

* * *

Appendix E

EXAMPLES OF EFFECTIVE MID-ARGUMENT ADVOCACY TECHNIQUES

1. Use Of Precedent

i. *Withrow v. Williams*, No. 91–1030, 1992 WL 687891 at *27–*30 (Nov. 3, 1992).

Oral Argument of Seth P. Waxman on Behalf of the Respondent

MR. WAXMAN: * * * My first point is that there was no challenge, though—there is no challenge in this Court to any aspects of the merits of the *Miranda* rulings below, and in our view the rule announced in *Stone v. Powell* should not and cannot be applied to violations of *Miranda*'s constitutional rules.

The rights protected by the Fifth Amendment privilege against self-incrimination are so unlike those under the Fourth Amendment, and the relationship of *Miranda* to the privilege is so different than the relationship between *Mapp* and the Fourth Amendment, that the concerns that inform this Court's decision in *Stone* and, we submit, no other concerns counsel favoring extension of that rule to *Miranda* claims. Indeed, those factors counsel against extending the rule in *Stone* to *Miranda*.

I'd like to briefly give the reasons why, and then explain in more detail why I say this. First, because in complete contrast to the Fourth Amendment exclusionary rule, *Miranda* is specifically designed to and does both prevent the constitutional violation from occurring and, if a violation does occur, it redresses the constitutional injury.

Second, unlike *Stone,* which reduce the burden on Federal courts and friction with State courts by taking Federal courts completely out of the business of adjudicating the constitutionality of the admission of physical evidence, depriving Federal habeas courts of the power to adjudicate Miranda claims will produce no such result, and third, unlike the Fourth Amendment exclusionary rule, *Miranda* is not unrelated to fairness and reliability at trial.

Before I elaborate on those three points, I would like to stress two points which I think are very fundamental in this case, one about *Stone* and one about *Miranda.*

Stone v. Powell is not a decision about the scope of the habeas corpus statute, it is a decision about the scope of the judge-made exclusionary rule designed to reinforce the Fourth Amendment. *Stone* itself makes this very clear, and this important distinction is apparent and reiterated in all of this Court's subsequent decisions that have declined to extend *Stone* beyond the strict confines of the Fourth Amendment and with good reason, because *Stone* is bound up in the unique status of the Fourth Amendment exclusionary rule.

With respect to *Miranda,* the contention that *Miranda v. Arizona* announced nothing more than nonconstitutional rules is wrong, and it critically obscures the issue in this case. We readily agree that one thing that *Miranda v. Arizona* did was to announce rules that are not required by the Constitution. The warnings themselves, for example, are not constitutionally required. *Miranda* says this, and that's what cases like *California v. Prysock* and *Duckworth v. Eagan* are about.

Similarly, the mere occurrence of unwarned custodial interrogation absent a use of the statements as evidenced at chief—at trial, while decried by *Miranda,* does not amount to a constitutional violation because the statements haven't been used against the defendant as testimony. This is the precise teaching of this Court's decisions in *Michigan v. Tucker* and *Oregon v. Elstad.*

These types of *Miranda* violations are not at issue in this case. They're not currently enforced on habeas corpus. They're not enforced against the States at all.

* * *

ii. **Glover v. United States**, No. 99–8576, 2000 WL 1770624 at *21–*22 (Nov. 27, 2000).

Oral Argument of Michael R. Dreeben on Behalf of the Respondent

* * *

MR. DREEBEN: The Court similarly believed that it was appropriate to give guidance to the lower courts by showing how the rule of law applies to the particular facts in *Brooke Group v. Brown & Williamson*, a 1993 decision where the Court took a novel antitrust principle and then applied it to the very intricate and specific facts of that case.

In *Siegert v. Gilley*, a 1991 decision, the Court actually affirmed the judgment on a ground that the lower court had not reached at all. There, the lower court had said there was a heightened pleading requirement for qualified immunity. This Court decided the case on the grounds that there was no underlying constitutional right that was asserted in the *Bivens* action at all, and in that case not only was that not the question presented, but the parties hadn't even briefed it or addressed it. So—

QUESTION: * * * [I]t seems to me that case—opinion perhaps represents a decision that a particular claim is logically antecedent to another one, and it seems to me you have a hard time saying that here.

MR. DREEBEN: I do have a hard time saying it's logically antecedent, but the third case that I would refer the Court to involves the elaboration of the additional implications of a claim that the court decided. That is *Colstad v. American Dental Association*, which was decided in 1999, and there the Court elaborated a standard for punitive damages in Title VII actions and then went on to give guidance to the lower courts about how agency principles apply, but then remanded—

* * *

iii. *Mickens v. Taylor*, No. 00–9285, 2001 WL 1412443 at *47–*53 (Nov. 5, 2001).

Oral Argument of Irving L. Gornstein on Behalf of the United States, as Amicus Curiae, Supporting the Respondent

MR. GORNSTEIN: Mr. Chief Justice, and may it please the Court:

When a district court has reason to know about a potential conflict and fails to initiate inquiry, the Sixth Amendment is violated only when there is a showing of an actual conflict and an adverse effect on the quality of performance. And we say that for three reasons.

First, it is a central tenet of this Court's Sixth Amendment jurisprudence that a Sixth Amendment violation does not occur unless there has been prejudice to the defense. It would be inconsistent with that basic principle to set aside a jury verdict and order a new trial with all the societal costs that entails when—

QUESTION: I must interrupt you here, though. The prejudice standards under—under *Strickland* is not the standard we're talking about here, is it?

MR. GORNSTEIN: It is not. Under *Sullivan*, there has to be an adverse effect on the quality of performance, but it is still—from that, there is inferred prejudice. It would be inconsistent with the central thrust of showing some kind of prejudice to reverse a conviction, set aside it, and—and order a new trial when there has been no showing that the quality of representation has been affected.

And in *Sullivan*, the Court held—

QUESTION: Well, let me just push that all the way. Supposing in—in *Holloway* itself the judge said, well, I—I really think you—he thought it through and said, I think you could represent both. Could he have just gone ahead and insisted on the lawyer representing them?

MR. GORNSTEIN: In—in *Holloway*, if there's no inquiry conducted by the judge, there's automatic reversal.

QUESTION: The question here is when does the judge have a duty of inquiry.

MR. GORNSTEIN: The judge—

QUESTION: Are you saying he never has a duty of inquiry unless there's going to be actual prejudice?

MR. GORNSTEIN: No. I—I think that what the Court said in *Wood* about the duty of inquiry and—and—this is somewhat vague, I will agree, but it said there has to be a clear possibility of a conflict.

QUESTION: All right. Supposing there's a clear possibility of prejudice, but no actual proof of prejudice, is that enough to impose a duty of—of inquiry on the judge?

MR. GORNSTEIN: There's a duty of inquiry, but if the duty is not fulfilled and a trial is held and a—there's a conviction and the defendant is seeking to overturn his conviction, at that point the defendant still must show an actual conflict and an adverse effect on the quality of his representation.

QUESTION: We've been trying to find a way to distinguish *Holloway* from this case. One way is to say that multiple representation is so fraught with difficulties that it's simply a separate category. Another is to say that the likelihood of an adverse effect is so significant, so serious that we'll presume it. Another is to say that the conflict itself is much more serious in most cases than—how would you—

MR. GORNSTEIN: I would say that there would—

QUESTION: How would—how would you have us deal with *Holloway*?

MR. GORNSTEIN: I would say that *Holloway* is a special case where prejudice was presumed conclusively based on two factors. The first is that deference to the contemporaneous judgment of counsel that he was operating under a disabling conflict, and when he's representing that he's operating under a disabling conflict, it's not just a representation that he has a conflict, but that this is going to affect his performance. He's not going to be able to represent the defendant adequately.

And the second is that prejudice inheres in the situation in which a judge orders a defense counsel, over his objection, to continue representation even though the attorney believes he is not going to be able to perform adequately.

And those two circumstances together create a per se rule of prejudice, and it's a carve-out from the *Sullivan* rule.

QUESTION: Does *Wood* stand for a similar proposition, or is *Wood* different?

MR. GORNSTEIN: Now, *Wood* is a situation where the *Sullivan* rule was applied in a case in which there was reason to know a clear possibility of an actual conflict. And what the Court said in that circumstance is that the Constitution would be violated if it was found that the lawyer had a—a conflict that influenced his basic strategic decisions. And that is the same exact test as the *Sullivan* test. There not only has to be a showing of an actual conflict but an effect on performance for there to be a Sixth Amendment violation.

QUESTION: Are you saying *Wood* is an effect case?

MR. GORNSTEIN: It is both an actual conflict and effect. That's what it directs when it says the words actual conflict—

QUESTION: So, you're saying in this case if the lawyer had said to the judge, my client doesn't trust me because I—I represented the decedent and he won't be candid with me, then the judge would have a duty to discharge counsel.

MR. GORNSTEIN: I'm not saying that they—he would have had a duty to discharge counsel. He can inquire—

QUESTION: Why would that case have been different from *Holloway*?

MR. GORNSTEIN: He can—first of all, *Holloway* is a situation where the lawyer himself is representing that he cannot adequately represent—

QUESTION: Correct. It's because my client doesn't trust me.

MR. GORNSTEIN: Well, if he represents that he cannot adequately represent the—the defendant, and then the district court has to conduct an inquiry. And if the inquiry reveals that in fact representation can be adequately given, then the judge need not dismiss. But if the judge concludes that adequate representation cannot be given, then the judge should dismiss.

QUESTION: No matter how severe the conflict. I mean, no matter how—in your view, no matter how severe the conflict, still unless you can show that it actually affected the lawyer's representation, it is not a constitutional error.

MR. GORNSTEIN: After a trial has been held and the defendant is seeking to overturn his conviction, that's correct.

QUESTION: Well, *Strickland* doesn't say that. *Strickland* says that it's important to maintain a fairly rigid rule of presumed prejudice for conflicts of interest.

MR. GORNSTEIN: Yes, but *Strickland* goes on—

QUESTION: Should we change *Strickland*?

MR. GORNSTEIN: No. No, because *Strickland* goes on to say that in that situation, prejudice is presumed only where there's been an actual effect on—on performance, both an actual conflict and an adverse effect on performance. What *Strickland* says is the defendant doesn't have to show the additional burden that is—that is present in most *Strickland* cases of showing there's a reasonable probability that the outcome of the trial would change. But what—*Strickland* reaffirms *Cuyler v. Sullivan*, which requires both an actual conflict and an effect—an adverse effect on performance.

2. Segues

i. *United States v. Microsoft Corp.*, Nos. 00–5212 & 00–5213, Oral Arg. Tr. at 74–75 (Feb. 26, 2001).

Oral Argument of Jeffrey P. Minear on Behalf of the Plaintiff–Appellee

THE COURT: What would their surveys show at a point where Navigator has 80 percent of the market and IE has 5 percent? They would show that no one has ever heard of IE; right?

MR. MINEAR: That may very well be the case, but what IE has to do is compete on the merits to show that they have a better product.

THE COURT: Which you can only do by persuading OEMs to carry it and the OEMs won't carry it and the OEMs won't carry it because of the market surveys, as you've just said.

MR. MINEAR: This is the same constraint that anyone is facing in a market that is subject to network effects. The key here is that you do not employ anticompetitive tactics as a monopolist to prevent your [competitor's] product from reaching the end user.

I would like to speak just very briefly to the IAP channel because I do think that that's important. The contracts that were involved there, I think, are clearly exclusionary, the AOL contracts that were mentioned before.

These contracts basically had four critical features. First, they required that the AOL distribute Internet Explorer as its default browser. If that alone were all that Microsoft had bargained for, that would not cause a problem. But in addition, these contracts prohibited organizations, such as America Online, to respond to questions, to provide an alternative browser unless a subscriber specifically asked for it and in addition put a cap on the number of copies of an alternative browser that AOL could provide.

Now, there was no competitive justification for these types of caps. Again, IE is a no-revenue product, so it can't be justified on increasing revenue here. And either browser is likely to improve the attractiveness of Windows. So the revenue-generating product, Windows, was enhanced by either browser. This is the type of exclusionary conduct that has traditionally been discouraged by Section 2.

On top of that, we also have types of threats and coercion that were directed to particular OEMs.

* * *

ii. ***United States v. Beggerly***, No. 97–731, 1998 WL 214900 at *8–*10 (Apr. 27, 1998).

Oral Argument of Paul R. Q. Wolfson on Behalf of the Petitioner

* * *

MR. WOLFSON: Right. If we win on the first issue, then I think we have a substantive defense, but on the—

QUESTION: Not any more. You waived it below. I mean—

MR. WOLFSON: Well, no.

QUESTION: *Res judicata* can be waived.

MR. WOLFSON: I don't—I have to say I don't think we waived it. I mean, it wasn't really presented in a way in which we were called upon to address it in the district court.

The respondents did not even amend * * * their complaint in order to raise a claim under the Quiet Title Act until after they filed for summary judgment, and the district court dismissed it as untimely, which should be reviewed in the court of appeals, I would think, under an abuse of discretion standard, so we strongly feel that we had no call to even address these matters.

It was only when the court of appeals, even while excusing the respondents for their 12–year delay in bringing their suit, rushed to the * * * ultimate merits of the case, reopened the judgment, concluded that everything—that the land claim was valid, and awarded title to the respondents, that we had to face the issue about whether the Quiet Title Act could be a basis for awarding the title [to] the respondents' land.

I think that that does * * * return me to my point about why the court of appeals' * * * rulings are so important. First, I mean, in terms of finality of judgments and sovereign immunity, the court of appeals essentially redetermined land title issues in a litigation against the United States that was a collateral attack on a final judgment where there was no waiver of sovereign immunity that would permit such a case to go forward.

Second, when the court of appeals, on the issue of whether there is tolling of the statute of limitations under the Quiet Title Act, when the court held that it should be tolled, I think it disregarded two very important policies about statute of limitations, both generally in the law and especially with regard to land title litigation: first, protecting parties against being forced to come into court to defend against stale, very stale land claims, and also to encourage plaintiffs who claim an interest in land to conduct prompt and thorough research on their claims.

I've spoken third about the court of appeals kind of prematurely judging the merits of the case. That, we submit, was error because it was—first of all because it was outside of the scope of the court of appeals.

QUESTION: Is it your position the court of appeals was wrong in saying that the independent action was just really a continuation of the earlier action?

MR. WOLFSON: Yes, it is. I think that's—that is essentially our primary submission.

3. Use Of Analogies

i. *Bray v. Alexandria Women's Health Clinic*, No. 90–985, 1992 WL 687912 at *11–*13 (Oct. 6, 1992).

Oral Argument of John G. Roberts, Jr., on Behalf of the United States, as *Amicus Curiae*, Supporting the Petitioners

* * *

Petitioners do not interfere with respondents' rights because respondents are women. Petitioners do what they do because they're opposed to an activity, the activity of abortion. They target their conspirators not because of who they are, but because of what they are doing. Respondents now seem to recognize this. In their brief on reargument they say that this is, quote, unlike the usual section 1985(3) case, end quote.

But it is not a section 1985(3) case at all, and the reason is that section 1985(3) is not concerned simply with the deprivation of Federal rights, however fundamental, however important. It is concerned with the discriminatory deprivation of Federal rights, and petitioners are perfectly nondiscriminatory, nondiscriminating, in their opposition to abortion.

Respondents' answer to this argument is that only women can exercise the right to an abortion, and therefore petitioners' antiabortion activities have a discriminatory impact on women. People intend the natural consequences of their acts, and therefore respondents argue, you can infer from the discriminatory impact that petitioners have a discriminatory purpose.

A few examples will show that the logic of that doesn't hold up. Consider, for example, an Indian tribe with exclusive fishing rights in a particular river. A group of ecologists get together who are opposed to fishing in the river, because they think it disturbs the ecology. They interfere with the Indians' rights.

The impact of their conspiracy is on a particular Indian group, but it would be quite illogical to infer from that they have any animus against Indians. They're opposed to fishing in the river, not Indians, even though only Indians can fish in the river. Petitioners are opposed to abortion, not women, even though only women can exercise the right to an abortion.

Another example. Suppose a group of men and women get together who are opposed to the draft and they interfere with registration. The direct impact of their conspiracy will be felt only by men, since only men are eligible for the draft. But, again, it would be quite wrong to infer from that impact that the conspirators have any animus against men. They're opposed to the draft, not men, even though only men are eligible for the draft.

ii. ***Chickasaw Nation v. United States***, No. 00–507, 2001 WL 1183439 at *26–*27 (Oct. 2, 2001).

Oral Argument of Edward C. Dumont on Behalf of the Respondent

* * *

QUESTION: What is a pull-tab? I've never pulled—

MR. DuMONT: A pull-tab is a little card about like this with three to five little windows, like an Advent calendar, that you can pull up and reveal something underneath them.

(Laughter.)

QUESTION: What a weird analogy.

(Laughter.)

MR. DuMONT: And if you find under it three angels, for instance, you may—

(Laughter.)

MR. DuMONT:—you may win something. So, you pay a dollar for the ticket. If you get the right combinations of symbols under the tickets, then you win something. If you don't, you don't.

QUESTION: Of course, in Calvinist theology, it's not weird at all.

(Laughter.)

4. *Handling Hypothetical Questions*

i. *Illinois v. Wardlow*, No. 98–1036, 1999 WL 1034479 at *24–*25 (Nov. 2, 1999).

Oral Argument of Malcolm L. Stewart for the United States, as *Amicus Curiae*, Supporting the Petitioner

* * *

QUESTION: But there—what do you make of the slippery slope argument that—that takes the—the situation one step further? It was made in at least one of the amicus briefs. As you say, the police certainly can properly ask a question of anybody on the street, and most people will answer the question or at least not behave rudely.

If the petitioner's petition—position is accepted, what do we do or what rule would we have in the case in which the individual who was accosted by the police on the street and asked a question, instead of answering it tells the officer to go to blazes or perhaps something stronger than that? Does that—is that going to be the equivalent of flight, *i.e.*, deviant response, and—and justify a *Terry* stop?

MR. STEWART: No. I think—I think flight is really different fundamentally in at least three respects from less extreme means of expressing a desire to avoid—

QUESTION: Let's assume the language is extreme.

MR. STEWART: Okay. One of the—one of the things that is distinctive about flight is that in many cases it is likely to connote a panicked reaction, an emotional reaction to the police presence. And—and panic is in our view more likely to signal consciousness of guilt than is an—an emphatic, salty expression of disdain for the police.

The second—the second, and perhaps the—the most fundamental difference is that flight expresses the desire not simply to refuse cooperation with the police, but to be free from any form of police observation or scrutiny. And that's really one of the reasons that we think the purposes of the *Terry* stop are particularly implicated in this situation; that is, the fundamental purpose of the *Terry* stop is to allow the police briefly to freeze the status quo while they undertake further inquiry to determine whether there [is danger to the officer or a crime afoot].

* * *

ii. ***Florida v. White***, No. 98–223, 1999 WL 183815 at *18–*19 (Mar. 23, 1999).

Oral Argument of Malcolm L. Stewart on Behalf of the United States, as *Amicus Curiae*, Supporting the Petitioner

* * *

MR. STEWART: The rule we're advocating—and I think it is supported by a number of this Court's decisions—is that when items of personal property are found in public areas, they may be seized by law enforcement officials based on probable cause without a prior judicial warrant.

Now, some of this Court's—

QUESTION: So—so, if the vehicle had been parked in the owner's driveway, could it have been seized?

MR. STEWART: The driveway is a close question. If it had been parked in the owner's garage, for instance, an area in which the owner would clearly have a reasonable expectation of privacy, the car could not have been seized on our view without a warrant.

QUESTION: So, what's your position on the driveway or the curtilage?

MR. STEWART: Our position on the—our position on the driveway, generally speaking, is that a driveway is not within the curtilage, and therefore the owner would not have a reasonable expectation of privacy in it.

There was actually a case in the Seventh Circuit, *United States v. Redman*, that involved a related issue in which law enforcement officials conducted a search of trash cans located at the—the point of the individual's driveway that was closest to the house. And the *en banc* Seventh Circuit split 8 to 5, held that the individual did not have a reasonable expectation of privacy in his driveway.

We think the same rule would apply to seizures of a vehicle from a driveway, but in fairness, given the way that the Seventh Circuit divided, we can't say that that's a settled question.

QUESTION: It depends on how much is left of the *Coolidge* decision.

MR. STEWART: That's correct. But—but at any rate, the dividing line would be as to any particular location, did the individual have a reasonable expectation of privacy in this place? The garage, clearly yes. A public parking lot, clearly no. The driveway is—is somewhere in between.

* * *

iii. ***Pennsylvania Department of Corrections v. Yeskey,*** No. 97–634, 1998 WL 222956 at *43–*48 (Apr. 28, 1998).

Oral Argument of Irving L. Gornstein on Behalf of the United States, as *Amicus Curiae*, Supporting the Respondent

MR. GORNSTEIN: Mr. Chief Justice, and may it please the Court:

The court of appeals correctly held that the ADA prohibits State prisons from discriminating against disabled inmates in their programs, services, and activities that they provide to inmates for three reasons:

First, the text of the act unambiguously prohibits such discrimination, second, the application of the ADA to prisons was a logical—State prisons was a logical extension of section 504 of the Rehabilitation Act's application to Federal prisons and to State prisons that receive Federal funding, and third, the interpretive principles that are relied on by petitioner do not support the creation of a nontextually based exemption to the act.

Beginning with the text, the act applies to any public entity that provides programs, services, or activities and, since the act defines a public entity to include any agency or department to a State, the State Department of Corrections is clearly covered. Nor is there any question that—

QUESTION: I think I'm very interested, Mr. Gornstein, if it does apply, how you interpret the accommodation that's required in the prison context.

MR. GORNSTEIN: Well, there would be two things you would look to. First of all, the backdrop of section 504, which this Court interpreted in *Southeastern Community College v. Davis* not to require accommodations that impose undue burdens and not to require accommodations that would lead to a fundamental alteration in the program, which in that case included lowering standards and substantially modifying a nursing program, and second of all you would look to a general principle that this Court has applied in section 504(2), to deferring to the reasonable medical judgments of health professionals.

By a parity of reasoning, in the prison context you would defer to the reasonable security judgments of correctional officials in the context of an ADA case.

* * *

QUESTION: Tell us a little bit more about how the boot camp might work. Let's suppose that a high school had a physical conditioning program, very rigorous, for its students 2 or 3 hours a day, and that a disabled student wanted to participate, and it would cost $5,000 a year per disabled student increase to run a separate track program for the disabled student.

The same with the boot camp. A disabled prisoner wants to participate in boot camp. It would cost $5,000 a year for the second track for the disabled prisoner.

Would the judge make the same determination in each case, or would he say, prison budgets are such that $5,000 is more significant for a prison than it is for schools?

MR. GORNSTEIN: I think that the real difference would not come in in measuring undue burden but would come in in the question of security, deferring to security interests. I'm not sure the case would look that much different when the question is just a financial one.

But I would add in response to your hypothetical—

QUESTION: Well, let's say in each case you can do it for $5,000, second track, a second track for the school $5,000, second track for the prisoners.

MR. GORNSTEIN: There's a question—

QUESTION: Is the calculus just the same?

MR. GORNSTEIN: There would be a question that would arise whether you have to do any sort of new and separate program at all, whether that—regardless of how much it might cost. Whether you would have to run a separate or new program, that would be a question.

QUESTION: Why wouldn't you in the boot camp hypothetical, if it's feasible to do for $5,000 a prisoner, or $5,000 a student?

MR. GORNSTEIN: I think that the question is whether you're being denied access to services or a program that is being provided by the institution. Here, the program or service is the boot camp program, and the question would be, would admission to that require fundamentally altering that program.

QUESTION: $5,000.

MR. GORNSTEIN: If rigorous physical exercise is an essential part of that program, and there is no—it wouldn't matter how much money it would cost to construct another one, it would be a different program.

QUESTION: Let's assume that we think it might work if it's altered for this person. We're not sure, but we're pretty sure it will work. It won't be as good, but it will certainly have some benefits. The same with the high school.

MR. GORNSTEIN: If it doesn't substantially change the nature of the program, then if it's not costly, then it may have to be provided under the ADA and section 504 as well. * * *

* * *

5. *Advancing A Reasonable, Limited Rule*

i. ***Dusenbery v. United States***, No. 00–6567, 2001 WL 1398611 at *29–*31 (Oct. 29, 2001).

Oral Argument of Jeffrey P. Minear on Behalf of the Respondent

* * *

MR. MINEAR: Yes. And—and with regard to the Federal Rules, they do recognize that service can be effected through mail—through the notice of waiver provisions that are set forth there, and we would defend the constitutionality of those provisions which allow the party to, in fact, accept service by notice.

QUESTION: If this Court writes a due process opinion, can we say that mail, routine mail, is always sufficient, or are there some cases in which you must have personal service?

MR. MINEAR: Well, the Court can certainly do that. We might caution that it's not necessary to do that in this case.

QUESTION: Well, I want to know what the principle is that you're—that controls our case, the beginning principle here.

MR. MINEAR: The Court has drawn these principles largely from common experience and knowledge about the instrumentalities that are used for purposes of service. And if we looked at the *Mullane* case, the Court cited that the mails had, through common experience, been determined to be a reasonable means for providing service in that type of proceeding.

Now, whether the Court would want to take the step of saying that the mails are always adequate in any proceeding is a step that's not necessary for the Court to take. And so, I'm hesitant to suggest to the Court that it ought to do so. It certainly does not need to do so in this case because this case involves procedures that are very similar to *Tulsa*, to *Mennonite*, to *Schroeder*, to—

QUESTION: All right. So, then you are relying on the fact that this is a forfeiture case and we're—there's this voice of the past of *in rem* versus *in personam* hanging over this—this argument of yours.

MR. MINEAR: Well, actually no, Your Honor. It's not the *in rem* nature of the proceedings, but rather it's a—it's an intersection of two factors.

One, this type of proceeding is similar to the proceedings this Court has dealt with previously that are not necessarily *in rem*. For instance, probate claims are not necessarily—would not necessarily be treated as *in rem* I think under—under traditional law. But it's—it's the intersection of the fact that these proceedings are similar to proceedings elsewhere that the Court has already ruled on and the fact that this Court can draw on its long experience [that] the mails are, in fact, as a practical matter, a reasonable means for providing service or providing notice.

* * *

6. *Clearly Articulating The Client's Position*

i. *Illinois v. Wardlow*, No. 98–1036, 1999 WL 1034479 at *21–*23 (Nov. 2, 1999).

Oral Argument of Malcolm L. Stewart on Behalf of the United States, as *Amicus Curiae*, Supporting the Petitioner

MR. STEWART: Mr. Chief Justice, and may it please the Court:

It's certainly true, as respondent and his *amici* point out, that individuals may, on some occasions, have innocent motives for fleeing the police. But the purpose of a *Terry* stop is not to apprehend individuals who are known to be guilty of criminal offenses; rather, it's to provide a means by which police may resolve ambiguities in situations where they have reasonable—reason to suspect criminal activity, but lack probable cause to make an arrest. And in our view, flight from identifiable police officers will ordinarily correlate sufficiently with likely involvement in criminal activity.

QUESTION: Well, Mr. Stewart—

QUESTION: What do you do—

QUESTION:—do you propose some per se rule, as Mr. Devine was arguing, or are you advising us to stick with the *Terry* reasonable suspicion/totality of the circumstances?

MR. STEWART: I think we—we believe you should look at the totality of the circumstances. I think in the end our position is not significantly different in—in substance from the petitioner's, although we may use different terminology. Our view is that ordinarily when an individual flees at the sight of an identifiable police officer, under circumstances in which the officer reasonably infers that the individual is running because of the officer's presence, rather than for some other reason, ordinarily that would raise a sufficient inference of guilt to justify a *Terry* stop. * * *

* * *

ii.   *Village of Willowbrook v. Olech*, No. 98–1288, 2000 WL 49179 at *25–*26 (Jan. 10, 2000).

Oral Argument of Irving L. Gornstein on Behalf of the United States, as *Amicus Curiae*

MR. GORNSTEIN: Mr. Chief Justice, and may it please the Court:

We have explained in our brief why we believe this is not an appropriate case for resolving the class-of-one issue, but if the Court reaches the question, it should hold that a class-of-one claim is subject to the same analysis as other equal protection claims.

That means that unless there is a fundamental right, or a suspect classification involved, rational basis review applies, and under rational basis review the relevant inquiry is an objective one into whether there is any conceivable rational basis for the alleged difference in treatment.

* * *

7. *Refuting Opposing Counsel's Argument*

 i. *Felker v. Turpin*, No. 95–8836, 1996 WL 306345 at
 *51–*52 (June 3, 1996).

 Oral Argument of Drew S. Days, III, on Behalf of the
 United States, as *Amicus Curiae*, Supporting the Respondent

 * * *

 GENERAL DAYS: * * * One of the things that I
 wanted to point out that I think is contrary to the
 State of Georgia. Georgia's position with respect to
 this circumvention and evasion is that Congress apparently did not see the continuation of this Court's
 jurisdiction over original habeas as being a circumvention. If one looks at section 103 of the act, that was a
 decision by Congress to amend Rule 22 of the Federal
 Rules of Appellate Procedure.

 QUESTION: Where do we find 10–that portion.

 GENERAL DAYS: That's at point 4 and 5a of the
 appendix to our brief, Mr. Chief Justice.

 What Congress did there is amend the jurisdiction of
 Federal circuit judges to grant original habeas, and
 basically said that that was no longer possible. It
 seems to us that Congress knows how to address
 original habeas jurisdiction when it wants to, and it
 concluded that it did not wish to do so insofar as the
 Supreme Court was concerned.

 And to us, this makes great sense, because after all
 Congress was legislating against a backdrop of this
 Court's decisions and its policies, and there are two
 things to note about those particular decisions and
 policies.

 One is that for over 70 years this Court has attempted
 to impose reasonable restrictions over the abuse of the
 writ, particularly second or successive petitions, and
 secondly, in dealing with original habeas petitions this
 Court has, as several of you on the bench, Mr. Chief
 Justice and others, have pointed out, this Court has
 imposed very stringent requirements before granting
 original habeas. There hasn't been one granted since
 Ex parte Grossman in 1925.

 Not only that, the statute 2241(b) that Mr. Justice
 Stevens just mentioned, 2242, which requires that

there be some showing of why the applicant hadn't gone to another court, and 2254(b), the old 2254(b), essentially indicated that no petition would be granted unless it could be shown that relief was not available any place else. * * *

* * *

ii. ***UNUM Life Ins. Co. v. Ward***, No. 97–1868, 1999 WL 115178 at *17–*18 (Feb. 24, 1999).

Oral Argument of Edwin S. Kneedler on Behalf of the United States as *Amicus Curiae*, Supporting Petitioner in Part and Respondent in Part

MR. KNEEDLER: Thank you, Mr. Chief Justice, and may it please the Court:

I'd like to address several things at the outset in terms of petitioner's argument that the notice prejudice rule conflicts with provisions of ERISA itself, before I get to the insurance savings clause. First, counsel mentioned or argued that the application of the notice prejudice rule would be inconsistent with the requirement that a fiduciary administer the plan in accordance with its terms. Actually, what section 1104(a)(1)(D) of Title 29 says, it should be administered in accordance with the documents and instruments governing the plan "insofar as such documents and instruments are consistent with the provisions of this subchapter."

This subchapter includes the insurance savings clause. So to the extent the insurance savings clause makes State law applicable to the plan, the administrator is required to comply with State law in the same way that the administrator would obviously be required to comply with Federal law.

QUESTION: So the argument based on, in effect, on the word "document" is essentially a circular argument?

MR. KNEEDLER: Yes, because the statute itself says only insofar as it's consistent with the subchapter, which itself incorporates State law.

The other point that's been argued is that section 503 of ERISA, which requires plans to have claims adjudication procedures in accordance with regulations of the Secretary, somehow occupies the field or ousts any notice—any application of a rule like the notice prejudice rule.

And we think that is also incorrect. Section 503 says nothing about the filing of claims. The Secretary's regulations under section 503 say nothing about the time period for the initial filing of a claim.

QUESTION: Could the Secretary adopt regulations like the notice prejudice rule and then occupy the field?

MR. KNEEDLER: We believe she could, but section 503 and certainly the regulations as they're now written do not occupy the field. The very first section of the regulations say that they establish minimum standards for claims, and that appears on page 105A of the appendix. The regulations establish minimum procedures. They don't address at all the time period for filing claims. And most significantly, they provide in three separate different subsections, (c), (d)(3), and (g)(3), that where the plan provides for an insurance company to administer—to administer the policy, that the claims process—excuse me—an insurance company that is subject to regulation under State law, that the claim may provide for claims to be adjudicated by the insurance company.

So the regulations themselves refer to the fact that insurance companies are subject to State regulations.

* * *

iii. *Kay v. Ehrler*, No. 90–79, 1991 WL 636562 at *29–*31 (Feb. 25, 1991).

Oral Argument of Robert A. Long, Jr., on Behalf of the United States, as *Amicus Curiae*, Supporting the Respondents

MR. LONG: Thank you, Mr. Chief Justice, and may it please the Court:

Let me begin with a point Mr. Dyk raised. He referred to *pro se* organizations, and there was also a question whether a partnership can litigate pro se. Our understanding is that the general rule is that organizations cannot litigate *pro se*. That is certainly true of corporations, and we think that is the majority rule as to partnerships and also as to unincorporated associations.

QUESTION: Corporations can't litigate *pro se* because the corporation can't come into court?

MR. LONG: It could not appear through its president or through some officer of the corporation. It has to hire a member of the bar to represent it.

QUESTION: Well, what if its vice president is a lawyer?

MR. LONG: I think that then the courts have allowed the attorney—

QUESTION: They don't need to go out and hire anybody. It's just part of his job.

MR. LONG: Well, that would be the in-house counsel situation, and that is certainly okay. I might add—

QUESTION: But how about a voluntary organization, say an environmental organization or, you know, any one of the groups that litigate. If they're simply an association, are they allowed to appear in court by one of their members who is not a lawyer?

MR. LONG: We think the general rule is they are not, and the cases on this are collected under 28 U.S.C. 1654, which is a statute we did not cite in our brief, but that is a statute that generally gives all parties in Federal courts a right to conduct their own cases personally or by counsel.

QUESTION: So, under your view an organization would have to be represented by an attorney, but it could be an attorney who was also a member of the organization?

MR. LONG: Yes, that's exactly right, Mr. Chief Justice. We think the language of Section 1988 which provides that a prevailing party other than the United

States may recover a reasonable attorney's fee as part of the costs answers the question presented in this case. The word "attorney" ordinarily denotes a person who is both licensed to practice law and who acts as the representative or agent of a client. Members of the bar generally do represent clients, but that does not mean that a lawyer who litigates a case *pro se* is functioning as an attorney. Standard dictionaries define attorney as the agent or representative of another. And representation is the essence of phrases such as attorney in fact and power of attorney. We also think other language in Section 1988 reinforces the conclusion that Congress used attorney in its usual sense.

* * *

8. *Candor to the Court*

i. *Securities and Exchange Commission v. Zandford*, No. 01–147, 2002 WL 485040 at *8–*9 (Mar. 18, 2002).

Oral Argument of Matthew D. Roberts on Behalf of the Petitioner

* * *

QUESTION: Mr. Roberts, there's one point in your reply brief that I didn't quite grasp. This action is brought by the SEC.

MR. ROBERTS: Yes.

QUESTION: And it hinges on the wrong that was done to the customer. Could the customer bring this very lawsuit, could the customer have sued the broker for a 10(b) violation?

MR. ROBERTS: In this circumstance, yes, the customer could have brought a private action against the broker, Your Honor. That wouldn't be true in every circumstance because the customer, a private plaintiff seeking damages[,] has to prove elements of a violation in addition to what the SEC must prove.

A customer has to show causation of the transaction and loss or damages to the customer. The customer also has to be an actual purchaser seller. In the situation where there's a sale by the broker of the customer's securities, the purchaser-seller requirement will be met. But there might not be the damages that are necessary unless the broker follows through with his scheme to misappropriate the proceeds of the sale.

QUESTION: But this time he did.

MR. ROBERTS: But he did.

* * *

ii. *Chickasaw Nation v. United States*, No. 00–507, 2001 WL 1183439 at *27–*29, *39–*43 (Oct. 2, 2001).

Oral Argument of Edward C. Dumont on Behalf of the Respondent

* * *

QUESTION: So, in any event, we're not talking here about Indian casinos, gambling casino operations, because they wouldn't be covered by the exemption in Title 35 even if it applied.

MR. DuMONT: That's correct. They would not be covered by the exemption. They would be covered by the tax.

QUESTION: Well, that depends on how broadly one construes the word lottery, and that's been broadly construed in some cases.

MR. DuMONT: That's true. There's a fairly specific—

QUESTION: But in any event, in this case we do have an Indian lottery.

MR. DuMONT: We have an Indian lottery. We—we are prepared to concede that, yes.

QUESTION: Well, is—are we talking about—is the excise tax, .25 percent on the amount of each wager in 4401(a)(1)—does that apply to Indian gaming? It says, there shall be imposed on any wager authorized under the law of the State in which accepted excise tax equal to 0.25 percent of the amount of such wager. Is that the kind we're talking about here?

MR. DuMONT: That's the tax. It's the .25 percent on any wager.

QUESTION: That is the tax we're talking about.

MR. DuMONT: That is the tax we're talking about. Now, wager—the definitions exclude most kinds of table games like blackjack and so on where, if you look at the definitions, which are on page 90—

QUESTION: See, that's—what I'm thinking of—what I'm thinking about is since 44(a)–4401(a)(1); *i.e.*, there shall be a quarter of 1 percent tax on every wager authorized under the law of the State, except later on, A, B, C, D. If that's what we're talking about in this case, I'm trying to understand the testimony to which they pointed by Mr. Lionell John who said, I object to that word taxation because it would impose—give authority to impose a tax on Indian tribes. But there already was that authority in 4401(a). Is that right?

MR. DuMONT: That's—that's certainly correct. This tax applies, by its terms, to anyone who accepts a wager and we would certainly say that includes a State or a tribe. Now, States are specifically exempted under chapter 35; tribes are not.

QUESTION: I can understand that. What I can't understand is the reference to chapter 35. You don't really have a good explanation for that, do you? What—what does the—what does the reference to chapter 35 cover that's of any relevance?

MR. DuMONT: We do not have a good explanation for that.

QUESTION: Thank you.

* * *

QUESTION: Mr. Dumont, before we get off of canons, we've just been talking about two, but there's a third one. Indians really have two canons on their side and the third one is, to my mind, the strongest and—and the one that's—that's the hardest for you to overcome.

And that is that you never read a statute so that any of its provisions is inoperative or senseless. And—

MR. DuMONT: I agree with you, Your Honor.

QUESTION: To be sure, the Indians' proposed interpretation here is strained, but you can do it; whereas there is no possible way to read section 35 on your interpretation as being relevant. What do you say to that? I really think you have the burden of showing that—that the Indians' interpretation is not only strained, but it's really so strained, it's just—it's just an impossible interpretation. Why is it an impossible interpretation using, you know, that A, B, using the or to mean—you know.

MR. DuMONT: Right. First of all, I agree with you that that's our biggest issue in this case.

Second, I also agree that our answer to that is that the statute is not ambiguous, and this gets back to the canon point. The statute is not ambiguous because it cannot be fairly read to—to impose the exemption that my colleagues want. And I would say that not only because it's not the natural reading, as you pointed out, Justice Scalia, of the statute, but also because you put several things together.

First of all, I'm looking at page—

QUESTION: 90a of the—

MR. DuMONT: 90a.

QUESTION:—of the appendix to the petition.

MR. DuMONT: But—page 90a.

[W]hat they want to do is to split gaming—winnings from gaming or wagering operations. Now, first of all, the very last line of the statute refers to State gaming and wagering operations, and there it is used as a phrase. And we submit that that's powerful evidence that it's used as a phrase a few lines up.

Second, in the very next breath from where it says, with respect to the winnings from gaming or wagering operations, the statute says, shall apply to Indian gaming operations. It doesn't—doesn't say, apply to

Indian gaming. It says, apply to Indian gaming operations. Again, clearly the statute is using those two together.

Third, even if we were to accept that interpretation, I'm not sure where it would get the tribes here because if you accept that interpretation, then you are divorcing winnings and gaming—or sorry—wagering and gaming. It means they don't mean the same thing. And all the statute confers is a right to have these provisions apply to Indian gaming operations conducted pursuant to this chapter in the same manner as it applies to the States.

Now, if we're going to divorce gaming from wagering operations, then having the provisions that apply to gaming by the States tells you nothing about chapter 35 because chapter 35 applies to wagering operations.

So—and—and finally, I think, as Justice Ginsburg and some of the other colloquies pointed out earlier, the implication of that reading would be that the reporting and withholding requirements that we all agree are central to this statute somehow only apply to the Indian gaming piece and they don't apply to the wagering operations piece. And that makes no sense out of the statute.

QUESTION: But—

MR. DuMONT: So, for all those reasons, I don't think it's just a strained reading; I think it's an impossible reading of the statute.

QUESTION: But you do concede that, as I believe Judge Dyk said, the only way to make sense out of the statute is to treat it as though the reference to chapter 35 were not there.

MR. DuMONT: I think that's right. I think in—in effect what one has to do is ignore the parenthetical, the examples in the parenthetical, and give effect instead to the—what we would call the operative statutory text. And as I said, if you took out the entire parenthetical, it wouldn't change anything about the—the effect of this statute on sections 1441, 3402(q), or 6041 because those are provisions of the

Internal Revenue Code concerning the reporting and withholding of taxes with respect to winnings, and so they would continue to apply even if we deleted the entire parenthetical.

What wouldn't continue to apply are these two inapt examples—or the one inapt example of chapter 35 and possibly 6050I. And in a particular situation like this, I take no joy in saying that there are some words that have no effect in the statute, but that is the position we're left with, and it is by far the better position of the two that are possible.

* * *

9. *Closing to Argument*

i. ***Custis v. United States***, No. 93–5209, 1994 WL 663719 at *47–*49 (Feb. 28. 1994)

Oral Argument of William C. Bryson on Behalf of the Respondent

* * *

QUESTION: Mr. Bryson, supposing the district court in this case took all these convictions into consideration, as the court of appeals said it could, and the defendant is then sent to prison for a number of years. Under our *Malang* decision, could he then in Federal habeas challenge one of his earlier convictions?

MR. BRYSON: Your Honor, our reading of *Malang* is that he could not, that those convictions he would not be in custody on those prior convictions, although there's language at the end of *Malang* that leaves open the question of just how you can challenge conviction A when you have been—when that has been used to enhance your sentence for conviction B.

If I may say one more word about the practical impacts and the burden of this, I think it is an increasing practice that we see increasing numbers of cases come in, and just recently I saw a case in which a defendant had 17 prior convictions and challenged every single one of them, and it is not limited—this problem is not limited—

QUESTION: Did he succeed on any of his challenges?

MR. BRYSON: He actually got a long opinion out of the court of appeals in which there was a split opinion as to whether he should have been granted relief or not, but the—

QUESTION: On 17?

MR. BRYSON: The point is that the mischief here— well, a number of them were not violent crimes.

QUESTION: He had to win on 15 in order to get under the three, didn't he?

MR. BRYSON: He managed to knock a number out on the ground that they were not violent crimes, others on other grounds and so forth, but he got down to a small number and attacked those on constitutional grounds.

But if I can just make one further point, this is not a principle that—if this Court adopts the principle petitioner seeks, that's limited just to enhancement proceedings. It would affect every sentencing proceeding in which somebody wants to use a prior conviction just as a factor going to whether the person should be sentenced in a particular way.

It also would affect, I assume, whether a prior conviction can be used for impeachment, so that when a prosecutor stands up after the defendant has testified and says, I want to impeach this guy with his prior conviction, he would be able to say, oh no, I had a bad lawyer, you can't use that, and you'd have to have a proceeding right there to decide whether or not the lawyer in that other case was ineffective.

I think one other area in which the same practical problem would arise is probation revocation. You've never been able to challenge your initial conviction in a revocation proceeding, but I assume that if the defendants are correct here, the defendant is correct, then you would be able to in a case like this.

QUESTION: Thank you, Mr. Bryson.

* * *

ii. *Conwood v. United States Tobacco Co.*, No. 00–
6267 (6th Cir.), Oral Arg. Tr. at 18–20 (Nov. 27, 2001).

Argument of Mark C. Hansen on Behalf of Plain-
tiff/Appellee Conwood Company, L.P.

* * *

MR. HANSEN: * * * The verdict should be affirmed.
It was a fair and appropriate trial, and the parties
should go on about their business. Thank you.

JUDGE CLAY: I know you're out of time there, but let
me ask you this. How do you respond to this argument
that the expert should have disaggregated legal from
illegal conduct, and that in part that seems to be
opposed to this *Daubert* issue. I don't know if you
think that's a *Daubert* issue or not, but how would you
address that?

MR. HANSEN: Four points, Your Honor. First, they
waived that argument. They didn't ask for a jury
instruction about it. They didn't ask for a special
verdict. It's sandbagging, frankly, to the District Judge
to come to this Court and say there should have been
further parsing out of the species of conduct that the
jury found wrongful. The jury was presented the case
on a general instruction, which they said was fine, and
on a general verdict form. And we cited the cases in
our brief that say that when a litigant does that, he
can't then come to the Court of Appeals and say
disaggregation, it needs to be all picked apart and
redone at $20 million a side.

Second, Leftwich did disaggregate. If there's one point
I can leave the Court with, it probably isn't presented
clearly in our brief, Leftwich did two studies, one of
which isn't even challenged. He took the defense expert's study, Professor Scheffman, who did a bad acts
analysis. He attempted to prove that wherever reported bad acts were high, there was no correlation with
low market share. Well, guess what? Leftwich took
that very study, Leftwich took Scheffman, their computer model, and ran it with better data, that is, the
contemporaneous sworn surveys of 241 Conwood sales

reps, as opposed to a piece of paper that Professor Scheffman couldn't describe other than he got it from UST counsel. When you ran the regression that way, he proved the damages independently of his other study. That was entirely disaggregated, because it was bad act specific. The very study they claimed—remarkably—in their brief that we didn't do, he did, and yet I can't find a word about it in either their opening brief or their reply brief.

Third, there was really nothing to disaggregate in that we said to the jury, and this was consistent throughout the trial—and it shows the distance from the trial to this appeal—we said to the jury, I said it in summation, and it's probably in the Joint Appendix: We are not asking you to award damages for anything they did to sell their products, to promote their products, to get the space they needed to sell. We are only asking you to give us damages, and find unlawful, things they admitted were improper. And those are three things: Going to stores and taking out our racks without permission; going to stores and using their power to get permission—either by ruse or other trickery—to take racks out; third, making deals with stores that required stores to let them take those out.

And then the fourth point is that, even if at the end of the day all those other arguments were to fail, and we submit they certainly can't, the Supreme Court in *Bigelow*, and this Court in *Elyria–Lorain* said the following: When an antitrust violator, a 70 percent monopolist pollutes the market with wrongful conduct, extensive, systematic wrongful conduct, it will not lie for the wrongdoer to come to the Court of Appeals and say parse out the damages, there might be some lawful conduct mixed in there. That is the very argument the Defendant made in *Bigelow* that was accepted by the Seventh Circuit. And the Supreme Court said that argument will not lie. It is always difficult to predict what would have happened in fair competition. It is not fair argument for the Defendant to say it's too imprecise, there may be lawful conduct swept into the mix. It's Defendant's fault that created this problem in the first place, created the need to make a reasonable estimate. And so long as the jury had the basis for a reasonable estimate, which I submit the jury more than amply did here, the jury verdict must stand.

JUDGE CLAY: I think we have the argument in hand.

MR. HANSEN: Thank you, Your Honor.

iii. *Rice v. Cayetano,* No. 98–818, 1999 WL 955376 at *17–*19 (Oct. 6, 1999).

Oral Argument of Theodore B. Olson on Behalf of the Petitioner

* * *

QUESTION: Let me ask a question that Justice Kennedy's question prompted. Supposing today we approach an island that we had previously not any political relationship with, but it's populated by a group of 1,000 people who are just all farmers. They don't even have a Government. Could we make an arrangement with that group that you can become a part of the United States and in exchange we give all of you and your descendants a tax exemption, say, or free baseball tickets to the World Series.

(Laughter.)

QUESTION: Some preference.

MR. OLSON: I don't think so, Justice Stevens.

QUESTION: You don't think—

MR. OLSON: I do not think so, and—

QUESTION: Congress would not have the power to make that kind of a deal.

MR. OLSON: I don't see where it would come from in the Constitution.

Secondly, what we have here is, and I'm going to put back into your hypothetical what we have here, which are remote descendants of the people. Now, let's move forward 200 years.

QUESTION: Right, I'm saying, we'll give this to you and all of your descendants.

MR. OLSON: Forever and ever and ever.

QUESTION: Right.

MR. OLSON: I don't think that that's consistent at all with the Fourteenth and Fifteenth Amendment to the Constitution, especially if it involved voting. If it didn't involve voting, we'd only be dealing with the Fourteenth Amendment to the Constitution.

This Court is required, with respect, if we step to the Fourteenth Amendment—

QUESTION: And make my hypothetical saying, and your descendants can vote when they're only 15 years old. That would be the vote.

MR. OLSON: Pardon?

QUESTION: To get voting into it, I'd say we give you, a) a tax exemption, and b) the right to have your children vote when they're 14 years old, and all your descendants. We could not make that—

MR. OLSON: I think that is a discrimination on the basis of ancestry which this Court has said over and over again is a discrimination on the basis of race. To the extent that there's a Fourteenth Amendment issue that will focus on, this Court has said racial classifications, and we don't need to look into motives here, or legislative history, or anything else. This is a racial classification on its face.

QUESTION: In Justice Stevens' hypothetical and my hypothetical, would the United States have power to pass legislation consistent with the Fourteenth and Fifteenth Amendment, and to make agreements with those people?

MR. OLSON: I think I answered that, and I think the answer is no. I don't know where the power, that power would come from.

QUESTION: The United States is simply powerless. That's a—

MR. OLSON: To—

QUESTION: Under the foreign affairs power?

MR. OLSON: Well, to make a distinction among citizens on the basis of race in the voting booth, I think that is precluded by the Fifteenth—

QUESTION: No, the hypothetical is, can they deal with them at all? Does the United States have power to deal with a people that is not organized?

MR. OLSON: No, I think that—yes. I think the answer is yes under the foreign policy powers of the United States. Yes, they can deal with this group of people. We're not talking about bringing them in and making them citizens.

QUESTION: The Government can annex territory. That was the Louisiana Purchase.

MR. OLSON: Of course. Of course. Let me just say, and I'd like to reserve the balance of my time for rebuttal, that there is nothing remotely close to a compelling governmental reason here even offered by respondent, except to justify, we have to have—limit people on the basis of race in the voting booth because we're going to limit people on the basis of race on the recipient end.

That is discrimination as an end justifying a discriminatory means. That cannot be a compelling justification. There's not remote narrow tailoring here. It's obvious overclassification and underclassification. It is unlimited in time, to use the words of the *Adarand* decision, and unlimited in terms of descendants from the individuals who are purportedly related to the class.

I will reserve the balance of my time, with the Court's permission.

Appendix F

MODEL REBUTTALS

1. *Toyota Motor Manufacturing v. Williams*, No. 00–1089, 2001 WL 1453954 at *49–*51 (Nov. 7, 2001).

Rebuttal Argument of John G. Roberts, Jr., on Behalf of the Petitioner

MR. ROBERTS: Thank you, Your Honor.

Justice Kennedy, it will not be enough to x out that one sentence on page 4a. You would also have to x out the sentence on page 5a saying that an individual is disabled if their impairment, quote, seriously reduces her ability to perform the manual tasks that are job-related. You would also have to x out the other sentence on page 4a that says a plaintiff is disabled if they're limited in performing, quote, manual tasks associated with an assembly line job, end quote. And you would have to x out the sentence on page 2a that says the key issue is whether the plaintiff in this case can use her arms, hands, and shoulders, quote, as required by her new job, end quote. I respectfully submit that by the time you get through x-ing out all those sentences, you should go one step further and x out the opinion as a whole by holding that it is reversed.

Thank you, Your Honor.

QUESTION: What about the other—the other two issues? I mean, the—the court of appeals did not purport to reach the working as a substantial life activity and what else? Lifting as a substantial life activity. How can we reverse it without addressing those issues also, which I don't think we have the tools to do here?

340

MR. ROBERTS: You can certainly reverse with respect to the summary judgment on performing manual tasks. The issues with respect to lifting and working were not addressed by the court of appeals.

QUESTION: So, you acknowledge we would have to remand for—for its consideration of those.

MR. ROBERTS: Unless the Court felt, given the fact that the issues with respect to working were insinuated into the case by the Sixth Circuit's approach, that it was appropriate to address that major life activity as well.

QUESTION: Even as to manual tasks, are you asking for a ruling in your favor on summary judgment on that, or are you saying it shouldn't have been effectively summary judgment for the plaintiff and then we go to the next stage, that—that it could be a jury question on manual tasks?

MR. ROBERTS: No, no. Summary judgment should be granted in favor of Toyota because you have, with respect to manual tasks, an undisputed factual record, and the question is whether that meets the legal standard of substantially limited with respect to a major life activity. A jury can decide things like whether can she lift 20 pounds or not, if there's a dispute, can she do this or that. But those facts are all undisputed with respect to manual tasks. It is a purely legal question whether she meets the statutory standard.

2. *Department of Army v. Blue Fox, Inc.*, No. 97–1642, 1998 WL 846720 at *55–*57 (Dec. 1, 1998).

Rebuttal Argument of Jeffrey A. Lamken on Behalf of the Petitioner

* * *

MR. LAMKEN: The basic principle that we believe should control this case is that anybody seeking money from the United States must show a waiver of immunity and a substantive source of law applicable to the United States giving them a right to the money.

In our view, neither section 702 nor *Pearlman* make equity a source of substantive law applicable to the

United States that gives rise to the right to money from the Treasury. In *Pearlman*, the United States was not a party and the rights that were recognized were rights to money that operated against only other private parties.

In fact, in *OPM v. Richmond*, there existed in that very case a waiver of immunity, but the Court rejected the notion that the—that the lower Federal courts could create a right to money under the theory of equitable estoppel. We think the same rule applies to creating rights to money under a theory of equitable liens.

QUESTION: May I just ask one question about the phrasing of the question presented in your cert petition? It asks whether section 702 permits respondent to bring an action, so forth and so on, which seems to me to raise squarely the sovereign immunity question whether this is a money damage case or not. I don't see that it raises the question whether there's any other source of—of law that would support the claim.

MR. LAMKEN: I think it squarely raises that question for two reasons. First, the—the way we read the Ninth Circuit decision—I think the proper way to read it—is that section 702 renders certain sources of law applicable to the United States and create the liens, so that section 702 in a real sense permits people to assert—

QUESTION: Well, it should have been permits or authorizes.

MR. LAMKEN: Permits or—permits—

QUESTION: But you're saying that they read it as an authorization statute, not merely as a waiver of sovereign immunity.

MR. LAMKEN: That's correct, but I think that the second answer is that that in fact is a sovereign immunity issue and the Court consistently has treated the creation of substantive monetary rights against the United States as an issue of sovereign immunity. It treated it—that as an issue of sovereign immunity in the *United States v. Testan*. It created—treated it as an issue in the *United States v. Nordic Village*, and it treated it again as an issue of sovereign immunity in *United States v. Idaho* because sovereign immunity has two inherent components. One is an immunity to suit, and the other is an immunity of the United States' property and its funds to seizure and encumbrances. And any plaintiff seeking to get money from the Treasury must overcome both. It must show both jurisdiction in the Federal court and that Congress has affirmatively intended money to be leaving the Treasury based on this source of law. And I—thank you.

CHIEF JUSTICE REHNQUIST: Thank you, Mr. Lamken. The case is submitted.

3. *INS v. National Center for Immigrants' Rights, Inc.*, No. 90–1090, 1991 WL 636247 at *45–*48 (Nov. 13, 1991).

Rebuttal Argument of Stephen J. Marzen on Behalf of the Petitioner

MR. MARZEN: Three points. First, Mr. Schey asserts that there are thousands of cases in which there are derivative citizenship claims. With the addition of the new case that he has litigated in the Ninth Circuit, we know now of a total of two such cases, one cited in our brief in 1961 and the one he just mentioned.

QUESTION: What do you do about those two cases?

MR. MARZEN: The second part of my point is at page 25 of our opening brief, footnote 16. There is an INS operating instruction which provides as follows; quote, individuals maintaining a colorable claim to U.S. citizenship will not normally be subject to the condition. There is an out for us if we think it's abusive or frivolous. But if you have a colorable claim, the regulation will not be applied to you.

QUESTION: It says will not normally be, but the language of the regulation would seem to apply.

MR. MARZEN: We do make an exception in the operating instruction for just this sort of case.

Secondly, the 1990 Immigration Act which Mr. Schey brings up as Congress legislating new authority to detain aliens which it didn't otherwise have is not quite what the 1990 act says. The 1990 act restricts the Attorney General's discretion to release people. Congress was dissatisfied with the Attorney General releasing aggravated felons pending a final determination of their deportability. So Congress reduced the Attorney General's preexisting authority to let these people out on bail.

QUESTION: What about the most recent amendment, does—if the statute means what you say it means, why was that needed, do you suppose?

MR. MARZEN: I'm referring to the most recent. And the reason it was needed is that Congress did not want to allow the release of aggravated felons. He took away the Attorney General's discretion to release them either on their own recognizance or on bond.

The Attorney General, under this law, cannot release aggravated felons under any bond condition unless he determines that they pose no risk of flight and no danger to the community.

My final point is with respect to the legislation—

QUESTION: Before you leave that one point, Mr. Marzen, the regulation to which you refer in the footnote 16 that you cited, when was that adopted? * * * Was that after this case began or was it in effect before the regulation was—

MR. MARZEN: I'm not sure. The date, the only date that it's attached to was an addendum on September 7, 1984. So it's several years ago, but I don't know whether it was announced contemporaneously with the regulation.

The legislative history of H.R. 10—I just will direct the Court, if I might, to the appendix to the petition in our reply brief which points out that subsection (c) which contains the legislative history to which he refers does limit detention. But that, that provision had lifetime detention for those four classes of aliens after a finding of deportability.

That same legislation, and that's on page 6A, the same act, H.R. 10 on pages 3A and 4A contains almost in haec verba the authority that the Attorney General has in current section 1252(a), pending a final determination of deportability, the alien, the Attorney General may in his discretion continue the alien custody or release him on conditions. The legislative history to which he cites refers to a very controversial provision which wasn't adopted. There was no controversy in any of the committee reports or any of the floor debate over the Attorney General's authority that is at issue in this case.

QUESTION: What do you say to *Carlson* and the other Supreme Court case that he cites?

MR. MARZEN: *Carlson* affirms that you can impose conditions that are unrelated to release. And we cite that as the strongest authority in our favor.

If there are no further questions.

CHIEF JUSTICE REHNQUIST: Thank you, Mr. Marzen, the case is submitted.

4. ***Reno v. Condon***, *No. 98–1464, 1999 WL 1075199 at *3–*4 (November 10, 1999).*

Rebuttal Argument of Seth P. Waxman on Behalf of the Petitioners

GENERAL WAXMAN: Thank you, Mr. Chief Justice. I'd like to make 3 points in my 3 minutes, if I may.

First of all, with respect to the *Usery–Garcia* point, Judge Easterbrook, writing the majority opinion in *Travis*, which is the companion case in the Seventh Circuit, found correctly, we think, and for the reasons we articulate in our reply brief at page 8, footnote 6, that this case, in any event, wouldn't be decided differently even under the regime in *Usery*.

And I commend the Court's attention to Judge Easterbrook's majority opinion and our analysis, which essentially takes off from the Chief Justice's concurrence in *South Carolina v. Baker*, where the Chief Justice emphasized that the more expansive conception of the Tenth Amendment espoused in *Usery* recognized that congressional action that, quote, operates to displace the State's freedom to structure integral operations in areas of traditional Government functions runs afoul of the authority granted by Congress.

Justice Scalia's hypothetical, where there was a bar on releasing any information that is in a State record, probably would raise very serious concerns under *Usery*, but a release in commerce on information that is personal and private that is provided by citizens we think doesn't implicate *Usery*.

With respect to the—Justice Kennedy's point and Justice Stevens' point about the category of one, I—if one looks at the environmental laws, for example, that Congress has regulated sludge and solid waste systems that are operated, if not exclusively, overwhelmingly by municipalities, and Congress—and it has regulated in a way that is different than it regulates other types of environmental issues, and the fact that Congress distinguishes—

QUESTION: I don't know that the Tenth Amendment applies with all its force to local governments as opposed to State governments. You're talking about the regulation applies to local governments.

GENERAL WAXMAN: Well, if it doesn't, Mr. Chief Justice, I'd sure like to take another shot at *United States v. Printz*, which involved sheriffs and—

(Laughter.)

GENERAL WAXMAN: I don't mean to be facetious. We have understood that in contrast to this Court's Eleventh Amendment jurisdiction, the Court has always construed its Tenth Amendment jurisdiction to include not only States but subordinate sovereign entities, or subordinate governmental entities.

I just want to point out, with respect to *South Carolina v. Baker*, which is always cited as a statute of general applicability, and perhaps in one sense correctly so, but only in the sense that this is, too, the section that—the statute that was at issue in *Baker*, section 310(b)(1) of the Tax Equity and Fiscal Responsibility Act applied only to State and local governments. It denied a tax exemption to unregistered bonds, a tax exemption that only applied to—ever only applied to State and local governments.

The Court pointed out in its opinion that this was part of a general system of law, a general law that did away with—it tried to address the problem of tax fraud through the use of unregistered bonds. It acted with respect to the Federal Government in a different way, and the same is true here.

CHIEF JUSTICE REHNQUIST: Thank you, General Waxman.

GENERAL WAXMAN: Thank you very much.

CHIEF JUSTICE REHNQUIST: The case is submitted.

*

Table of West Research Guides

Researching Supreme Court and Appellate Advocacy: Mastering Oral Argument

§ 1 Introduction

Supreme Court and Appellate Advocacy: Mastering Oral Argument provides a strong base for analyzing even the most complex problem involving issues related to oral arguments at the appellate level. Whether your research requires examination of case law, statutes, expert commentary, or other materials, West books and Westlaw are excellent sources of information.

To keep you informed of current developments, Westlaw provides frequently updated databases. With Westlaw, you have unparalleled legal research resources at your fingertips.

Additional Resources

If you have not previously used Westlaw or have questions not covered in this appendix, call the West Reference Attorneys at 1–800–REF–ATTY (1–800–733–2889). The West Reference Attorneys are trained, licensed attorneys, available 24 hours a day to assist you with your Westlaw search questions. To subscribe to Westlaw, call 1–800–344–5008 or visit westlaw.com at **www.westlaw.com**.

§ 2 Westlaw Databases

Each database on Westlaw is assigned an abbreviation called an *identifier*, which you use to access the database. You can find identifiers for all databases in the online Westlaw Directory and in the printed *Westlaw Database Directory*. When you need to know more detailed information about a database, use Scope. Scope contains coverage information, lists of related databases, and valuable search tips.

The following chart lists Westlaw databases that contain information pertaining to oral argument at the appellate level. For a complete list of litigation-related databases, see the online Westlaw Directory or the printed *Westlaw Database Directory*. Because new information is continually being added to Westlaw, you should also check the tabbed Westlaw page and the online Westlaw Directory for new database information.

Selected Appellate Procedure, Rules, Oral Argument, and Related Databases on Westlaw

Database	Identifier	Coverage
United States Supreme Court		
Supreme Court Case Law	SCT	Begins with 1945
Supreme Court Case Law– Before 1945	SCT–OLD	1790–1944
United States Law Week	UNLW	Begins with 1986
Preview of U.S. Supreme Court Cases	SCT–PREVIEW	Begins with December 1989
Westlaw Bulletin–U.S. Supreme Court	WLB–SCT	Current Data
U.S. Supreme Court Briefs	SCT–BRIEF	Meris Briefs: Begins with 1990–91 Term Amicus briefs: begins with 1995– 96 Term
Transcripts of U.S. Supreme Court Oral Arguments	SCT–ORALARG	Begins with 1990-91 Term
Federal and State Case Law Combined		
Federal and State Case Law	ALLCASES	Begins with 1945
Federal and State Case Law–Before 1945	ALLCASES–OLD	1789–1944
Individual Circuit Federal and State Cases	CTAXX–ALL (where XX is a circuit number or DC)	Varies by court
Federal Case Law		
Federal Case Law	ALLFEDS	Varies by court
U.S. Courts of Appeals Cases	CTA	Begins with 1945
U.S. Court of Appeals for Individual Circuit Cases	CTAXX (where XX is a circuit number, DC, or F)	Begins with 1945
U.S. District Courts Cases	DCT	Begins with 1945
U.S. District Court Cases for Individual Circuit States	DCTXX (where XX is a circuit number or DC)	Begins with 1945
State Case Law		
State Case Law	ALLSTATES	Begins with 1945
Individual State Cases	XX–CS (where XX is a state's two-letter postal abbreviation)	Varies by state
Federal Statutes and Rules		
United States Code Annotated®	USCA	Current data
Federal Rules	US–RULES	Current data
Federal Orders	US–ORDERS	Current data
State Statutes and Rules		
State Statutes–Annotated	ST–ANN–ALL	Current data

Database	Identifier	Coverage
Individual State Statutes–Annotated	XX–ST–ANN (where XX is a state's two-letter postal abbreviation)	Current data
Individual State Court Rules	XX–RULES (where XX is a state's two-letter postal abbreviation)	Current data
Individual State Court Orders	XX–ORDERS (where XX is a state's two-letter postal abbreviation)	Current data

Legal Texts, Periodicals, Practice Materials, and Related Materials

American Journal of Trial Advocacy	AMJTA	Selected coverage begins with 1982 (vol. 6) Full coverage begins with 1993 (vol. 17)
Association of Trial Lawyers of America–Convention Reference Materials	ATLA–CLE	Begins with 2000
Death Penalty–Texts and Periodicals	DP–TP	Varies by publication
Individual State Practice Series	XXPRAC (for selected states where XX is a state's two-letter postal abbreviation	Current data
Journal of Appellate Practice and Process	JAPPPR	Full coverage begins with 1999 (vol. 1)
Legal Practice Database	LAWPRAC	Varies by publication
Litigation–Law Reviews, Texts, and Bar Journals	LTG–TP	Varies by publication
Suffolk Journal of Trial and Appellate Advocacy	SFKJTAA	Full coverage begins with 1995 (vol. 1)
Supreme Court Review	SCTR	Full coverage begins with 1993 (vol. 1993)
Transcripts of U.S. Supreme Court Oral Arguments	SCT–ORALARG	Begins with 1990–91 Term
Trial	JTLATRIAL	Selected coverage begins with 1997 (vol. 33, no. 11)
Trial Magazine	TRIAL–MAG	Begins with January 1995

Directories

West Legal Directory®	WLD	Current data
West Legal Directory–Litigation	WLD–LIT	Current data
	AFJ WLD–JUDGE WLD–CLERK	
West Dockets Databases for US Courts of Appeals		

§ 3 Retrieving a Document with a Citation: Find and Hypertext Links

§ 3.1 Find

Find is a Westlaw service that allows you to retrieve a document by entering its citation. Find allows you to retrieve documents from anywhere in Westlaw without accessing or changing databases. Find is available for many documents, including case law (state and federal), the *United States Code Annotated*, state statutes, administrative materials, and texts and periodicals.

To use Find, simply type the citation in the *Find this document by citation* text box on the tabbed Westlaw page and click **GO**. The following list provides some examples:

To Find This Document	Access Find and Type
Gregory v. U.S. 109 F. Supp. 2d 441 (E.D.Va. 2000)	**109 fsupp 2d 441**
U.S. v. Elizalde–Adame 262 F.3d 637 (7th Cir. 2001)	**262 f3d 637**
Fed. R. App. P. 10	**frap rule 10**
N.Y. Ct. Rules § 670.20	**ny ct rule s 670.20**

For a complete list of publications that can be retrieved with Find and their abbreviations, click **Find** on the toolbar and then click **Publications List**.

§ 3.2 Hypertext Links

Use hypertext links to move from one location to another on Westlaw. For example, use hypertext links to go directly from the statute, case, or law review article you are viewing to a cited statute, case, or article; from a headnote to the corresponding text in the opinion; or from an entry in a statutes index database to the full text of the statute.

§ 4 Searching with Natural Language

Overview: With Natural Language, you can retrieve documents by simply describing your issue in plain English. If you are a relatively new Westlaw user, Natural Language searching can make it easier for you to retrieve cases that are on point. If you are an experienced Westlaw user, Natural Language gives you a valuable alternative search method.

When you enter a Natural Language description, Westlaw automatically identifies legal phrases, removes common words, and generates variations of terms in your description. Westlaw then searches for the concepts in your description. Concepts may include significant terms, phrases, legal citations, or topic and key numbers. Westlaw retrieves the 20 documents that most closely match your description, beginning with the document most likely to match.

§ 4.1 Natural Language Search

Access a database, such as Journals and Law Reviews (JLR). In the *Natural Language description* text box, type a description such as the following:

what is the standard of review for excusable neglect

§ 4.2 Browsing Search Results

Best Mode: To display the best portion (the portion that most closely matches your description) of each document in a Natural Language search result, click the **Best** arrow at the bottom of the page.

Term Mode: Click the **Term** arrow at the bottom of the page to display portions of the document that contain search terms.

Previous/Next Document: Click the left or right **Doc** arrow to view the previous or the next document in the search result.

Citations List: The citations list in the left frame lists the documents retrieved by the search. Click a hypertext link to display a document in the right frame.

§ 4.3 Next 20 Documents

Westlaw displays the 20 documents that most closely match your description, beginning with the document most likely to match. If you want to view an additional 20 documents, click the right arrow in the left frame.

§ 5. Searching with Terms and Connectors

Overview: With Terms and Connectors searching, you enter a query, which consists of key terms from your issue and connectors specifying the relationship between these terms.

Terms and Connectors searching is useful when you want to retrieve a document for which you know specific details, such as the title or the fact situation. Terms and Connectors searching is also useful when you want to retrieve documents relating to a specific issue.

§ 5.1   Terms

Plurals and Possessives: Plurals are automatically retrieved when you enter the singular form of a term. This is true for both regular and irregular plurals (e.g., **child** retrieves *children*). If you enter the plural form of a term, you will not retrieve the singular form.

If you enter the nonpossessive form of a term, Westlaw automatically retrieves the possessive form as well. However, if you enter the possessive form, only the possessive form is retrieved.

Compound Words, Abbreviations, and Acronyms: When a compound word is one of your search terms, use a hyphen to retrieve all forms of the word. For example, the term **news-stand** retrieves *news-stand, newsstand,* and *news stand.*

When using an abbreviation or acronym as a search term, place a period after each of the letters to retrieve any of its forms. For example, the term **u.s.a.** retrieves *USA, U.S.A., U S A,* and *U. S. A.* Note: The abbreviation does *not* retrieve *United States of America,* so remember to add additional alternative terms to your query such as **"united states"**.

The Root Expander and the Universal Character: When you use the Terms and Connectors search method, placing the root expander (!) at the end of a root term generates all other terms with that root. For example, adding the ! to the root *advoca* in the query

advoca! /s oral /s argument

instructs Westlaw to retrieve such terms as *advocacy, advocate, advocated,* and *advocating.*

The universal character (*) stands for one character and can be inserted in the middle or at the end of a term. For example, the term

withdr*w

will retrieve *withdraw* and *withdrew.* Adding three asterisks to the root *elect*

elect* * *

instructs Westlaw to retrieve all forms of the root with up to three additional characters. Terms such as *elected* or *election* are retrieved by this query. However, terms with more than three letters following the root, such as *electronic,* are not retrieved. Plurals are always retrieved, even if more than three letters follow the root.

Phrase Searching: To search for an exact phrase, place it within quotation marks. For example, to search for references to *standard of review*, type **"standard of review"**. When you are using the Terms and Connectors search method, you should use phrase searching only if you are certain that the terms in the phrase will not appear in any other order.

§ 5.2 Alternative Terms

After selecting the terms for your query, consider which alternative terms are necessary. For example, if you are searching for the term *good faith*, you might also want to search for the terms *nonfrivolous* or *meritorious.* You should consider both synonyms and antonyms as alternative terms. You can also use the Westlaw thesaurus to add alternative terms to your query.

§ 5.3 Connectors

After selecting terms and alternative terms for your query, use connectors to specify the relationship that should exist between search terms in your retrieved documents. The connectors are described below:

Use:	To retrieve documents with:	Example:
& (and)	both terms	**"plain error" & "harmless error"**
or (space)	either term or both terms	**non-frivolous good-faith**
/p	search terms in the same paragraph	**"summary judgment" /p certiorari**
/s	search terms in the same sentence	**revers** /s prejudice**
+s	the first search term preceding the second within the same sentence	**merits +s brief**
/n	search terms within *n* terms of each other (where *n* is a number)	**defect! /5 indictment**
+n	the first search term preceding the second by *n* terms (where *n* is a number)	**appeal +5 right**

Use:	To retrieve documents with:	Example:
" "	search terms appearing in the same order as in the quotation marks	**"standard of review"**

Use:	To exclude documents with:	Example:
% (but not)	search terms following the % symbol	**r.i.c.o.** % **"puerto rico"**

§ 5.4 Field Restrictions

Overview: Documents in each Westlaw database consist of several segments, or fields. One field may contain the citation, another the title, another the synopsis, and so forth. Not all databases contain the same fields. Also depending on the database, fields with the same name may contain different types of information.

To view a list of fields for a specific database and their contents, see Scope for that database. Note that in some databases not every field is available for every document.

To retrieve only those documents containing your search terms in a specific field, restrict your search to that field. To restrict your search to a specific field, type the field name or abbreviation followed by your search terms enclosed in parentheses. For example, to retrieve a U.S. Supreme Court case titled *PGA Tour, Inc. v. Martin,* access the U.S. Supreme Court Cases database (SCT) and search for your terms in the title field (ti).

ti(p.g.a. & martin)

The fields discussed below are available in Westlaw case law databases you might use for researching issues related to appellate oral arguments.

Digest and Synopsis Fields: The digest (di) and synopsis (sy) fields, added to case law databases by West's attorney-editors, summarize the main points of a case. The synopsis field contains a brief description of a case. The digest field contains the topic and headnote fields and includes the complete hierarchy of concepts used by West's editors to classify the headnotes to specific West digest topic and key numbers. Restricting your search to the synopsis and digest fields limits your result to cases in which your terms are related to a major issue in the case.

Consider restricting your search to one or both of these fields if

- you are searching for common terms or terms with more than one meaning, and you need to narrow your search; or

- you cannot narrow your search by using a smaller database.

For example, to retrieve state family law cases that were reversed and remanded for abuse of discretion by the trial court and which discuss the clear and convincing standard of evidence, access the California Cases database (CA–CS) and type the following query:

sy,di("clear and convincing" & abuse* /5 discretion & reversed /5 remanded)

Headnote Field: The headnote field (he) is part of the digest field but does not contain topic numbers, hierarchical classification information, or key numbers. The headnote field contains a one-sentence summary for each point of law in a case and any supporting citations given by the author of the opinion. A headnote field restriction is useful when you are searching for specific statutory sections or rule numbers. For example, to retrieve headnotes from Florida cases that cite section 59.06 of the Florida Statutes, access the Florida Cases database (FL–CS) and type the following query:

he(59.06)

Topic Field: The topic field (to) is also part of the digest field. It contains hierarchical classification information, including the West digest topic names and numbers and the key numbers. You should restrict search terms to the topic field in a case law database if

- a digest field search retrieves too many documents; or

- **you want to retrieve cases with digest paragraphs classified under more than one topic.**

For example, the topic Appeal and Error has the topic number 30. To retrieve state criminal cases that discuss the court ordering a new trial *sua sponte*, access the Texas Cases database (TX–CS) and type a query like the following:

to(30) /p "new trial" /p "sua sponte"

For a complete list of West digest topics and their corresponding topic numbers, access the Custom Digest by choosing **Key Numbers and Digest** from the *More* drop-down list.

Note: Slip opinions and cases from topical services do not contain the digest, headnote, and topic fields.

Prelim and Caption Fields: When searching in a database containing statutes, rules, or regulations, restrict your search to the prelim (pr) and caption (ca) fields to retrieve documents in which your terms are important enough to appear in a section name or heading. For example, to retrieve Ohio statutes regarding making a motion for a new trial, access the Ohio Statutes–Annotated database (OH–ST–ANN) and type the following:

pr,ca(new /5 trial & motion)

§ 5.5 Date Restrictions

You can use Westlaw to retrieve documents *decided* or *issued* before, after, or on a specified date, as well as within a range of dates. The following sample queries contain date restrictions:

da(2002) & oral /p argu!

da(aft 1998) & role job purpose /s attorney lawyer /p appellate /p advoca!

da(8/2002) & judge justice bench panel court /p question /p oral /3 argument

You can also search for documents *added to a database* on or after a specified date, as well as within a range of dates. The following sample queries contain added-date restrictions:

ad(aft 1999) & "midnight deadline" /p settl!

ad(aft 12/31/2000 & bef 6/1/2002) & preserv! /s argument /s appeal

§ 6 Searching with Topic and Key Numbers

To retrieve cases that address a specific point of law, use topic and key numbers as your search terms. If you have an on-point case, run a search using the topic and key number from the relevant headnote in an appropriate database to find other cases containing headnotes classified to that topic and key number. For example, to search for state cases containing headnotes classified under topic 30 (Appeal and Error) and key number 867(4) (Review of Verdict, Findings or Judgment), access the State Case Law database (ALL-STATES) and enter the following query:

30k867(4)

For a complete list of West digest topics and their corresponding topic numbers, access the Custom Digest by choosing **Key Numbers and Digest** from the *More* drop-down list.

Note: Slip opinions and cases from topical services do not contain West topic and key numbers.

§ 6.1   Custom Digest

The Custom Digest contains the complete topic and key number outline used by West attorney-editors to classify headnotes. You can use the Custom Digest to obtain a single document containing the case law headnotes that are related to your legal issue from a particular jurisdiction.

Access the Custom Digest by choosing **Key Numbers and Digest** from the *More* drop-down list on the toolbar. Select up to 10 topics and key numbers from the easy-to-browse outline and click **GO**. Then follow the on-screen instructions.

For example, to research issues involving appeals, scroll down the Custom Digest page until topic 30, *Appeal and Error*, is displayed. Click the plus symbol (+) to display key number information. Select the check box next to each key number you want to include in your search, then click **GO**. Select the jurisdiction from which you want to retrieve headnotes and, if desired, select a date restriction and type additional search terms. Click **Search**.

§ 6.2   KeySearch

KeySearch is a research tool that helps you find cases and secondary sources in a specific area of the law. KeySearch guides you through the selection of terms from a classification system based on the West Key Number System® and then uses the key numbers and their underlying concepts to formulate a query for you. To access KeySearch, click **KeySearch** on the toolbar. Then browse the list of topics and subtopics and select a topic or subtopic to search by clicking the hypertext links. For example, to search for cases that discuss preserving an issue for appeal, click **Civil Procedure** at the first KeySearch page. Then click **Appeal and Review** and **Preservation of Error** on the next two pages.

§ 7   Verifying Your Research with Citation Research Services

Overview: A citation research service, such as they KeyCite service, is a tool that helps you ensure that your cases are good law; helps you retrieve cases, legislation, or articles that cite a case, rule, or statute; and helps you verify that the spelling and format of your citations are correct.

§ 7.1   KeyCite for Cases

KeyCite for cases covers case law on Westlaw, including unpublished opinions. KeyCite for cases provides

- direct appellate history of a case, including related references, which are opinions involving the same parties and facts but resolving different issues

- negative indirect history of a case, which consists of cases outside the direct appellate line that may have a negative impact on its precedential value

- the title, parallel citations, court of decision, docket number, and filing date of a case

- **citations to cases, administrative decisions, and secondary sources on Westlaw that have cited a case**

- **complete integration with the West Key Number System so you can track legal issues discussed in a case**

§ 7.2   KeyCite for Statutes and Federal Regulations

KeyCite for statutes and federal regulations covers the *United States Code Annotated* (USCA®), the *Code of Federal Regulations* (CFR), and statutes from all 50 states. KeyCite for statutes provides

- links to session laws amending or repealing a statute

- statutory credits and historical notes

- citations to pending legislation affecting a federal statute or a statute from California or New York

- citations to cases, administrative decisions, and secondary sources that have cited a statute

§ 7.3   KeyCite for Administrative Materials

KeyCite for administrative materials includes

- National Labor Relations Board decisions beginning with 1935

- Board of Contract Appeals decisions (varies by agency)

- Board of Immigration Appeals decisions beginning with 1940

- Comptroller General decisions beginning with 1921

- Environmental Protection Agency decisions beginning with 1974

- Federal Communications Commission decisions beginning with 1960

- Federal Energy Regulatory Commission (Federal Power Commission) decisions beginning with 1931 (history only)

- Internal Revenue Service revenue rulings beginning with 1954

- Internal Revenue Service revenue procedures beginning with 1954

- Internal Revenue Service private letter rulings beginning with 1954

- Internal Revenue Service technical advice memoranda beginning with 1954

- Public Utilities Reports beginning with 1974 (history only)

- U.S. Merit Systems Protection Board decisions beginning with 1979

- U.S. Patent and Trademark Office decisions beginning with 1987

- U.S. Tax Court (Board of Tax Appeals) decisions beginning with 1924

- U.S. patents beginning with 1976

§ 7.4 KeyCite Alert

KeyCite Alert monitors the status of your cases or statutes and automatically sends you updates at the frequency you specify when their KeyCite information changes.

§ 8 Researching with Westlaw—Examples

§ 8.1 Retrieving Law Review Articles

Recent law review articles are often a good place to begin researching a legal issue because law review articles serve 1) as an excellent introduction to a new topic or review for a stale one, providing terminology to help you formulate a query; 2) as a finding tool for pertinent primary authority, such as rules, statutes, and cases; and 3) in some instances, as persuasive secondary authority.

Suppose you need to gain background information on the kinds of questions judges ask during oral arguments.

Solution

- To retrieve recent law review articles relevant to your issue, access the Journals and Law Reviews database (JLR). Using the Natural Language search method, enter a description like the following (place alternative terms in parentheses, following the primary term):

questions judges (court panel bench justice) ask during oral argument

- If you have a citation to an article in a specific publication, use Find to retrieve it. For more information on Find, see Section 3.1 of this appendix. For example, to retrieve the article found at 35 Ind. L. Rev. 451, access Find and type

35 ind l rev 451

- If you know the title of an article but not which journal it appeared in, access the Journals and Law Reviews database (JLR) and search for key terms using the title field. For example, to retrieve the article "Preparation and Delivery of Oral Argument in Appellate Courts," type the following Terms and Connectors query:

ti(prepar! & deliver! & oral /5 argument)

§ 8.2 Retrieving Case Law

Suppose you need to retrieve state cases discussing whether communication between judge and jury is reversible error and therefore grounds for a new trial.

Solution

- Access the State Case Law database (ALLSTATES). Type a Natural Language description such as the following:

judge jury communications require new trial because reversible error

- When you know the citation for a specific case, use Find to retrieve it. For more information on Find, see Section 3.1 of this appendix. For example, to retrieve *Del'Ostia v. Strasser*, 798 So. 2d 785 (Fla. Dist. Ct. App. 2001), access Find and type

798 so2d 785

- If you find a topic and key number that is on point, run a search using that topic and key number to retrieve additional cases discussing that point of law. For example, to retrieve New York state cases containing headnotes classified under topic 275 (New

Trial) and key number 47 (Communications by or with Jurors), access the New York Cases database (NY–CS) and type the following query:

275k47

- To retrieve cases written by a particular judge, add a judge field (ju) restriction to your query. For example, to retrieve cases written by Judge Spain that contain headnotes classified under topic 275 (New Trial), type the following query:

ju(spain) & to(275)

- You can also use KeySearch and the Custom Digest to help you retrieve cases and headnotes that discuss the issue you are researching.

§ 8.3   Retrieving Statutes and Regulations

Suppose you need to retrieve Florida statutes addressing making oral argument via teleconference calls.

Solution

- Access the Florida Statutes–Annotated database (FL–ST–ANN). Search for your terms in the substantive-doc field (sd) (includes the citation, prelim, caption, text, and credit fields) using the Terms and Connectors search method:

sd(oral /5 argument & tele-conferenc!)

- When you know the citation for a specific statute or regulation, use Find to retrieve it. For example, to retrieve section 35.22 of the Florida Statutes, access Find and type

fl st s 35.22

- To look at surrounding sections, use the Table of Contents service. Click the **TOC** tab in the left frame. To display a section listed in the Table of Contents, click its hypertext link. You can also use Documents in Sequence to retrieve the section following section 35.22 even if that subsequent section was not retrieved with your search or Find request. Select **Docs in Seq** from the drop-down list at the bottom of the right frame and click **GO**.

- When you retrieve a statute on Westlaw, it will contain a message if legislation amending or repealing it is available online. To display this legislation, click the **KeyCite** link in the message.

Because slip copy versions of laws are added to Westlaw before they contain full editorial enhancements, they are not retrieved with the update feature. To retrieve slip copy versions of laws, access the United States Public Laws database (US–PL) or a state's legislative service database (XX–LEGIS, where XX is the state's two-letter postal abbreviation). Then type **ci(slip)** and descriptive terms, e.g., **ci(slip) & "new trial"**. Slip copy documents are replaced by the editorially enhanced versions within a few working days. The update feature also does not retrieve legislation that enacts a new statute or covers a topic that will not be incorporated into the statutes. To retrieve this legislation, access US–PL or a legislative service database and enter a query containing terms that describe the new legislation.

§ 8.4   Using KeyCite

Suppose one of the cases you retrieve in your case law research is *Cooper v. Griffin*, 455 F.2d 1142 (5th Cir. 1972). You want to determine whether this case is good law and to find other cases or sources that have cited this case.

Solution

Use KeyCite to retrieve direct and negative indirect history for *Cooper v. Griffin*.

Use KeyCite to display citing references for *Cooper v. Griffin*.

§ 8.5   Following Recent Developments

If you are preparing for an appellate oral argument, it is important to keep up with recent developments. How can you do this efficiently?

Solution

One of the easiest ways to stay abreast of recent developments in the U.S. Supreme Court is by accessing the Westlaw Bulletin–U.S. Supreme Court database (WLB–SCT). The WLB–SCT database contains summaries of recent U.S. Su-

preme Court cases, rules, orders, and other legal activity. When you access WLB–SCT, you automatically retrieve a list of documents added to the database in the last month.

You can also use the WestClip® clipping service to stay informed of recent developments of interest to you. WestClip will run your Terms and Connectors queries on a regular basis and deliver the results to you automatically. You can run WestClip queries in legal and news and information databases. More information about WestClip is available at **www.westgroup.com/documentation**.

Table of Cases

N

National Aeronautics and Space Admin. v. Federal Labor Relations Authority, 527 U.S. 229, 119 S.Ct. 1979, 144 L.Ed.2d 258 (1999)—§ **4.4;** § **4.4, n. 1.**

National Aeronautics and Space Administration v. Federal Labor Relations Authority, 1999 WL 183821 (U.S.Oral.Arg.1999)—§ **4.4, n. 2.**

National Bellas Hess, Inc. v. Department of Revenue of State of Ill., 386 U.S. 753, 87 S.Ct. 1389, 18 L.Ed.2d 505 (1967)—§ **8.5;** § **8.5, n. 7.**

National Collegiate Athletic Ass'n v. Smith, 525 U.S. 459, 119 S.Ct. 924, 142 L.Ed.2d 929 (1999)—§ **7.4;** § **7.4, n. 1.**

National Collegiate Athletic Ass'n v. Smith, 1999 WL 32847 (U.S.Oral. Arg.1999)—§ **7.4, n. 3.**

National Credit Union Admin. v. First Nat. Bank & Trust Co., 522 U.S. 479, 118 S.Ct. 927, 140 L.Ed.2d 1 (1998)— § **7.5;** § **7.5, n. 6;** § **9.3;** § **9.3, n. 2.**

National Credit Union Admin. v. First Nat. Bank & Trust Co., 1997 WL 611828 (U.S.Oral.Arg.1997)—§ **7.5, n. 7;** § **9.3, n. 3.**

National Federation of Federal Employees, Local 1309 v. Department of Interior, 526 U.S. 86, 119 S.Ct. 1003, 143 L.Ed.2d 171 (1999)—§ **4.2, n. 24.**

National Federation of Federal Employees, Local 1309 v. Department of Interior, 1998 WL 792045 (U.S.Oral. Arg.1998)—§ **4.2, n. 23.**

New Jersey v. New York, 523 U.S. 767, 118 S.Ct. 1726, 140 L.Ed.2d 993 (1998)—§ **4.2;** § **4.2, n. 12;** § **7.1;** § **7.1, n. 6.**

New Jersey v. New York, 1998 WL 15118 (U.S.Oral.Arg.1998)—§ **4.2, n. 14;** § **7.1, n. 7.**

Nichols v. United States, 511 U.S. 738, 114 S.Ct. 1921, 128 L.Ed.2d 745 (1994)—§ **7.2;** § **7.2, n. 6.**

Nichols v. United States, 1994 WL 663472 (U.S.Oral.Arg.1994)—§ **7.2, n. 7.**

Norman v. Consolidated Edison Co. of New York, 89 F.2d 619 (2nd Cir. 1937)—§ **2.4, n. 12.**

O

Ogden v. Saunders, 25 U.S. 213, 6 L.Ed. 606 (1827)—§ **2.1;** § **2.1, n. 27.**

Ohio v. Robinette, 519 U.S. 33, 117 S.Ct. 417, 136 L.Ed.2d 347 (1996)—§ **9.1;** § **9.1, n. 2.**

Ohio v. Robinette, 1996 WL 587659 (U.S.Oral.Arg.1996)—§ **9.1, n. 5.**

Osborn v. Bank of United States, 22 U.S. 738, 6 L.Ed. 204 (1824)—§ **2.1;** § **2.1, n. 35.**

P

Pennsylvania v. Mimms, 434 U.S. 106, 98 S.Ct. 330, 54 L.Ed.2d 331 (1977)— § **7.4, n. 5;** § **9.1, n. 7.**

PGA Tour, Inc. v. Martin, 532 U.S. 661, 121 S.Ct. 1879, 149 L.Ed.2d 904 (2001)—§ **4.2;** § **4.2, n. 1.**

PGA Tour, Inc. v. Martin, 2001 WL 41011 (U.S.Oral.Arg.2001)—§ **4.2, n. 2.**

Posters 'N' Things, Ltd. v. United States, 511 U.S. 513, 114 S.Ct. 1747, 128 L.Ed.2d 539 (1994)—§ **7.2;** § **7.2, n. 12.**

Posters 'N' Things, Ltd. v. United States, 1993 WL 757642 (U.S.Oral. Arg.1993)—§ **7.2, n. 13.**

Proprietors of Charles River Bridge v. Proprietors of Warren Bridge, 36 U.S. 420, 9 L.Ed. 773 (1837)—§ **2.1;** § **2.1, n. 29.**

Q

Quill Corp. v. North Dakota, 504 U.S. 298, 112 S.Ct. 1904, 119 L.Ed.2d 91 (1992)—§ **8.5;** § **8.5, n. 6.**

Quill Corp. v. North Dakota, 1992 WL 687848 (U.S.Oral.Arg.1992)—§ **8.5, n. 8.**

R

Ramirez, United States v., 523 U.S. 65, 118 S.Ct. 992, 140 L.Ed.2d 191 (1998)—§ **1.2, n. 2;** § **5.6;** § **5.6, n. 3.**

Ramirez, United States v., 1998 WL 15476 (U.S.Oral.Arg.1998)—§ **1.2, n. 2;** § **5.6, n. 5.**

R.A.V. v. City of St. Paul, Minn., 505 U.S. 377, 112 S.Ct. 2538, 120 L.Ed.2d 305 (1992)—§ **4.4;** § **4.4, n. 5.**

R.A.V. v. St. Paul, Minn., 1991 WL 636263 (U.S.Oral.Arg.1991)—§ **4.4, n. 6.**

*

About the Author

David C. Frederick has argued twelve cases in the Supreme Court of the United States, including *Idaho v. United States*, 533 U.S. 262 (2001); *United States v. Locke*, 529 U.S. 89 (2000); *Carter v. United States*, 530 U.S. 255 (2000); and *California v. Deep Sea Research*, 523 U.S. 491 (1998). In 2001, he represented the United States in oral arguments before the U.S. Court of Appeals for the D.C. Circuit in *United States v. Microsoft Corporation*, 253 F.3d 34 (D.C. Cir. 2001) (en banc) (per curiam). He has argued cases in the First, Fifth, Sixth, Eleventh, D.C., and Federal Circuits. A recipient of the Coast Guard Medal for Distinguished Public Service (2000) for his advocacy in the *Locke* case, and of the Attorney General's Distinguished Service Award (1998), Frederick was an Assistant to the Solicitor General at the United States Department of Justice from 1996 to 2001. He was graduated from the University of Pittsburgh (B.A.); the University of Oxford (D. Phil.), where he was a Rhodes Scholar; and the University of Texas (J.D.). Frederick was a law clerk to the Honorable Byron R. White, Supreme Court of the United States, and to the Honorable Joseph T. Sneed, U.S. Court of Appeals for the Ninth Circuit. In addition to numerous articles, he is the author of *Rugged Justice: The Ninth Circuit Court of Appeals and the American West, 1891–1941* (Berkeley: University of California Press, 1994). Frederick is a partner at Kellogg, Huber, Hansen, Todd & Evans, P.L.L.C., in Washington, D.C.

*

Index